T0304248

GLOBAL SUPPLY CHAIN QUALITY MANAGEMENT

Product Recalls and Their Impact

SUPPLY CHAIN INTEGRATION
Modeling, Optimization, and Applications

Sameer Kumar, Series Advisor
University of St. Thomas, Minneapolis, MN

Global Supply Chain Quality Management: Product Recalls and Their Impact
Barbara B. Flynn and Xiande Zhao
ISBN: 978-1-4398-1554-0

Humanitarian Logistics and Supply Chains: Case Studies and Research Issues
Dave Goldsman
ISBN: 978-1-4665-4253-2

**Internet Retail Operations: Integrating Theory and Practice
for Managers**
Timothy M. Laseter and Elliot Rabinovich
ISBN: 978-1-4398-0091-1

**Human-Computer Etiquette: Cultural Expectations and the Design Implications
They Place on Computers and Technology**
Caroline C. Hayes and Christopher A. Miller
ISBN: 978-1-4200-6945-7

**Closed-Loop Supply Chains: New Developments to Improve the Sustainability
of Business Practices**
Mark E. Ferguson and Gilvan C. Souza
ISBN: 978-1-4200-9525-8

Connective Technologies in the Supply Chain
Sameer Kumar
ISBN: 978-1-4200-4349-5

Financial Models and Tools for Managing Lean Manufacturing
Sameer Kumar and David Meade
ISBN: 978-0-8493-9185-9

Supply Chain Cost Control Using Activity-Based Management
Sameer Kumar and Matthew Zander
ISBN: 978-0-8493-8215-4

GLOBAL
SUPPLY CHAIN QUALITY
MANAGEMENT

Product Recalls and Their Impact

Edited by Barbara B. Flynn and Xiande Zhao

CRC Press
Taylor & Francis Group
Boca Raton   London   New York

CRC Press is an imprint of the
Taylor & Francis Group, an **Informa** business

CRC Press
Taylor & Francis Group
6000 Broken Sound Parkway NW, Suite 300
Boca Raton, FL 33487-2742

© 2015 by Taylor & Francis Group, LLC
CRC Press is an imprint of Taylor & Francis Group, an Informa business

No claim to original U.S. Government works

Printed on acid-free paper
Version Date: 20140930

International Standard Book Number-13: 978-1-4398-1554-0 (Hardback)

Visit the Taylor & Francis Web site at
http://www.taylorandfrancis.com

and the CRC Press Web site at
http://www.crcpress.com

Contents

Acknowledgments

The research described in this book is substantially supported by a joint research grant of the Hong Kong Research Grant Council (project no. N_CUHK461/09) and the Natural Science Foundation of China (NSFC) (project no. 70931160446). It is also supported by an NSFC major program grant (project no. 71090403/71090400). The authors also acknowledge the support provided by the Indiana University Center for International Business Education and Research and the Kelley School of Business.

Editors

Dr. Barbara B. Flynn is the Richard M. and Myra Louise Buskirk Professor of Manufacturing Management at the Kelley School of Management, Indiana University. She earned her DBA in operations management from Indiana University; MBA, with an emphasis in operations management and managerial economics, from Marquette University; and BA in psychology from Ripon College. Dr. Flynn's previous academic appointments have been at Wake Forest University, Iowa State University, and Louisiana State University. She is a fellow of the Decision Sciences Institute and a recipient of the Distinguished Service Award from the Decision Sciences Institute and the Distinguished Scholar Award from the Operations Management division of the Academy of Management.

Dr. Flynn has received more than $1 million in research funding from the National Science Foundation, the U.S. Department of Education, and the Center for Innovation Management Studies. She is director of the High Performance Manufacturing research group, which studies the relationship between manufacturing practices and performance in various organizational and national cultures. Other research interests include global supply chain management, quality management, operations strategy, just-in-time (JIT), and group technology. She has published articles in *Management Science, Decision Sciences, Journal of Operations Management, International Journal of Operations Management,* and other leading journals, as well as a book and numerous book chapters.

Dr. Flynn is former editor-in-chief and founding editor of *Decision Sciences Journal of Innovative Education* and former editor-in-chief of *Quality Management Journal.* She is an associate editor of *Journal of Operations Management* and *Decision Sciences.* She serves on the Editorial Review Board of *International Journal of Applied Quality Management, Production and Operations Management,* and *Benchmarking for Quality Management and Technology.* Dr. Flynn is a past president of the Decision Sciences Institute and has held leadership positions within the Decision Sciences Institute, Academy of Management, The Institute for Management Sciences (TIMS), and American Production and Inventory Control Society. She previously served as director of the Indiana University Center for International Business Education and Research.

At Indiana University, Dr. Flynn teaches MBA courses in project management, service operations management, and operations management.

Dr. Xiande Zhao is professor of Operations and Supply Chain Management at the China Europe International Business School and at South China University of Technology. He was formerly professor of Operations Management in the Department of Decision Sciences and Managerial Economics and the director of the Center of Supply Chain Management/Logistics, Li & Fung Institute of Supply Chain Management/Logistics at the Chinese University of Hong Kong (2005 to 2012).

During the past 25 years, Dr. Zhao has been affiliated with a number of universities, where he held several academic and administrative positions. In 2011, Dr. Zhao was specially appointed as "One Thousand Talent Professor" under China's Global Search of One Thousand Talent Theme and served as director of the Institute for Supply Chain Integration and Service Innovation at South China University of Technology. Previously, he worked as an associate professor at City University of Hong Kong, Hampton University, and University of Utah. He also held joint appointments, as honored professor or visiting professor at Fudan University, Xi'an Jiao Tong University, Wuhan University, Nankai University, and Tianjin University.

Professor Zhao earned his PhD in business administration with a major in operations management and a minor in international business from the University of Utah in the U.S. He also earned his MBA and MSc in chemistry from the same university and a bachelor's degree in chemistry from Nankai University in China.

Professor Zhao's expertise is in the areas of operations and supply chain management. His teaching and research interests focus on innovation, quality, and productivity improvements in manufacturing and service organizations. He applies empirical methodologies mainly to investigate problems, issues, and challenges of managing supply chain and operations in China. He has conducted research in the areas of supply chain management, quality management, service operations management, service innovation and design, and high-performance manufacturing. Dr. Zhao has published more than 60 articles in refereed journals, including *Journal of Operations Management*, *Journal of Consumer Research*, *Production and Operations Management*, *European Journal of Operational Research*, and *International Journal of Production Research*. He has conducted a number of research projects on service innovation and design, supply chain integration, supply chain quality management, innovation, and supply chain learning funded by the National Natural Science Foundation of China and Hong Kong Research Grant Council.

Dr. Zhao has also provided training and consulting services for business corporations including China Mobile, China Telecom, DHL, Japan Airline, Ninjom, GlaxoSmithKline, Towngas, Kerry Properties, Guang Zhou Steel Group, and Beijing Commercial Bank.

Contributors

Jie Chen
University of Bath
Bath, United Kingdom

Jiangang Du
Nankai University
Tianjin, China

Xiucheng Fan
Fudan University
Shanghai, China

Barbara B. Flynn
Indiana University
Indianapolis, Indiana

and

Fundacáo Getulio Vargas
Sao Paulo, Brazil

Dennis A. Gioia
Pennsylvania State University
University Park, Pennsylvania

Haiju Hu
Yanshan University
Qinhuangdao, China

Baofeng Huo
Zhejiang University
Hangzhou, China

F. Robert Jacobs
Indiana University
Bloomington, Indiana

Fujun Lai
University of Southern Mississippi
Hattiesburg, Mississippi

Junfeng Li
Chongqing University of Technology
Chongqing, China

Yina Li
South China University of
  Technology
Guangzhou, China

Xueyuan Liu
Wuhan University
Wuhan, China

Yong Long
Chongqing University
Chongqing, China

Li Luo
South China University of Technology
Guangzhou, China

Stephen Ng
Hang Seng Management College
Hong Kong

John Z. Ni
University of Rhode Island
Kingston, Rhode Island

Kim Hua Tan
Nottingham University
Nottingham, United Kingdom

Ying Kei Tse
University of York
York, United Kingdom

Dongming Ye
Shantou Advance Management
    Consulting
Shantou, China

Thomas Kwan-Ho Yeung
South China University of Technology
Guangzhou, China

TingTing Zhao
Fudan University
Shanghai, China

Xiande Zhao
China Europe International Business
    School
Shanghai, China

and

South China University of Technology
Guangzhou, China

Bochao Zhuang
Hauqiao University
Quanzhou, China

INTRODUCTION TO SECTION I: BACKGROUND

In Section I, we provide an introduction to the topic of product safety hazards and the product recalls that may result. Chapter 1 provides a description of the importance of product safety issues, both from the perspective of researchers and from the perspective of companies, investors, and consumers. It introduces the concept of supply chain quality management as one of the causes of product safety issues and gives an overview of existing research related to product recalls.

Chapter 2 provides an overview of how product recalls are handled in the United States, giving a summary of the five government agencies that are responsible for working with companies and consumers to determine when a product recall is necessary and administer it. Examples of five memorable product recalls in the United States are given (Extra-Strength Tylenol, Ford Pinto, Sanlu, Mattel, and Toyota) and are used as the foundation for a discussion of the causes of product safety hazards. Notably, some product hazards are caused by elements of supply chain management, in addition to those that are related to design- or manufacturing-related issues. These are the types of hazards that we will focus on most closely in this book, as we consider ways to ensure product safety and quality throughout a supply chain.

The topic of product safety and recalls in developing countries is the subject of Chapter 3. Although the United States has a well-developed government infrastructure for administering product recalls, this is not the case in most developing countries, which are characterized by a lack of government infrastructure for product recalls and a more general lack of experience with recalls. This lack of experience is related to the priority that is placed on consumer protection, which seems to have a higher priority in more developed countries. In China, there is actually a decent foundation of consumer protection legislation; however, the judicial support for it is often lacking. In the absence of a strong consumer protection infrastructure in developing countries, informal methods for consumer protection may develop. Chapter 3 particularly highlights the role of social media in publicizing product safety hazards and providing an opportunity for affected consumers to tell their stories. Although the use of social media for consumer reviews is popular across the world, it serves a particularly important role in the absence of a strong government infrastructure for consumer protection.

Chapter 4 examines product safety from the perspective of risk, drawing upon the literature on risk and risk mitigation. This literature is described and applied to the product safety context, developing a framework for studying supply chain quality management and product recalls from the perspective of risk.

Chapter 1

Introduction

Barbara B. Flynn and Xiande Zhao

Contents

1.1 Introduction: Importance of Product Safety Issues

The topic of product recalls and the safety issues that precipitate them is of critical importance to both managers and researchers. Many product harm crises ultimately lead to a product recall, in response to government, society, and organizational concerns for removing dangerous products from the market, due to their health and safety implications. The number of product recalls due to quality and safety problems has been surging in recent years. Today's intense global competition and high customer expectations have led to a number of highly publicized recent recalls in the United States for products including vehicles (Toyota), toys (Mattel), and food (pet food, spinach), which have raised numerous concerns among the public. Safety issues and product recalls are not limited to the United States, however. For example, during 2006–2009, the total number of product recalls in E.U. countries doubled from 893 to 1686.

In particular, there have been a number of incidents involving products that were made in China or that had supply chains that passed through China. Of the 152 consumer products recalled by the U.S. Product Safety Commission during the first half of 2007, 68% were made in China (Roth et al. 2008). In 2008, 72% of the 86 consumer products recalled in the United Kingdom were made in China (Rapex 2010). Out of the 1686 consumer products recalled in the European Union in 2009, 58% of them were made in China. As a result, food and drug safety issues became the topic of a Chinese government report in 2009 (Wen 2008), indicating that it was putting more emphasis on food and drug safety.

1.1.1 Causes of Product Safety Issues

1.1.1.1 Product Design

Although product safety hazards are often blamed on manufacturers, other parties can also be responsible. For example, many product safety hazards are a result of poor product design. Design issues can include toys with sharp points or with small parts that can fall off in a child's mouth. These can also include factors such as the placement of various parts within an item. The case of the Ford Pinto in the early 1970s was a notorious example of poor product design. Among the first small, energy-efficient automobiles to be produced in the United States during a very energy-conscious era, Pintos were quite popular among Americans because of their size and cost. However, the fuel tank was located between the rear bumper and the rear axle, such that studs protruding from the rear of the axle housing could puncture the fuel tank upon impact. In a number of cases, the spilled gasoline was then ignited by sparks, causing the vehicle to go up in flames, even after a very low-speed impact. Although this was a safety issue that had been known at Ford, its focus on keeping costs very low caused the design issue to go unrepaired for a long period of time, with devastating consequences for a number of unfortunate Pinto owners and, ultimately, for Ford.

1.1.1.2 Supply Chains

An important source of product safety issues that has gone virtually unnoticed during the recent years are supply chains. Investigation into recent product recalls reveals that manufacturing firms are particularly vulnerable to product quality and safety problems in situations where goods and materials have been sourced via a global supply chain characterized by poor visibility. Often, a manufacturing firm lacks information on the true origin of the materials provided by a supplier and the quality of those materials.

Perhaps the most notorious example of a supply chain as the source of product safety issues is the case of the melamine-tainted milk products in China. This is particularly interesting because the incident occurred within China, with Chinese consumers and their babies suffering the consequences. In 2008, raw milk that contained melamine, an industrial chemical used in Formica and as a fire retardant additive in paint, plastics, and paper, among other things, was discovered in the milk supply of a number of leading Chinese producers of milk powder for baby formula. Upon investigation, it was found out that some farmers had discovered that another use for melamine was to increase the apparent protein content of raw milk. In order to make sure that the milk they supplied to large dairy producers passed inspection, they had intentionally added melamine to their raw milk in order to simulate higher protein levels. This caused kidney stones among the infants who consumed the baby formula, leading to the deaths of six Chinese babies. One of the critical issues in dealing with this problem, however, was that it was impossible to determine which farmers were guilty of the tampering, since raw milk was collected at collection stations, where dairy farmers would dump their raw milk into large vats, where it was mixed with raw milk from other dairy farmers.

The melamine-tainted milk incident illustrates the problem of supply chain transparency. Because it was impossible to know which dairy farmers were responsible for the tampering, they all suffered as large dairy producers addressed the problem by moving from using small, independent dairy farmers as a source of supply to their own vertically integrated dairy farms as their suppliers of raw milk. While this was an effective way of removing the source of a very serious supply chain quality issue, it also caused many innocent farmers to lose their livelihood.

The Mattel case provides a similar example of lack of supply chain transparency. Although Mattel very clearly specified the types of paint to be used in its products and used only suppliers that it had certified, it was not aware of some other common supply chain practices in China. Since its accession to the World Trade Organization, many Chinese companies have experienced dramatic growth by serving as suppliers to large multinational firms like Mattel. They were reluctant to ever turn down an order from a large multinational, even during peak periods when they may not have sufficient capacity, because they viewed supplying multinationals as the key to their future success. Thus, during an unexpected peak in demand, it is not unusual for a Chinese supplier to re-outsource some of its production to a different Chinese company. That company, in turn, may re-outsource some of its production to yet another Chinese company, and supply chain transparency quickly disappears. Like children's game of "telephone," detailed product specifications for components such as paint may get lost along the way. Such was the case with Mattel, when one of its long-trusted Chinese suppliers inadvertently used some yellow paint that its long-trusted paint supplier had re-outsourced during a capacity crisis. The rest of the story is history.

In both the case of Mattel and the case of the Chinese dairy producers, it was the brand owner (Mattel or the Chinese dairy companies) that ultimately suffered the consequences of what transpired in its supply chain. Even though both Mattel and the Chinese dairy producers had acted in good faith and had taken what they believed to be appropriate precautions to ensure the quality of the materials provided by their suppliers, they were unaware of activities that were occurring in the trenches. It was their names and reputations that were destroyed due to the negligence of their supply chain members. Ultimately, several of the Chinese dairy companies went bankrupt, and all of Mattel's toys took a huge hit in the market (not just those that used the tainted yellow paint).

1.1.2 Research on Product Recalls

The recent surge in product recalls of U.S. and Chinese-made products has attracted substantial attention from both government and academia due to their danger to consumers. A product recall is removal from the market or replacement of a product that has been found to be defective and potentially hazardous. It is a response to a product harm crisis, which is defined as a "discrete, well-publicized occurrence wherein products are found to be defective or dangerous" (Dawar and Pillutla 2000, p. 215). Product harm crises have increased in frequency due to globalization, increasing complexity of products, higher consumer demand, and more stringent product safety legislation (Dawar and Pillutla 2000). They have been described as "among a firm's worst nightmares" (Heerde et al. 2007, p. 230) because they can cause consumer panic and are very costly, as illustrated by the Chinese melamine-tainted milk powder crisis, which led to Sanlu filing for bankruptcy and to death sentences or life imprisonment for some of the key players. A product recall not only can ruin carefully cultivated brand equity and tarnish a company's reputation but also can result in major revenue and market share losses (Chen et al. 2009). It can disrupt channel and supplier relationships, make a company vulnerable to opportunistic competitors, invite regulatory interference, and cause an otherwise solid organization to become unstable (Smith et al. 1996).

Product defects can be caused by design or manufacturing issues (Bapuji 2011; Beamish and Bapuji 2008; Lyles et al. 2008), transportation and handling problems, supply chain problems, and other issues. Design flaws occur when product designers fail to consider potential hazards posed by a product. For instance, Mattel's Batman Batmobile cars had hard plastic pointed ends that could cause laceration injuries, resulting in their recall in 2004 (Bapuji 2011). Manufacturing defects are related to deviations from design specifications or incorrect assembly (Bapuji 2011). Recent examples include toys that were recalled because they contained high levels of lead paint (Hora et al. 2011).

Regardless of the cause of a product defect, a product recall induces both direct and indirect costs for a manufacturer. Direct costs include the cost of notification of consumers and correction of defects, both of which are short-run in nature (Barber and Darrough 1996). Indirect cost is the loss associated with reduced "brand name capital" due to damage to the product's reputation and loss of consumers' goodwill (Klein and Dawar 2004; also see Davidson and Worrell 1992; Pruitt and Peterson 1985).

Although there has been a substantial amount of prior research on manufacturing and design-related product hazards and product quality, there has been very little related to supply chain product hazards and how they translate into supply chain quality management, which is the primary focus of this book. Most quality management initiatives have been myopic, focusing only on internal quality operations. The cases described above illustrate, however, the need to develop quality management strategies that encompass upstream and downstream supply chain partners, as well as internal operations.

Lyles et al. (2008) describe how these issues are exacerbated in long supply chains. Chinese supply chains are not substantially different from Western supply chains, except for the greater distances involved. However, in China, the process of subcontracting has been built into the manufacturing process since the 1980s, partly as a way of fulfilling *guanxi* obligations to reciprocate and return favors. Consequently, longer supply chains may occur not for production efficiency but because of a cultural expectation.

Even for a supply chain of the same length, the greater distance translates into much longer lead times when supply chains extend across the Pacific. Their sheer length and relatively slow movement of events and inventory make it difficult for partners to monitor and control the actions of their upstream and downstream partners. As a result, relationships are particularly important in Chinese supply chains. From the Western perspective, a manufacturer offshoring production to China is looking for stable, trustworthy partners capable of planning months into the future and holding large quantities of inventory. Chinese suppliers, on the other hand, seek downstream North American partners with access to large consumer markets, dependable forecasts, and the ability to pay for and disseminate large amounts of finished goods inventory. In such supply chains, even relatively minor infractions can cause serious tensions between partners. From a Chinese supplier's perspective, a U.S. partner's extended payments or inability to accept large quantities of inventory is reason for concern. From a U.S. partner's perspective, a Chinese partner's use of questionable raw materials or labor practices is similarly bad. Trust helps overcome these issues. When upstream and downstream partners build a relationship whereby suppliers are assured of future demand and retailers are assured of future supply, everyone reaps benefits in terms of greater stability and profitability.

1.2 Overview of This Book

In this book, we take a deep dive into product safety issues and the product recalls that can result from them. We focus, in particular, on supply chain product quality issues, although we consider also other sources of product hazards. Similarly, we focus on many examples from China, although we consider some leading examples also from other parts of the world.

This book is first and foremost a compilation of research findings from a significant global research project on product safety and recalls headed by Professor Xiande Zhao. It is unique in that it examines these issues from a wide variety of perspectives and using a wide variety of methodologies. These methodologies include detailed case research on both examples of poor practices and best practices, first-hand accounts by several key players in well-known product recalls, event study methodology to determine the financial impact of a product recall announcement, controlled experiments to determine the effect of various recall strategies on consumers, and surveys to determine the relationship among key factors related to product safety hazards and product recalls. This allows readers to synthesize the findings from different perspectives, leading to the development of frameworks and guidelines for managers. Much of the technical details of the research reported here are contained in chapter appendices for reference in order to keep the material in the chapters at a level that is easily accessible.

1.2.1 Section I: Background

The research reported in this book is divided into multiple sections. Section I provides background based on the extant research. Chapter 2 describes general background about key regulatory agencies in the United States that are responsible for product safety and initiation of a product recall. It then moves into short descriptions of a number of highly publicized product recalls, including Ford Pinto, Extra Strength Tylenol, melamine-tainted milk, Mattel, and Toyota. Each of these demonstrates key themes that the book builds upon, including various sources of product hazards and critical factors for dealing with them. Chapter 2 then lays the foundation for research on design hazards, upstream supply chain management issues, and downstream supply chain management issues that will be elaborated upon in subsequent chapters. It concludes with a summary of research findings about product recalls from various perspectives, including the financial perspective, the consumers' perspective, the crisis management and public relations perspective, and the supply chain and quality management perspective.

Chapter 3 extends the discussion in Chapter 2 to developing countries. Consumer protection issues often take the backseat in emerging economies, which are more focused on the rapid development of their production capabilities and their establishment as a player in the multinational playing field. Chapter 3 begins with a discussion of the development of consumer protection legislation in developing countries, with a particular focus on China and the legislation that it has developed recently. Although many developing countries are making substantial headway in developing sound consumer protection legislation, issues often arise in the enforcement of this legislation. Because of this, informal mechanisms arise for disseminating news about product safety issues and giving consumers the opportunity to express their frustrations and opinions. The second part of Chapter 3 describes the role of social media as an informal consumer protection mechanism, focusing on its use during the melamine-tainted milk incident in China. It illustrates how, in the absence of strong protection by a government and its courts, other less formal mechanisms will take their place.

Chapter 4 describes research on product safety as part of a larger body of research on risk and risk management. It begins with the development of risk construct from several perspectives, including decision theory vs. the managerial perspective on risk, the difference between risk and uncertainty, and the difference between subjective and objective risk. It then develops a model of perceived risk that can be used as a foundation for studying product safety. Chapter 4 then proceeds to develop the notion of supply chain quality risk, elaborating on its sources, including insufficient supply chain transparency, product complexity and testability, and cutting corners. Implications for supply chain risk management include strategies for the reduction of variability and for acquisition of information.

1.2.2 Section II: Dark Side of Product Safety

Section II provides detailed research case studies of some classic examples of what not to do in the event of a product safety hazard. These are used to develop a framework for studying product safety hazards and product recalls.

We begin with the Chinese toy recalls in Chapter 5. This chapter provides detailed information about the global toy industry and the toy industry in China, highlighting the unique set of pressures faced by this industry. It then describes key safety issues in toy supply chains and the regulations that affect members of toy supply chains in China. Chapter 5 then describes in depth the Mattel case, providing the story both from Mattel's side and from the perspective of Lee Der, one of Mattel's most trusted Chinese suppliers. It illustrates the unintended consequences of re-outsourcing on both Mattel and Lee Der. Chapter 5 then provides the detailed, first-hand, and frank perspective of the Mattel crisis provided by Robert Eckert, who was the chief executive officer of Mattel during the time of this crisis.

Chapter 6 describes in detail the melamine-tainted milk crisis in China, drawing on contemporaneous news reports. It analyzes these reports from the perspective of supply chain quality management, drawing especially upon prior research in supply chain governance structures and strategic supply chain design. Chapter 6 also discusses these events in the context of quality management, describing the relationship between the prevention, appraisal, internal defect, and external costs associated with this incident. It uses this perspective to develop recommendations based on making investments in prevention through strategic supply chain design.

In Chapter 7, Dennis Gioia tells the story of his experience as Ford's recall coordinator during the Pinto crisis, when he was a recent MBA graduate. He describes the set of decisions made by Ford, including using a cost–benefit analysis that incorporated the value of a human life, to determine when it was appropriate to issue a recall announcement, as well as his personal reflections on the incident. Interestingly, Gioia went on to become a business ethics professor at Pennsylvania State University, perhaps partly because of his experience with Ford. In the second part of Chapter 7, he describes his research on how humans develop script schemas for processing information, which can blind decision makers to important information.

In Chapter 8, we synthesize the stories of the cases in Section II and use them to develop a research framework for supply chain quality management. This framework provides the foundation for the research that is reported in the remaining sections of the book.

1.2.3 Section III: Bright Side of Product Safety: Exemplar Cases

In Section III, we examine a different set of research case studies, which provide exemplars for dealing with product safety issues and risk. They describe companies that have developed approaches for preventing quality and safety issues, particularly in their product design and supply chain operations. Each of these cases is set in China, providing a nice contrast with the sometimes negative perceptions that are, on certain occasions, associated with manufacturing and supply chain operations in China.

Chapters 9 and 10 are set in the automobile industry in China and provide very detailed discussions of the approaches taken by two Chinese companies that are involved in international joint ventures. Chapter 9 highlights the system used at Dongfeng-Peugeot-Citroen Automobile Co. Ltd. (DPCA), focusing on its internal integration, in particular. Chapter 10 focuses on Changan Ford Mazda Automobile Co., Ltd. (CFMA) and the systems that it has developed for administering product recalls. While DPCA has always had a strong reputation for quality, CFMA has been the subject of a number of significant recalls since 2010. Both companies have developed strong systems for developing and ensuring product quality and safety, as well as structured procedures for determining when to issue a product recall and how to administer it. Chapters 9 and 10 give an inside view of these systems, providing detailed descriptions of them, taken from company documents.

Chapter 11 focuses on Bright Dairy, one of the key players in the melamine-tainted milk product recalls in China, based on visits to several of Bright Dairy's factories and interviews with company executives. Chapter 11 describes the comprehensive quality management system used within its factories, as well as Bright's involvement in farm management, in order to ensure supply chain quality. This is challenging, since the level of education of small-scale farmers in China is very low and the farmers are often illiterate. Through development of innovations like barcoded ear tags on the cows, Bright Dairy has developed technological solutions to recording information about the yields, feed, veterinary treatment, medications, and other important information for every cow, helping the small-scale farmers to learn about the importance of quality and contribute raw milk that meets Bright's high standards. Chapter 11 also describes the important role that the Shanghai Dairy Association plays in helping small-scale farmers in the Shanghai area to ensure that they are delivering high-quality raw milk to dairy producers.

We look at a similar situation in Chapter 12, which describes the CHIC Group Global Company, Ltd. CHIC is a Chinese world-class provider of processed fruit to leading brand owners, such as Del Monte, Heinz, and Yum! Brands, globally. Because it deals with an agricultural commodity in rural areas characterized by poor infrastructure and poorly educated peasant farmers, it faces similar challenges to Bright Dairy. Chapter 12 describes the highly innovative technology and social approaches used by CHIC to help its suppliers learn about quality and ensure that the raw fruit that they provide is of the highest quality. This synergistic relationship benefits both CHIC and its suppliers and provides a very interesting Chinese quality success story.

1.2.4 Section IV: Financial Perspective on Product Recalls

Section IV contains a collection of event studies on the stock market reaction to the announcement of a product recall by a company. The event study approach, commonly used by accounting, finance, and economics researchers, quantifies the difference between the "normal" stock market returns experienced by a company and the "abnormal" returns following a specific event. This difference provides a powerful way of examining the impact of a product recall announcement on the financial value of a company.

In Chapter 13, we return to the melamine-tainted milk powder crisis in China, examining the cumulative abnormal returns for publically traded dairy companies whose stock is traded in the Shanghai, Hong Kong, and New York Stock Exchanges. Through examining the returns of both companies that were found to have melamine in their milk products and those that were not, the researchers looked at whether there was a spillover effect of the negative publicity about dairy products to dairy producers that did not have any melamine issues with its products. The researchers also examined the longer-term implications of the product recall announcements to determine whether there was a long-lasting effect on the financial value of the involved firms and how quickly firms with different supply chain designs were able to recover.

Chapter 14 applies event study methods to the toy industry in the United States. Toys are a particularly interesting product group to study since toy customers (typically parents) and toy consumers (children) are not the same. Toy customers act as agents for toy consumers, and each group has very different priorities.

While product safety is very important for parents, it is of little interest to children. In addition to examining the short-term financial impact of a product recall announcement on the financial value of a toy company, the researchers also examine key factors that may influence this impact, including brand, source transparency, firm size, and degree of product hazard.

Chapter 15 examines the financial impact of a product recall announcement on an often forgotten member of supply chains: retailers. Although the manufacturer of a product typically reimburses retailers for the direct costs associated with collecting consumer products that have been recalled for a safety issue, there are a number of indirect costs that are not always considered. Customers may be confused about who holds the responsibility for product safety and quality, particularly when the product bears the retailer's private brand. Using data from U.S. Consumer Product Safety Commission recall announcements, this research establishes that there are significant negative cumulative abnormal returns for retailers following the announcement of a product recall. Chapter 15 then delves more deeply into the causes of this reaction, including comparing national and private brands, various types of recall strategy (repair, replacement, or refund), and different levels of product hazard, in order to determine which are the most important factors.

1.2.5 Section V: Consumer Perspective on Product Recalls

Section V describes two controlled experiments for developing a better understanding of the impact of various product recall strategies on consumer perceptions of a company. In a controlled experiment, typical consumers are asked to read a short scenario that contains factors that can exist at several different levels. For example, one respondent might read a scenario where the level of product hazard is low, the product is recalled immediately, and consumers are compensated at a high level for returning the recalled product. Another respondent might be given a scenario that is exactly the same, except that the level of product hazard is high, the company did not recall the product until forced to by a government agency, and consumers are compensated at a low level for returning the recalled product. Using controlled experiment allows researchers to isolate the effect of the manipulated variable to learn more about their effects in a controlled setting.

In Chapter 16, the effectiveness of various recall strategies is tested with consumers of an orange juice drink product. The strategies include the use of a proactive (voluntary) vs. passive (mandated) recall announcement and the level of compensation that consumers received for their issues related to the product recall. These are studied in the context of two different theories that offer conflicting explanations for how consumers will react.

Chapter 17 looks at the role of fear in consumers' reaction to a product recall announcement. Using several different products in its scenarios, it assesses the relationship between consumers' subjective estimate of risk and the actual risk of a product hazard, as well as the perceptions of potential consumers who did not actually purchase the affected product but who might be well acquainted with those who did purchase it. Combined, Chapters 16 and 17 provide useful insights for managers in understanding consumer reactions to a product recall announcement, which can help to mitigate these.

1.2.6 Section VI: Supply Chain Quality Management and Performance

The research reported in Section VI uses survey methodology to gather data on a variety of factors in organizations. Statistical analysis is used to assess the relationship between various factors, in order to learn about which are the most critical, providing insights for managers who are involved with ensuring quality in supply chains.

Chapter 18 examines potential drivers of supply chain quality integration, including the degree of competitive intensity in an industry and the use of an approach to quality management that extends across an entire organization. While both quality management and supply chain integration have been extensively studied in the past, quality management is very different in the context of a supply chain, where it can be very challenging to ensure the quality of supply chain partners and their partners. Thus, this research synthesizes the previously independent research streams on quality management and supply chain integration. By breaking supply chain integration into internal integration, customer integration, and supplier integration, this research isolates the effect of specific factors on each of the dimensions of supply chain integration and the performance that results.

In Chapter 19, the focus is on customer orientation, an important factor in supply chain quality integration. It describes how customer orientation is a set of unique, organization-specific capabilities that function as a resource and can lead to a competitive advantage. Using data collected from across China, in conjunction with the China Quality Management Association, this research examines the relationship among customer orientation, process management and product, process, and financial performance.

Finally, Chapter 20 examines the framework for supply chain quality management that was proposed in Chapter 8. Using data from manufacturers in the toy, food, automobile, and pharmaceutical industries in China, these relationships are tested. This research focuses, in particular, on the role of the company that functions as the leader of a supply chain, with considerable influence over the other members of the supply chain.

We close with Chapter 21, which synthesizes the findings from the entire book and provides additional reflection and discussion of the key findings and their implications for both academic researchers and practicing managers.

References

Bapuji, H. 2011. *Not Just China: The Rise of Recalls in the Age of Global Business.* New York: Palgrave-Macmillan.

Barber, B.M. and M.N. Darrough. 1996. Product reliability and firm value: The experience of American and Japanese automakers, 1973–1992. *J. Pol. Econ.* 104(5): 1084–1099.

Beamish, P.W. and H. Bapuji. 2008. Toy recalls and China: Emotion vs. evidence. *Mgmt. Org. Rev.* 4(2): 197–209.

Chen, Y., S. Ganesan and Y. Liu. 2009. Does a firm's product-recall strategy affect its financial value: An examination of strategic alternatives during product-harm crises. *J. Mrktg.* 73: 214–226.

Davidson, W.N. and D.L. Worrell. 1992. The effect of product recall announcements on shareholder wealth. *Strat. Mgmt. J.* 13: 467–473.

Dawar, N. and M. Pillutla. 2000. Impact of product-harm crises on brand equity: The moderating role of consumer expectations. *J. Mrktg. Res.* 37: 215–226.

Heerde, H.V., K. Kelsen and G. Marnik. 2007. The impact of a product harm crisis on marketing effectiveness. *Mrktg. Sci.* 26(2): 230–284.

Hora, M., H. Bapuji and A.V. Roth. 2011. Safety hazard and time to recall: The role of recall strategy, product defect type, and supply chain player in the U.S. toy industry. *J. Ops. Mgmt.* 29: 766–777.

Klein, J. and N. Dawar. 2004. Corporate social responsibility and consumers' attributions and brand evaluations in a product-harm crisis. *Int. J. Res. Mrktg.* 18: 864–872.

Lyles, M.A., B.B. Flynn and M.T. Frohlich. 2008. All supply chains don't flow through: Understanding supply chain issues in product recalls. *Mgmt. Org. Rev.* 4: 167–182.

Pruitt, S.W. and D.R. Peterson. 1985. Security price reactions around product recall announcements. *J. Fin. Res.* 20: 113–122.

Rapex. 2010. Keeping European customers safe 2010: Annual report on the operation of the rapid alert system for non-food dangerous products. Available at http://ec.europa.eu/consumers/safety/raoex/stats_reports_en.html.

Roth, A.V., A.A. Tsay, M.E. Pullman and J.V. Gray. 2008. Unraveling the food supply chain: Strategic insights from China and the 2007 recalls. *J. Supp. Chain Mgmt.* 44: 22–39.

Smith, N.C., R.J. Thomas and J.A. Quelch. 1996. A strategic approach to managing product recalls. *Harvard Bus. Rev.* 74: 102–112.

Wen, J. 2008. *Report on the work of the government* [online]. Available from http://news.xinhuanet.com/english/2008-03/19/content_7818043.htm (Accessed March 19, 2009).

Chapter 2

Importance of Product Recalls

John Z. Ni, Yina Li, and Barbara B. Flynn

Contents

2.1 Introduction: Background

Consumer protection is a set of laws and organizations that were developed to ensure the rights and safety of consumers. Although commonly developed as a response to various crises and emergencies that led to public outrage, going back to the nineteenth century common law, modern consumer protection in the United States began with the promotion of the Consumer Bill of Rights by President Kennedy, the "Great Society" program of the Johnson administration, and the efforts of consumer activist lawyer Ralph Nader.

A product recall is a form of consumer protection aimed at removing unsafe products from the hands of consumers. In this chapter, we provide general background about how product recalls are administered in the United States. We describe several well-known product recall incidents and use them as the basis for a discussion of the causes of the product hazards that lead to the need for a product recall. We end with a brief summary of different types of prior research on product recalls, setting the stage for the research described in this book.

2.2 Product Recall Agencies and Procedures in the United States

2.2.1 Regulatory Agencies

In the United States, there are five major federal agencies that manage product recall campaigns:

1. National Highway Traffic Safety Administration (NHTSA)
2. Food Safety and Inspection Service (FSIS)
3. Food and Drug Administration (FDA)
4. Consumer Product Safety Commission (CPSC)
5. Environmental Protection Agency (EPA)

These agencies apply regulations to address the problems arising from information asymmetries between manufacturers and consumers. For example, the NHTSA of the U.S. Department of Transportation provides information about vehicle and transportation equipment recalls. Pursuant to the National Traffic and Motor Vehicle Safety Act, the responsibilities of NHTSA include

1. Establishing minimum federal safety performance standards for motor vehicles and equipment
2. Verifying that motor vehicles and equipment satisfy the safety standards
3. Investigating possible motor vehicle safety noncompliance
4. In situations of noncompliance, directing recall campaigns to ensure that all vehicle and equipment comply with safety standards

The NHTSA's jurisdiction includes motor vehicle products that have experienced a safety-related defect or did not comply with federal motor vehicle safety standards. According to NHTSA reports, there were 4399 recall campaigns involving over 140 million motor vehicles between 1973 and 1992, with the majority voluntarily initiated by American companies. The defects that triggered these recalls varied from relatively minor defects, such as rusty fenders and ill-fitting shoulder harnesses, to serious defects, such as brake problems and engines prone to fire. In 2009, 16.4 million vehicles were recalled in 492 announcements by the NHTSA.

The FSIS of the U.S. Department of Agriculture monitors meat, poultry, and egg products produced by federally inspected establishments, while the FDA monitors other food products, as well as pet food and animal feed products. The CPSC is responsible for more than 15,000 kinds of consumer products used in and around the home, in sports, in recreation, and in schools. The EPA monitors emission-related components and systems of motor vehicles.

2.2.2 Recall Procedures

Each of these government agencies follows similar procedures. As an example, we describe the procedures followed by the NHTSA and the CPSC. When a motor vehicle safety defect or noncompliance is discovered by a manufacturer, the manufacturer voluntarily files a Defect and Noncompliance Information Report with the NHTSA, detailing the affected population, problem description, chronological summary, proposed remedy, and recall schedule. Upon its receipt, the NHTSA writes a formal acknowledgement letter providing an identification number and additional information on the scheduling of the recall. This information is then entered into the NHTSA database, which is accessible to the public through its website. The public is also notified by a notification letter or press release from the manufacturer.

When a manufacturer of a consumer product discovers a product with "a substantial risk of injury to the public" (CPSC 2012), it must notify the CPSC. After a report is filed, the manufacturer and the CPSC's compliance staff negotiate alternative courses of action for removing the hazardous product from the market. Most often, a plan of action is voluntarily adopted by the manufacturer, and a joint press release is issued; however, if an agreement is not reached, the CPSC can litigate. Publicly available on the CPSC's website, recall notices contain information about the product being recalled; the company recalling the product; where the product was recalled; the hazard associated with the recalled product; sales details such as the number of units sold, sales locations, sale period, and sale price; the procedure for returning the product; and the remedy offered by the manufacturer. Depending on the agreement, the manufacturer's remedy may include paying a refund to purchasers, repairing the defect, replacing the item with a new one, or sending a warning notice to consumers.

2.2.3 Classification of Product Hazards

Product recalls can be classified based on the level of hazard posed by the defect, ranging from situations where the use of a defective product could lead to serious health consequences or death to situations where the use of the product is not likely to cause any adverse health consequences. The NHTSA classifies product hazards into three categories based upon their severity. Hazards considered to be minor are classified as Type I. These include such problems as mislabeled or missing placards. Type II hazards, considered to be intermediate in nature, involve problems such as loosened or missing bolts in major assemblies and windshield wiper problems. Type III hazards are the most severe in magnitude and include safety problems that can result in vehicle fires or loss of steering and braking functions, as well as problems that severely affect vehicle drivability, such as repeated engine stalling. Similarly, the CPSC classifies hazards into three categories. A Class A hazard exists when the risk of death or grievous injury or illness is likely or very likely or serious injury or illness is very likely. A Class B hazard exists when the risk of death or grievous injury or illness is not likely but is possible, or when serious injury or illness is likely, or when moderate injury or illness is very likely. A Class C hazard exists when the risk of serious injury or illness is not likely but is possible or when moderate injury or illness is not likely but is possible.

Another way to categorize product recalls is by their initiation: involuntary or voluntary. An involuntary (also known as passive) recall is mandated by the federal or state government or one of their agencies. A voluntary recall, on the other hand, originates with the product's manufacturer or brand owner. A voluntary recall may reassure consumers that the manufacturer willingly stands behind its products, while a government-ordered recall may indicate to consumers that the product is so defective that the government had to step in to correct the situation. Almost all NHTSA recalls have been voluntary; only eight times since its founding has the NHTSA mandated a recall for alleged safety defects by an automobile manufacturer.

2.3 Highly Publicized Product Recalls and Their Impact

Although there have been many widely publicized recent examples of automotive, toy, and food recalls, the foundation was laid by the Ford Pinto and Tylenol recall cases in the United States during the 1970s. These cases served as a wakeup call to the American public, which began demanding higher safety standards related to design, manufacturing, and packaging. More recent well-known recalls have included China's recall of melamine-tainted dairy products, Mattel's toy recalls, and Toyota's automotive recalls. The year 2007 was a bellwether for product recalls. High-profile recalls, ranging from tainted pet food to toothpaste and from toys to faulty tires, resulted in widespread outrage among consumers. According to the CPSC, there were 472 product recalls in FY 2007, one of the highest totals in its history.

The following examples of notorious product recalls are important because of their ultimate impact on consumer awareness and legislation. In addition, each illustrates a different product hazard cause, ranging from design and manufacturing causes to causes related to supply chain monitoring. It is important to note that the brand owner is typically ultimately held responsible for a recall by consumers and investors, even if it was not the source of the cause.

2.3.1 Ford Pinto

Designed during the summer of 1967, the Ford Pinto was one of the second generation of subcompact cars in the United States. It appeared on the market in 1970, and sales were strong for the first few years. At that point, however, reports started surfacing that Pintos leaked fuel and were prone to catching on fire after a relatively low-speed rear-end collision. The negative publicity was exacerbated by the publication of an article in September 1977 entitled "Pinto Madness" in the magazine *Mother Jones* (Dowie 1977). The article asserted that Ford engineers had discovered, during preproduction testing, that low-speed rear-end collisions could rupture the fuel system extremely easily. However, because the production equipment had already been tooled when this was discovered, Ford officials decided to manufacture the car anyway. Later, internal memos were discovered that applied cost–benefit analysis to justify the decision by placing a value of $200,000 on an adult human life ($100,000 per child). Because the cost of a production fix would be $137 million and the associated benefit was only $49.5 million, no production fix was undertaken.

Responding to the rash of consumer complaints, the NHTSA began recall proceedings, ultimately resulting in the 1978 determination that a safety defect existed in the fuel systems of 1971–1976 Ford Pintos. After an 8-year delay and following 38 rear-end collisions and fires, 27 deaths, and 24 cases of nonfatal burns, Ford announced the recall of approximately 1.5 million Pintos and 30,000 Mercury Bobcats. Many of the victims or their relatives sued Ford in civil lawsuits in order to recover damages for the effects of wrongful or negligent actions. For example, in a highly publicized damage suit by a Californian teenager badly burned in a rear-end Pinto collision, the jury awarded $128 million in damages. The Ford Pinto case is described in greater detail in Chapter 7 in an insider report written by Ford's recall coordinator at the time of the incident.

2.3.2 Extra-Strength Tylenol

In the mid-1970s, Tylenol became the biggest selling item in drug, food, and mass merchandising outlets, breaking the 18-year dominance by Proctor & Gamble's Crest toothpaste. However, this dominance took a drastic turn in 1982. During a 3-day period in late September and early October, seven Chicago residents died after taking Extra-Strength Tylenol capsules that were laced with cyanide. Within days, it became clear to investigators that tampering had occurred at the retail level. Apparently, a few bottles of Extra-Strength Tylenol had been removed from store shelves, cyanide was added to the capsules (which could be easily opened and closed), and the bottles were returned to the shelves. The perpetrator was never found, and the poisoning became an event without precedent in American business, reported in 125,000 stories in the print media alone. On October 5, 1982, Johnson & Johnson ordered a nationwide recall of Tylenol capsules, halted its production, and spent more than $100 million to withdraw the product from the market and cover other expenses arising from the contamination of the capsules. Ultimately, the Tylenol recall resulted in the development of the tamper-proof and tamper-evident packaging that is required for over-the-counter medications today, as well as the complete elimination of encapsulated medication.

2.3.3 Melamine-Tainted Milk

On September 11, 2008, China's Ministry of Health released a preliminary investigation confirming that contaminated Sanlu baby milk powder was the cause of kidney stones in infants. The Sanlu Group had discovered that some of its products were contaminated with melamine, an industrial chemical that simulates higher levels of nitride content in milk and that can cause kidney stones and kidney failure in children (Lu et al. 2009). Some of its upstream supply chain members (farmers and raw milk collection stations) had attempted to deceive Sanlu's milk protein testers by adding melamine-laced "protein powder" to their substandard milk so that it would pass inspection. Sanlu responded by announcing a recall to purge all batches of its baby milk powder produced before September. Expanding the scope of their investigation, Chinese inspectors found melamine in baby milk powder produced by 22 companies nationwide on September 16, 2008, and Chinese authorities immediately ordered an immediate halt to the sale of products from these companies.

The consequences of the melamine-tainted milk crisis were dire. Hundreds of children became ill from ingesting melamine, and six died. Tian Wenhua, Sanlu's president and chief executive officer (CEO), was sentenced to life imprisonment and a $2.9 million fine. The distributor of the fake protein powder also was sentenced to life imprisonment. Both Zhang Yunjin, the producer of the fake protein powder, and the farmer who used it to alter the nitride content of his milk were sentenced to death. The melamine-tainting crisis is described in greater detail in Chapters 6 and 13.

2.3.4 Mattel Toys

On August 1, 2007, the world's largest toy maker, Mattel, stunned the world by issuing an unprecedented recall of 967,000 toys made by its Fisher-Price unit due to concerns that they contained hazardous levels of lead paint. Despite Mattel's specifications for the paint, a Chinese paint supplier had substituted a less expensive paint, containing lead, in an attempt to cut costs. Less than a month later, Mattel announced its second recall of 436,000 cars tainted with lead paint and more than 18 million toys containing small magnets that could be swallowed by children. Mattel's problems intensified on September 4 when it announced its third major 2007 recall, which involved 775,000 lead paint-tainted accessories associated with Barbie, Mattel's signature brand. The case of Mattel and its Chinese suppliers is discussed further in Chapter 5.

The ripple effect caused by these widely publicized recalls was significant. Shortly after the initial recall, Mattel announced a $30 million charge to cover the cost. In December 2008, it paid $12 million as part of a multistate settlement to resolve charges that it shipped toys containing lead paint to the United States. In addition, Mattel and its wholly owned subsidiary, Fisher-Price, were fined a $2.3 million civil penalty by the CPSC for violating the federal lead paint ban. These recalls also resulted in an orgy of China bashing, as consumers and the press worried about the safety and labor practices of overseas suppliers. This spate of recalls also led to intensified calls from consumer advocates and politicians for stricter safety standards, as well as tougher penalties for companies. As a result, the Consumer Product Safety Improvement Act was passed by a wide margin in Congress and signed into law by then-President Bush, marking America's most important regulatory advance against toxic chemicals in many years.

2.3.5 Toyota

For decades, Toyota had been the gold standard for automotive quality and customer satisfaction. However, this reputation was shattered in September 2009, when Toyota initiated its largest recall ever (4.2 million cars) amid reports that the accelerator pedal could become trapped under the floor mat, causing a vehicle to accelerate, even after the driver has lifted his or her foot off the pedal. This followed a widely publicized fatal crash in San Diego in which a Californian Highway Patrol officer was killed, along with three family members, when his Lexus suddenly accelerated out of control. Complaints about the speed control problem surged after the first recall. Less than 2 months later, Toyota issued its second large recall for sticking gas pedals, this time involving a total of 2.3 million cars and trucks from model years 2005 through 2010. On January 27, 2010, an additional 1.1 million vehicles were recalled due to the floor mat issue. On February 9, Toyota's reputation for quality and reliability suffered further damage when it announced the recall of 437,000 cars, including its flagship Prius, for a brake problem. Under the mounting pressure from consumers and the federal government, Toyota's CEO and grandson of founder Kiichiro Toyoda, Akio Toyoda, apologized to customers and testified in a public hearing held by the U.S. Congress, stating "I fear the pace at which we have grown may have been too quick.... Priorities became confused, and we were not able to stop, think, and make improvements as much as we were able to before" (Rooney 2010). More than 300 lawsuits were filed against Toyota, and the financial impact could total more than $5 billion, including increased incentive campaigns, litigation costs, and marketing efforts.

2.4 Causes of Product Hazards

These examples illustrate a number of different causes of product hazards that ultimately led to product recalls. Although it is tempting to blame the manufacturer for product hazards, not one of these examples deals with a hazard for which the manufacturer was responsible. Rather, these cases present stories of design defects and hazards that are related to long, complex supply chains.

2.4.1 Design Issues

Mattel's use of small magnets is an example of a design defect. The small magnets in some of its toys could easily fall off when a baby chews on a toy. Because of their size, they are easily swallowed. This can present a significant problem if the magnets in different parts of a baby's stomach are attracted to each other and stick together. Announced in the middle of Mattel's product recalls for lead paint, it was easy to blame Mattel's Chinese manufacturing operations for yet another product recall. However, the manufacturers were simply following the specifications provided to them by Mattel's toy designers; in this case, it was the designers who were negligent, not the manufacturers.

Similarly, the Pinto case illustrates a design defect. Although its designers knew that the fuel system could easily rupture, due to its location in the vehicle, they opted to proceed with production anyway because of cost considerations. Ironically, Ford already owned a patent on a gas tank that was known to be much safer. However, the early 1970s was the period when small economy cars were first introduced to the U.S. domestic market, and Ford was reluctant to do anything that could jeopardize the low cost of its popular Pintos.

The cause of Toyota's sticking gas pedals has yet to be determined. It is believed to be due to a design defect, but it may also be a consumer hoax, in order to collect settlement funds from Toyota.

2.4.2 Upstream Supply Chain Issues

The Chinese milk tampering case illustrates issues with inadequate monitoring of long and complex supply chains. Although Sanlu had originally owned its own dairy farms, it had more recently reorganized to focus primarily on marketing and distribution, outsourcing its milk production primarily to small farmers. Other Chinese dairy companies had followed a similar strategy in order to meet the needs of the rapidly expanding market for dairy products in China, as the disposable income of its consumers increased and they were introduced to Western foods, such as pizza and cheeseburgers. Small farmers in China have very small dairy operations, typically in the range of one to five cows, and the farmers are often illiterate and poorly educated about product safety. As they grew in size, the large dairy companies lost control over their upstream supply chain for their primary raw material.

Mattel's story is similar. Like many large toy companies, the majority of its toys are made in China, either by Mattel-owned operations or subcontractors. Although it provides its Chinese subcontractors with detailed specifications and certifies them for safety, Mattel did not realize that its subcontractors would often subcontract some of their work to other suppliers, essentially re-outsourcing. Eager for Mattel's work, certified subcontractors would accept all orders that Mattel offered, regardless of their available capacity. In a bind to meet Mattel's deadlines, they would sometimes re-outsource their work to a subtier supplier, which might further re-outsource it to a different subtier supplier. When Mattel discovered the problems with lead paint on some of its toys, it found that it was unable to even trace through its supply chain to the source of the problems. Thus, Mattel had also lost control over its upstream supply chain.

2.4.3 Downstream Supply Chain Issues

Tylenol's story is somewhat different, indicating a different type of supply chain problem. While Sanlu and Mattel suffered from inadequate upstream supply chain monitoring, Tylenol suffered from intentional tampering, which occurred after its products were in its downstream supply chain, on the shelf in retail establishments. Although this was the first major case of downstream supply chain tampering, there have been many other more recent examples. Some, like the Tylenol case, have injuring consumers as their intent. Other examples of downstream supply chain tampering have an economic motive; for example, large pharmaceutical companies like Eli Lilly have had problems with the intentional substitution of counterfeit pharmaceuticals into their supply chain; the actual products were then sold on the black market.

2.5 Prior Research on Product Recalls

The existing research on product harm crises and recalls comes from varying perspectives, drawing upon different theoretical foundations and methodologies. The financial perspective draws upon efficient market theory and uses event study methodology to examine the stock market reaction to a recall announcement, while the marketing perspective is based on consumer behavior theories and primarily uses controlled experiments. The supply chain management perspective uses survey methodology, while the crisis management literature takes a primarily qualitative approach to studying communication strategies during a product hazard crisis.

2.5.1 Financial Perspective

The financial perspective focuses on investor perceptions of a recall announcement by developing an understanding of how the stock market reacts to it. These studies use objective data collected from secondary sources, such as the *Wall Street Journal* and reports from governmental regulators, employing event study methodology. The theoretical underpinnings of event study methodology state that, in an efficient market, the financial impact of any unanticipated event will be immediately reflected in the stock price (Fama 1970; Pruitt and Peterson 1986).

Most prior event study research reveals that the stock market responds quickly and efficiently to the information content of a product recall announcement but does not react persistently (Bromiley and Marcus 1989; Chu et al. 2005; Davidson and Worrell 1992; Haunschild and Mooweon 2004; Hoffer et al. 1988; Jarrell and Peltzman 1985; Pruitt and Peterson 1985; Rhee and Haunschild 2006). The stock market overreacts immediately following an announcement, and this reaction seems to be based on all potential losses associated with the recall (Govindaraj et al. 2004). However, the firms engaged in a product recall tend to recover their market value as more information on actual costs becomes available (Cheah et al. 2007; Chu et al. 2005; Govindaraj et al. 2004; Pruitt and Peterson 1986; Rhee and Haunschild 2006).

Whether a recall announcement triggers a spillover effect to the stock price of competitors is another focus of the financial perspective. A spillover effect (Balachander and Ghose 2003) is the extent to which external information (e.g., a product harm crisis) about a brand changes attitudes about other brands that were not directly involved. For example, Johnson & Johnson's 1982 Tylenol recall led to a \$4.06 billion wealth decline for other (nonaffected) over-the-counter drug companies, in addition to the \$2.11 billion loss suffered by Johnson & Johnson shareholders (Mitchell 1989). Conversely, some researchers have found that the competitors are likely to gain at the cost of firms whose products are recalled because their products could be substituted for the recalled products (Barber and Darrough 1996; Dowdell et al. 1992; Govindaraj et al. 2004; Reilly and Hoffer 1983). This effect seems to be industry dependent, with a negative spillover effect in the drug and food industries (Freedman et al. 2009; Heede et al. 2007; Jarrell and Peltzman 1985) but a positive spillover effect in the tire industry (Govindaraj et al. 2004).

These results may be explained by signaling theory (Ahmed et al. 2002; Akerlof 1970; Spence 1973). When the news of a recall is broken, investors who are unable to distinguish between firms with and without a product hazard will price all stocks by averaging across all firms. As a result, similar firms suffer a negative "spillover" from the affected firm. However, as more information becomes available, investors are able to differentiate between the affected company and its unaffected competitors. Therefore, the market value of these competitors increases. Signaling theory posits that a rival's stock price will eventually react in a direction opposite to that of the affected firm.

Researchers have also investigated how decisions about how to conduct a recall impact the stock market. Rupp (2001) found that involuntary recalls, which were hypothesized to present a low-quality signal and elicit more damage to shareholders than voluntary recalls do, were not found to be associated with greater shareholder losses. Chen et al. (2008), however, found that a voluntary product recall strategy had a negative effect on a firm's financial value when compared to an involuntary strategy. Examples of product recall research from the financial perspective are contained in Section IV. Chapter 13 studies the stock market effect of product recall announcements in several industries in China, while Chapter 14 examines the financial impact of toy recall announcements in the United States. Chapter 15 describes the effect of product recall announcements on retailers, which are often neglected in supply chain management research.

2.5.2 Consumers' Perspective

The consumers' perspective focuses on consumer reactions to a recall announcement in terms of their future expected purchasing behavior and perceptions of brand equity. It makes use of primary data collected from scenario experiments, where researchers isolate cause-and-effect relationships, allowing them to observe, under controlled conditions, the effects of systematically varying one or more variables (Christensen 1991). A text is used to describe different scenarios, and participants are instructed to imagine these conditions happening to themselves.

Studies focusing on consumer behavior reactions to a product recall examine antecedent variables that determine outcomes, such as consumers' perception of the crisis (Laufer et al. 2006b), their repurchase intention (Marsh et al. 2004; Matos and Rossi 2006; Weinberger et al. 1980), and their impression of the company (Laufer et al. 2006a; Mowen 1980; Mowen et al. 1981). Antecedent variables of interest include country of manufacture (Laufer et al. 2006a), brand and company reputation (Laufer et al. 2006a; Mowen 1980; Siomkos and Kurzbard 1994), consumer age (Laufer et al. 2006c), knowledge of the recall by other companies (Mowen 1980; Mowen et al. 1981), perceived corporate responsibility of the company engaged in the product recall (Matos and Rossi 2006; Mowen et al. 1981), the source of information about the product and product type (Siomkos and Kurzbard 1994; Weinberger et al. 1980), the actions of the regulators (Mowen 1980), perceived seriousness of the crisis (Laufer et al. 2005; Mowen et al. 1981), and whether other companies have had similar product hazards (Mowen 1980; Mowen et al. 1981).

Other studies focus on the impact of product recalls on brand equity (Dawar and Pillutla 2000; Klein and Dawar 2004; Lei et al. 2005) and examine the reaction of consumers to brand equity in the face of a product recall. Dawar (1998) argued that brand equity can potentially be devastated by a product harm crisis, forcing the firm to either undertake massive expenditures for recall, restitution, and communication or forsake the brand and not invest any further in salvage measures. Dawar (2000) described the enduring effects of a product harm crisis as dependent on consumers' perceptions of the relevance of the crisis to key brand associations and the firm's response to it. Both effects are contingent upon consumer knowledge. Lei et al. (2005) found that a spillover effect occurred relative to a brand portfolio. That is, the strength of association among subbrands is a significant predictor of the spillover effect of a product harm crisis. Detailed examples of scenario experiments studying the consumers' perspective are contained in Section V. Chapter 16 examines the effect of different recall strategies on consumers' perceptions of a brand and repurchase intentions, while Chapter 17 deals with the role of emotions, particularly fear, in consumer reactions to a recall announcement.

2.5.3 Crisis Management and Public Relations Perspective

The crisis management and public relations perspective focuses on the way product harm crises and product recall information are communicated (e.g., Berman 1999; Burnett 1998; Gurau and Serbian 2005; Kabak and Siomkos 1991, 1992; Malickson 1983; Pearson and Clair 1998; Siomkos and Kurzbard 1994), prescribing practices to follow in dealing with a product harm crisis. Described organizational crises, such as a product harm crises, as evolving over a number of phases. The incubation phase is where early-warning signals may be present. Once the precipitating event has occurred and the crisis is manifest, the onset phase occurs. Finally, there are rescue and salvage efforts and full cultural adjustment. To manage a crisis like a product harm crisis effectively, management should strive for "minimizing potential risk before a triggering event. In response to a triggering event, effective crisis management involves improvising and interacting by key stakeholders so that individual and collective sense making, shared meaning, and roles are reconstructed" (Macdonald 2008). Thus, the best approach is avoiding a product harm crisis through investments in prevention. If a product harm crisis does occur, however, provision of relevant and timely information to consumers and investors is critical.

Siomkos and Kurzbard (1994) found that consumers' perception of the degree of danger was heavily influenced by external entities, including regulatory agencies (Eagle et al. 2005; Gibson 1995; Pearson and Mitroff 1993) and the press. In addition, consumers' future purchases of the company's other products will not be influenced by the present crisis if external reactions to the company's responses are positive and when the company's recall response was voluntary or a super effort, instead of denial.

2.5.4 Supply Chain Quality Management Perspective

A research perspective that has recently emerged addresses product harm crises and product recalls from the perspectives of supply chain management and quality management. While it has been suggested that quality management should be closely associated with supply chain management (e.g., Carter et al. 1998; Kannan and Tan 2005; Lin et al. 2005; Lo and Yeung 2006; Sroufe and Curkovic 2008; Tan et al. 1998; Theodorakioglou et al. 2006; Yeung 2008), most research still regards quality management and supply chain management as distinct. Robinson and Malhotra (2005, p. 319) defined supply chain quality management (SCQM) as "the formal coordination and integration of business processes involving all partner organizations in the supply channel to measure, analyze and continually improve products, services, and processes in order to create value and achieve satisfaction of intermediate and final customers in the marketplace." Foster (2008, p. 461) defined SCQM as "a systems-based approach to performance improvement that leverages opportunities created by upstream and downstream linkages with suppliers and customers." Thus, SCQM extends quality management principles from the individual firm to the entire supply chain. There remains a lack of conceptualization about quality management through the lens of supply chain management. But as Robinson and Malhotra (2005, p. 315) noted, "quality practices must advance from traditional firm centric and product-based mindsets to an inter-organizational supply chain orientation involving customers, suppliers, and other partners."

SCQM is different from other research perspectives on product recalls in its specific orientation toward the *prevention* of product harm crises and product recalls. As Robinson and Malhotra (2005, p. 315) noted, "[w]hile the importance of quality management is universally recognized, academic researchers need a more focused approach in evaluating quality management issues within the internal and external supply chain contexts." Thus, SCQM moves the focus of quality management beyond the walls of a single company to the role that suppliers and customers and their extended networks play in quality management. The SCQM perspective is described in greater detail in Section VI. Chapter 18 examines the impact of supply chain integration on performance, while Chapter 19 looks specifically at the customer orientation component of downstream customer integration. Chapter 20 examines the relationship of supply chain quality management with performance.

References

Ahmed, P., J. Gardella, and S. Nanda. 2002. Wealth effect of drug withdrawals on firms and their competitors. *Fin. Mgmt.* 31(3): 21–41.

Akerlof, G.A. 1970. The market for "Lemons": Quality uncertainty and the market mechanism. *Q. J. Econ.* 84(3): 488–500.

Balachander, S., and S. Ghose. 2003. Reciprocal spillover effects: A strategic benefit of brand extensions. *J. Mktg.* 67(1): 4–13.

Barber, B.M., and M.N. Darrough. 1996. Product reliability and firm value: The experience of american and japanese automakers, 1973–1992. *J. Pol. Econ.* 104(5): 1084–1099.

Berman, B. 1999. Planning for the inevitable product recall. *Bus. Horizons* March–April: 69–78.

Bromiley, P., and A. Marcus. 1989. The deterrent to dubious corporate behavior: Profitability, probability and safety recalls. *Strat. Mgmt. J.* 10(3): 233–250.

Burnett, J.J. 1998. A strategic approach to managing crises. *Pub. Rel. Rev.* 24(4): 475–488.

Carter, J.R., L. Smeltzer, and R. Narasimhan. 1998. The role of buyer and supplier relationships in integrating TQM through the supply chain. *Eur. J. Purch. Supp. Mgmt.* 4: 223–234.

Cheah, E.T., W.L. Chan, and C.L.L. Chieng. 2007. The corporate social responsibility of pharmaceutical product recalls: An empirical examination of U.S. and U.K. markets. *J. Bus. Ethics* 76: 427–449.

Chen, Y., S. Ganesan, and Y. Liu. 2008. Does a firm's product recall strategy affect its financial value? An examination of strategic alternatives during product harm crises. *J. Mktg.* 73(6): 24–226.

Christensen, T.W. 1991. Crisis leadership. A study of leadership practice. Capella University, UMI Dissertations Publishing, Ann Arbor, Michigan.

Chu, T.H., C.C. Lin, and L.J. Prather. 2005. An extension of security price reactions around product recall announcements. *Q. J. Bus. Econ.* 44(3/4): 33–48.

CPSC (Consumer Product Safety Commission). 2012. *CPSC Recall Handbook*. CPSC Office of Compliance.

Davidson, W., and D. Worrell. 1992. Research notes and communications: The effect of product recall announcements on shareholder wealth. *Strat. Mgmt. J.* 13(6): 467–473.

Dawar, N. 1998. Product-harm crises and the signaling ability of brands. *Int. Stud. Mgmt. Org.* 28(3): 109–119.

Dawar, N. 2000. *An Examination of Nuanced Effects of Product-Harm Crises on Brand Equity*. Richard Ivey School of Business working paper, University of Western Ontario, London.

Dawar, N., and M.M. Pillutla. 2000. Impact of product-harm crises on brand equity: The moderating role of consumer expectations. *J. Mktg. Res.* 37(2): 215–226.

Dowdell, T.D., S. Govindaraj, and P.C. Jain. 1992. The tylenol incident, ensuing regulation, and stock prices. *J. Fin. Quant. Anal.* 27(2): 283–301.

Dowie, M. 1977. Pinto madness. *Mother Jones.* September/October Issue.

Eagle, L., L.C. Rose, P.J. Kitchen, and Hawkins, J. 2005. Regulatory oversight or lack of foresight? Implications for product recall policies and procedures. *J. Cons. Pol.* 28: 433–460.

Fama, E.F. 1970. Efficient capital markets: A review of theory and empirical work. *J. Fin.* 15: 383–417.

Foster, S.T. 2008. Towards an understanding of supply chain quality management. *J. Ops. Mgmt.* 26: 461–467.

Freedman, S., M.S. Kearney, and M. Lederman. 2009. Product recalls, imperfect information, and spillover effects: Lessons from the consumer response to the 2007 toy recalls. *NBER Working Paper Series*, w15183 (July 2009).

Gibson, D.C. 1995. Public relations considerations of consumer product recall. *Pub. Rel. Rev.* 21(3): 225–240.

Govindaraj, S., B. Jaggi, and B. Lin. 2004. Market overreaction to product recall revisited—The case of Firestone tires. *Rev. Quant. Fin. Acctg.* 23(1): 31–54.

Gurau, C., and A. Serbian. 2005. The anatomy of the product recall message: The structure and function of product recall messages published in the UK press. *J. Comm. Mgmt.* 9(4): 326–338.

Haunschild, P.R., and M. Rhee. 2004. The role of volition in organizational learning: The case of automotive product recalls. *Mgmt. Sci.* 50(11): 1545–1560.

Heede, H.V., K. Helsen, and M.G. Dekimpe. 2007. The impact of a product-harm crisis on marketing effectiveness. *Mrktg. Sci.* 26(2): 230–245.

Hoffer, G.E., S.W. Pruitt, and R.J. Reilly. 1988. The impact of product recalls on the wealth of sellers: A reexamination. *J. Pol. Econ.* 96(3): 663–670.

Jarrell, G., and S. Peltzman. 1985. The impact of product recalls on the wealth of sellers. *J. Pol. Econ.* 93(3): 512–536.

Kabak, I.W., and G.J. Siomkos. 1991. Replacement after a product harm crisis. *Ind. Mgmt.* September/October: 25–26.

Kabak, I.W., and G.J. Siomkos. 1992. Monitoring recovery after a product harm crisis. *Ind. Mgmt.* May/June: 11–12.

Kannan, V.R., and K.C. Tan. 2005. Just in time, total quality management, and supply chain management: Understanding their linkages and impact on business performance. *OMEGA* 33: 153–162.

Klein, J., and N. Dawar. 2004. Corporate social responsibility and consumers' attributions and brand evaluations in a product-harm crisis. *Int. J. Res. Mrktg.* 21: 203–217.

Laufer, D., K. Gillespie, B. McBride, and S. Gonzalez. 2005. The role of severity in consumer attributions of blame: Defensive attributions in product-harm crises in Mexico. *J. Int. Cons. Mktg.* 17(2/3): 33–50.

Laufer, D., K. Gillespie, and D.H. Silvera. 2006a. The impact of country of manufacture and brand on consumer's attributions of blame in a product harm crisis. *Adv. Cons. Res.* 1:187.

Laufer, D., D.H. Silvera, and T. Meyer. 2006b. Exploring differences between older and younger consumers in attributions of blame for product harm crises. *Acad. Mrktg. Sci. Rev.* 7.

Laufer, D., D.H. Silvera, and T. Meyer. 2006c. The impact of aging on consumer attributions of blame for a product harm crisis. *Adv. Cons. Res.* 33: 704–705.

Lei, J., N. Dawar, and J. Lemmink. 2005. The spillover effects of product harm crisis in a brand portfolio. *Am. Mrktg. Assn.* Winter: 72(3): 288–289.

Lin, C.H., I.H. Lin, and C.T. Lin. 2005. The relationship between service failures, service recovery strategies and behavioral intentions in hotel industry. *Bus. Rev., Cambridge*, 8(1): 141–147.

Lo, V.H.Y., and A. Yeung. 2006. Managing quality effectively in supply chain: A preliminary study. *Supp. Chain Mgmt.* 11(3): 208–215.

Lu, H.Y., H.Y. Hou, T.H. Dzwo, Y.C. Su, J.E. Andrews, S.T. Weng, M.C. Lin, and J.Y. Lu. 2009. Factors influencing intentions to take precautions to avoid consuming food containing dairy products. *Brit. Food J.* 112(9): 919–933.

Macdonald, J.R. 2008. Supply chain disruption management: A conceptual framework and theoretical model. College Park, MD, University of Maryland.

Malickson, D.L. 1983. Are you ready for a product recall? *Bus. Horizons* Jan–Feb: 31–35.

Marsh, T.L., T.C. Schroeder, and J. Mintert. 2004. Impacts of meat product recalls on consumer demand in the USA. *Appl. Econ.* 36: 897–909.

Matos, C.A. de, and C.A.V. Rossi. 2006. Consumer reaction to product recalls: Factors influencing product judgment and behavioural intentions. *Int. J. Cons. Stud.* 31(1): 109–116.

Mitchell, M.L. 1989. The impact of external parties on brand-name capital: The 1982 tylenol poisonings and subsequent cases. *Econ. Inq.* 27(4): 601–618.

Mowen, J.C. 1980. Further information on consumer perceptions of product recalls. Planning for and implementing a product recall. *Adv. Cons. Res.* 7: 519–523.

Mowen, J.C., D. Jolly, and G.S. Nickell. 1981. Factors influencing consumer responses to product recalls: A regression analysis approach. *Adv. Cons. Res.* 8: 405–407.

Pearson, C.M., and J.A. Clair. 1998. Reframing crisis management. *Acad. Mgmt. Rev.* 23(1): 59–76.

Pearson, C.M., and I.I. Mitroff. 1993. From crisis prone to crisis prepared: A framework for crisis management. *Acad. Mgmt. Exec.* 7(1): 48–59.

Pruitt, S.W., and D.R. Peterson. 1985. Security price reactions around product recall announcements. *Financial Rev.* 20(3): 99.

Pruitt, S.W., and D.R. Peterson. 1986. Security price reactions around product recall announcements. *J. Fin. Res.* 9(2): 113–122.

Reilly, R.J., and G.E. Hoffer. 1983. Will retarding the information flow on automobile recalls affect consumer demand? *Econ. Inq.* 21(3): 444–447.

Rhee, M., and P.R. Haunschild. 2006. The liability of good reputation: A study of product recalls in the U.S. automobile industry. *Org. Sci.* 17(1): 101–117.

Robinson, C.J., and M.K. Malhotra. 2005. Defining the concept of supply chain quality management and its relevance to academic and industrial practice. *Int. J. Prod. Econ.* 96: 315–337.

Rooney, B. 2010. Toyoda: Our rush to grow led to safety issues. *CNN.* February 23, 2010.

Rupp, N.G. 2001. Are government initiated recalls more damaging for shareholders? Evidence from automotive recalls, 1973–1998. *Econ. Lett.* 71: 265–270.

Siomkos, G., and G. Kurzbard. 1994. The hidden crisis in product-harm crisis management. *Eur. J. Mrktg.* 28(2): 30–41.

Spence, M. 1973. Job market signaling. *Q. J. Econ.* 87(3): 355–374.

Sroufe, R., and S. Curkovic. 2008. An examination of ISO 9000:2000 and supply chain quality assurance. *J. Ops. Mgmt.* 26: 503–520.

Tan, K.C., R.B. Handfield, and D.R. Krause. 1998. Enhancing the firm's performance through quality and supply base management: An empirical study. *Int. J. Prod. Res.* 36(10): 2813–2837.

Theodorakioglou, Y., K. Gotzamani, and G. Tsiolvas. 2006. Supplier management and its relationship to buyers' quality management. *Supp. Chain Mgmt.* 11(2): 148–159.

Weinberger, M.G., C.T. Allen, and W.R. Dillon. 1980. The impact of negative marketing communications: The consumers union/Chrysler controversy. *J. Adv.* 10(4): 20–47.

Yeung, C.L. 2008. Strategic supply management, quality initiatives, and organizational performance. *J. Ops. Mgmt.* 26: 490–502.

Chapter 3

Consumer Protection in Developing Countries

TingTing Zhao and Barbara B. Flynn

Contents

3.1 Introduction: Consumer Protection in Developing Countries

The term "consumer protection" refers to a group of laws and organizations that are designed to ensure the rights of consumers. The underlying rationale is that consumers need special protection because of the unbalanced relationship that exists between them and business organizations (Shigang and Guangyan 2012). First, consumers are individual people, who are scattered and not organized. Second, the business organizations that sell them products and services hold most of the technical information; consumers are information deprived, without sufficient evidence of consumer rights issues that they may have suffered.

According to the *West Encyclopedia of American Law* (Lehman and Phelps 2005), a consumer is someone who acquires goods or services for his or her direct use or ownership, rather than for resale or use in production and manufacturing (Gale and Lehman 2011). Although this seems like a clear definition, it is subject to question on several levels, which can make the enforcement of consumer laws challenging to enforce. For example, what is meant by direct use? Does this apply to collectors of antiques, for example, who many not actually use the products that they purchase? Does it apply to people who purchase items for use by others (e.g., parents who purchase toys and food for their children)? In developed countries, these questions have been dealt with and progressively refined over a period of many years of legislation and litigation (Overby 2006). In developing countries, however, the development of consumer protection legislation has taken place only recently, and enforcement often lags behind. In this chapter, we discuss consumer protection legislation in China, describing key laws and how they have been implemented, paralleling China's rapid emergence as a consumer society. We then describe how social media serves as a consumer protection mechanism in China, filling the vacuum caused by challenging implementation and enforcement of consumer protection laws.

3.1.1 Consumer Protection in Developed Countries

Consumer protection has a long history in developed countries. The earliest known consumer protection legislation was the *Lex Julia de Annona* statute implemented by the government of Rome around 50 B.C. It provided legal protection for commercial operations, as well as consumer protection for Roman citizens, including prevention of commercial monopolies and of predatory and discriminatory pricing. In the United States, the antitrust and antimonopoly laws of 1890 and early in the twentieth century were aimed primarily at preventing commercial monopolization. However, they also protected consumers from unethical pricing, exploitation of commercial markets, and violations of constitutionality.

In the United States, the Consumer Product Safety Act established the Consumer Product Safety Commission, giving it the power to develop safety standards and administer (and sometimes mandate) recalls for unsafe products, as described in

Chapter 2. As the wave of consumerism took place in developed countries, the role of the government in consumer protection was set forth; the government is required to meet its responsibility to consumers in the exercise of their rights. These rights include (1) the right to safety; (2) the right to be informed; (3) the right to choose; and (4) the right to be heard. Other important consumer protection legislation in the United States includes (Eigen 2009).

1. The Federal Trade Commission Act, which gave the Federal Trade Commission the ability to prevent unfair competition and deceptive acts and regulate trade
2. The United States National Do Not Call Registry, which gives consumers in the United States the right to limit telephone calls from telemarketers
3. The Pure Food and Drug Act, which created the U.S. Food and Drug Administration, in order to regulate food, drugs, and related products
4. The Communications Act of 1934, which created the Federal Communications Commission to regulate radio and interstate cable, telephone, and satellite communications
5. The Fair Credit Reporting Act, which regulates consumer credit information collection, dissemination, and use
6. The Fair Debt Collection Practices Act, which targets abusive consumer practices and ensures fairness in debt collection
7. The Truth in Lending Act, which requires disclosure of all key terms of loan arrangements and costs
8. The Real Estate Settlement Procedures Act, which disallows kickbacks and requires good faith estimates of lending costs
9. The Health Insurance Portability and Accountability Act, which provides consumer protection for health information
10. The Digital Millennium Copyright Act, which disallows the production or sale of devices or services intended to circumvent copyright measures

This legislation was developed and refined over a period of more than a century, as consumer protection issues occurred and were tested. It is typical of the types of consumer protection that exist in developing countries, where there is strong legislation and enforcement.

3.1.2 Consumer Protection in China

In order to understand consumer protection in China, we begin by stepping back a half century to the time when the concept of "consumer" did not exist in China. During China's Cultural Revolution (1966–1976), all Western influences were rejected, and there was little room for consumers, ideologically. The economy was centrally planned, with little thought to individual consumers. The planned economy focused on perceived needs, rather than the actual desires of consumers, and the state was the principal supplier of goods, housing, and services. Coupons were the means of exchange for most consumer goods, with little opportunity for consumer choice. Thus, there were no mechanisms for consumers to complain about consumer problems, or even the recognition that consumers might have problems. Thus, the concept of a consumer is relatively new in China, beginning with Deng Xiaoping's market liberalization during 1978–1979 (Ho 1997).

In preparation for China's accession to the World Trade Organization in 2001, there was a significant amount of consumer protection legislation developed (Overby 2006). China is now the largest consumer market in the world, with a radically altered competitive landscape. It is the target for foreign businesses that seek to tap into its large market and take advantage of its dramatic economic growth rates and rising personal incomes. Thus, in a relatively short period of time, compared with developed economies, China made the transition from having no consumer economy to being the largest consumer market in the world (Overby 2006). However, the rapid growth of consumerism also unveiled a number of problems that Chinese consumers had with the goods and services that they had purchased, including counterfeit medicines, tainted food products, shoddy and fake products, and false advertising.

This progression is not necessarily typical of an emerging market, nor was it similar to the development of consumer protection in a Western industrialized country. China's recent history is unique because, although it was a developing country with a developing legal system, it had a booming economy with a vast number of consumers (Overby 2006).

Interestingly, the notion that consumers merited special protection was not difficult to promote in China. Even before there was a strong acceptance of Western market values, China's Confucian heritage was built on a strong mistrust of the merchant class (Tong 1992), who had the lowest status in Chinese society:

> [their] low status was partially due to a general belief that merchants do not create real value, but simply dawdle or pass on things which have been created by other people. In this sense, they are parasites of the society and believed to be unethical. (Tong 1992, p. 344)

There are a number of important consumer laws in China. In the following, we describe two of the most important to consumer product safety.

3.1.2.1 Law of the People's Republic of China on the Protection of Consumer Rights and Interests

The Law of the People's Republic of China on the Protection of Consumer Rights and Interests (CRIL) became effective in January 1994 and remained the same until 2013, when it was updated. It is China's primary consumer protection statute, covering nine basic rights of consumers (Overby 2006):

1. The right to the inviolability of personal and property safety
2. The right to obtain true information regarding goods and services received
3. The right to free choice of goods and services
4. The right to a fair deal
5. The right to demand compensation when personal injury or property damage occurs
6. The right to form public organizations for the maintenance of consumers' legitimate rights and interests, according to the law
7. The right to acquire knowledge concerning consumption and the protection of consumer rights and interests
8. The right to have human dignity, national customs, and habits to be respected when purchasing and using goods and when receiving services
9. The right to raise charges against state organs and functionaries and to raise criticism of and proposals for the protection of consumer rights and interests

Within CRIL, Article 22 is of particular interest to the study of product safety:

> **Article 22.** Business operators shall guarantee the quality, functions, usage and terms of validity which the commodities or services they supply should possess under normal operations or acceptance, except that consumers are aware of the defects before they buy the commodities or receive the services. For product defects that cause personal injuries, the business owner is responsible for medical and other related expenses.

Perhaps the principal weakness of CRIL is that it fails to address the legal consequences for a business owner who fails to comply with its obligations. It lists a number of ways to deal with this situation but positions them only as suggestions, not as mandates:

1. Resolution of disputes through settlement
2. Conciliation
3. Mediation through consumer associations
4. Appeal to the relevant administrative department
5. Referral to arbitration
6. Legal proceedings

Another interesting part of CRIL is Article 49, which requires increased compensation in the amount that was paid to the business operator that engages in fraudulent activities in supplying goods and services.

Although this legislation seems comprehensive, the primary issue is how and when it should be enforced. It is more of a set of broad standards than a guideline for effective action.

> …unless specific liability is provided for in Chapter VII, it is unclear whether a breach of obligations or an infringement of rights under the earlier Chapters would be the basis for civil liability. Because of this, the effectiveness of the broad statements in the earlier Chapters of the CRIL that recognize consumer rights and business operators' obligations is significantly undercut. The rights and obligations become general principles unsupported by any effective legal enforcement apparatus. (Overby 2006)

3.1.2.2 Law of the People's Republic of China on Product Quality

The Law of the People's Republic of China on Product Quality (PQL) was adopted in 1993 (Overby 2006) and amended by the Standing Committee of the National People's Congress in 2000. It provides a strong foundation for consumer protection.

> **Article 14:** Producers shall be liable for the quality of the products they produce. The products shall meet the following quality requirements:
>
> 1. Constituting no unreasonable threats to personal safety or safety to property, and conforming to the national standards or the sectoral standards for ensuring human health, personal safety and safety of property, where there are such standards.
> 2. Possessing the properties as required, except for those with directions stating their functional defects, and
> 3. Conforming to the product standards marked on the products or on the packages thereof, and to the quality conditions indicated by way of product directions, samples, etc. (Han 2003).

If a seller provides a product that fails to meet these standards, it is obligated to

1. Repair or replace the good
2. Refund the purchase price
3. Pay for consequential losses resulting from the nonconformity

Furthermore, the seller has the right to recover its own losses from the producer or an intermediate seller if one of those parties is liable.

Although the PQL states that the seller is liable for compensation when personal property or property losses are incurred due to a defective product, this is somewhat open to interpretation. For example, is this a strict liability standard or a fault-based standard (Overby 2006)? In addition, there are a number of routes for the defense to take in such a case. For example, if the defect could not be found at the time that the product was in circulation, due to "scientific and technological reasons" (Overby 2006), the seller is not liable. The period of limitation for filing a complaint is 2 years from the time that the consumer knew or should have known that there had been an infringement of his or her rights.

3.1.2.3 China Consumers Association

The China Consumers Association was founded in 1984, with state support and linkages (Overby 2006). It provides many of the functions of a consumer protection agency like the U.S. Consumer Product Safety Commission. It also serves as the base for thousands of additional local agencies and organizations. Although it has no enforcement power, the China Consumers Association serves a number of important functions:

1. Promotes consumer issues and education
2. Offers dispute resolution services
3. Monitors quality of goods and services
4. Advises government authorities on matters related to consumer affairs
5. Research on consumer issues
6. Investigates consumer concerns; the results may indicate areas where law reform is warranted

3.1.2.4 Issues with Consumer Protection in China

Despite having well-documented laws in books, there are a number of issues with consumer protection in China. First, there are obstacles to enforcement of consumer protection laws (Zhao 2002). According to Overby (2006, p. 370), "The mere existence of laws does not speak powerfully to their utility or their impact." The general law reform that has taken place in China in recent years has resulted in a myriad of new laws, such that consumers may not be aware of all of these laws or fully understand their rights under them.

Second, China's judicial system is in its infancy, making enforcement of laws like consumer protection laws challenging (Overby 2006). It has not progressed at the same pace as recent economic advances in China. During the 1990s, the focus was on the development of appropriate legislation, rather than its enforcement (Shigang and Guangyan 2012). The courts are overburdened, making it difficult to even get a hearing for a consumer rights case. There is no small-claims court, as there is in the United States, making it difficult for individual consumers to move forward with a consumer protection case. Furthermore, there is not a simplified procedure for judicial resolution of consumer disputes, as there is in the United

States. Thus, the judicial system has not been strong in enforcing consumer protection legislation.

In addition, Chinese people are generally reluctant to rely upon the law to protect their rights (Overby 2006). They are more likely to seek less formal means for resolving their disputes. Maxims like "minimize the consequences" and "better none than less" are deeply rooted in the Chinese culture (Shigang and Guangyan 2012), causing Chinese consumers to be reluctant to turn to the courts to settle their issues.

Furthermore, although CRIL is sound, it was static and had not been updated since its enactment in 1993. It was based upon three principles, which may be conflicting:

1. Protecting the legitimate rights and interests of consumers
2. Maintaining socioeconomic order
3. Promoting healthy development of the Socialist market economy

CRIL was eventually updated in 2013, increasing consumer powers, adding rules for Internet shopping, and increasing the punishment for businesses that mislead shoppers; compensation for retailers who violate the law was increased to three times the amount of damages (Jourdan 2013). The 2013 update also strengthened the role of the China Consumers Association, so that it is now able to represent groups of consumers in class action lawsuits against retailers.

CRIL and other related laws have been enacted at a superficial level (Shigang and Guangyan 2012). They lack specific rules for dealing with consumers in a consumer setting. Consumers are not always able to get adequate, immediate, and effective support. The five listed methods for dealing with disputes (consultation, reconciliation, mediation, appeal, and arbitration) are limited in their application and can drag on, often leading to no resolution. CRIL protects a limited scope of rights and mostly describes the rights that consumers have, rather than how they can specifically realize those rights (Shigang and Guangyan 2012); there are no detailed procedural regulations.

The compensation provision required business operators to pay double (quadruple, as of late 2013) if they have committed a fraud on consumers; however, the burden of proof is on the consumers (Huixing 2005). Consumers may lack the sort of skills needed to prove the cause of a defect, the type of defect, and which defects led to the actual damage (Shigang and Guangyan 2012). For example, in the melamine-tainted milk case, customers did not have any way of knowing that there was melamine in the milk powder that they had purchased or how it got there; all that they knew was that their babies became ill after consuming milk made from the powder. In addition, burden of proof and litigation expenses can be substantial, preventing consumers with limited incomes from moving forward with consumer protection cases.

Furthermore, there have been some notable examples of consumers who took advantage of the provisions of these laws, making the courts somewhat skeptical of consumer protection complaints. The most famous example is Wang Hai (Overby 2006), a citizen who made a very successful career out of CRIL's Article 49. In 1995, he began to buy fake products then demanded double compensation after receiving verification from the manufacturers that they were phony. Fearful of reprisals, he took to wearing dark glasses, which eventually became his trademark (Asia: A shopper's friend 2001). He quickly became a national celebrity, leading to a number of Wang Hai imitators. In 1995, he set up Da Hai Commercial Consultancy Corp. and, later, Wanghai Online Information Consulting, companies that specialized in purchasing fake products then suing the offending manufacturers and retailers. Although he readily admitted that his primary goal was personal financial gain, Wang Hai became China's most powerful consumer activist. In 1999, courts in Nanjing and Beijing ruled that he could not assert his rights under CRIL because he knew that the items that he bought were fake when he bought them, and they excluded from "consumer" status any parties who buy for a reason other than real consumption. However, the Wang Hai phenomenon did help the growing awareness that ordinary citizens have consumer rights, even if they are reluctant to exercise them.

To summarize, although there has been a substantial amount of consumer protection legislation in China, it is broad and challenging to enforce. There is a growing awareness of the right to consumer protection among ordinary consumers, however. In the following, we describe how social media has been used to fill the gaps in consumer protection enforcement in China, allowing a grassroots consumer protection movement to develop.

3.2 Social Media as a Form of Consumer Protection

3.2.1 Overview

Nearly 17 years ago, Ozanne and Murray (1995) attempted to create a new discourse for consumers, suggesting that public policy can help consumers become aware of their power to define and fulfill their own needs. They argued that, in a postmodern society, people maneuver through an information-rich environment in which their relationships with other people were increasingly being mediated by forces such as television, VCRs, computers, and information highways. They further suggested the development of a different kind of consumer, one who is empowered to reflect on his or her social conditions to decide how to live.

With the emergence of social media, that new kind of consumer is easily seen in society today, 19 years after the research of Ozanne and Murray (1995). Social media empowers consumers by satisfying their need to be informed and to be heard. The communications world is dramatically moving in a digital direction (Weber 2007).

Social media deliver web-based information created by people with the intention of facilitating communication, representing one of the major sources of social interaction, as people share stories and experiences with each other (Wright and Hinson 2009). Anyone with an opinion about anything can create, in a matter of minutes, his or her own website for publishing news, opinions, commentary, and links to other sites (Key 2005).

According to Media System Dependency Theory, media system dependency is defined as "a relationship in which the capacity of individuals to attain their goals is contingent upon the information resources of the media system." Those information resources can be categorized as the ability to create and gather, process, and disseminate information. According to a previous study, "media system dependency theory assumes that the more a person depends on having his or her needs met by media use, the more important will be the role that media play in the person's life, and therefore the more influence those media will have on the person." In an environment where the mass media fails to provide equal access to each consumer, not allowing him or her to be informed and to be heard, social media can take the place of the mass media to allow these things to happen.

Social media provides equal access to consumers to communicate anything they want to;. thus, these empowered consumers rely on social media to protect their right to be informed and to be heard in an increasingly complex marketplace. This is of particular importance in developing countries, where government and industry may fail to meet their responsibility for consumer protection.

3.2.2 Role of Mass Media in Consumer Protection

There are three critical functions of the mass media. The first is its political function, which includes monitoring and surveillance, while the second is its economic function, which includes the provision of information related to buyers and sellers and interpretation of information. The third function of the mass media is its general sociological function, because it expresses social norms and coordinates the behavior of the masses. From a theoretical perspective, all three aspects of the mass media's function contribute to the protection of consumer rights. However, the reality is that, in the mass media–dominant age, consumers do not have equal access to obtaining information from the mass media.

Knowledge-gap theory provides an explanation for this phenomenon. The knowledge-gap hypothesis theory suggests that each new medium increases the gap between the information rich and the information poor, because of differences in their access to the medium and in their control over its use. As the infusion of mass media information into a social system increases, the segments of a population with higher socioeconomic status tend to acquire information at a faster rate than those in the lower status segments. Thus, the gap in knowledge between socioeconomic segments tends to increase, rather than decrease.

3.2.3 Emergence of Social Media

Social media (Wright and Hinson 2009) is changing how people and organizations communicate. This has increased as social media has developed into a number of different forms, including text, images, audio, and video, and through the development of forums, message boards, photo sharing, video sharing, Wikis, social networks, and microblogging sites. According to a recent report, the number of users of social media giants Facebook and Twitter has reached 750 million and 100 million, respectively. More than half of all Internet users have joined a social network; social networks have become the number one platform for creating and sharing content (Young 2009). Social media satisfies consumers' need to be heard, provides them with a platform to reach more people than ever before, and enables consumers to advocate for and promote the brands and topics they feel strongly about.

The popularity of social media has grown not only in developed countries but also in developing countries. India has 1.17 billion Internet users, with 68.5% of its online population visiting social networking sites. In the past decade, the number of Internet users in China has grown from millions to billions. According to the statistics of the China Internet Network Information Center, the number of Internet users in China is 4.2 billion; among them, 2.77 billion people are mobile Internet users. Internet penetration has increased rapidly not only in cities but also in rural areas.

3.2.4 Social Media in China

To Chinese people, the Internet not only is a tool for checking e-mail and getting information but also provides a form of social identification and interactive engagement. As a result of government censorship, China's digital media landscape is dominated by local players, which makes China's digital media market unique. Most of its netizens are urban; however, there are more than 95 million rural netizens, and the number is increasing. Evidence shows that Chinese netizens are looking for ways to express their freedom on the Internet. According to a recent survey, 73% of Chinese netizens agreed with the statement, "Online, I feel free to say and do things I would not do or say offline," compared to only 32% of U.S. netizens (Liu 2012).

The digital media in China is dominated by several social media giants. As one of the biggest social-networking sites social media networks in China, Renren, which has a very similar function to Facebook, has a total of more than 100 million registered users; 24 million people visit it each day. It provides interactive experiences and word-of-mouth communications, which builds and maintains close relationships between customers. The number of registered users of Sina Weibo, which serves a similar function to Twitter, is nearly 75 million.

Growing media and Internet penetration are playing a significant role in changing how China's consumers see the world. They no longer passively receive information from the traditional mass media. Rather, the rapid development of social media enables them to be informed and to be heard about their opinions on products and services. Every day, millions of Chinese consumers converse in online communities, discussion boards, blogs, and social networks. They turn to the Internet to share opinions, advice, grievances, and recommendations.

Furthermore, Chinese consumers are increasingly relying on social media to express their voice and protect their rights. Consumers in different locations can build up close attachments through various social networks. When their rights have been harmed, consumers can virtually unite through the platform of social media to express their voices and form a strong base of power, which is much more powerful in encouraging the government to take actions to protect consumer rights.

3.3 Social Media in the Chinese Milk Powder Scandal

3.3.1 Mass Media and Social Media Perspectives

No Chinese consumer will ever forget the Sanlu milk powder contamination incident that happened in 2008, which aroused Chinese consumers awareness about consumer rights and product safety. The way that the rights of affected consumers were protected during the incident also illustrates the role of social media as an institutional supplement for protecting consumer rights. The formal version of the incident, as reported by the mass media, is as follows:

> In 2008, Sanlu, a Chinese dairy firm, was accused of producing melamine contaminated milk. After drinking this milk formulation, nearly 53,000 infants across the country were affected with 13,000 infants immediately hospitalized. (Macartney 2008)

Social media can help us to learn more about the underlying mechanisms of the incident. We used the online ethnographic method to study the milk powder contamination incident. Qualitative research studies were conducted through ethnographic editing of data from virtual social spheres such as chat rooms, virtual communities, and museums (Sudweek and Simoff 1999). Ethnography is based primarily on analysis of texts and chats (Mitra and Cohen 1999) or on interactive online studies as a participant–observer. Interviews and recording of actions in Internet communication groups, such as forums and communities, supply clear boundaries (Kendall 1999; Sharf 1999).

We used the Tianya community for conducting our research. As the largest online community in China, Tianya has more than 4,736,2421 registered users around the world. Tianya had a total of 22,755 posts regarding the milk powder contamination incident, which enabled us to get a better picture of what transpired in 2008.

The first piece of evidence about the milk powder contamination appeared in the mass media on September 6, 2008. Several months earlier, however, affected consumers' complaints had already been posted in Tianya, starting on May 20, 2008, when the father of an affected baby complained in his post about the low quality of Sanlu powder, which caused his daughter's unusual urine. Social media was the only way for him to complain, since mass media in China is monitored by the government. Because Sanlu was a state-owned enterprise, with a good reputation, any sort of negative information regarding it would not normally appear in the coverage by the mass media.

Several months later, the number of affected babies was increasing in different cities in China. All these babies were drinking formula made from Sanlu powder; however, Sanlu again stated that its powder had absolutely no quality issues. This was the source of great concern by netizens in their social media posts. A large number of people participated in the online discussion, posing many posts that cited Sanlu's irresponsibility. This established a way for people to become more powerful by joining their voices with the voices of other concerned netizens, which drove the government to take actions to investigate the issue, compensate harmed consumers, and punish Sanlu and other members of its supply chain that were responsible.

Thus, faced with an immature judicial system and imperfect institutions for the protection of consumer rights, the will of the people eventually drove the government to make decisions that were beneficial to the rights of consumers. During the discussion of the milk contamination issue, the role of social media became much clearer. In addition to this case, other stories have been put forth on various social media platforms, allowing consumers to express their negative experiences with product or service failures and thus help themselves to protect their own rights.

3.3.2 Discussion

The story of the milk powder contamination incident illustrates the important role of social media as an institutional supplement to the government in protecting consumer rights. Without social media, the affected consumers would not have been able to express their opinions; thus, they would not have been heard by the government and other consumers.

Social media served two main functions in this case. First, it enabled the affected consumers' opinions to be heard. Sanlu's customers were relatively low in social status and income; thus, there would have been no way for them to complain without the existence of social media. Second, social media enabled other consumers to be informed about something that was very important to them (the health of their babies). At the same time, these consumers had the opportunity to express their opinions about the incident and have an impact on how it was ultimately handled.

Legislation and enforcement of consumer protection provisions still have a long way to go in China and other developing countries. The emergence of social media as an institutional supplement for the protection of consumer rights empowers consumers, especially those who are of lower socioeconomic status. This allows them to express their opinions regarding their rights, which could easily have been ignored by the government and Sanlu, prior to the emergence of their power to join their voices with other consumers that was provided by social media. Social media connects consumers in different locations and transforms them from independent individuals to a powerful group, in order to work together to protect their rights as consumers.

The role of social media and the way that it empowers consumers bring new challenges for companies. It is important for future research to study the role of social media and consumer protection in developing countries. Our research contributes to the early foundation for research on social media and consumer protection in developing countries, providing insights to the Western world regarding social media in China and the unique role that it plays there.

References

Asia: A shopper's friend. Consumer protection in China. *The Economist* 361(8248), November 17, 2001.

Davidson, M.J. 1994. *Trade Practices and Consumer Protection*. Butterworths.

Eigen, L.D. 2009. A solution to the problem of consumer contracts that cannot be understood by consumers who sign them. *Scriptamus*.

Gale, T. and Lehman. 2011. *West Encyclopedia of American Law*, vols. 13 Farmington Hills, MI: Gale Group.

Han, L. 2003. The product quality law in China: A proper balance between consumers and producers? *J. Chinese Comp. Law*, 43.

Ho, S.C. 1997. The emergence of consumer power in China. *Bus. Horizons* September–October.

Huixing, L. 2005. Consumer policy and legislation of China. *Law Mag.* 5.

Jiang, P. 1995. Chinese legal reform: Achievement, problems and prospects. *J. Chinese Law* 67.

Johnston, C.F. 1996. Consumer welfare and competition policy. *Competition Cons. Law J.* 3(3): 45–260.

Jourdan, A. 2013. China overhauls consumer protection laws. October 25.

Kendall, L. 1999. Recontextualizing 'cyberspace': Methodological considerations for online research. In S. Jones (Ed.), *Doing Internet Research*. London: Sage.

Key, R.J. 2005. How the PR profession can flourish in this new digital age: Why you must challenge old PR models. *Pub. Rel. Tactics* November: 18–19.

Laws.com. n.d. The Truth Behind the History of Consumer Protection Laws. http://consumer .laws.com/consumer-protection-laws.

Lehman, J. and Phelps, S.I. 2005. *West Encyclopedia of American Law*. Farmington Hills, MI: Gale Cengage.

Liu, C. 2012. *People in developing countries love social media more*. Available at http://it.21cn.com/mi/a/2012/1213/11/20110610.shtml, retrieved December 15, 2012.

Lu, H. 2000. To be relatively comfortable in an egalitarian society. In D. Davis (Ed.), *The Consumer Revolution in Urban China*. Berkeley: The University of California Press.

Macartney, J. 2008. China baby milk scandal spreads as sick toll rises to 13,000. *The Times (London)*, September 22. Retrieved April 2, 2010.

Overby, A.B. 2006. Consumer protection in China after accession to the WTO. *Syracuse J. Int. Law Commer.* 33(2): 347–392.

Ozanne, J.L. and Murray, J.B. 1995. Uniting critical theory and public policy to create the reflexively defiant consumer. *Am. Behav. Sci.* 38(4): 516–525.

Sharf, B.J. 1999. Beyond netiquette: The ethics of doing naturalistic discourse research on the internet. In S. Jones (Ed.), *Doing Internet Research*. London: Sage.

Shigang, L. and Z. Guangyan. 2012. The problems of China's consumer protection law in legal practice. *Int. J. Bus. Soc. Sci.* 3(14): 65–72.

Tong, G. 1992. Chinese consumer protection policy. *J. Cons. Policy* 337: 343–344.

Wright, D.K. and Hinson, M.D. 2009. An updated look at the impact of social media on public relations practice. *Pub. Rel. J.* 3(2): 1–27.

Young, R. 2009. Social media: How new forms of communications are changing job search and career management: *Be Heard*. Newsletter of the Toronto Chapter of the International Association of Business Communicators.

Zhao, G. 2002. Chinese product liability law: Can China build another Great Wall to protect its consumers? *Wash. U. Glob. Stud. Law Rev.* 1(1): 581–586.

Chapter 4

Quality Risk in Global Supply Networks

Kim Hua Tan, Ying Kei Tse, and Jie Chen

Contents

4.1 Introduction: Importance of Supply Chain Risk

The rapid increase in quality risk in global supply chains not only brings new challenges in supply chain quality management for policy makers and managers but also provides new research opportunities for the academic world, especially for the field of operations management and supply chain management (Sodhi et al. 2012). Quality management research in the supply chain arena provides researchers an opportunity to apply, extend, and challenge existing risk management and quality management theories and frameworks. In particular, the risks associated with product quality and safety in supply chains are only partially understood in the extant literature.

Supply chain quality risk is an ambiguous concept. There is no unified definition of supply chain risk (Tang and Musa 2011), and it lacks "an overarching typology to delineate exactly what constitutes supply chain risk" (Rao and Goldsby 2009). This has resulted in disparate studies and fragmented literature, which hinders managing supply chain risk using a systematic and structured approach (Khan and Burnes 2007; Rao and Goldsby 2009; Ellis et al. 2011).

This chapter contributes to the literature in two important ways. First, we clarify some confusion and paradoxes in the extant risk management literature, leading to the development of an integrated model of risk. Second, we develop a clearer understanding of supply chain risk, contributing to the supply chain risk management literature. The Theory of Swift, Even Flow (Schmenner and Swink 1998) is applied as a theoretical lens to help better understand the nature of supply chain risk management. This research also provides a foundation for the development of meaningful measures (Wacker 2004) of supply chain risk for empirical studies and for further development of theory related to this important construct.

4.2 Risk and Supply Chain Quality Risk

4.2.1 Concept of Risk

Risk has been widely studied in diverse fields, including economics (Davidson 1991), finance (Schinasi and Drees 1999), accounting (Hakansson 1969), strategy (Baird and Thomas 1985), marketing (Cook and Page 1987), and operations management (Lewis 2003). However, it is difficult to define. As Fishhoff (1985) observed, "People disagree more about what risk is than about how large it is." There is substantial tension in the literature between decision theorists and managerial researchers about questions related to the nature of risk, the difference between risk and uncertainty, and the debate over whether risk is objective or subjective. We focus on each of these in the following and then propose an integrated model of risk.

4.2.2 Decision Theory vs. Managerial Perspective

The starting point for many discussions about risk is the variance-based view, which is dominant in the classic decision theory literature (Miller 1992; Peck 2006). It defines risk as "variation in the distribution of possible outcomes, their likelihoods, and their subjective values" (March and Shapira 1987). This view can be traced back to the work of Markowitz in 1952 (Rao and Goldsby 2009), who equated risk with estimated variance (Markowitz 1952) in his research on investment portfolios. This view has been widely accepted (Rao and Goldsby 2009; Cheng et al. 2012) in finance and strategic management research (Miller and Reuer 1996). The innate association between risk and variance lies in the fundamental statistical attributes of variance. The wider the dispersion of data around its mean, the greater the variance. High variance lowers confidence that the observed value is close to the mean and is thus an indicator of unpredictability (Melnyk et al. 1992; Fredendall and Melnyk 1995). Therefore, variance has been the cornerstone of the concept of risk (Shapira 1995). Inherent in the variance-based view is the notion that risk entails both the possibility of loss and the possibility of gain (Moore 1983).

However, managers may view risk differently (March and Shapira 1987; Miller and Reuer 1996). For managers, risk is typically viewed only as downside risk, which is loss or danger (Shapira 1995; Miller and Reuer 1996). The downside of risk is articulated through many definitions in the management literature. For example, in the organizational management literature, Mitchell (1995) defines risk as the product of the probability of loss and the significance of that loss. In the strategic management literature, Das and Teng (1998) define risk as unanticipated negative variation. In the operations management literature, Lewis (2003) regards risk as negative consequences or losses generated from an operation.

As a result, there is "considerable tension" within the academic literature on the nature of risk (Rao and Goldsby 2009). On one side, classic decision theorists regard risk as the prospect of different results that could be obtained, while on the other side, management researchers view risk only as potential loss. There is a "persistent tension between 'risk' as a measure (e.g., the variance) and 'risk' as a danger or hazard" (March and Shapira 1987, p. 1407). This conflict resulted in the development of the deficiency of variance risk measure (Miller and Reuer 1996).

4.2.3 Risk vs. Uncertainty

Another source of confusion about the concept of risk is whether there is a difference between risk and uncertainty (Knight 1921; Yates and Stone 1992; Mun 2004; Khan and Burnes 2007). Uncertainty is considered to be "of the same species" as risk (Mun 2004), and these two terms are often regarded as synonyms and are used interchangeably (Peck 2006; Ritchie and Brindley 2007); however, distinctions between these two concepts have been suggested. For instance, Mun (2004) suggests that uncertainties become risks only if they affect outcomes. Knight (1921) proposes that risk implies known probabilities, while uncertainty implies unknown probabilities. Luce and Raiffa (1957) offer a more refined distinction that risk occurs when each action leads to a few known outcomes, each of which is associated with a known probability; however, which outcome will occur is uncertain. In contrast, uncertainty is where each action leads to a set of consequences with unknown probabilities.

Managers see risk less precisely than decision theorists do (March and Shapira 1987). For managers, risk is not primarily a probability concept (Mitchell 1995); this abstract mathematics concept is difficult for managers to get their hands around (Duncan 1972). Kaplan and Garrick (1981) proposed a simple, clear distinction between risk and uncertainty, illustrating the difference by an example of an heir waiting for the news of how much inheritance he will receive. He knows that he will inherit but does not know in what amount. In this case, there is uncertainty, but no risk. Thus, the notion of risk involves uncertainty and loss or damage. Kaplan and Garrick (1981) symbolize this as risk = uncertainty + damage. Thus, the notion of risk entails possible loss, which is absent from the concept of uncertainty.

4.2.4 Subjective vs. Objective Risk

Another ongoing debate is about whether the nature of risk is objective or subjective (Moore 1983; Yates and Stone 1992; Bernstein 1996). The objective view regards risk as measureable by quantitative scientific means, while the subjective view regards it as completely personal (Khan and Burnes 2007); what is loss to one individual could be gain to another. Thus, the subjective view of risk considers it as an "interaction between the alternative and the risk taker" (Yates and Stone 1992, p. 5). The fundamental question here is actually a philosophical question: to what extent can the past foretell the future (Bernstein 1996)? The objective view believes in "the uniformity and timeless consistency of nature" (Davidson 1991, p. 135) and regards the future as a statistical reflection of the past. However, the subjective view questions this consistency differently. To what extent do we feel more confident about the uniformity of the universe than to simply say "we do not know?" This debate is not easily resolved, but it is necessary to recognize its impact on the attitude and methods used in risk management (Khan and Burnes 2007).

In our view, risk has both objective and subjective components. Its objective nature is based on the probability that can be obtained from our knowledge of the past (Davidson 1991); without it, there is no meaning of the accumulation of knowledge. However, because complete information and perfect knowledge are never fully available (Mitchell 1995; Lewis 2003), it is impossible to specify a precise objective probability (Savage 1954); risk is always "assessed" or "perceived" using human judgment, which is inherently subjective.

4.2.5 Model of Perceived Risk

Perceived risk has three key elements: the probabilistic estimate of the level of uncertainty, the controllability of the uncertainty, and the level of confidence in the estimates (Sitkin and Weingart 1995). The higher the level of uncertainty is, the higher the level of risk becomes. However, if the uncertainty can be easily controlled, then the level of risk is reduced. Conversely, the higher the level of controllability, the lower the level of risk. Risk is also associated with confidence in the estimates of both the controllability of the uncertainty and the level of uncertainty. The lower the level of confidence is, the higher the level of risk will be.

Because uncertainty is an element of risk (Yates and Stone 1992), it can be caused by external volatility (Premus and Sanders 2008); unplanned or unpredicted changes in the external environment create uncertainty (Vargo and Lusch 2004). The volatility aspect of uncertainty echoes the variance-based view of risk, both of which are based on the notion that high variance or high volatility is associated with low predictability (Gifford et al. 1979).

Another major cause of uncertainty is lack of information (Lawrence and Lorsch 1967; Duncan 1972; Rowe 1977; Milliken 1987). Uncertainty occurs because people do not have enough information to make accurate predictions (Premus and Sanders 2008); thus, Downey and Slocum (1975) state that uncertainty is "a counterpart to information." Incomplete information not only increases the level of uncertainty but also lowers managers' confidence in the controllability of uncertainty as well as their estimates of it (Luce and Raiffa 1957; Mitchell 1995; Zsidisin 2003). A model of perceived risk is displayed in Figure 4.1. For simplicity, we use "risk" to denote "perceived risk" throughout this chapter.

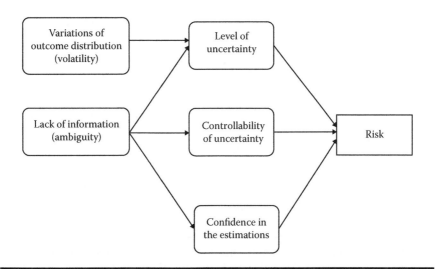

Figure 4.1   Model of risk.

This model clearly demonstrates the two key elements that increase risk. Variability stems from the volatility of external environment and reflects the objective nature of risk. It increases the level of uncertainty and thus increases risk. Lack of information indicates ambiguity in the decision-making process and reflects the subjective nature of risk. It not only increases the level of uncertainty but also lowers the controllability of uncertainty and confidence in the estimates.

4.3 Supply Chain Quality Risk

In the context of a product harm crisis, quality risk is the extent to which there are discrete, well-publicized occurrences wherein products are found to be defective or dangerous. As such, a product harm crisis is the most serious type of quality defect. Such cases have been well documented in the marketing literature (Siomkos and Kurzbard 1994; Dawar and Pillutla 2000; Heerde et al. 2007; Chen et al. 2009). Gray et al. (2011) define quality risk as "the propensity of a manufacturing establishment to fail to comply with good manufacturing practices." However, this is a somewhat narrow definition that focuses solely on manufacturing defects, while quality risks can also result from design issues, supply chain practices, and other factors.

We focus on quality risk in the supply chain context. Figure 4.2 illustrates the concept of supply chain quality risk. Using the example of a simple supply

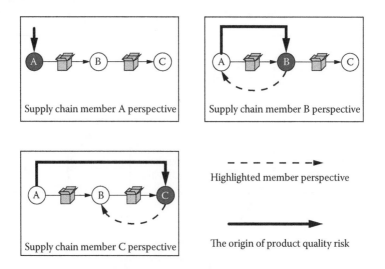

Figure 4.2 Quality risk in supply chains. (From Tse, Y.K. et al., Managing product quality risk in global supply chain. *3rd Int. Conf. on Ops. and Supp. Chain Mgmt.*, 2009.)

chain with three members, A finds a quality problem and discovers its cause, after a period of time. However, because of the time lapse, A has already distributed defective products to the downstream supply chain members. While A perceives that this was due to an internal problem in its production process, B views this as an external problem with a component that it received from A. For C, this is viewed as B's quality problem, since A is a subtier supplier to C, unknown to C. However, supply chain member C may ultimately be held responsible for the quality problem by consumers and investors, since its name is on the product, similar to the Sanlu and Mattel scenarios described in Chapter 2. Figure 4.2 illustrates how quality risk is viewed differently in different parts of a supply chain.

Thus, quality risk in a supply chain focuses on quality problems in a supply chain context, rather than in a manufacturing context. Supply chain quality risk is the inherent quality uncertainty about raw materials, ingredients, production, logistics, or packaging in any of the supply chain members, which can trigger a cascading effect that spreads through a multitier supply network.

Because supply chain members are located in different positions in a supply chain and have different perspectives of quality risk, supply chain quality risk cannot be mitigated by a single unified risk management framework, since the foci of risk management strategies can be very different from one member to another. For example, a brand owner needs to ensure the quality of production and keep track of who did what, and when, to affect the final quality of products in the upstream supply chain, in order to better monitor product quality. On the other hand, a supply chain member located in the beginning of the supply chain will simply need to ensure quality of its production and raw materials.

A global supply chain consists of different parties, including retailers, wholesalers, distributors, manufacturers, suppliers, logistics service providers, customs inspectors, etc., linked together in a supply network that may stretch across thousands of miles. All parties must coordinate their efforts to turn raw materials into finished goods and eventually sell them to end customers (Lyles et al. 2008). This supply chain structure is an inherent source of a number of uncertainties; however, as more parties become involved, it unavoidably complicates quality assurance along the supply chain.

4.4 Causes of Supply Chain Quality Risk

Many companies follow a global sourcing strategy, which can complicate the severity and complexity of product quality and safety risks (Roth et al. 2008). Consider, for example, the sourcing strategy for a portable media player (iPod), which contains a total of 451 parts (Dedrick et al. 2009). On one hand, the manufacturing company can realize an economic benefit by lowering its material costs. On the other hand, however, it may have difficulty in ensuring the quality of the materials or parts from suppliers that are located far apart in different countries.

There are multiple geographical factors that can erode the economic advantages it obtains from its global sourcing, inducing unanticipated costs and risks in its supply chain.

Moreover, it is not uncommon that the production of branded products is outsourced to vendor plants, which may further exercise global sourcing, perhaps unknown to the branded product manufacturer. Thus, to the branded product manufacturer, quality may deteriorate when its vendors re-outsource some of their jobs to other suppliers (Lyles et al. 2008) that may not follow the same selection practices as the branded product manufacturer and may fail to adequately convey production standards during re-outsourcing.

4.4.1 Insufficient Supply Chain Transparency

A multitiered supply chain with low transparency is particularly vulnerable to quality risk. Although manufacturers may have systems to identify and assess supplier risks, the effectiveness of the risk management strategies depends on the quality and quantity of useful information obtained from the supplier (Yang et al. 2009). Information asymmetry between buyer (manufacturer) and seller (supplier) companies will affect the effectiveness of quality control between them (Tomlin 2006). Information asymmetry is a condition where relevant information is known to some, but not all, parties involved. Typically, the buyer does not have enough information for its decision making.

For example, Menu Foods Corp., a pet food manufacturer in Canada, recalled more than 60 million cans in 2007 because one of its suppliers, ChemNutra, had re-outsourced its production to a supplier in China, which used a toxic chemical in its ingredients. Menu Foods had low supply chain transparency in that it did not know that ChemNutra had re-outsourced its production to the Chinese supplier (Yang et al. 2009). Thus, the risk management measures put into place by Menu Foods Corp. would likely be different if it knew that ChemNutra had outsourced its ingredients to the Chinese supplier.

In practice, sellers usually have more and better information about their production quality than do the buyers they serve because of their knowledge about product quality, including the quality level of finished goods, the quality of materials, the origins of materials, and so forth. Such information may not be shared with buyers, so material quality is unobservable in such a low transparency environment.

4.4.2 Product Complexity and Testability

Products are composed of components made by a manufacturer and its suppliers (Balachandran and Radhakrishnan 2005). When a product is composed of many parts and components, its supply chain becomes more complex, creating inherent difficulties in assessing the quality of the components. Thus, testability is one of the major factors affecting the impact of quality risk. Since quality testing is the last line of defense for preventing harmful products from reaching the marketplace, manufacturers must either invest in their in-house testing ability or employ a third-party inspector in order to ensure the quality of incoming materials and finished products.

However, some kinds of products do poorly with respect to testability. For example, contamination with unwanted foreign substances had not been previously encountered in China's dairy supply chain (Roth et al. 2008); thus, it was not expected that an industrial chemical like melamine might be added to a food product and this possibility was thus not tested for. Low testability can be mitigated by improving risk perception, knowledge, and information sharing with supply chain members.

4.4.3 Cutting Corners

While companies may reduce their manufacturing cost by outsourcing production to developing countries such as China, product quality may be sacrificed by substitution of cheaper or unsafe components. For example, E.U. and U.S. toy retailers that place unrelenting pressure on their Chinese toy suppliers for even lower prices bear some of the responsibility in the lead paint incidents. Because the toy importers focus primarily on cost, rather than quality or supply chain and product integrity, they may inadvertently send the signal to their suppliers that low prices are paramount. This can cause suppliers to use lead paint to lower their production cost, since paint with higher levels of lead often sells for a third of the cost of paint with low levels (Barboza 2007), and the suppliers want to attract future business from the manufacturer. Supply chain managers and purchasing managers who are rewarded for short-term profitability may seek low-cost suppliers (Gray et al. 2007; Roth et al. 2008), so the supplier that quotes low and quietly cuts corners on quality will get the order (Midler 2007). However, the honest supplier, which quotes a higher price and offers better quality product, will lose out in the competition. Chinese suppliers may also resort to using cheaper, counterfeit, or unauthorized materials to lower cost.

4.5 Implications for Supply Chain Risk Mitigation

As displayed in the proposed model of risk (Figure 4.1), there are two key elements that increase the level of risk: variability and lack of information. Therefore, in order to mitigate supply chain risk, there are two key drivers: reduction of variations in supply chain flows and acquisition of information from across the chain. Based on these key drivers, a model of supply chain risk mitigation is proposed and displayed in Figure 4.3.

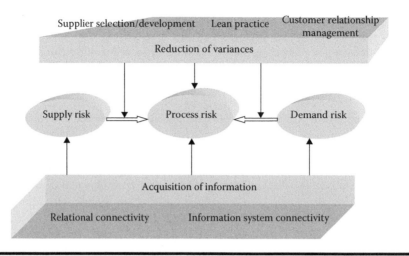

Figure 4.3   Model of supply chain risk mitigation.

4.5.1 Reduction of Variability

Bowersox and Closs (1996) described variance reduction as a basic objective of logistical performance. To reduce variation in a supply chain, the continuity of supply needs to be secured, demands on the production process need to be smoothened, and the production process itself should be even and regular (Schmenner and Swink 1998). To reduce supply variation, proactive activities related to supplier selection and development can improve suppliers' performance and help secure the supply (Krause 1997; Kannan and Keah 2006). Suppliers selected for their focus on quality and delivery service (Choi and Hartley 1996) work with a manufacturer to help solve problems that could potentially disrupt the supply (Balsmeier and Voisin 1996). To reduce process variation, lean practices such as reducing setup time, using smaller lot sizes, and continuous quality improvement can be implemented to ensure uninterrupted flow (Womack and Jones 1996). Reducing setup time and using smaller lot sizes can shorten throughput time, making the process operate more consistently and assisting in reducing quality variance. Quality control and continuous improvement are essential in avoiding congestion in the process and reducing process variability (Schmenner and Swink 1998).

It is important to note that efforts to reduce variation should be extended across the entire supply because the effect of variability is amplified across supply chain levels (Germain et al. 2008). The variability that originates in one company can impact the variability of other companies along the supply chain. This amplification effect highlights the importance of controlling the variability of the entire supply chain, including supply, internal, and demand processes.

4.5.2 Acquisition of Information

Getting relevant information lies at the heart of managing risk (Peck 2005) because information is the antidote to uncertainty and risk (Downey and Slocum 1975). The availability of relevant information improves predictability, enhances confidence in estimation, and enables companies to react to changes in a supply chain in a timely manner and thus reducing possible damages.

To acquire information and gain supply chain visibility, there are two pillars: information system connectivity and relational connectivity. Information technology has greatly improved information exchanges between supply chain partners (Constant et al. 1994; Barua et al. 1997); however, most organizations are reluctant to give away information (Berry et al. 1994). Thus, the physical connectivity between information systems cannot trigger information flows without relational connectivity (Fawcett et al. 2007). Partners are more willing to exchange information in an accurate and timely manner when engaged in a trust-based relationship (e.g., Li and Lin 2006; Barratt and Oke 2007; Fawcett et al. 2007; Frazier et al. 2009).

4.6 Conclusions

In this chapter, we discussed the quality risk that is inherent in global supply networks, clarifying the concept of supply chain quality risk. The large number of recent product recalls exemplifies how globalization has led to complex supply chain structures; that is, the more entities that are involved in a supply network, the more uncertainty there is in final product quality. This causes an amplification of quality variance across the supply chain due to the increasing level of information asymmetry among supply chain members. As the level of information asymmetry increases, it is more difficult to detect the emergence of risk.

Companies face different challenges in handling quality risk. Even with the use of existing quality management systems, quality risk is unavoidable because there are other factors, such as the corporate social responsibility of supply chain members, that can lead to the development of product hazards. Nevertheless, the effective use of risk management strategies can mitigate the potential for quality risk. Managers should identify the root causes of supply chain quality risk and establish relevant strategies for mitigating it, so as to reduce the occurrence of product harm crises. Moreover, since there is no one single formula for managing quality risk in a supply chain, organizations should always be prepared for the potential for a product harm crisis and equip themselves with supply chain risk management and supply chain quality management strategies so that they can prevent a product harm crisis or at least not panic during a recall.

58 ■ *Kim Hua Tan, Ying Kei Tse, and Jie Chen*

References

Baird, I.S. and H. Thomas. 1985. Toward a contingency model of strategic risk taking. *Acad. Mgmt. Rev.* 10(2): 230–243.

Balachandran, K.R. and S. Radhakrishnan. 2005. Quality implications of warranties in a supply chain. *Mgmt. Sci.* 51(8): 1266–1277.

Balsmeier, P.W. and W. Voisin. 1996. Supply chain management: A time-based strategy. *Ind. Mgmt.* 38(5): 24–27.

Barboza, D. 2007. Why lead in toy paint? It's cheaper. *New York Times* September 11.

Barratt, M. and A. Oke. 2007. Antecedents of supply chain visibility in retail supply chains: A resource-based theory perspective. *J. Ops. Mgmt.* 25(6): 1217–1233.

Barua, A., S. Ravindran, and A.B. Whinston. 1997. Effective intra-organizational information exchange. *J. Info. Sci.* 23(3): 239–248.

Bernstein, P. 1996. *Against the Gods: The Remarkable Story of Risk.* Chichester, Wiley.

Berry, D., D.R. Towill, and N. Wadsley. 1994. Supply chain management in the electronics products industry. *Int. J. Phys. Dist. Log. Mgmt.* 24(10): 20–32.

Bowersox, D. and D. Closs. 1996. *Logistical Management.* Singapore, McGraw-Hill.

Chen, Y., S. Ganesan, and Y. Liu. 2009. Does a firm's product-recall strategy affect its financial value? An examination of strategic alternatives during product-harm crises. *J. Mktg.* 73: 214–226.

Cheng, T.C.E., F.K. Yip, and A.C.L. Yeung. 2012. Supply risk management viaguanxiin the Chinese business context: The buyer's perspective. *Int. J. Prod. Econ.* 139(1): 3–13.

Choi, T.Y. and J.L. Hartley. 1996. An exploration of supplier selection practices across the supply chain. *J. Ops. Mgmt.* 14: 333–343.

Constant, D., S. Kiesler, and L. Sproull. 1994. What's mine is ours, or is it? A study of attitudes about information sharing. *Info. Sys. Res.* 5(4): 400–421.

Cook, J.V.J. and J.R. Page. 1987. Assessing marketing risk. *J. Bus. Res.* 15(6): 519–530.

Das, T.K. and B.S. Teng. 1998. Resource and risk management in the strategic alliance making process. *J. Mgmt.* 24(1): 21–42.

Davidson, P. 1991. Is probability theory relevant for uncertainty? A post Keynesian perspective. *J. Econ. Persp.* 5(1): 129–143.

Dawar, N. and M. Pillutla. 2000. The impact of product-harm crises on brand equity: The moderating role of consumer expectations. *J. Mrktg. Res.* 37: 215–226.

Dedrick, J., K.L. Kraemer, and G. Linden. 2009. Who profits from innovation in global value chains?: A study of the ipod and notebook pcs. *Ind. Corp. Change* 19(1): 81–116.

Downey, H.K. and J.W. Slocum. 1975. Uncertainty: Measures, research, and sources of variation. *Acad. Mgmt. J.* 18(3): 562–578.

Duncan, R.B. 1972. Characteristics of organizational environments and perceived environmental uncertainty. *Adm. Sci. Q.* 17(3): 313–327.

Ellis, S.C., J. Shockley, and R.M. Henry. 2011. Making sense of supply disruption risk research: A conceptual framework grounded in enactment theory. *J. Supp. Chain Mgmt.* 47(2): 65–96.

Fawcett, S.E., P. Osterhaus, G.M. Magnan, J.C. Brau, and M.W. McCarter. 2007. Information sharing and supply chain performance: The role of connectivity and willingness. *Supp. Chain Mgmt. Int. J.* 5(12): 358–368.

Fishhoff, B. 1985. Managing risk perceptions. *Issues Sci. Tech.* 2(1): 83–96.

Frazier, G.L., E. Maltz, K.D. Antia, and A. Rindfleisch. 2009. Distributor sharing of strategic information with suppliers. *J. Mrktg.* 73(4): 31–43.

Fredendall, L.D. and S.A. Melnyk. 1995. Assessing the impact of reducing demand variance through improved planning on the performance of a dual resource constrained job shop. *Int. J. Prod. Res.* 33(6): 1521–1534.

Germain, R., C. Claycomb, and C. Dröge. 2008. Supply chain variability, organizational structure, and performance: The moderating effect of demand unpredictability. *J. Ops. Mgmt.* 26(5): 557–570.

Gifford, W.E., H.R. Bobbit, and J.W. Slocum Jr. 1979. Message characteristics and perceptions of uncertainty by organizational decision makers. *Acad. Mgmt. J.* 22(3): 458–481.

Gray, J.V., A.V. Roth, and M.J. Leiblein. 2011. Quality risk in offshore manufacturing: Evidence from the pharmaceutical industry. *J. Ops. Mgmt.* 29(7–8): 737–752.

Gray, J.V., B. Tomlin, and A.V. Roth. 2007. The effect of power and path-dependencies on manufacturing outsourcing decisions. Ohio State University Working Paper.

Hakansson, N.H. 1969. An induced theory of accounting under risk. *Acctg. Rev.* 44(3): 495–514.

Heerde, H.V., K. Helsen, and M.G. Dekimpe. 2007. The impact of a product-harm crisis on marketing effectiveness. *Mktg. Sci.* 26(2): 230–245.

Kannan, V.R. and C.T. Keah. 2006. The impact of supplier selection and buyer–supplier engagement on relationship and firm performance. *Int. J. Phys. Dist. Log. Mgmt.* 36(10): 755–775.

Kaplan, S. and B.J. Garrick. 1981. On the quantitative definition of risk. *Risk Anal.* 1(1): 11–27.

Khan, O. and B. Burnes. 2007. Risk and supply chain management: Creating a research agenda. *Int. J. Log. Mgmt.* 18(2): 197–216.

Knight, F. 1921. *Risk, Uncertainty and Profit.* New York, Harper and Row.

Krause, D.R. 1997. Supplier development: Current practices and outcomes. *Int. J. Purch. Mat. Mgmt.* 33(2): 12–19.

Lawrence, P.R. and J.W. Lorsch. 1967. *Organization and Environment: Managing, Differentiation and Integration.* Sage Publications, Homewood, IL.

Lewis, M.A. 2003. Cause, consequence and control: Towards a theoretical and practical model of operational risk. *J. Ops. Mgmt.* 21(2): 205–224.

Li, S. and B. Lin. 2006. Accessing information sharing and information quality in supply chain management. *Dec. Supp. Sys.* 42(3): 1641–1656.

Luce, R.D. and H. Raiffa. 1957. *Games and Decisions: Introduction and Critical Surveys.* New York, Wiley.

Lyles, M.A., B.B. Flynn, and M.T. Frohlich. 2008. All supply chains don't flow through: Understanding supply chain issues in product recalls. *Mgmt. Org. Rev.* 4(2): 167–182.

March, J.G. and Z. Shapira. 1987. Managerial perspectives on risk and risk taking. *Mgmt. Sci.* 33(11): 1404–1418.

Markowitz, H.M. 1952. Portfolio selection. *J. Fin.* 7(1): 77–91.

Melnyk, S.A., D.R. Denzler, and L. Fredendall. 1992. Variance control vs. dispatching efficiency. *Prod. Inv. Mgmt. J.* 33(3): 6–13.

Midler, P. 2007. Quality fade: China's great business challenge. Knowledge@Wharton, July 25.

Miller, K.D. 1992. A framework for integrated risk management in international business. *J. Int. Bus. Stud.* 23(2): 311–331.

Miller, K.D. and J.J. Reuer. 1996. Measuring organizational downside risk. *Strat. Mgmt. J.* 17(9): 671–691.

Milliken, F.J. 1987. Three types of perceived uncertainty about the environment: State, effect, and response uncertainty. *Acad. Mgmt. Rev.* 12(1): 133–143.

Mitchell, V.W. 1995. Organisational risk perception and reduction: A literature review. *Brit. J. Mgmt.* 6(2): 115–133.

Moore, P.G. 1983. *The Business of Risk.* Cambridge, Cambridge University Press.

Mun, J. 2004. *Applied Risk Analysis.* Hoboken, NJ, John Wiley & Sons.

Peck, H. 2005. Drivers of supply chain vulnerability: An integrated framework. *Int. J. Phys. Dist. Log. Mgmt.* 35(3/4): 210–232.

Peck, H. 2006. Reconciling supply chain vulnerability, risk and supply chain management. *Int. J. Log. Res. Appl.* 9(2): 127–142.

Premus, R. and N.R. Sanders. 2008. Information sharing in global supply chain alliances. *J. Asia-Pacific Bus.* 9(2): 174–192.

Rao, S. and R.J. Goldsby. 2009. Supply chain risks: A review of typology. *Int. J. Log. Mgmt.* 20(1): 97–123.

Ritchie, B. and C. Brindley. 2007. Supply chain risk management and performance: A guiding framework for future development. *Int. J. Ops. Prod. Mgmt.* 27(3): 303–322.

Roth, A.V., A.A. Tsay, M.E. Pullman, and J.V. Gray. 2008. Unraveling the food supply chain: Strategic insights from china and the 2007 recalls. *J. Supp. Chain Mgmt.* 44(1): 22–39.

Rowe, W. 1977. *An Anatomy of Risk.* New York, Wiley.

Savage, L. 1954. *The Foundations of Statistics.* New York, Wiley.

Schinasi, G.J. and B. Drees. 1999. Managing global finance and risk. *Fin. Dev.* 36(4): 38–41.

Schmenner, R.W. and M.L. Swink. 1998. On theory in operations management. *J. Ops. Mgmt.* 17(1): 97–113.

Shapira, Z. 1995. *Risk Taking: A Managerial Perspective.* New York, Russell Sage Foundation.

Siomkos, G.J. and G. Kurzbard. 1994. The hidden crisis in product-harm crisis management. *Eur. J. Mktg.* 28(2): 30–41.

Sitkin, S.B. and L.R. Weingart. 1995. Determinants of risky decision-making behavior: A test of the mediating role of risk perceptions and propensity. *Acad. Mgmt. J.* 38(6): 1573–1592.

Sodhi, M.S., B.G. Son, and C.S. Tang. 2012. Researchers' perspectives on supply chain risk management. *Prod. Ops. Mgmt.* 21(1): 1–13.

Tang, O. and S.N. Musa. 2011. Identifying risk issues and research advancements in supply chain risk management. *Int. J. Prod. Econ.* 133(1): 25–34.

Tomlin, B. 2006. On the value of mitigation and contingency strategies for managing supply chain disruption risks. *Mgmt. Sci.* 52(5): 639–657.

Tse, Y.K. and K.H. Tan. 2011. Managing product quality risk in a multi-tier global supply chain. *Int. J. Prod. Res.* 49(1): 139–158.

Tse, Y.K., K.H. Tan, and S. Ng. 2009. Managing product quality risk in global supply chain. *3rd Int. Conf. on Ops. and Supp. Chain Mgmt.* Hong Kong.

Vargo, S.L. and R.F. Lusch. 2004. Evolving to a new dominant logic for marketing. *J. Mktg.* 68(1): 1–17.

Wacker, J.G. 2004. A theory of formal conceptual definitions: Developing theory-building measurement instruments. *J. Ops. Mgmt.* 22(6): 629–650.

Womack, J. and D. Jones. 1996. *Lean Thinking.* New York, Simon and Schuster.

Yang, Z.B., G. Aydýn, V. Babich, and D.R. Beil. 2009. Supply disruptions, asymmetric information, and a backup production option. *Mgmt. Sci.* 55(2): 192–209.

Yates, J.F. and E. Stone. 1992. *The Risk Construct.* Chichester, Wiley.

Zsidisin, G.A. 2003. A grounded definition of supply risk. *J. Purch. Supp. Mgmt.* 9(5–6): 217–224.

INTRODUCTION TO SECTION II: DARK SIDE OF PRODUCT SAFETY

In Section II, we use detailed case studies to provide an in-depth discussion of the dark side of product safety hazards. Each of the case studies in this section describes product safety issues that were poorly handled. In addition to reflecting the impact of product safety issues, these case studies provide a foundation for developing a framework for studying product hazards and highlight important issues to consider.

We begin with a discussion in Chapter 5 of Mattel and its recalls during 2007. We provide background about the global toy industry and the role of Mattel and its Chinese suppliers in this industry. Although Mattel had several major product recalls during 2007, we focus in particular on its recalls that were due to lead paint, since these highlight important supply chain quality management issues. We look at the Mattel story from two perspectives. First is the perspective of Lee Der, one of Mattel's most trusted Chinese suppliers, with which it had had a long and successful relationship—right up until the time that high levels of paint were found in the products that it produced for Mattel. Second is the perspective of Bob Eckert, who was Mattel's chief executive officer during the 2007 crisis. These perspectives highlight the importance of supply chain transparency and the responsibility that is ultimately with the brand owner.

In Chapter 6, we highlight a different example of the importance of supply chain transparency and introduce the concept of supply chain traceability. This chapter focuses on the melamine-tainted milk products that were produced in China during 2008 and sold to Chinese consumers. Melamine is an industrial chemical that has the curious side benefit of simulating high protein levels when added to raw milk. Sanlu and other manufacturers of baby milk formula used protein levels as a criterion for whether to accept raw milk from small-scale farmers. The temptation to tamper with the raw milk was high since these farmers often had genetically inferior cattle, low-quality feed, poor veterinary care, and a low level of education. Melamine can cause kidney stones in infants and ultimately led to the death of six Chinese babies. We describe how supply chain design was related to the presence of melamine in the milk supply and the importance of supply chain transparency and traceability in addressing this severe product safety hazard.

Chapter 7 describes the classic Ford Pinto case, which occurred during the early 1970s. It is described by Dennis Gioia, who was the young MBA who served as Ford's Field Recall Coordinator. The Ford Pinto was developed in response to the Arab Oil Embargo and the sudden popularity of small, foreign cars in the United States. It was one of the first small and efficient U.S.-made cars, and thus, keeping it light and cheap were of paramount importance in its design. The location of its fuel tank could cause it to rupture during a low-speed accident, bursting into flames after a relatively minor collision. Gioia describes why the Pintos were not initially recalled, despite knowledge of this defect, and Ford's analysis that ultimately resulted in a discounted cash flow analysis that placed a value on a human life. He then goes on to describe how human decision makers develop cognitive schema that can cause them to overlook what may seem to others as obvious factors in making decisions. This chapter illustrates the importance of information systems to gather and objectively analyze data, in addition to the analysis done by decision makers, in order to help them avoid making poor decisions because of their decision making biases and heuristics.

In Chapter 8, we draw upon these detailed cases and the brief examples from Section I to highlight the most critical factors in supply chain quality management. This framework provides the foundation for explaining the best practice cases in Section III and the structure for our research that is described in Sections IV through VI.

Chapter 5

Chinese Toy Recalls

Dongming Ye, Stephen Ng, Thomas Kwan-Ho Yeung, and Barbara B. Flynn

Contents

5.1 Introduction: Background

On August 2, 2007, Mattel, the largest toy company in the world, announced a massive recall of tens of millions of its Fisher Price toys that had been produced by a Chinese manufacturer that applied paint with excessive amounts of lead in them. This led to crumbling of the public's confidence in Mattel, toys in general, and, ultimately, Chinese-made products and products that contained Chinese-made components.

In this chapter, we take a deep dive into the toy industry, focusing in particular on the situation that Mattel found itself in during the summer of 2007. We begin by setting the stage for the toy recall incidents by describing the global toy market in 2007. From there, we describe the case of Mattel and Lee Der, the supplier of the products that were tainted with lead paint. In Section 5.5, we provide a first-hand account of the incident from Bob Eckert, who was the chairman of the board and chief executive officer (CEO) of Mattel in 2007.

5.2 Toy Market

5.2.1 Global Toy Industry

The global toy market in 2007 had an estimated size of $71 billion, with 36% concentrated in North America. European markets accounted for another 30% of global toy sales, while Asian markets had grown by 12% in 2006 and were expected to grow by 25% in 2007. A large part of the Asian growth was expected to occur in China and India, whose burgeoning middle classes were thriving on double-digit economic growth.

The U.S. toy industry had a large number of players in 2007, with about 800 companies operating in the dolls, toys, and games manufacturing industry. The industry was dominated by a few key players, including Mattel, Hasbro, RC2, JAAKS Pacific, Marvel, and Lego. The industry leaders were Mattel and Hasbro, with combined sales of $8.7 billion, while the combined sales of the other players were under a billion dollars. There were also numerous small toy companies, approximately 70% of which employed less than 20 persons.

Like today, big retailers like Wal-Mart and Target were the major players in the retail toy market in 2007, with the top five retailers accounting for more than 60% of U.S. toy sales. They not only sell the products of toy companies such as Mattel, Hasbro, and Lego but also source their own toys directly from China, selling them under their private labels. For example, Wal-Mart sells its toys under its Kid-Connection brand, while Target sells toys under its Play Wonder brand. As the big-box retailers like Wal-Mart have gained share, specialty toy retailers such as Toys 'R Us have steadily lost market share.

Although the major retail markets for toys are in the United States and Europe, production is concentrated in Asia, primarily China. U.S. and Europe domestic operations focus on product design, marketing, research and development, and high-value activities, with only 10% or so of U.S. demand for toys actually produced in the United States. More than 60% of toys sold in the world are made in China.

The toy industry is not only highly competitive but also highly seasonal. Every year, about 70% of toy sales occur during the Christmas holiday period. This creates a challenge for toy manufacturers in that there is a significant production peak during the first quarter, so that the last shipment can occur by the end of the second quarter, in order to arrive in the retail stores in time for the important holiday sales period. Unbalanced capacity requirements may lead to subcontracting in order to meet peak demand.

Regulatory pressure is substantial in the toy sector. The world's largest toy markets in the United States, Japan, and the European Union have the most stringent safety regulations. For example, the scope of chemical content regulation has recently expanded to include a larger number of chemicals; the new Toy Safety Directive in the European Union now includes, among other things, fragrances. Lead in products accessible to children should not be greater than 600 ppm, as stipulated in Consumer Product Safety Commission (CPSC) 16 CFR, and 90 ppm in soluble, as stipulated in ASTM F963 (the U.S. standard). For most countries outside the United States, Japan, and the European Union, however, the guidelines for chemicals, apart from selected phthalates, seem to be more voluntary in nature.

5.2.2 Toy Supply Chain Players

The major players in the global toy supply chain are the toy companies, retailers, and traders. Each plays a different role and operates its supply chain with a different structure. Large toy companies control their supply chains by exerting substantial pressure on their suppliers. Their supplier audits cover a wide range of activities, including engineering capacity, quality management systems, subtier supplier management, control of incoming materials, manufacturing equipment and process controls, personnel training, and in-house testing expertise. They also audit raw materials suppliers, monitoring their production and product testing. Because the majority of toy suppliers are small firms that source a wide variety of materials, they do not individually exert much buying power for raw materials, such as wood, metal, textiles, paint, or coatings. Some rely on repurposed materials, while those that are somewhat larger may be able to establish cooperative arrangements with raw material suppliers.

Most retailers are not involved in toy development and buy whatever is available on the market; thus, they have only limited influence over product design. Nevertheless, larger retailers may make a significant effort to control the safety of the toys that they buy, including supplier auditing, prototype testing, and final product testing. Smaller retailers typically employ fewer dedicated safety personnel, and safety-related contacts with vendors are less frequent. The involvement of retailers in product safety and recalls, including the special case of retailers with privately branded toys, is further explored in Chapter 15.

Traders, who serve as the intermediary between toy companies and retailers, typically have no influence on either toy design or manufacturing. Combined with the small size of most trading companies and the fact that they typically import many other types of products in addition to toys, it is difficult for them to be aware of all relevant requirements, and they may not have the capacity to influence toy quality in any meaningful way. As a result, traders rely almost entirely on toy manufacturers and the test reports they provide in order to ensure that the toys they trade are safe.

5.2.3 Toy Industry in China

Thanks to its political reform and seemingly endless supply of inexpensive labor, toys have become China's largest export. There are more than 26,000 toy companies in mainland China, including toy manufacturers, trading companies, and retailers. Among them, 8000 manufacturers employ more than 350 million workers. Most toy manufacturers are concentrated in the southeast part of China in Guangdong and Zhejiang province.

Although China's toy industry is fairly well established, it faces many challenges. On the one hand, domestic toy production costs keep rising, and China's price advantage is further eroded by competition from developing countries like Vietnam and African countries. Difficult conditions such as soaring material and labor costs, shortages of power, and land supply all present significant challenges. On the other hand, there is great anxiety about the massive volume of China-made toys exported worldwide. International toy companies and associations have put increasing pressure on their local governments to set up trade tariffs. New requirements such as the Restriction of Hazardous Substances Directive (RoHS) and Waste Electrical and Electronic Equipment Directive (WEEE) directives from the European Union, antiterrorism policies from the United States, and ethical standards from the International Toys Association all build barriers to China's toy exports. Chinese toy manufacturers claim that it is difficult for them to understand the legislative approach in the European Union, where conformity to a standard does not necessarily mean that the product is in compliance with all applicable safety requirements set out in the legislation. Although efforts from E.U. and Chinese authorities, as well as the European toy industry, to better inform Chinese toy manufacturers about applicable regulations and develop harmonized safety standards have resulted in greater awareness, there is still a need to improve understanding of the requirements that are required in non-toy-specific legislation, such as for certain phthalates and azo colorants.

Ironically, the Chinese toy industry has been seriously affected by the policy of multinational corporations of selecting the lowest priced supplier. In order to ensure the lowest price, short-term orders are placed, making relationships primarily transactional. Furthermore, orders are often spilt into many smaller orders to create more competition. Prices are quoted based on long-term forecasts, but there is no commitment to individual suppliers. If the goods sell well, then a large order could be forthcoming. Although late shipments may face substantial penalties, Chinese subcontractors will generally accept all orders in order to avoid jeopardizing potential future orders. In addition, Chinese factories may accept multiple orders from different multinational companies. Thus, if there is sudden increase in demand or it looks like a deadline will not be met, Chinese subcontractors often resort to reoutsourcing part of their production to even smaller factories.

5.3 Toy Safety

Table 5.1 presents an overview of toy recalls made by the CPSC since 1988. More than 80% of recent toy recalls have involved toys made in China, with most due to excess lead content in surface paint. Despite stringent restrictions, lead is widely used in paint because paint with high lead content is heavy and bright, making products more appealing to consumers. Lead in children's products poses a serious hazard because exposure can affect almost every organ and system in the human body, leading to IQ deficits, attention deficit/hyperactivity disorder, motor skill impairment, and reduced reaction times. Because of this, many countries have limited the permissible amount of lead in products, including the paint on their surfaces.

5.3.1 Safety Issues in Global Toy Supply Chains

Global toy supply chains are complicated in that they are often quite lengthy and may cut across a number of countries and continents. This increases the effort needed for monitoring and product testing. Inspection costs may be surprisingly high in a global supply chain because of the effort that has to be put into quality management, in order to ensure that inappropriate supplier behavior will be promptly detected. However, the length and geographical dispersion of toy supply chains may make it impossible for downstream supply chain members to know who their actual suppliers are. Re-outsourcing exacerbates this further. This can cause difficulties in tracing upstream to the source of a safety hazard. In addition to being long, toy supply chains can also be wide because toy manufacturers, retailers, and traders may strive to reduce supply risk by contracting with several suppliers, so as to take advantage of competitive bidding among potential suppliers. This increases the risk of supply inconsistency and escalation of monitoring and reconciliation costs.

Another problem in toy supply chains is that retailers and traders may not be fully aware of or understand the specific safety regulations in the importing country. Because retailers are not usually involved in the development and manufacturing of toys, they have no influence over the safety-related design and manufacturing aspects

Table 5.1   Toy Recalls by the CPSC

Year	Total Number of Recalls	Recalls of Chinese-Made Toys	
		Number	Percentage
1988	29	1	3
1989	52	4	8
1990	31	14	45
1991	31	8	26
1992	25	13	52
1993	20	8	40
1994	29	16	55
1995	35	19	54
1996	26	13	50
1997	22	9	41
1998	29	12	41
1999	20	4	20
2000	31	15	48
2001	23	12	52
2002	25	11	44
2003	15	10	67
2004	15	13	87
2005	19	16	84
2006	35	26	79

Source: Bapuji, H., Beamish, P. *Toy Recalls: Is China Really the Problem?*, Asia Pacific Foundation of Canada, Vancouver, Canada, 2007. With permission.

of products. However, recent E.U. legislative requirements stipulate that retailers bear the same responsibilities relating to toy safety as the manufacturers do (European Toy Safety Directive 2009). Traders are usually more remotely located from the manufacturers and the production of the toys, generally buying toys off the shelf.

As a result, the responsibility for toy safety ultimately falls on the manufacturers, which are typically Chinese. In general, smaller manufacturers have less ability to influence product safety. Although the larger players often have significant in-house capabilities for dealing with safety issues, medium-sized manufacturers may have less well-developed product safety systems. The smallest often struggle to even guarantee consistent product safety, relying primarily on the local authority's export licensing and product testing to ensure and demonstrate their compliance. In order to fulfill their responsibility, Chinese manufacturers increasingly rely on third-party independent testing laboratories to perform the necessary tests and certify the safety and reliability of the toys and give them international credibility. These laboratories serve as the source of the most up-to-date information about the import country's safety regulations for the original equipment manufacturers (OEMs) and their suppliers, retailers, and traders.

5.3.2 China's Export Regulations for Toy Monitoring

China Entry-Exit Inspection and Quarantine (CIQ) is the national authority responsible for monitoring exports. As stipulated by law, exporting of toys is monitored by a permit system. Toys listed on the permit list must be tested according to the standards and regulations of the importing countries. If the regulations of the importing country are found to be poorly defined or unavailable, then the goods will be tested according to China's current standards, such as GB6675. In addition to quality checking, Chinese manufacturers must also comply with production and management requirements. Before issuing a release order, sampling checks of the goods are conducted. If there are more than two claims or returns within a year for reasons that are found to be the responsibility of the manufacturer, the CIQ will revoke the quality permit.

5.4 Mattel Crisis

The key players in the Mattel crisis are Mattel (the foreign importer), Lee Der (its Chinese subcontractor), Dongxin New Energy Co. (its paint supplier), and Dongguan Zhong Xin Colorants, which supplied some colorants to Dongxin New Energy Co. during a peak demand period, unknown to either Lee Der or Mattel.

5.4.1 Mattel

With a vision of producing "the world's premiere toy brands—today and tomorrow," Mattel "designs, manufactures, and markets a broad variety of toy products worldwide through sales to its customers and directly to consumers." Mattel employs over 30,000 employees, has sales organizations in 43 countries, sells products in more than 150 countries, and is the largest toy company in the world. Mattel develops and designs toys at its headquarters, producing its core brands, such as Barbie and Hot Wheels, in company-owned manufacturing facilities located in

China, Indonesia, Thailand, Malaysia, and Mexico and its noncore brands in third-party manufacturers in a number of countries including the United States and Mexico. About half of Mattel's sales are through three major retailers: Wal-Mart, Toys 'R Us, and Target.

Mattel's China head office, which was initially located in Hong Kong, is responsible for managing the operations of its facilities in Shenzhen, Dongguan, and Foshan province. In 2004, the U.S. worldwide headquarters moved its China head office to Guanyao in Foshan province, where Mattel had contracts with approximately 37 principal subcontractors. According to some estimates, about 3000 Chinese companies make Mattel products (Barboza 2007).

5.4.2 Lee Der

Foshan Leader Toy Co., Ltd. (Lee Der) was established in 1993 as an equal-share joint venture company between Foshan Fenjiang Industry Company in mainland China and Lee Der Industrial Company Limited, a Hong Kong–based industrial company. According to the contract, the mainland side did not have the power to interfere with operations. On the Hong Kong side, the two shareholders, Chiu Kwai-Chuen and Cheung Shu-Hung, owned the company in equal shares. Mr. Chiu was quite elderly, so almost all of Lee Der's business and operations were handled by 50-year-old Cheung Shu-Hung. Because Lee Der sustained losses for its first few years and the mainland side refused to provide further financial support, the partners kept on investing. In 1993, Mattel placed a small educational toy order with Lee Der, which it filled satisfactorily, leading to additional Mattel orders. Lee Der soon became a trusted supplier of plastic toys to Mattel, with a good production record for decades. It was awarded Mattel's Reliable Supplier certificate in 1997. Lee Der rapidly expanded in 1998, and the buildings from another toy manufacturer were rented for production; thus, Lee Der had three production facilities in Foshan by 1998, with 2500 employees.

The Foshan government took great pride in Lee Der's RMB2 billion in sales in 2006, which ranked second in Foshan city. Lee Der became the role model for Foshan's export-oriented companies, setting a goal for itself of RMB3 billion in annual sales. In 2007, Lee Der was on the brink of opening a new $5 million plant.

5.4.3 The Crisis

In mid-June 2007, a report from the third-party Shenzhen CTI (China) testing company shocked Lee Der's management (*Singpao Daily* 2012). Shenzhen CTI (China) was mainland China's largest third-party privately owned testing laboratory and was one of the Mattel-authorized testing agents. The report revealed that five samples of toys produced by Lee Der were found to have paint with excessive lead levels. It was the first time that a paint test had been failed since Lee Der's establishment in 1993. Liang Jiacheng, a Foshan native who was described as Cheung's best friend and business partner, had set up the Dongxin Industrial Printing and Packing

Company Ltd. in 2001, becoming Lee Der's major paint supplier. The company changed its name to Dongxin New Energy Co., Ltd., in 2004, building its factory next door to one of Lee Der's factories. Lee Der management immediately called for a meeting with its paint supplier. After reading the report, Liang was also confused. He immediately had the sample retested by the Guangdong Entry-Exit Inspection and Quarantine Bureau (CIQ). The results indicated that the lead level for yellow paint was 22,380 ppm, which was 36.3 times higher than the permissible limit of 600 ppm.

On June 27, Mattel's call center in the United States received a report from a consumer stating that a home test kit had found excessive lead in some of Mattel's toys. These were toys that had been made by Lee Der. On July 3, Mattel was informed that another toy made by Lee Der was also found with lead above the permissible limits. Further tests on the toy samples collected from Lee Der were conducted on July 9 in Mattel's own laboratories, revealing that 9 of the 23 samples of Lee Der toys contained excess lead in the surface paint. On July 12, Mattel stopped importing from Lee Der due to the lead paint issue. All three of Lee Der's factories were forced to cease production immediately, leaving 2500 workers with no work.

Under the guidance of Mattel, Cheung and the Lee Der management quickly carried out a proactive investigation. They traced through the upstream supply chain to Dongxin, finding that it had failed to comply with Lee Der's standard purchasing procedures. Dongxin had been a trusted paint supplier to Lee Der for the previous 4 years, during which no quality problems had ever been detected. However, in April 2007, Dongxin unexpectedly ran short of yellow colorants. In order to quickly rectify the situation, Dongxin turned to the Internet and bought about 500 kg of colorants from Zhong Xin Colorants in the nearby city of Dongguan. Zhong Xin had presented Dongxin with a false business registration and lead-free certificates. According to Mattel's standard procedures, all color pigment was required to be tested by a third-party laboratory prior to production. Since no such laboratory was available in Foshan, however, this would have had to be done in Guangzhou, requiring an additional 5 to 10 days. Because even a 1-day delay would bring losses to Lee Der by shutting down its production, Dongxin management made the decision to skip the third-party lab test.

As a result, parts painted with lead-tainted yellow paint were inadvertently used by Lee Der. After the situation came to light, seven employees of Zhong Xin disappeared, while the police hunted for them. The Dongguan Quality Supervision Bureau could find no corporate representative for Zhong Xin, and the Dongguan Industrial and Commercial Office confirmed that Zhong Xin was nowhere to be found on the corporate registry list. The company had simply disappeared.

During June and July, Lee Der kept on producing as usual. Orders escalated in June, and Lee Der planned to hire more workers by July. After Mattel's ban on importing was announced in July, there was break in production, but it soon resumed. Production was on and off during July and started again in earnest in August. By mid-August, there was HKD16 million worth of toys sitting in Lee Der's warehouses, since Mattel was no longer accepting them. During the remediation process, 3000 cartons of lead-tainted toys were sealed and were awaiting destruction by government officials. In the meantime, Mattel designated Hengchang Petrochemical Co., Ltd. as its new paint supplier.

Mattel approved the results of Lee Der's month-long quality system improvements. It placed a new order with Lee Der on August 2, using paint from Hengchang, and Cheung Shu-Hung was eager to resume exporting as soon as possible. On August 3, he submitted a report to the Foshan CIQ updating the current status of the Mattel product recall issue. A second report was submitted on August 6. Both of Lee Der's reports appealed to the authorities to resume its export permit. To his disappointment, however, there was no feedback from the CIQ. Cheung Shu-Hung was also concerned about when all the toys piling up in his warehouse would be shipped to the United States.

Mattel had refused to disclose Lee Der's identity, stating that it was inappropriate to do so while the investigation was still underway. Due to mounting pressure, however, Mattel announced on August 7 that the toymaker was Lee Der. More broadly, the reputation of China's manufacturers was at risk after the rounds of toy recalls, and, thus, massive pressure was placed on Cheung.

On August 8, Cheung Shu-Hung suffered a heavier blow, as the CIQ temporarily banned Lee Der and Hangchang from exporting. No exports would be allowed unless satisfactory remediation had taken place. Possible judiciary investigation would also be carried out if criminal offense was found. On the afternoon of August 11, Cheung Shu-Hung took his own life. His body was found by his employees in Lee Der's warehouse. On August 14, Mattel issued a global recall for hundreds of thousands of toys made in China because of danger to children from lead paint. The heavy media coverage of the multiple lead paint toy recalls added to consumers' fears. American parents were particularly worried about excessive lead in Chinese-made painted toys that were already on the shelves.

Ultimately, the lead paint crisis moved from being a financial issue to becoming a political issue. During the 2008 U.S. presidential election campaign, Democratic candidates took aim at China's food safety issues, calling for a tough stance on China over trade and human rights. According to *Financial Times*, U.K., Senator Hillary Clinton, in an open letter to President George W. Bush, urged him to raise safety standards: "I don't want to eat bad food from China or have my children having toys that are going to get them sick. We have to have tougher standards on what they import into this country" (Ward and Luce 2007).

5.5 Mattel Perspective*

This section describes the Mattel crisis from the perspective of Bob Eckert, who was the chairperson of the Board and CEO of Mattel, Inc., during the time of the crisis.

---

* Heavily excerpted from Lyles (2008).

Although there has been some minor editing and rearrangement of thoughts, the words are all his, excerpted from an interview that originally appeared in *Business Horizons* (Lyles 2008).

> Mattel has been manufacturing in China for about 30 years. At one point, we manufactured our entire line of toys in Taiwan, but then the industry evolved into Hong Kong. Then, as Hong Kong became more of a financial center, we moved into mainland China. Mattel was, in fact, one of the early manufacturing/production systems to go into China. We started with manufacturing; then, over time, we started doing more supply chain things from China, particularly engineering. We are heavy users of production molds, because we mold a lot of plastic. So, we started making molds and tools in China, and thus engineering in China. Within the last five or ten years, we've started doing our product design directly in China, instead of doing it all in the U.S. Very recently, within the last three or four years, we have also been selling and marketing in China. Right now at Mattel, about half of our business is done outside of the United States, and about half of our sales come from outside the United States.
>
> Mattel's physical supply chain is a lot longer than a lot of other companies' supply chains. We have a business that is volatile in predicting demand, so there's the phenomenon of the hot toy. I can't just pick up the phone and call Indiana and get more of a hot toy. If we've got a hot toy, we've got to call Indonesia or Malaysia or China or Thailand, or some other place where we make toys, and order it. So, the length of the supply chain for companies manufacturing in China makes a difference.

5.5.1 Mattel Recalls

Last year, Mattel was in the wake of the supply chain disruptions, including product recalls and production chain breakdowns. Eckert made the following clarifications about what happened.

> There were really two types of recalls we faced [in 2007]. In the nature of the toy business, it's not unusual to have one recall, or even two or three, in the course of a given year, when we're creating 8,000 new products. But the recalls were more pronounced [in 2007], and there were two things that happened. The first was related to lead paint. We do lead paint tests and check for lead paint, and we never had failures in lead paint testing until this year. Lead paint is one of those things that shouldn't be on a product for kids. We have some toys that were produced with a small amount of lead paint on a small part, but the fact is, it shouldn't have been there.

The second area is tiny, high-powered, rare-earth magnets. During the last four or five years, we've been using these small magnets in toys. These magnets are pretty ubiquitous, and we've used them in toys to create quite magical experiences for children. The problem is, however, that if the magnets become dislodged, these things can be dangerous. When the industry started using these magnets four or five years ago, if a magnet becomes dislodged from the plastic toy, we viewed it as a quality issue. We would use better glue, or somehow better affix the magnet to the toy. Unfortunately, a couple of years ago, a child ingested a magnet from one of our competitors' toys and then several minutes later ingested a second magnet. These magnets are so powerful that they worked to find one another in the child's intestine, and he died. That was a wake-up call to everybody in the toy business that this isn't just a quality issue; this is a safety issue, and we've got to find a way to make sure those magnets stay affixed to those toys.

We've worked hard to come up with a new system that really embeds the magnet in the plastic. We thought it was a big change, and the industry has now adopted this system. Even though the risk of a child getting into trouble under the old process was low, because the risk was so important we said, "You know what? We want to notify the people who bought these toys three or four or five years ago that we're retroactively applying today's standards to those products we made several years ago," and we recalled them. So, last year there were two very different, but equally important, issues which generated a lot of publicity.

5.5.2 Lead Paint Issue

The surprising discovery of adverse supply chain issues generated negative headlines for Mattel. Eckert continued to share the unexpected experience on the large size of recalls that took place in 2007.

> [We did not] anticipate the large size of recalls because we test products for lead paint routinely, and over the years we didn't find failures. But we had a failure in the summer of 2007 on a product and, as a result of that, we had a recall. The way our system works is when we have a failure like that, we look for the root cause. We determine in which plant that product was made, what dates were involved, what other products were made in that plant at that time, and in the case of these painted toys with unacceptable levels of lead, where the paint came from and how it was used. We trace back to the very root cause of the problem, which takes a little bit of time, but allows us to make sure that we go out and rectify the problem as quickly as we can.

What happened in the case of these lead paint issues is that we have vendor plants—we manufacture about half our toys in Mattel plants, and about half are outsourced in plants that we don't own—and one of those vendor plants subcontracted a part of a toy to some other plant, and it was at that level that somebody made a mistake and used the wrong paint. So, we had to track down who did what, when and then find the ultimate cause.

This problem with lead paint shouldn't happen again. The recall only impacted about one-half of one percent of all the toys Mattel made. That's what the recall was, but that number *should* be zero. So, we have added redundant processes to ensure that lead paint doesn't get used, and if somehow it does get used, that we find it before it gets to consumers, so we don't have recalls and don't have parents worrying about these issues. As an example, today a vendor or even a Mattel plant can only use paint from one of our certified paint suppliers, I believe there are eight of them that we've certified now in China. Second, before a manufacturing plant—whether it's a Mattel plant or an outside vendor plant—can use the paint that came from a certified supplier that we know does good quality control, they've got to re-test it, and confirm that it does not have heavy elements like lead. Third, we've increased our personnel presence at these vendor plants. So, there's a Mattel person or some sort of auditor watching the manufacturing process. Fourth, and very importantly, before every production batch of toys reaches the shelves or consumers, we again test for lead paint. It's a redundant system; knowing where the paint came from, testing it, watching it get used, and testing it again before it hits the shelf.

It's hard for me to imagine—although I've learned never to say "never" in life—that this could happen again. That's very important from a consumer standpoint. What we've found is if we apologize for what happened, if we explain what happened and, most importantly, if we tell people what we're doing to prevent it from happening in the future, they'll say, "Hey, okay, I get it, and I'll continue buying your products." We've had several vendors make mistakes, so some of them are short-term relationships. Others, including one vendor that I can recall, we have worked with for 25 years. So, we have some very long-standing relationships. We're particularly surprised when someone with whom we've worked with for many years has a problem like this. We have had a very good relationship, making thousands or millions of high-quality toys over decades, so when a problem like this happens, it's almost akin to something happening in one of our own plants. So, we need to look very hard for what was the root cause.

Sometimes, it appears an honest mistake was made; somebody was supposed to test paint and they didn't, not because they were trying to circumvent the system, but because accidents happen. They didn't test that batch of paint, and it was a bad batch of paint. That's one kind of mistake. Another kind of mistake is when you are purposefully circumventing our system. We have very, very simple requirements for things like paint and what kind of testing you do and how you do it, and those sorts of things. If you are purposefully circumventing our system, we don't want to work with you anymore. There's a difference between someone who makes an honest mistake and someone who's cheating. As such, we work very hard, in every instance, to get to the root cause of the problem.

5.5.3 Dealing with the Backlash

Eckert continued to illustrate a story on public apology, as he believed that it was a risky but necessary move.

First, we've apologized in the United States and Washington, D.C. I've testified in front of the U.S. Senate when it was looking at the issues of toy quality and safety for children, and I remember my opening comment was, "Let me start by apologizing to you here and to those watching on television today," because parents shouldn't have to worry about these kinds of issues. That's our job. The first thing we do is apologize; I don't care where we are and with whom we are speaking: "We're sorry this happened." So, when we go to China and we're talking to the Chinese government about these issues, we start with, "We're sorry this happened." The second thing we talk about is what happened, and the third thing is what we're doing to prevent it from happening in the future. But, there is an additional element to what we said in China, and that is: "We're sorry to all the parents here in China that have purchased these products and have to send them back now or have to deal with them." Again, I don't care where you live, I'm sorry this happened.

We've been working with government agencies and regulators all over the world: in Washington, D.C., in Brussels and in Beijing. We've been active at many levels because one of the things we would like to do is better harmonize the various standards around the world. For example, there is a certain level of lead paint that is acceptable here in the United States, which is different than what is acceptable in the European Union. And the way we test for the presence of lead paint is different in the U.S. than in Europe. It seems to us that it would be easier if everybody could agree on one standard, and agree on one way to test that standard. It would make manufacturing easier because, the fact is, more of our businesses are global today. To have different standards and different processes country-by-country is not particularly efficient.

5.5.4 Moving Forward

Eckert highlighted his corporate value of keeping balance of triple bottom line (people-profit-planet), staying focused on supply chain quality assurance and moving forward from the past to achieving sustainable goals. He continued with the discussions on how to move forward with improvements.

> Can we find a way to come together? We're having a lot of success in the United States with the Consumer Product Safety Commission, and with the Secretary of Health and Human Services. We're working at that level of the administration, coordinating across industries—the toy industry, food industry, and others—trying to coordinate across countries. I foresee a day when we'll have a much more efficient and effective regulatory system that will better recognize the global nature of business today.
>
> My thinking has evolved over the last 30 years. We try to balance people, planet and profits. Just looking at profits alone is too short-sighted. One of the things I've learned about business is that, for some constituents, there'll never be enough profits. Don't get me wrong, profits are important; but, we also have a responsibility to society in other ways. As an example, the toy industry does an awful lot of manufacturing in relatively under-developed markets. We tend to be labor-intensive and have low value-added products. We were one of the early industries to go into a place like mainland China 30 years ago. When we're there, we acknowledge a responsibility to not abuse people and to help people move up the socio-economic ladder.
>
> It's hard for us to impose our American standards today on these countries, which are probably in the same place that America was two or three generations ago. But clearly, we need to impose standards that are different than the standards which were imposed on our immigrant grandparents when they came to this country and were abused. We have a stated policy in manufacturing, for example, of how we run a facility or how one of our vendor plants runs a facility, what kind of people are employed, nobody under-age, no forced labor, how they're paid and when they're paid. We have a checklist of 200 standards, and if anybody wants to log on to www.mattel.com, he/she will see that we have outside, independent auditors who go into our facilities and monitor our compliance with these standards. It's not just about making money; it's about making sure that we are building people's skills and responsibilities, and are treating them fairly. I think that's a responsibility of business today.
>
> We're always rethinking our manufacturing strategy. Today, Mattel manufactures in Mexico, Malaysia, Indonesia, Thailand and China, and we're constantly looking at our manufacturing footprint and trying to optimize it. I believe almost 80% of the world's toys are currently

made in southern China, and it's harder for us to find employees in southern China. If you stood in front of a toy factory 20 years ago, there was empty land beside it. Now, you can look to your left and see a cell phone plant or some sort of electronics plant, and look to your right and see an auto manufacturer. There is increasing higher value-added competition for us in labor and wages in southern China, and so I see the toy industry moving again, over the years, to some other place. It might be further inland, or in northern China. It might be to another emerging market like Vietnam or someplace like that. Just as the toy industry moved from Taiwan to Hong Kong to southern China, I see the continued evolution of our manufacturing. I don't know exactly where we'll go. But if we do move, I don't think it's related to the short-term events of the past year. It's part of a longer strategic plan.

I see more [design and development work] being done in China [in the future]. There are two things influencing this trend. One is simply the natural evolution of China's economy and labor force. The country now has very high quality engineers graduating, and we can employ them locally on the ground in our manufacturing facilities. The skill set of the labor force is evolving. The second thing impacting all this is the digitization of the supply chain. When I started out in business, products were designed by drawings using a pad and pencil. Today, it's done on a screen with a stylus. The file we create can be transferred electronically to any place in the world, and worked on in any place in the world. There are always nuances in culture, and differences in how people communicate with and deal with one another. Mattel has been very successful in China for decades, and I suspect we'll be there for decades to come. Appreciating and understanding cultural differences are important; whether you're working with someone in China, in Mexico or wherever, there exist cultural nuances that are important to understand.

In addition, the regulatory and legal environment is somewhat different. The intellectual property challenge is always an issue in emerging countries. Here in the United States, we're much more sophisticated and advanced regarding intellectual property protection, so we don't really worry about counterfeit goods in the U.S. But one needs to worry about counterfeit goods when they're manufacturing overseas. Still, I don't think there's anything remarkable or new, based on our experience. It's just a reminder that it's a big world out there, and you need to be very vigilant in your standards.

Chinese manufacturing was under a little bit of a siege that summer, and part of it was related to recalls. Certainly, some of the recalls had nothing to do with the manufacturing process at all. Again, when I talk about these small, high-powered magnets, what happened is we changed our design and our engineering of how we affix or embed the magnet into the plastic. We decided to use today's standards retroactively. It made no difference where those toys were produced or when they were produced. A lot of the media, I think, confused the issue a little bit and said, "This magnet issue, that's another example of poor Chinese manufacturing quality." It had nothing to do with manufacturing quality. So, we said to the officials and the regulators in China, "I'm sorry that the second set of recalls, which had to do with the magnet-based toys, was somehow associated with you. It shouldn't have been."

5.5.5 Conclusions

Countries don't make products, companies do. It just so happens that the majority of toys today are made in China; hence, most of the toys recalled in any given year come from there. That's not a surprise to me. Probably the largest recall that Mattel ever undertook was a product made in Indiana. So, again, we can make mistakes in manufacturing regardless of where the physical plant is. That said, I think it's important to have good oversight, regardless of whether you're manufacturing in China or Eastern Europe or here in the United States. To me, it's the same control system that the company needs to be responsible for. I don't like to rely on regulators to monitor our compliance. I think that's our job.

References

Barboza, D. 2007. Scandal and Suicide in China: A Dark Side of Toys. *New York Times*, August 23.

European Toy Safety Directive 2009/48/EC. Available at http://eur-lex.europa.eu/LexUriServ /LexUriServ.do?uri=OJ:L:2009:170:0001:0037:EN:PDF.

Lyles, M.A. 2008. Appreciating cultural differences in China: An interview with Robert A. Eckert, Chairperson of the Board and CEO of Mattel, Inc. *Business Horizons*, 51: 463–468.

Singpao Daily. 2012. The Death of Zhang Shuhong, A Hong Kong Businessman. Available at http://www.singpao.com/xw/yw/201211/t20121101_398588.html (retrieved August 22, 2014).

Ward, A. and Luce, E. 2007. Democratic rivals united in tough line on Beijing. *Financial Times*, August 16. Available at http://www.ft.com/cms/s/0/548767ee-4b90-11dc-861a -0000779fd2ac.html#axzz3B4h4d5cY (retrieved August 22, 2014).

Chapter 6

Chinese Milk Powder Crisis

Xiande Zhao, Yina Li, Barbara B. Flynn,
and Stephen Ng

Contents

6.1 Introduction: Importance of the Chinese Milk Crisis

The Chinese melamine-tainted milk powder recall was one of the most notorious in recent history. The series of events related to this product recall received a great deal of media coverage all over the world and caused the public to focus greater attention on the quality and safety of Chinese products than ever before. Moreover, this incident served as a wakeup call for manufacturers everywhere.

Through a detailed analysis of the events leading up to and following the melamine-tainted milk powder crisis, this chapter examines several key issues related to supply chain quality management. First, how was supply chain design related to the quality problems? Did supply chain design contribute to the product harm crisis? Second, how was the supply chain quality assurance (QA) system related to the quality problems? Third, what strategies can supply chain decision makers adopt, following a product harm crisis, in order to prevent future incidents?

Examination of these issues ultimately leads to the need to develop a comprehensive approach for managing supply chain quality. On the basis of concepts related to the total cost of quality, we discuss the design of supply chains based on prevention of product harm crises, in order to mitigate the frequency and severity of product recalls. This has important implications for preventing product harm crises, mitigating their effect through effective supply chain designs and supply chain quality management systems.

6.2 Supply Chain Design and Cost of Quality

6.2.1 Supply Chain Design

The growing focus on supply chain management in an increasingly intense competitive environment calls for more effective coordination and cooperation across the firms that comprise a supply chain. Hence, considerable effort has been devoted to gaining a better understanding of supply chain design (Stock et al. 2000; Gereffi et al. 2005; Gellynck and Molnar 2009). Supply chain designs vary on a continuum from the spot market to full vertical integration. We focus on the supply chain design proposed by Stock et al. (2000), which is composed of two dimensions: the relationship between a firm and its suppliers and customers and the extent of vertical integration present in the supply chain. In China's relationship-based environment, a stronger relationship between a dairy company and its raw milk suppliers could have helped to reduce the raw milk suppliers' temptation to engage in inappropriate behaviors, such as tampering with product quality, thus reducing transaction costs for the dairy company. A nonvertically integrated supply chain may focus more on price adjustments and risk shifting than on product quality. Successful vertical coordination (through the enhanced access to inputs and improved management) could help a dairy company source sufficiently high-quality raw milk supplies and can thus have a positive effect on supplier productivity and quality (Dries et al. 2009).

The dairy industry in China is broad, encompassing the agriculture, manufacturing, and service industries. A problem in any tier will cause a failure for the dairy company. The longer the supply chain is, the more difficult it is for a manufacturer to keep track of who did what and when and the final quality of the products (Lyles et al. 2008). After the dairy crisis, the Chinese government reformed the production, purchasing, processing, and sales sectors of the dairy industry, to help them come back to normal.

Because of the geographic distribution differences between the raw milk supply base and dairy product consumption market, Chinese dairy companies can be divided into two categories: resource-based companies, represented by Mengniu Dairy and Yili Dairy, and urban-based companies, represented by Bright Dairy and Sanyuan Dairy (Xinhuanet 2006). The core competency of the resource-based companies is their control of complex nationwide distribution channels. In contrast, the competitive advantage of the urban-based companies lies in their control of the milk sources for the core market and direct distribution networks (cold chain logistics system); they rely only on limited milk sources around the city.

6.2.2 Quality-Related Costs

To better understand the cost impact on companies that are faced with a product harm crisis, we draw upon the cost of quality perspective to provide a holistic picture. Quality-related costs can be categorized as prevention, appraisal, internal failure, and external failure costs (Nandakumar et al. 1993; Foster 1996; Ritzman and Krajewski 2004). Prevention costs are the costs related to designing and maintaining a QA system to prevent defects before they occur. Appraisal costs are the costs of inspection and testing, including receiving inspection, in-process inspection, and final inspection. Internal failure costs include losses from defects that are found within a production facility, including scrap, spoilage, repair, and rework costs. External failure costs arise when a defect is discovered after customers have purchased a product, including warranty and replacement costs, customer complaint handling costs, recall costs, litigation costs, and the loss of future revenues and profits. As a company designs its supply chain quality management system, it makes trade-offs among prevention, appraisal, and failure costs.

To understand how this trade-off is made, it is necessary to explore the way that QA systems are designed. QA systems are concerned with quality planning and defect prevention (Garvin 1988; Collins 1994), and an integrated QA system focuses on quality throughout an entire supply chain. QA systems are increasingly more important in integrated food supply chains that extend from primary production to the consumer (Turner and Davies 2002). An integrated QA system should integrate quality-related functions at all levels; it should not simply be a set of independent, tier-specific QA systems (Nookabadi and Middle 2006). Integrated QA systems have two dimensions: intrasystem integration and intersystem integration (Kolarik 1995); in other words, integrated QA systems focus on quality planning and defect prevention both within each tier in a supply chain and across the tiers.

6.3 Background

To gain further insight into the relationships among supply chain design, QA systems, and quality-related costs, the Chinese melamine-tainted milk powder crisis was investigated using focus group interviews, in-depth case studies, and secondary information and data from various sources, including newspapers, magazines, government reports, and academic experts in quality management. To deepen our understanding of what led to the crisis, we focused on the Sanlu Group, which was at the heart of the melamine scandal, and six Chinese publicly traded dairy companies: Yili, Bright Dairy, and Sanyuan (listed in the China A Shares stock market), Mengniu (listed in the Hong Kong stock market), Synutra International, Inc., and American Dairy, Inc. (listed in the U.S. stock market). Sanlu, Yili, Bright Dairy, Mengniu, and Synutra were found to have melamine-tainted milk products, while Sanyuan and American Dairy were not. Please see Chapter 2 for details about how the melamine-tainted milk incident transpired.

6.4 Supply Chain Design

The raw milk supplied to Chinese dairy companies comes from two categories of sources: outsourced suppliers and vertically integrated suppliers. The former includes three sources: small-scale independent farmers, small dairy farm complexes, and cooperative dairy farms, which are corporate owned. More details about these suppliers are summarized in Table 6.1.

There is a variety of raw milk sources among the dairy companies that we studied, summarized in Table 6.2. Sanlu obtained 100% of its raw milk supply from third parties (Lu and Tao 2009), and more than 90% of the raw milk used by Yili and Mengniu was provided by third parties. These consisted primarily of small-scale independent farmers scattered across the country, who took their milk to independent milk collection stations (Ding 2009), with the remainder provided by cooperative dairy farms. Synutra owns six factories in China: three in Heilongjiang, with raw milk provided by its own corporate-owned dairy farms, and three in Mongolia and Hebei, which use raw milk provided by small-scale independent farmers.

In contrast, 95% of the raw milk used by Bright Dairy is provided by its own corporate-owned dairy farms and small dairy farm complexes; only 5% of its raw milk is provided by small-scale independent farmers (Li 2008). Four large dairy supply bases provide all raw milk for American Dairy, including two that are corporate-owned dairy farms and two that are cooperative dairy farms operated by

Table 6.1 Comparison of Raw Milk Suppliers by Structure

	Outsourced Suppliers			Vertically Integrated Suppliers
	Small-Scale Independent Farmers	Small Dairy Farm Complexes	Cooperative Dairy Farms	Corporate-Owned Dairy Farms
Ownership	Individual farmer	Government or privately owned company owns the facilities; individual farmers own cattle	Jointly owned by farmers, milk dealers, government agencies, dairy companies	Dairy company
Type of cattle	Genetically inferior	Somewhat inferior	Good	Good
Nutrition	Independent, unscientific	Centralized, somewhat scientific	Centralized, scientific	Centralized, scientific
Milking process	Manual	Centrally, by machine	Centrally, by machine	Centrally, by machine
Cleanliness	Unstandardized, insufficient	Somewhat standardized and sufficient	Standardized, sufficient	Strongly enforced standards and clean
Epidemic inspection and prevention	Independent, unstandardized	Somewhat uniform and standardized	Uniform, standardized	Uniform, standardized

(continued)

Table 6.1 Comparison of Raw Milk Suppliers by Structure (Continued)

| | Outsourced Suppliers | | | Vertically Integrated Suppliers |
	Small-Scale Independent Farmers	Small Dairy Farm Complexes	Cooperative Dairy Farms	Corporate-Owned Dairy Farms
Numbers of suppliers	Thousands of small-scale suppliers	Hundreds of independent suppliers, located together on the small dairy farm complex	Fewer larger suppliers	Internal control
Relationship with suppliers	Arm's length, short-term relationship	Somewhat closer	Long-term, close relationship	Internal control
Raw milk quality	Not guaranteed, tends to be the worst	Somewhat better	Good	Best
Distribution channel	Sold in the spot market or to milk dealers	Sold through the complex to dairy companies	Sold through the cooperative to dairy companies	Vertically controlled by dairy companies

Table 6.2 Comparison of the Supply Chain Structure

	% from Small-Scale Farmers	% from Small Dairy Farm Complexes	% from Cooperative Dairy Farms	% from Corporate-Owned Dairy Farms	Melamine Tainted?
Sanlu	100	0	0	0	Yes
Mengniu	90	10			Yes
Yili	90	10			Yes
Synutra	50	0	0	50	Yes
Bright Dairy	5	95			Yes
American Dairy	0	0	50	50	No
Sanyuan	0	0	20	80	No

American Dairy and other dairy companies. Sanyuan owns and operates 27 large-scale farms that supply 80% of its raw milk (Sun and Chen 2009). The other 20% of its raw milk is provided by cooperative dairy farms, with none supplied by small-scale independent farmers (Yang 2009).

6.5 QA Systems

Since the problems with melamine-tainted milk were originally detected in the Sanlu Group, and since its products were found to contain the highest level of melamine contamination, Sanlu provides an example to help better understand the QA systems of the companies with the most serious melamine issues. The Sanlu Group, Inc., began as a self-sufficient, fully integrated organization, which owned both its farms and dairy cattle. As China's growing income per capita and demand for Western food, such as pizza and cheeseburgers, increased, the demand for dairy products increased dramatically. Sanlu found that its growth was limited by its raw milk supply and lack of focus on R&D and production.

In 1987, Sanlu underwent a reorganization that separated its farming and processing into distinct operations. As part of this initiative, Sanlu provided financing to small-scale independent farmers, to allow them to own their cattle, while it focused on the research and development, production, marketing, and brand building side of things. Sanlu also introduced milk collection stations, which acted as a middleman for buying raw milk from the independent farmers. Thus, Sanlu shifted its focus from farming to mass production and marketing. This strategic move significantly increased its scale of production, reducing Sanlu's costs and subsequently increasing its market share and profitability, as well as providing opportunities for small-scale independent farmers to develop their businesses. Sanlu went on to become China's largest producer of milk powder for baby formula. Because of the success of this business model, it was quickly imitated by other dairy companies.

Quality control was not originally a problem for Sanlu, since the dairy market was a buyer's market, and Sanlu had the power to refuse deliveries of unqualified raw milk. However, from 2000 to 2007, as dairy consumption in China grew at the stunning rate of 23% annually, and many new dairy companies sprang up across the country, the aggregate raw milk supply fell short of demand, turning the dairy industry into a seller's market. Because they were no longer vertically integrated, the dairy companies found themselves competing with each other to secure a supply of raw milk. There was no unified control system or government agency in charge of supervising the milk collection stations and small-scale independent farmers. This led to opportunistic behavior by some suppliers, and some avoided investing in capital equipment and the medication and feed additives that are important in ensuring milk quality levels (Enderwick 2009). In addition, the milk collection stations began to tamper with the raw milk by adding melamine before selling it to the dairy companies in order to ensure that their raw milk would not be rejected for substandard protein levels.

Moreover, the Chinese government's exemption of checking certification may have encouraged Sanlu to forgo testing its incoming raw milk supplies. The small-scale independent farmers had little knowledge about optimal feed for their cattle and had no incentive to improve the effectiveness of their farming practices or the quality of their raw milk (Enderwick 2009). These combined to lead to Sanlu's failure to control the quality of its raw milk. Ultimately, Sanlu's products were found to contain the highest level of melamine contamination in China, 5125 times higher than the E.U. safety standard.

6.6 Implications

6.6.1 Role of Supply Chain Design

As shown in Tables 6.1 and 6.2, as the number of suppliers increased, the relationship between the dairy companies and their outsourced suppliers changed from a close relationship to an arm's-length relationship. Small-scale farms are very small in China, typically housing five or fewer cattle; this is hard to picture in the United States, where a small dairy farm may have 75–100 cattle. Chinese dairy farmers are often illiterate, limiting their ability to keep records of feed, medication, yield, and so forth. It is very difficult for dairy companies to manage and keep tabs on thousands of small-scale farmers when they have an arm's-length relationship with them.

However, for the dairy companies that instead designed their supply chains to focus on fewer larger suppliers, such as the cooperative dairy farms, it was much easier to establish long-term, close relationships and work with suppliers to develop effective systems for record keeping and monitoring. The raw milk provided by the corporate-owned dairy farms was of the best quality, followed by that provided by the cooperative dairy farms, the small dairy farm complexes, and finally the small-scale independent farmers, which was of the worst quality. All of the companies studied that used raw milk provided by small-scale independent farmers (Sanlu, Yili, Mengniu, Synutra, and Bright Dairy) were found to have melamine-tainted milk products, while their counterparts using raw milk provided by farms other than the small-scale independent farmers (Sanyuan and American Dairy) were found to be free of tainted milk. Thus, strategic supply chain design has strong quality and safety implications.

Changing the supply chain design by removal of an unsafe supply base (e.g., small-scale independent farmers) may help to improve supply chain quality. Reduction of the number of supply chain tiers toward full vertical integration may also contribute to improvement of dairy supply chain quality. The dairy companies that used raw milk supplies from the corporate-owned dairy farms had better control over their raw milk sources and reduced their quality risk because the middleman layer was eliminated from their supply chain design. In contrast, a multitier supply chain environment is characterized by a long chain of suppliers; the risk associated with product quality is increased due to the need to monitor a greater number of tiers and greater product uncertainties.

Table 6.3 highlights the difficulties for dairy companies in managing a long supply chain, which is characterized by poor visibility and low traceability of material origin. Thus, the longer the supply chain becomes (i.e., the more the tiers in the supply chain or the greater the number of suppliers in each tier), the more difficult it is for producers to keep track of who did what and when and the final quality of the products (Lyles et al. 2008).

Following the melamine crisis, the Chinese government developed regulations for restructuring the dairy industry and its supply chains. Since October 2011, 30% of the cattle must be raised on large farms, and dairy companies are expected to obtain 70% of their raw milk from farms that they own themselves (General Office of the State Council of the People's Republic of China 2008). This is expected to rationalize the current system of small independent farmers whose milk previously reached the production facilities via a web of unaccountable middlemen.

Table 6.3 Supply Chain Quality Risks

Supply Chain Segment	Issues	Sources	Risks
Dairy farms	Quality of cattle	Genetically inferior	More prone to diseases
			Lower protein levels in raw milk
	Cattle feed	Unscientific feed blending	Higher incidence of diseases
		Inferior additives	Higher bacterial levels in raw milk
		Tainted feed	Lower protein levels in raw milk
		Substandard veterinary pharmaceuticals	
	Processing and handling	Contaminated containers	Lower protein levels in raw milk
		Contamination due to hand milking	Higher bacterial levels in raw milk
		Intentional chemical additives	Tainted raw milk
		Insufficient cleanliness	Adulterated raw milk
Raw milk dealers	Infrastructure	Collection equipment	Poor raw milk quality
		Transportation equipment	Higher bacterial levels in raw milk
		Testing equipment	Inability to track to the source of raw milk
		Storage equipment	
		Cleanliness and sterilization procedures	
		Mixing of raw milk from different sources	

	Technology	Cleanliness and sterilization Technological know-how Process and production capability	Inability to track to the source of raw milk Inability to detect failures Spoiled raw milk Tainted raw milk Adulterated raw milk
	Opportunistic behavior	Rapidly growing demand for dairy products Insufficient supply of raw milk Price-based competition Profit-seeking behavior	Spoiled raw milk Tainted raw milk Adulterated raw milk Higher bacterial levels in raw milk Falsification of records
	Practices	Lack of best practices Unclean conditions Poor sterilization habits	Spoiled raw milk Tainted raw milk Higher bacterial levels in raw milk
Dairy companies (manufacturers)	Inbound logistics	Mixing of raw milk from various sources Supplier selection Supplier inspection Cold chain transportation practices Transportation equipment Visibility and traceability systems	Adulterated raw milk Tainted raw milk Spoiled raw milk Substandard final milk products Lower protein levels in raw milk

(continued)

Table 6.3 Supply Chain Quality Risks (Continued)

Supply Chain Segment	Issues	Sources	Risks
	Internal processes	Processing standards Quality of employees Processing equipment Packaging Additive mix	Adulterated raw milk Tainted raw milk Spoiled raw milk Substandard final milk products Lower protein levels in raw milk
	Outbound logistics	Cold chain transportation practices Transportation equipment Quality of packaging Visibility and traceability systems	Lower percentage of protein and other beneficial elements in dairy products Adulterated dairy products
Distributors and retailers	Infrastructure	Delivery equipment Storage equipment Cold chain systems Customer errors and handling Purchasing from substandard suppliers Lack of quality monitoring Inadequate inventory management	Expired dairy products Deteriorated dairy products Packaging damage Undetected problems

6.6.2 *Role of QA in Prevention*

Figure 6.1 shows the QA system that Bright Dairy developed after the melamine scandal. It introduced the most advanced technology for ensuring traceability and QA, from the farm to the supermarket. We use the findings from our visit to Bright Dairy's Shanghai-based no. 8 dairy plant and interviews with its operations managers to illustrate the QA system now used by Bright Dairy. This provides an example of how investments in prevention lead to reduced internal failures, external failures,

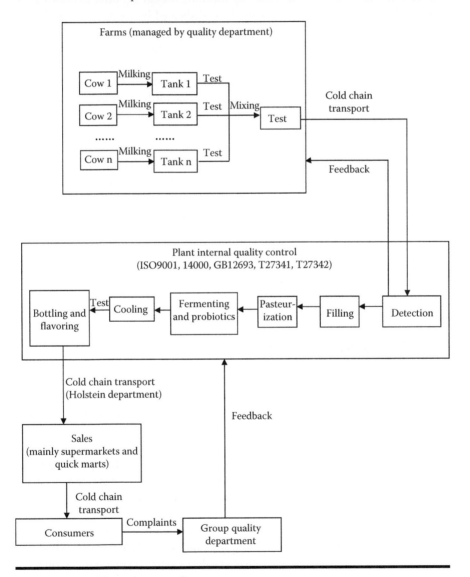

Figure 6.1 Bright Dairy's quality assurance system.

and appraisal costs and, ultimately, a lower cost of quality. Bright Dairy's QA system is featured in Chapter 11.

Bright Dairy attaches an ear tag to each cow in its corporate-owned dairy farms, providing a unique identifier for every cow. Through the use of a barcode scanning gun, data on veterinary treatment, testing of cow welfare, and all feed given to the cow are automatically transferred to Bright's computer system. Bright Dairy uses automated milking machines, with each cow milked three times a day. The cow and its history are identified by scanning the ear tag prior to milking. The milk is then collected in a single container (dedicated by cow) for raw milk sampling, bacteriological testing, and other inspections. Information about any problems encountered with the raw milk provided by a particular cow is sent back to the farm of origin, and if there is any evidence of intentional tampering, the partnership with the farm of origin will be permanently terminated. Only after the tests on the individual containers of milk have been satisfactorily completed will raw milk from different cattle be mixed together. Another round of tests is then executed in order to ensure bulk milk quality.

All of Bright Dairy's raw milk is shipped within 12 hours to ensure its freshness after testing and recording all the detailed indicators. Each bulk milk hauler, supported by Bright Dairy's professional cold chain and GPS, ensures that all the shipping documents and records are accurate, in order to minimize potential security risks. Upon the arrival of bulk raw milk at the Bright Dairy processing facility, the information on the shipping documents is verified and samples of the bulk milk are tested. If there is any quality or safety problem that was not detected initially but was found later, a product recall will be immediately launched. More information about Bright Dairy's innovative systems for preventing safety problems through investments in prevention is provided in Chapter 11.

6.7 Relationship among Supply Chain Governance, QA, and Cost

Product quality risk potentially exists in all tiers of the dairy supply chain; a problem in any tier can cause a failure for the dairy company. For example, although some small-scale independent farmers added melamine to their raw milk without the knowledge of the dairy companies, it was the reputation of dairy companies like Sanlu that was ultimately damaged. Thus, it is critical to incorporate QA principles into the supply chain design. We use the cost of quality perspective to analyze prevention, appraisal, internal failure, and external failure costs by supply chain tiers, as shown in Table 6.4.

On the basis of our previous discussion of the Sanlu and Bright Dairy cases, we describe the relationship among supply chain design, QA system, and quality-related costs. When Sanlu put its emphasis on developing and marketing products, it changed from vertical integration to an outsourcing model for obtaining all of its raw

Table 6.4   Costs of Quality in the Chinese Dairy Supply Chain

	Costs of Quality			
	Prevention Cost	*Appraisal Cost*	*Internal Failure Cost*	*External Failure Cost*
Dairy farmers	Outsourced suppliers Provision of loans for cattle and equipment Provision of quality guidance on critical inputs Cost of hiring experts to offer guidance Promotion of best farming practices Training of farmers Incentives for quality production Vertically Integrated Suppliers Investment in superior cattle Development of cattle breeding centers Development of large-scale farming bases	Investment in testing equipment Cost of testing Final inspection Field testing Independent third-party testing Training inspection staff	Yield losses due to destroyed raw milk Rework costs Discounts due to selling downgraded raw milk at lower prices Problem-solving costs	Handling of consumer complaints Provision of replacement products Compensation for medical expenses Liability litigation costs Loss of customer goodwill Opportunity costs related to lost sales Supply chain disruptions Public relations costs Loss of shareholder wealth

(continued)

Table 6.4   Costs of Quality in the Chinese Dairy Supply Chain (Continued)

	Costs of Quality			
	Prevention Cost	*Appraisal Cost*	*Internal Failure Cost*	*External Failure Cost*
	Centralized feed purchasing Development of identification and traceability systems for individual cattle Investment in automated milking and processing equipment Investment in refrigerated containers			
Raw milk dealers	Outsourced suppliers Independent third-party testing Emphasis on quality, rather than quantity Selection based on quality, rather than price Process training and education	Investment in testing equipment Cost of testing Final inspection Field testing Independent third-party testing Training inspection staff	Yield losses due to destroyed raw milk Rework costs Discounts due to selling downgraded raw milk at lower prices Problem-solving costs	Handling of consumer complaints Provision of replacement products Compensation for medical expenses Liability litigation costs Loss of customer goodwill

Testing of raw milk prior to mixing		Opportunity costs related to lost sales
Selection of high-quality dealers		Supply chain disruptions
Development of long-term relationships with dealers		Public relations costs
Monitoring quality through check and sure system		Loss of shareholder wealth
Monitoring		
Promotion of best practices		
Vertically Integrated Suppliers		
Investment in automated milking equipment		
Investment in refrigeration systems		
Elimination of raw milk dealers (purchase directly from farmers)		
Establishment of long-term relationships with farmers		
Improvement of traceability to monitor raw milk quality		

(continued)

Table 6.4 Costs of Quality in the Chinese Dairy Supply Chain (Continued)

	Costs of Quality			
	Prevention Cost	*Appraisal Cost*	*Internal Failure Cost*	*External Failure Cost*
Dairy companies (manufacturers)	Cultivation of social responsibility Employee involvement Increased vertical integration Supplier selection, monitoring, and management Monitoring of supplier processes	Development of purchasing standards Investment in testing equipment Final inspection	Yield losses due to destroyed raw milk Rework costs Discounts due to selling downgraded raw milk at lower prices Problem-solving costs	Handling of consumer complaints Provision of replacement products Compensation for medical expenses Liability litigation costs Loss of customer goodwill Opportunity costs related to lost sales Supply chain disruptions Public relations costs Loss of shareholder wealth

Distributors and retailers			
Direct delivery to customers	Development of purchasing standards	Yield losses due to destroyed raw milk	Handling of consumer complaints
Training	Investment in testing equipment	Rework costs	Provision of replacement products
Irregularly scheduled testing	Final inspection	Discounts due to selling downgraded raw milk at lower prices	Compensation for medical expenses
Investment in equipment and facilities		Problem-solving costs	Liability litigation costs
Investment in inventory management			Loss of customer goodwill
Investment in monitoring			Opportunity costs related to lost sales
Supplier selection, monitoring, and management			Supply chain disruptions
Supplier visits			Public relations costs
Damage handling			Loss of shareholder wealth

milk supply from small-scale independent farmers and did not invest in equipment and techniques to prevent problems or to test the quality of its incoming raw milk supplies. Thus, Sanlu's prevention and appraisal costs were quite low. However, because dairy products are nondiscrete and produced in batches (Jansen-Vullers et al. 2003), the raw milk from various small-scale independent farmers with different quality attributes was mixed together, making it impossible to track and trace back to the source of a problem (Tse and Tan 2012), increasing the number of potentially recalled products and leading to significant external failure costs. Sanlu's external failure costs were so substantial that these ultimately led to its bankruptcy. Because Sanlu focused on minimizing its prevention and appraisal costs, it neglected their trade-off with internal and external failure costs, which ultimately led to irreversible disaster.

On the other hand, the QA system that Bright Dairy developed after the melamine scandal included an effective coordination protocol between its processing plants and farms to overcome market imperfections at the farm level, leading to improvements in the quality and productivity of the farms. With the help of its intraorganization and interorganization supply chain QA system, Bright Dairy enhanced traceability and quality throughout its entire supply chain, from farm to table. Thus, although Bright Dairy's prevention and appraisal costs have substantially increased, its internal and external failure costs have significantly decreased. As a result, its total cost of quality (the sum of prevention, appraisal, internal failure, and external failure costs) was reduced.

6.8 Conclusions

On the basis of our findings, we developed a supply chain quality management framework that encompasses supply chain design, QA system, cost of quality, and the resulting bottom line, as shown in Figure 6.2. The supply chain design that we have described is based on the extent of vertical integration and the relationship with outside upstream suppliers. The QA system includes interorganization and intraorganization QA systems, and the cost of quality includes prevention, appraisal, internal, and external failure cost; companies' bottom line includes both their financial and social bottom line. This framework can help to provide direction to decision makers in setting up a suitable supply chain quality management system, such as allocating supply chain resources to supply chain design and QA systems, so as to minimize and prevent product quality risk in the entire supply chain, thus improving supply chain performance and, hence, supply chain health.

Due to the large number of recalls of Chinese-made products, there are global concerns about the quality of products made in China. Since Chinese companies produce a large percentage of consumer products in many industries, designing a supply chain to prevent quality problems and handle product recalls is becoming increasingly important. This chapter used the case of the 2008 melamine-tainted

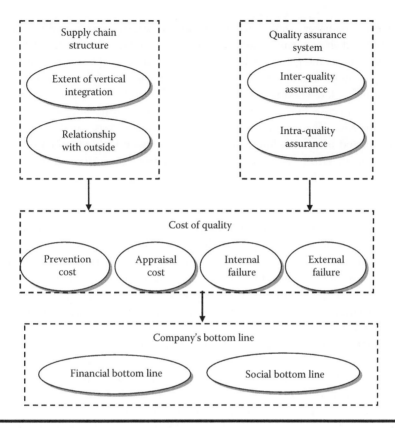

Figure 6.2 Proposed future research framework.

milk powder recalls to investigate supply chain quality and product recalls in China. Using case studies, media reports, interviews, and anecdotal information about the Chinese melamine-tainted milk powder crisis and Chinese major dairy companies, we established that companies that have a more vertically integrated supply chain and a better relationship with upstream suppliers, as well as better interorganization and intraorganization QA systems, invest more in prevention and appraisal costs in order to prevent the potential quality risks. Thus, their internal and external failure costs are significantly reduced.

We examined how supply chain design and QA systems influence the cost of quality and product quality. We found that those dairy companies that emphasized prevention by investing in development of their raw milk supply base, more vertically integrated supply chains, and better relationships with suppliers, as well developing interorganization and intraorganization QA systems, had better control of quality over their entire supply chain and were thus less likely to experience a product harm crisis (a significant external failure cost).

Hence, managers should include quality considerations in making decisions concerning their company's supply chain design, supplier selection, and QA system. Although outsourcing and neglecting to develop a tight QA system may result in lower prevention and appraisal costs, it runs the risk of high variation in product quality and lack of control and visibility of quality problems. This can cause serious product harm crises in the supply chain, leading to very significant internal and external failure costs. These costs, particularly external failure costs, can dwarf prevention, appraisal, and internal failure costs, leading to a much higher total cost of quality. Such risks can have a serious negative effect on a firm's financial performance or even cause it to go bankrupt, as Sanlu did. Prevention is a better approach for ensuring product quality, both within a factory and within a supply chain. Companies should develop a long-term supply chain quality management strategy for preventing product harm crises and for improving and sustaining their supply chain competitiveness.

However, the study of supply chain quality management is still in its infancy (e.g., Robinson and Malhotra 2005; Foster 2008). Future researchers should move beyond traditional firm-centric quality management to an interorganizational approach to supply chain quality management. While supply chain quality management embraces the traditional quality management paradigm, it extends the conceptual domain by including upstream and downstream quality and placing additional emphasis on issues such as supply chain leadership, external process integration (Robinson and Malhotra 2005), supplier development and integration (Lo and Yeung 2006; Carvalho and Costa 2007), supply chain transparency, traceability, testability, trust (Roth et al. 2008), and safety (Foster 2008), in order to prevent product harm crises and improve competitiveness.

While effective supply chain design, QA systems, and supply chain quality management systems may help to prevent most product harm crises, no system is completely safe. Therefore, companies should proactively design and implement effective product recall strategies and tactics for remedying a product harm crisis in order to avoid substantial external failure costs. For example, Cadbury's customers "forgave" it because it took a series of rapid and effective recall actions after its product harm crisis related to Salmonella contamination in 2007. To help evaluate the effectiveness of proactive strategies for handling product recalls, future research should examine consumers' reactions to alternative recall strategies and tactics using controlled experiments such as those described in Chapters 16 and 17.

References

Carvalho, R.A., and H.G. Costa. 2007. Application of an integrated decision support process for supplier selection. *Enterprise Info. Sys.* 1(2): 197–216.

Collins, P. 1994. Approaches to quality. *TQM Mag.* 6(3): 39–43.

Ding, L. 2009. Bright Dairy should have a turnaround [online]. Available from http://finance.jrj.com.cn/2009/01/2014503391111.shtml (Accessed January 20, 2009).

Dries, L., E. Germenji, N. Noev, and J. Swinnen. 2009. Farmers, vertical coordination, and the restructuring of dairy supply chains in central and Eastern Europe. *World Dev.* 37(11): 1742–1758.

Enderwick, P. 2009. Managing "quality failure" in China: Lessons from the dairy industry case. *Int. J. Emerg. Market* 4(3): 220–234.

Foster, S.T. Jr. 1996. An examination of the relationship between conformance and quality-related costs. *Int. J. Qual. Rel. Mgmt.* 13(4): 50–63.

Foster, S.T. 2008. Towards an understanding of supply chain quality management. *J. Ops. Mgmt.* 26(4): 461–467.

Garvin, D.A. 1988. *Managing Quality: The Strategic and Competitive Edge.* New York, Free Press.

Gellynck, X., and A. Molnar. 2009. Chain structures: The European traditional food sector. *Brit. Food J.* 111(8): 762–775.

General Office of the State Council of the People's Republic of China. 2008. The planning outlines for the rectifying and revitalization of Chinese dairy industry [online]. Available from http://news.xinhuanet.com/newscenter/2008-11/19/content_10383502.htm (Accessed November 19, 2008).

Gereffi, G., J. Humphrey, and T. Sturgeon. 2005. The governance of global value chains. *Rev. Int. Pol. Econ.* 12(1): 78–104.

Jansen-Vullers, M.H., C.A. Van Dorp, and A.J. Beulens. 2003. Managing traceability information in manufacture. *Int. J. Info. Mgmt.* 23(5): 395–413.

Kolarik, W.J. 1995. *Quality Concepts, Systems, Strategies, and Tools.* New York, McGraw-Hill.

Li, R. 2008. Bright Dairy: Neither building new factory nor expanding the scale of production without qualified milk sources [online]. Available from http://jjckb.xinhuanet .com/gnyw/2008-10/30/content_125338.htm (Accessed October 30, 2008).

Lo, V.H.Y., and A. Yeung. 2006. Managing quality effectively in supply chain: A preliminary study. *Supp. Chain Mgmt.* 11(3): 208–215.

Lu, J.Y., and Z.G. Tao. 2009. *Sanlu's Melamine-Tainted Milk Crisis in China.* Hong Kong, University of Hong Kong, Asia Case Research Centre.

Lyles, M.A., B.B. Flynn, and M.T. Frohlich. 2008. All supply chains don't flow through: Understanding supply chain issues in product recalls. *Mgmt. Org. Rev.* 4(2): 167–182.

Nandakumar, P., S. Datar, and R. Akella. 1993. Models for measuring and accounting for cost of conformance quality. *Mgmt. Sci.* 39(1): 1–16.

Nookabadi, A.S., and J.E. Middle. 2006. An integrated quality assurance information system for the design-to-order manufacturing environment. *TQM Mag.* 18(2): 174–189.

Ritzman, L., and L. Krajewski. 2004. *Foundations of Operations Management.* Upper Saddle River, New Jersey, Pearson Higher Education.

Robinson, C.J., and M.K. Malhotra. 2005. Defining the concept of supply chain quality management and its relevance to academic and industrial practice. *Int. J. Prod. Econ.* 96(3): 315–337.

Roth, A.V., A.A. Tsay, M.E. Pullman, and J.V. Gray. 2008. Unravelling the food supply chain: Strategic insights from China and the 2007 recalls. *J. Supp. Chain Mgmt.* 44(1): 22–39.

Stock, G.N., N.P. Greis, and J.D. Kasarda. 2000. Enterprise logistics and supply chain structure: The role of fit. *J. Ops. Mgmt.* 18(5): 531–547.

Sun, F., and S.F. Chen. 2009. *Sanlu Group and the Tainted Milk Crisis.* London, Ontario, University of Western Ontario, Richard Ivey School of Business.

Tse, Y.K., and K.H. Tan. 2012. Managing product quality risk and visibility in multi-layer supply chain. *Int. J. Prod. Econ.* 22(8): 1002–1013.

Turner, J.C., and W.P. Davies. 2002. The modern food chain: Profiting from effective integration. *Trade Partners UK and Ministry of Agriculture "Modern Food Chain" Seminar*, Kuala Lumpur, Malaysia, March 26, 1–37.

Xinhuanet. 2006. Would the word "fresh banning" of liquid milk abort due to benefit [online]? Available from http://news.xinhuanet.com/fortune/2006-06/01/content_4632824.htm (Accessed June 1, 2006).

Yang, S.J. 2009. Sanyuan: Keep on "Sanyuan Mode," control product quality strictly [online]. Available from http://www.bj.xinhuanet.com/bjpd-wq/2009-03/04/content_16505202.htm (Accessed March 4, 2009).

Chapter 7

Ford Pinto Recall*

Dennis A. Gioia

Contents

7.1 Introduction: Background

In 1973, Dennis Gioia became Ford Motor Co.'s field recall coordinator. He was in charge of the operational coordination of all the recall campaigns currently underway and also in charge of tracking incoming information to identify developing problems. Gioia's responsibility included viewing files containing field reports of alleged component failure that had led to accidents. He is now chair of the Department of Management and Organization and the Robert & Judith Klein Professor of Management in the Smeal College of Business at Pennsylvania State University.

---

* Heavily excerpted from Gioia, D. *J. Bus. Ethics*, 11, 379–390, 1992. With permission.

7.2 Dennis Gioia's Background

In the summer of 1972, I made one of those important transitions in life, the significance of which becomes obvious only in retrospect. I left academe with a BS in Engineering Science and an MBA to enter the world of big business. I joined Ford Motor Company at World Headquarters in Dearborn, Michigan, fulfilling a long-standing dream to work in the heart of the auto industry. I felt confident that I was in the right place at the right time to make a difference.

I found myself on the fast track at Ford, participating in a "tournament" type of socialization (Van Maanen 1978), engaged in a competition for recognition with other MBAs who had recently joined the company. And I quickly became caught up in the game. The company itself was dynamic; the environment of business, especially the auto industry, was intriguing; the job was challenging and the pay was great. The psychic rewards of working and succeeding in a major corporation proved unexpectedly seductive. I really became involved in the job.

By the summer of 1973, I was pitched into the thick of the battle. I became Ford's Field Recall Coordinator—not a position that was particularly high in the hierarchy but one that wielded influence far beyond its level. I was in charge of the operational coordination of all of the recall campaigns currently underway and also in charge of tracking incoming information to identify developing problems. Therefore, I was in a position to make initial recommendations about possible future recalls. The most critical type of recalls was labeled "safety campaigns"— those that dealt with the possibility of customer injury or death. These ranged from straight-forward occurrences, such as brake failure and wheels falling off vehicles, to more exotic and faintly humorous failure modes, such as detaching axles that announced their presence by spinning forward and slamming into the startled driver's door and speed control units that locked on, and refused to disengage, as the car accelerated wildly while the spooked driver futilely tried to shut it off. Safety recall campaigns, however, also encompassed the more sobering possibility of on-board gasoline fires and explosions.

7.3 Pinto Case

In 1970, Ford introduced the Pinto, a small car that was intended to compete with the then current challenge from European cars and the ominous presence on the horizon of Japanese manufacturers. The Pinto was brought from inception to production in the record time of approximately 25 months (compared to the industry average of 43 months), a time frame that suggested the necessity for doing things expediently. In addition to the time pressure, the engineering and development teams were required to adhere to the production "limits of 2000" for the diminutive car: it was not to exceed either $2000 in cost or 2000 pounds in weight. Any decisions that threatened these targets or the timing of the car's introduction were discouraged. Under normal conditions, design, styling, product planning, engineering, etc., were completed prior to production tooling. Because of the foreshortened time frame, however, some of these usually sequential processes were executed in parallel.

As a consequence, tooling was already well under way (thus "freezing" the basic design) when routine crash testing revealed that the Pinto's fuel tank often ruptured when struck from the rear at a relatively low speed (31 mph in crash tests). Reports (revealed much later) showed that the fuel tank failures were the result of some rather marginal design features. The tank was positioned between the rear bumper and the rear axle (a standard industry practice for the time). During impact, however, several studs protruding from the rear of the axle housing would puncture holes in the tank; the fuel filler neck also was likely to rip away. Spilled gasoline then could be ignited by sparks. Ford had in fact crash tested 11 vehicles; 8 of these cars suffered potentially catastrophic gas tank ruptures. The only 3 cars that survived intact had each been modified in some way to protect the tank. These crash tests, however, were conducted under the guidelines of Federal Motor Vehicle Safety Standard 301 which had been proposed in 1968 and strenuously opposed by the auto industry. FMVSS 301 was not actually adopted until 1976; thus, at the time of the tests, Ford was not in violation of the law.

There were several possibilities for fixing the problem, including the option of redesigning the tank and its location, which would have produced tank integrity in a high-speed crash. That solution, however, was not only time consuming and expensive, but also usurped trunk space, which was seen as a critical competitive sales factor. One of the production modifications to the tank, however, would have cost only $11 to install, but given the tight margins and restrictions of the "limits of 2000," there was reluctance to make even this relatively minor change. There were other reasons for not approving the change, as well, including a widespread industry belief that all small cars were inherently unsafe solely because of their size and weight. Another more prominent reason was a corporate belief that "safety doesn't sell." This observation was attributed to Lee Iacocca and stemmed from Ford's earlier attempt to make safety a sales theme, an attempt that failed rather dismally in the marketplace.

Perhaps the most controversial reason for rejecting the production change to the gas tank, however, was Ford's use of cost–benefit analysis to justify the decision. The National Highway Traffic Safety Association (NHTSA, a federal agency) had approved the use of cost–benefit analysis as an appropriate means for establishing automotive safety design standards. The controversial aspect in making such calculations was that they required the assignment of some specific value for a human life. In 1970, that value was deemed to be approximately $200,000 as a "cost to society" for each fatality. Ford used NHTSA's figures in estimating the costs and benefits of altering the tank production design. An internal memo, later revealed in court, indicates the following tabulations concerning potential fires (Dowie 1977):

COSTS: $137,000,000
(Estimated as the costs of a production fix to all similarly designed cars and trucks with the gas tank aft of the axle [12,500,000 vehicles × $11/vehicle])

BENEFITS: $49,530,000
(Estimated as the savings from preventing [180 projected deaths × $200,000/
   death] + [180 projected burn injuries × $67,000/injury] + [2100 burned cars ×
   $700/car])

The cost–benefit decision was then construed as straightforward: no production
fix would be undertaken. The philosophical and ethical implications of assigning
a financial value for human life or disfigurement do not seem to have been a major
consideration in reaching this decision.

7.3.1 Pintos and Personal Experience

When I took over the Recall Coordinator's job in 1973, I inherited the oversight
of about 100 active recall campaigns, more than half of which were safety-related.
These ranged from minimal in size (replacing front wheels that were likely to break
on 12 heavy trucks) to maximal (repairing the power steering pump on millions
of cars). In addition, there were quite a number of safety problems that were under
consideration as candidates for addition to the recall list.

One of these new files concerned reports of Pintos "lighting up" (in the
words of a field representative) in rear-end accidents. There were actually very
few reports, perhaps because component failure was not initially assumed. These
cars simply were consumed by fire after apparently very low speed accidents.
Was there a problem? Not as far as I was concerned. My cue for labeling a case
as a problem either required high frequencies of occurrence or directly traceable
causes. I had little time for speculative contemplation on potential problems that
did not fit a pattern that suggested known courses of action leading to possible
recall. I do, however, remember being disquieted by a field report accompanied
by graphic, detailed photos of the remains of a burned-out Pinto in which several
people had died. Although that report became part of my file, I did not flag it as
any special case.

It is difficult to convey the overwhelming complexity and pace of the job of
keeping track of so many active or potential recall campaigns. It remains the
busiest, most information-filled job I have ever held or would want to hold.
Each case required a myriad of information-gathering and execution stages. I
distinctly remember that the information-processing demands led me to con-
fuse the facts of one problem case with another on several occasions because the
telltale signs of recall candidate cases were so similar. I thought of myself as a
fireman—a fireman who perfectly fit the description by one of my colleagues:
"In this office, everything is a crisis. You only have time to put out the big fires
and spit on the little ones." By those standards, the Pinto problem was distinctly
a little one.

It is also important to convey the muting of emotion involved in the Recall
Coordinator's job. I remember contemplating the fact that my job literally involved

life-and-death matters. I was sometimes responsible for finding and fixing cars NOW, because somebody's life might depend on it. I took it very seriously. Early in the job, I sometimes woke up at night wondering whether I had covered all the bases. Had I left some unknown person at risk because I had not thought of something? That soon faded, however, and of necessity, the consideration of people's lives became a fairly removed, dispassionate process.

To do the job "well," there was little room for emotion. Allowing it to surface was potentially paralyzing and prevented rational decisions about which cases to recommend for recall. On moral grounds, I knew I could recommend most of the vehicles on my safety tracking list for recall (and risk earning the label of a "bleeding heart"). On practical grounds, I recognized that people implicitly accept risks in cars. We could not recall all cars with potential problems and stay in business. I learned to be responsive to those cases that suggested an imminent, dangerous problem.

Pinto reports continued to trickle in, but at such a slow rate that they really did not capture particular attention relative to other, more pressing safety problems. However, I later saw a crumpled, burned car at a Ford depot where alleged problem components and vehicles were delivered for inspection and analysis (a place known as the "Chamber of Horrors" by some of the people who worked there). The revulsion on seeing this incinerated hulk was immediate and profound. Soon afterwards, and despite the fact that the file was very sparse, I recommended the Pinto case for preliminary department-level review concerning possible recall. After the usual round of discussion about criteria and justification for recall, everyone voted against recommending recall, including me. It did not fit the pattern of recallable standards; the evidence was not overwhelming that the car was defective in some way, so the case was actually fairly straightforward. It was a good business decision, even if people might be dying. (We did not then know about the pre-production crash test data that suggested a high rate of tank failures in "normal" accidents [cf. Perrow 1984] or an abnormal failure mode.)

Later, the existence of the crash test data did become known within Ford, which suggested that the Pinto might actually have a recallable problem. This information led to a reconsideration of the case within our office. The data, however, prompted a comparison of the Pinto's survivability in a rear end accident with that of other competitors' small cars. These comparisons revealed that, although many cars in this subcompact class suffered appalling deformation in relatively low speed collisions, the Pinto was merely the worst of a bad lot.

Furthermore, the gap between the Pinto and the competition was not dramatic in terms of the speed at which fuel tank rupture was likely to occur. On that basis, it would be difficult to justify the recall of cars that were comparable with others on the market. In the face of even more compelling evidence that people were probably going to die in this car, I again included myself in a group of decision makers who voted not to recommend recall to the higher levels of the organization.

7.3.2 Epilogue: Pinto Case

Subsequent to my departure from Ford in 1975, reports of Pinto fires escalated, attracting increasing media attention, almost all of it critical of Ford. Anderson and Whitten (1976) revealed the internal memos concerning the gas tank problem and questioned how the few dollars saved per car could be justified when human lives were at stake. Shortly thereafter, a scathing article by Dowie (1977) attacked not only the Pinto's design, but also accused Ford of gross negligence, stonewalling, and unethical corporate conduct by alleging that Ford knowingly sold "firetraps" after willfully calculating the cost of lives against profits (see also Gatewood and Carroll 1983). Dowie's provocative quote speculating on "how long the Ford Motor Company would continue to market lethal cars were Henry Ford II and Lee Iacocca serving 20 year terms in Leavenworth for consumer homicide" (1977, p. 32) was particularly effective in focusing attention on the case. Public sentiment edged toward labeling Ford as socially deviant because management was seen as knowing that the car was defective, choosing profit over lives, resisting demands to fix the car, and apparently showing no public remorse (Swigert and Farrell 1980–1981).

Shortly after Dowie's (1977) exposé, NHTSA initiated its own investigation. Then, early in 1978, a jury awarded a Pinto burn victim $125 million in punitive damages (later reduced to $6.6 million), a judgment upheld on an appeal that prompted the judge to assert that "Ford's institutional mentality was shown to be one of callous indifference to public safety" (quoted in Cullen et al. 1987, p. 164). A siege atmosphere emerged at Ford. Insiders characterized the mounting media campaign as "hysterical" and "a crusade against us" (personal communications). The crisis deepened. In the summer of 1978, NHTSA issued a formal determination that the Pinto was defective. Ford then launched a reluctant recall of all 1971–1976 cars (those built for the 1977 model year were equipped with a production fix prompted by the adoption of the FMVSS 301 gas tank standard). Ford hoped that the issue would then recede, but worse was yet to come.

The culmination of the case and the demise of the Pinto itself began in Indiana on August 10, 1978, when three teenage girls died in a fire triggered after their 1973 Pinto was hit from behind by a van. A grand jury took the unheard of step of indicting Ford on charges of reckless homicide (Cullen et al. 1987). Because of the precedent-setting possibilities for all manufacturing industries, Ford assembled a formidable legal team, headed by Watergate prosecutor James Neal, to defend itself at the trial. The trial was a media event; it was the first time that a corporation was tried for alleged criminal behavior. After a protracted, acrimonious courtroom battle that included vivid clashes among the opposing attorneys, surprise witnesses, etc., the jury ultimately found in favor of Ford. Ford had dodged a bullet in the form of a consequential legal precedent, but because of the negative publicity of the case and the charges of corporate crime and ethical deviance, the conduct of manufacturing businesses was altered, probably forever. As a relatively minor footnote to the case, Ford ceased production of the Pinto.

7.3.3 Personal Reflections on the Pinto Case

In the intervening years since my early involvement with the Pinto fire case, I have given repeated consideration to my role in it. Although most of the ethically questionable actions that have been cited in the press are associated with Ford's intentional stonewalling after it was clear that the Pinto was defective (see Cullen et al. 1987; Dowie 1977; Gatewood and Carroll 1983)—and thus postdate my involvement with the case and the company—I still nonetheless wonder about my own culpability. Why didn't I see the gravity of the problem and its ethical overtones? What happened to the value system I carried with me into Ford? Should I have acted differently, given what I knew then? The experience with myself has sometimes not been pleasant. Somehow, it seems I should have done something different that might have made a difference.

In retrospect, I know that in the context of the times, my actions were legal (they were all well within the framework of the law); they probably also were ethical according to most prevailing definitions (they were in accord with accepted professional standards and codes of conduct); the major concern for me is whether they were moral (in the sense of adhering to some higher standards of inner conscience and conviction about the "right" actions to take). This simple typology implies that I had passed at least two hurdles on a personal continuum that ranged from more rigorous, but arguably less significant criteria, to less rigorous, but more personally, organizationally, and perhaps societally significant standards.

It is that last criterion that remains troublesome.

Perhaps these reflections are all just personal revisionist history. After all, I am still stuck in my cognitive structures, as everyone is. I do not think these concerns are all retrospective reconstruction, however. Another telling piece of information is this: The entire time I was dealing with the Pinto fire problem, I owned a Pinto (!). I even sold it to my sister. What does that say?

7.4 What Happened Here?

I, of course, have some thoughts about my experience with this damningly visible case. At the risk of breaking some of the accepted rules of scholarly analysis, rather than engaging in the usual comprehensive, dense, arms-length critique, I would instead like to offer a rather selective and subjective focus on certain characteristics of human information processing relevant to this kind of situation, of which I was my own unwitting victim. I make no claim that my analysis necessarily "explains more variance" than other possible explanations. I do think that this selective view is enlightening in that it offers an alternative explanation for some ethically questionable actions in business.

To me, there are two major issues to address. First, how could my value system apparently have flip-flopped in the relatively short space of 1–2 years? Second, how could I have failed to take action on a retrospectively obvious safety problem when I was in the perfect position to do so? To begin, I would like to consider several possible explanations for my thoughts and actions (or lack thereof) during the early stages of the Pinto fire case.

One explanation is that I was simply revealed as a phony when the chips were down; that my previous values were not strongly inculcated; that I was all bluster, not particularly ethical, and as a result acted expediently when confronted with a reality test of those values. In other words, I turned traitor to my own expressed values. Another explanation is that I was simply intimidated; in the face of strong pressure to heel to company preferences, I folded—put ethical concerns aside, or at least traded them for a monumental guilt trip and did what anybody would do to keep a good job. A third explanation is that I was following a strictly utilitarian set of decision criteria (Velasquez et al. 1983) and, predictably enough, opted for a personal form of Ford's own cost–benefit analysis, with similar disappointing results. Another explanation might suggest that the interaction of my stage of moral development (Kohlberg 1969) and the culture and decision environment at Ford led me to think about and act upon an ethical dilemma in a fashion that reflected a lower level of actual moral development than I espoused for myself (Trevino 1986, 1992). Yet another explanation is that I was co-opted; rather than working from the inside to change a lumbering system as I had intended, the tables were turned and the system beat me at my own game. More charitably, perhaps, it is possible that I simply was a good person making bad ethical choices because of the corporate milieu (Gellerman 1986).

I believe, however, on the basis of a number of years of work on social cognition in organizations, that a viable explanation rests on a recognition that even the best-intentioned organization members organize information into cognitive structures or schemas that serve as (fallible) mental templates for handling incoming information and as guides for acting upon it. Of the many schemas that have been hypothesized to exist, the one that is most relevant to my experience at Ford is the notion of a script (Abelson 1976, 1981).

My central thesis is this: My own schematized (scripted) knowledge influenced me to perceive recall issues in terms of the prevailing decision environment and to unconsciously overlook key features of the Pinto case, mainly because they did not fit an existing script. Although the outcomes of the case carry retrospectively obvious ethical overtones, the schemas driving my perceptions and actions precluded consideration of the issues in ethical terms because the scripts did not include ethical dimensions.

7.5 Script Schemas

A schema is a cognitive framework that people use to impose structure upon information, situations, and expectations to facilitate understanding (Gioia and Poole

1984; Taylor and Crocker 1981). Schemas derive from consideration of prior experience or vicarious learning that results in the formation of "organized" knowledge—knowledge that, once formed, precludes the necessity for further active cognition. As a consequence, such structured knowledge allows virtually effortless interpretation of information and events (cf. Cantor and Mischel 1979). A script is a specialized type of schema that retains knowledge of actions appropriate for specific situations and contexts (Abelson 1976, 1981). One of the most important characteristics of scripts is that they simultaneously provide a cognitive framework for understanding information and events, as well as a guide to appropriate behavior to deal with the situation faced. They thus serve as linkages between cognition and action (Gioia and Manz 1985).

The structuring of knowledge in scripted form is a fundamental human information processing tendency that, in many ways, results in a relatively closed cognitive system that influences both perception and action. Scripts, like all schemas, operate on the basis of prototypes, which are abstract representations that contain the main features or characteristics of a given knowledge category (e.g., "safety problems"). Protoscripts (Gioia and Poole 1984) serve as templates against which incoming information can be assessed. A pattern in current information that generally matches the template associated with a given script signals that active thought and analysis are not required. Under these conditions, the entire existing script can be called forth and enacted automatically and unconsciously, usually without adjustment for subtle differences in information patterns that might be important.

Given the complexity of the organizational world, it is obvious that the schematizing or scripting of knowledge implies a great information processing advantage—a decision maker need not actively think about each new presentation of information, situations, or problems; the mode of handling such problems has already been worked out in advance and remanded to a working stock of knowledge held in individual (or organizational) memory. Scripted knowledge saves a significant amount of mental work, savings that in fact prevent the cognitive paralysis that would inevitably come from trying to treat each specific instance of a class of problems as a unique case that requires contemplation. Scripted decision making is thus efficient decision making, but not necessarily good decision making (Gioia and Poole 1984).

Of course, every advantage comes with its own set of built-in disadvantages. There is a price to pay for scripted knowledge. On the one hand, existing scripts lead people to selectively perceive information that is consistent with a script and thus to ignore anomalous information. Conversely, if there is missing information, the gaps in knowledge are filled with expected features supplied by the script (Bower et al. 1979; Graesser et al. 1980). In some cases, a pattern that matches an existing script, except for some key differences, can be "tagged" as a distinctive case (Graesser et al. 1979) and thus be made more memorable. In the worst case scenario, however, a situation that does not fit the characteristics of the scripted perspective for handling problem cases often is simply not noticed. Scripts thus offer a viable explanation for why experienced decision makers (perhaps especially experienced decision makers) tend to overlook what others would construe as obvious factors in making a decision.

Given the relatively rare occurrence of truly novel information, the nature of script processing implies that it is a default mode of organizational cognition. That is, instead of spending the predominance of their mental energy thinking in some active fashion, decision makers might better be characterized as typically not thinking, i.e., dealing with information in a mode that is akin to "cruising on automatic pilot" (cf. Gioia 1986). The scripted view casts decision makers as needing some sort of prod in the form of novel or unexpected information to kick them into a thinking mode—a prod that often does not come because of the wealth of similar data that they must process. Therefore, instead of focusing on what people pay attention to, it might be more enlightening to focus on what they do not pay attention to.

7.5.1 Pinto Problem Perception and Scripts

It is illustrative to consider my situation in handling the early stages of the Pinto fire case in light of script theory. When I was dealing with the first trickling-in of field reports that might have suggested a significant problem with the Pinto, the reports were essentially similar to many others that I was dealing with (and dismissing) all the time. The sort of information they contained, which did not convey enough prototypical features to capture my attention, never got past my screening script. I had seen this type of information pattern before (hundreds of times!); I was making this kind of decision automatically every day. I had trained myself to respond to prototypical cues, and these didn't fit the relevant prototype for crisis cases. The frequency of the reports relative to other, more serious problems (i.e., those that displayed more characteristic features of safety problems) also did not pass my scripted criteria for singling out the Pinto case. Consequently, I looked right past them.

Overlooking uncharacteristic cues also was exacerbated by the nature of the job. The overwhelming information overload that characterized the role, as well as its hectic pace, actually forced a greater reliance on scripted responses. It was impossible to handle the job requirements without relying on some sort of automatic way of assessing whether a case deserved active attention. There was so much to do and so much information to attend to that the only way to deal with it was by means of schematic processing. In fact, the one anomaly in the case that might have cued me to the gravity of the problem (the field report accompanied by graphic photographs) still did not distinguish the problem as one that was distinctive enough to snap me out of my standard response mode and tag it as a failure that deserved closer monitoring.

Even the presence of an emotional component that might have short-circuited standard script processing instead became part of the script itself. Months of squelching the disturbing emotions associated with serious safety problems soon made muffled emotions a standard (and not very salient) component of the script for handling any safety problem. This observation, that emotion was muted by experience, and therefore de-emphasized in the script, differs from Fiske's (1982) widely accepted position that emotion is tied to the top of a schema (i.e., is the most salient and initially tapped aspect of schematic processing). On the basis of my experience, I would argue that, for organization members trained to control emotions to perform the job role (cf. Pitre 1990), emotion is either not a part of the internalized script, or at best becomes a difficult-to-access part of any script for job performance.

The one instance of emotion penetrating the operating script was the revulsion that swept over me at the sight of the burned vehicle at the return depot. That event was so strong that it prompted me to put the case up for preliminary consideration (in theoretical terms, it prompted me cognitively to "tag" the Pinto case as a potentially distinctive one). I soon "came to my senses," however, when rational consideration of the problem characteristics suggested that they did not meet the scripted criteria that were consensually shared among members of the Field Recall Office. At the preliminary review, other members of the decision team, enacting their own scripts in the absence of my emotional experience, wondered why I had even brought the case up. To me, this meeting demonstrated that, even when controlled analytic information processing occurred, it was nonetheless based on prior schematization of information. In other words, even when information processing was not automatically executed, it still depended upon schemas (cf. Gioia 1986). As a result of the social construction of the situation, I ended up agreeing with my colleagues and voting not to recall.

The remaining major issue to be dealt with, of course, concerns the apparent shift in my values. In a period of less than two years I appeared to change my stripes and adopt the cultural values of the organization. How did that apparent shift occur? Again, scripts are relevant. I would argue that my pre-Ford values for changing corporate America were bona fide. I had internalized values for doing what was right as I then understood "rightness" in grand terms. They key is, however, that I had not internalized a script for enacting those values in any specific context outside my limited experience. The insider's view at Ford, of course, provided me with a specific and immediate context for developing such a script. Scripts are formed from salient experience and there was no more salient experience in my relatively young life than joining a major corporation and moving quickly into a position of clear and present responsibility. The strongest possible parameters for script formation were all there, not only because of the job role specifications but also from the corporate culture. Organizational culture, in one very powerful sense, amounts to a collection of scripts writ large. Did I sell out? No. Were my cognitive structures altered by salient experience? Without question. Scripts for understanding and action were formed and reformed in a relatively short time in a way that not only altered perceptions of issues but also the likely actions associated with those altered perceptions.

I might characterize the differing cognitive structures as "outsider" versus "insider" scripts. I view them also as "idealist" versus "realist" scripts. I might further note that the outsider/idealist script was one that was more individually based than the insider/realist script, which was more collective and subject to the influence of the corporate milieu and culture. Personal identity, as captured in the revised script, became much more corporate than individual. Given that scripts are socially constructed and reconstructed cognitive structures, it is understandable that their content and process would be much more responsive to the corporate culture, because of its saliency and immediacy.

The recall coordinator's job was serious business. The scripts associated with it influenced me much more than I influenced it. Before I went to Ford, I would have argued strongly that Ford had an ethical obligation to recall. After I left Ford, I now argue and teach that Ford had an ethical obligation to recall. But, while I was there, I perceived no strong obligation to recall, and I remember no strong ethical overtones to the case whatsoever. It was a very straightforward decision, driven by dominant scripts for the time, place, and context.

7.5.2 Whither Ethics and Scripts?

Most models of ethical decision making in organizations implicitly assume that people recognize and think about a moral or ethical dilemma when they are confronted with one (cf. Kohlberg 1969; Trevino 1992). I call this seemingly fundamental assumption into question. The unexplored ethical issue for me is the arguably prevalent case where organizational representatives are not aware that they are dealing with a problem that might have ethical overtones. If the case involves a familiar class of problems or issues, it is likely to be handled via existing cognitive structures or scripts—scripts that typically include no ethical component in their cognitive content.

Although we might hope that people in charge of important decisions like vehicle safety recalls might engage in active, logical analysis and consider the subtleties in the many different situations they face, the context of the decisions and their necessary reliance on schematic processing tends to preclude such consideration (cf. Gioia 1989). Accounting for the subtleties of ethical consideration in work situations that are typically handled by schema-based processing is very difficult indeed. Scripts are built out of situations that are normal, not those that are abnormal, ill-structured, or unusual (which often can characterize ethical domains). The ambiguities associated with most ethical dilemmas imply that such situations demand a "custom" decision, which means that the inclusion of an ethical dimension as a component of an evolving script is not easy to accomplish.

How might ethical considerations be internalized as part of the script for understanding and action? It is easier to say what will not be likely to work than what will. Clearly, mere mention of ethics in policy or training manuals will not do the job. Even exhortations to be concerned with ethics in decision making are seldom likely to migrate into the script. Just as clearly, codes of ethics typically will not work. They are too often cast at a level of generality that cannot be associated with any specific script. Furthermore, for all practical purposes, codes of ethics often are stated in a way that makes them "context-free," which makes them virtually impossible to associate with active scripts, which always are context bound.

Tactics for script development that have more potential involve learning or training that concentrates on exposure to information or models that explicitly display a focus on ethical considerations. This implies that ethics be included in job descriptions, management development training, mentoring, etc. Tactics for script revision involve learning or training that concentrates on "script-breaking" examples. Organization members must be exposed either to vicarious or personal experiences that interrupt tacit knowledge of "appropriate" action so that script revision can be initiated. Training scenarios, and especially role playing, that portray expected sequences that are then interrupted to call explicit attention to ethical issues can be tagged by the perceiver as requiring attention. This tactic amounts to installing a decision node in the revised scripts that tells the actor "Now think" (Abelson 1981). Only by means of similar script-breaking strategies can existing cognitive structures be modified to accommodate the necessary cycles of automatic and controlled processing (cf. Louis and Sutton 1991).

The upshot of the scripted view of organizational understanding and behavior is both an encouragement and an indictment of people facing situations laced with ethical overtones. It is encouraging because it suggests that organizational decision makers are not necessarily lacking in ethical standards; they are simply fallible information processors who fail to notice the ethical implications of a usual way of handling issues. It is an indictment because ethical dimensions are not usually a central feature of the cognitive structures that drive decision making. Obviously, they should be, but it will take substantial concentration on the ethical dimension of the corporate culture, as well as overt attempts to emphasize ethics in education, training, and decision making before typical organizational scripts are likely to be modified to include the crucial ethical component.

References

Abelson, R.P. 1976. Script processing in attitude formation and decision-making, in Carroll, J.S. and J.W. Payne (eds.), *Cognition and Social Behavior.* Hillsdale, NJ, Erlbaum: 33–45.
Abelson, R.P. 1981. Psychological status of the script concept. *Am. Psychologist* 36: 715–729.
Anderson, J. and L. Whitten. 1976. Auto maker shuns safer gas tank. *Wash. Post* December 30: B-7.
Bower, G.H., J.B. Black, and T.J. Turner. 1979. Scripts in memory for text. *Cog. Psych.* 11: 177–220.
Cantor, N. and W. Mischel. 1979. Prototypes in person perception, in Berkowitz, L. (ed.), *Advances in Experimental Social Psychology*, Vol. 12. New York, Academic Press: 3–51.

Cullen, F.T., W.J. Maakestad, and G. Cavender. 1987. *Corporate Crime under Attack.* Chicago, Anderson Publishing Co.

Dowie, M. 1977. How Ford put two million firetraps on wheels. *Bus. Soc. Rev.* 23: 46–55.

Fiske, S.T. 1982. Schema-triggered affect: Applications to social perception, in Clark, M.S. and S.T. Fiske (eds.), *Affect and Cognition.* Hillsdale, NJ, Erlbaum: 55–78.

Gatewood, E. and A.B. Carroll. 1983. The anatomy of corporate social response: The Rely, Firestone 500, and Pinto cases. *Bus. Hor.* 24(5): 9–16.

Gellerman, S. 1986. Why "good" managers make bad ethical choices. *Harv. Bus. Rev.* 64: July–August: 85–90.

Gioia, D.A. 1986. Symbols, scripts, and sensemaking: Creating meaning in the organizational experience, in Sims, H.P. Jr. and D.A. Gioia (eds.), *The Thinking Organization: Dynamics of Organizational Social Cognition.* San Francisco, Jossey-Bass: 49–74.

Gioia, D.A. 1989. Self-serving bias as a self-sensemaking strategy, in Rosenfeld, P. and R. Giacalone (eds.), *Impression Management in the Organization.* Hillsdale, NJ, LEA: 219–234.

Gioia, D.A. and C.C. Manz. 1985. Linking cognition and behavior: A script processing interpretation of vicarious learning. *Acad. Mgmt. Rev.* 10: 527–539.

Gioia, D.A. and P.P. Poole. 1984. Scripts in organizational behavior. *Acad. Mgmt. Rev.* 9: 449–459.

Graesser, A.C., S.G. Gordon, and J.D. Sawyer. 1979. Recognition memory for typical and atypical actions in scripted activities: Test of script pointer and tag hypothesis. *J. Verb. Lrng. Verb. Beh.* 18: 319–332.

Graesser, A.C., S.B. Woll, D.J. Kowalski, and D.A. Smith. 1980. Memory for typical and atypical actions in scripted activities. *J. Exp. Psych.* 6: 503–515.

Kohlberg, L. 1969. Stage and sequence: The cognitive-development approach to socialization, in Goslin, D.A. (ed.), *Handbook of Socialization Theory and Research.* Chicago, Rand-McNally: 347–480.

Louis, M.R. and R.I. Sutton. 1991. Switching cognitive gears: From habits of mind to active thinking. *Hum. Rel.* 44: 55–76.

Perrow, C. 1984. *Normal Accidents.* New York, Basic Books.

Pitre, E. 1990. Emotional control. Working paper, Pennsylvania State University.

Swigert, V.L. and R.A. Farrell. 1980–1981. Corporate homicide: Definitional processes in the creation of deviance. *Law Soc. Rev.* 15: 170–183.

Taylor, S.E. and J. Crocker. 1981. Schematic bases of social information processing, in Higgins, E.T., C.P. Herman, and M.P. Zanna (eds.), *Social Cognition.* Hillsdale, NJ, Erlbaum: 89–134.

Trevino, L. 1986. Ethical decision making in organizations: A person–situation interactionist model. *Acad. Mgmt. Rev.* 11: 601–617.

Trevino, L. 1992. Moral reasoning and business ethics: Implications for research, education and management. *J. Bus. Ethics* 11: 445–459.

Van Maanen, J. 1978. People processing: Strategies of organizational socialization. *Org. Dynamics.* 7(1): 19–36.

Velasquez, M., D.J. Moberg, and G.F. Cavanagh. 1983. Organizational statesmanship and dirty politics: Ethical guidelines for the organizational politician. *Org. Dynamics.* 12(2): 65–80.

Chapter 8

Conceptualization of Supply Chain Quality Management

Haiju Hu, Barbara B. Flynn, and Xiande Zhao

Contents

8.1 Introduction: Important Themes

There were a number of important themes that emerged in Sections I and II. The chapters in Section I provided important background material for developing an understanding of supply chain quality management (SCQM), while the cases in

Section II illustrated a number of organizations that had problems with various aspects of SCQM, with very serious implications. We will draw upon these themes to develop a framework for SCQM, which will be used as a foundation for the remaining chapters in this book.

8.2 Elements of SCQM

From the key themes in Sections I and II, we developed a set of six critical elements of SCQM. Each is described in the following, along with examples from the literature reviewed in Section I and the cases described in Section II.

8.2.1 Internal Quality Integration

Internal quality integration is the effort of a company to facilitate quality improvement in its supply chains by integrating its own departments and internal processes. It is important as the starting point for improving SCQM. Companies that have a difficult time integrating quality management (QM) across their own internal functions will experience difficulties leading quality efforts across the external members of their supply chains.

Conceptually, it seems like internal quality integration should be simple, compared with external quality integration between a company and its customers and suppliers and their supply chains. However, internal quality integration can be quite challenging to implement because of what Bowersox et al. (1999) refer to as the "great operating divide" among the priorities, objectives, and terminology of different functional areas within an organization. The operations-facing side (procurement and manufacturing) of most organizations is typically driven by the cost to provide goods. The priorities of these areas revolve around establishing predictable demand patterns, minimizing changeovers, maximizing production run length, standardizing products (Sabath and Whipple 2004), and minimizing variability. In contrast, the customer-facing side (logistics and marketing) focuses on the cost to serve. The priorities of these groups are on providing tailored product offerings to meet customer requirements (sometimes through holding high levels of inventory), which is often supported by stock-keeping unit proliferation and the need for flexibility. Thus, the priorities of the operations-facing and customer-facing side of many organizations are in sharp contrast to each other. Fawcett and Magnan (2002) suggest that it is critical that an organization should first become effective in spanning its own internal boundaries, which Kanter (1994) describes as "learning to cooperate."

> Companies that have a difficult time navigating the "waters of their own harbor" must spend the majority of their time and resources on these issues, rather than collaborating with supply chain partners. (Fawcett and Magnan 2002, p. 347)

An internally integrated organization is able to achieve consensus in the strategic decisions that affect internal quality integration, developing a "one-plan" mentality, with common policies, procedures, and practices across all of its functions (Sabath and Whipple 2004). There is internal transparency between the operations-facing and customer-facing areas, which lays the foundation for transparency with external supply chain partners, including customers, suppliers, and their customers and suppliers. The notion of internal quality integration as the foundation for customer and supplier quality integration is supported by stage theory, which stresses that external uncertainties and linkages with other supply chain members must be internally absorbed into the proper places in the internal structure (Morash and Clinton 1997). Thus, internal quality integration provides the foundation for customer and supplier integration.

The Ford Pinto case provides a vivid example of the issues that arise when the internal functions of an organization are not well integrated. The Pinto was developed with a strong focus on development speed and low cost; the "limits of 2000" dictated that it could not exceed 2000 lb. in weight or cost more than $2000. Ford typically used a serial process to develop design, styling, production planning, and engineering details prior to developing production tooling, with each building on the efforts of the previous group. However, these processes were executed in parallel for the Pinto, with little communications between groups. When the safety department found that the Pinto failed just about every crash test because of the location of its fuel tank, this information did not move beyond the safety department. Even when the design problem became known, it was addressed by the finance department putting a value on a human life in its net present value (NPV) analysis. Clearly, better communications between Ford's finance department and its customer-facing departments could have led to a very different outcome.

Chapter 4's view of internal quality integration through the lens of risk provides details about the importance of internal quality integration. The focus of operations-facing departments on the cost to provide goods can be compromised by the inclusion of cheaper or unsafe components, particularly when decisions about them are made without consultation with the customer-facing departments. Similarly, an unrelenting emphasis on variance minimization by the operations-facing departments may run counter to the customer-facing departments' priority on development of products that meet the needs of specific customer segments. While there may be information system connectivity between the operations-facing and customer-facing sides of an organization, nurturing relational connectivity is much more of a challenge because of the different priorities and organizational cultures of these groups. Critical information may be lost, reducing internal quality integration.

Thus, it is important that companies work toward cross-functional collaboration in their quality assurance practices. The Ford Pinto case illustrates the problem of functional areas working at cross-purposes against each other, while Bob Eckert's comments indicate his focus on quality across all functional areas as the chief executive officer (CEO) of Mattel. In Section III, Chapter 9 describes the way that Dongfeng-Peugeot-Citroen Automobile Co. Ltd. explicitly designs its processes to facilitate internal integration.

8.2.2 Upstream QM System

The cases discussed thus far illustrate many critical problems related to upstream QM. In the case of Sanlu, its quality problems were caused by farmers who intentionally tampered with their raw milk in order to simulate higher protein content. In the Mattel case, a supplier had re-outsourced to another supplier, unknown to Mattel, that did not follow its standards for lead content in paint. Other examples of upstream QM issues include the defective batteries that Apple and Toshiba sourced from Sony and the defective ingredients in the pet food that Menu Foods outsourced from China.

These cases illustrate a number of problems associated with poor upstream QM systems. One is supply chain transparency. It is important that downstream customers understand what the upstream suppliers are doing. For example, Dong Xin's re-outsourcing to Zhongxing, without Lee Der's or Mattel's knowledge, led to massive toy recalls and destruction of both Mattel's brand image and Lee Der's credibility as a supplier. If Lee Der had known about Dong Xin's re-outsourcing to Zhongxing, there is every reason to believe that it would have made sure that Zhongxing had the appropriate certifications and understood what Mattel's standards for lead were.

A related issue arises in industries with a strong seasonal component. Because the toy industry faces a very significant demand increase in anticipation of Christmas holiday sales, the pressure on the suppliers to large multinational brand owners increases. Chinese suppliers, not wanting to jeopardize future business, tend to accept all orders, whether or not they have the capacity to produce them. They then re-outsource, sometimes to friends and relatives, who are similarly reluctant to say no and who may then also re-outsource production. It is easy for the original safety standards to get lost in the shuffle. This is a problem in any long supply chain, but it is worse when there has been re-outsourcing in parts of the chain without the knowledge of other parts.

As described in Chapter 2, an emphasis on cost cutting may send the wrong message to upstream suppliers. Chinese suppliers know that they were selected because of the low price that they charge. They may substitute different materials in an effort to keep their costs low, perhaps sincerely believing that they are doing what their customer wants. While price may be Mattel's order winner, the small suppliers do not always understand that quality and safety are order qualifiers; suppliers that do not meet safety standards will not even be considered for future work for Mattel, no matter how inexpensive its components are or how quickly they are provided (Lyles et al. 2008). This illustrates confusion of order winners and order qualifiers. Although large multinational corporations may select suppliers because of their low price (the order winner), they do not always convey that there is an important order qualifier: all components and products must meet their safety specifications.

A related issue, described in Chapter 3, is that orders are often split into smaller orders and sent to many suppliers. Those that are able to fill them quickly may then be awarded with larger orders in the future. Thus, suppliers may be faced with many small orders, each with different, unfamiliar standards, perhaps from companies in different countries. Because of the pressure of potential future orders, they may rush the work and cut corners. There is a multitude of safety regulations across different countries. For example, although most industrialized countries have banned lead paint on children's products, the exact standards for allowable lead content are different in each country. This may lead to confusion among suppliers, particularly those that supply companies in a number of different countries. The lack of harmonized safety standards across countries may actually contribute to supply chain quality problems through lack of consistency, particularly with relatively inexperienced suppliers in emerging economies.

Supplier selection can be challenging in a supply chain, since each link in the supply chain may have its own criteria. Supply chain members strive to balance their own priorities with the priorities of the supply chain, which may be in conflict. For example, although a primary goal for Mattel is the production of safe toys, it often deals with small suppliers whose primary goal is to be selected for future business with Mattel by providing components as quickly and cheaply as possible. Clearly, supplier selection (compounded by lack of transparency) was a major issue for both Mattel and the Chinese dairy producers.

Supplier development is also important to upstream QM. Supplier development refers to an organization's efforts to improve its suppliers' capabilities for the long-term mutual benefit of both parties (Hahn et al. 1990). Through collaborating with its suppliers, the organization can learn from them and from their more distant supply chain partners.

8.2.3 Downstream QM System

In traditional quality management (QM) theory, customer involvement is an important element (Flynn et al. 1994). It is based on the notion that companies should listen to the voice of their customers, build customer relationships, and use customer information (Criteria 2011–2012). However, customers can also be an important source of information on quality and product design, thus providing an opportunity for learning in a supply chain. Learning from customers includes obtaining guidance for the production process and information from customers about their quality and other needs.

It is easy to think of the responsibility for quality and safety as resting with the manufacturer and its suppliers; however, downstream QM can also have a negative impact on product quality. For example, a product like milk or frozen food needs to be stored at the proper temperature, during shipment and at the retail level. This may seem obvious, but it has been an issue in China due to the rapid increase in popularity of milk and dairy products as disposable income levels have increased; retail store managers have needed to be educated about proper storage practices. In Section III (Chapter 9), we describe how Dongfeng-Peugeot-Citroen makes sure that its dealers educate their customers (many of whom have never owned a car before) about the safe operation of their new vehicles.

The Tylenol case illustrates a different example of the importance of down-stream SCQM. Its products were removed from the shelves at the retail level, tampered with, then returned to the shelves. Although similar problems were ultimately prevented through the design of tamper-proof packaging, vigilance at the retail level is also important.

Downstream quality and safety issues can also occur during the distribution process. In the pharmaceutical industry, entire truckloads of expensive drugs are sometimes stolen and replaced with a counterfeit version of the product. The counterfeit products are typically inert, so the safety hazard they cause is related to preventing patients from receiving the medication that they need. However, there can be other problems with counterfeit products. For example, a woman in the United Kingdom was prescribed a painkiller by her physician, who instructed her that it was okay to take a second tablet if the first did not bring her relief. Not realizing that her pharmacy had inadvertently filled her prescription with an inert, counterfeit painkiller, she eventually got into the habit of taking five to six tablets at a time, since they did not seem to be very effective. When she refilled her prescription (this time with the genuine painkiller) and took her usual handful of tablets, she was dead within a few minutes.

The importance of downstream QM has not attracted the research attention that upstream QM has. Soltani et al. (2011) conducted a qualitative study on two supply chains and concluded that, to achieve competitiveness, both upstream cooperation and downstream cooperation were important. Kabadayi and Lerman (2011) found that manufacturers could minimize the negative effect of recalls if they used retailers that were trusted by consumers. In Section IV, in Chapter 15, we include an example of research on the financial impact of a product recall announcement on retailers.

8.2.4 Product Recall Strategy

As supply chains increase in length and become more geographically dispersed, it can be difficult to determine the source of a quality problem after it has occurred. However, traceability is a critical component of an SCQM system because it facilitates finding the source of a problem and rectifying it. The story of Mattel and its lead paint illustrates this well. Mattel had outsourced toys from Lee Der, which had outsourced pigments to Dong Xin. However, neither Mattel nor Lee Der had any idea that Dong Xin was reoutsourcing to Zhongxing when there was a need for surge capacity. Thus, Mattel's supply chain was not transparent because of the unknown re-outsourcing that was taking place within it.

A related issue are practices that destroy traceability. This is illustrated by the case of Sanlu and other milk producers that used collection stations. By allowing the raw milk from multiple farmers to be combined into the same vat, traceability was destroyed. Although the sources of the raw milk were known, the evidence that allowed tracing to a particular farmer was destroyed by the practice of dumping raw milk from all farmers into a vat at the collection stations. This type of approach is typical for agricultural products. For example, fruit processors dump truckloads of fruit into large bins, from which they are fed to the processing line, as illustrated by the well-known National Cranberry case (HBS #688122), where truckloads of berries from different farmers are dumped into bins, from which they are fed into a hopper. Similarly, truckloads of grain produced by different farmers are emptied into large storage silos at flour mills. To prevent these types of problems, a tracking and tracing system should be established throughout the supply chain (Kuman and Schmitz 2011; Roth et al. 2008). There are two types of tracking systems (Zhang et al. 2011). The goal of a backward tracking system is to minimize the number of potential sources of deficiencies from upstream suppliers, while the goal of a forward tracking system is to reduce the number of potentially affected products in the hands of consumers. In Section III, Chapters 11 and 12 describe innovative uses of technology in backward tracking, while Chapters 9 and 10 describe the systems used by automobile manufacturers in China.

Another important element of product recall systems is record keeping and information systems. Unlike agricultural products, a car is a discrete product with a unique vehicle identification number (the VIN); thus, traceability is much easier in the automobile industry. A strong information system will associate each part with the VIN of the car it was installed on; if the part is later recalled, the manufacturer should be able to identify the owner of each vehicle that was affected. As pointed out in Chapter 7, information systems and good record keeping are particularly important because of the way managers organize information into cognitive structures; their existing script schemas can bias them, so they may overlook a safety issue. With good data and analysis, patterns may emerge more quickly, pointing out the deficiencies in script schemas and highlighting the need for a product recall sooner.

An effective SCQM system should also have a plan for administering a product recall, should one be required. A product recall can serve as both a recovery measure for a product failure and a feedback system to guide future improvements. During a product recall, there are a number of key decisions, including how to identify the source of the defect, how to manage the recall, and how to reduce the negative effect of the recall announcement in the minds of the affected customers. In Section III, Chapter 10 provides a detailed description of the strategy of Changan-Ford Automobile Co. Ltd. for dealing with product defects and administration of product recalls.

To mitigate the negative effects of a product recall and recover promptly from the crisis, a response strategy is necessary. Critical elements of a response strategy include whether the recall is initiated proactively, when an issue is uncovered, or passively, when mandated. In Section IV, the financial effects of proactive and passive strategies are discussed in Chapter 13. In Chapters 16 and 17, in Section V, we describe experimental research that isolates the effects of important factors related to product recalls, in order to better understand their importance. Compensation is an important element of the response strategy. For instance, if an automobile part is found to be defective, the manufacturer may replace or repair the defective part for free and may also provide a loaner for the time that the car is being repaired. Compensation strategies typically fall into the categories of repair, refund, or replacement. Chapter 15 discusses the pros and cons of these strategies and studies their financial impact on a manufacturer.

8.2.5 Strategic Supply Chain Design for Quality

Supply chain design is defined as "the process of planning a supply chain in order to guarantee smooth and efficient supply chain planning and execution as to meet the targets set by supply chain management in terms of cost, time, quality, and service aspects" (Freiwald 2005). Strategic supply chain design for quality issues is well illustrated by the cases in Section II. Pinto's placement of the fuel tank in a dangerous location, in order to save money, and Ford's subsequent refusal to change it led to the loss of several lives and tremendous damage to Ford's reputation. The case of the Chinese dairy producers illustrates several different types of supply chain designs. Those that were designed to have tighter control over their raw milk supply, through vertical integration, had no problems with melamine tampering. Those designed to have less control over suppliers experienced correspondingly more tampering. Designing a supply chain to tightly control quality can be extremely challenging, particularly in the agriculture industry and in an emerging market, where the level of education of small suppliers can be quite low. Chapter 12 provides a model of how to do this well, in its description of CHIC's strategic supply chain design for quality in China's fresh fruit industry. Similarly, Chapter 11 nicely describes the approach that was developed by Bright Dairy following the melamine incident. Both Bright and CHIC make extensive use of technology, including barcoded ear tags on cows and GPS systems attached to farm equipment, in order to monitor and educate the small farmers, who are the primary source of supply. These are examples of investing in prevention. When the supply chain leader invests in prevention, it will drive down its need for extensive inspection and result in higher levels of quality.

8.2.6 Supply Chain Leadership for Quality

Supply chain leadership is the ability of one organization in a supply chain to exert influence over other member organizations, in order to increase their compliance with and commitment to the leader's vision for the entire supply chain (Sinha and Kohnke 2009). Usually, an organization will be identified as the supply chain leader based on the resources or power possessed by the organization (Richey et al. 2004). For example, Ford and Mattel were the leaders of their supply chains. Supply chain leadership for quality refers to the extent of importance that the supply chain leader attaches to quality. The existence of a supply chain leader that places a high value on quality is important to the success of the supply chain, in order to avoid chaos among the member organizations (Lambert et al. 1998).

Supply chain leadership for quality can be very challenging. Cheung Shu-Hung appeared to have taken all of the right steps at Lee Der in order to ensure the quality of the parts that it supplied to Mattel; it had been a supplier to Mattel since 1993 and was certified as a reliable supplier by Mattel in 1997. All color pigment that was used on Lee Der's components was tested by third-party laboratories prior to production. Once the lead paint was detected, Cheung immediately launched a proactive investigation.

Similarly, Bob Eckert's comments in Chapter 5 describe effective leadership for quality. As the CEO of Mattel, he described the importance of looking for the root cause of every failure, the development of redundant processes, and the importance of investments in prevention. Extending these concepts to a supply chain, he described the importance of knowing where all components came from, testing them, watching the process, then testing the products again before they are put on the shelves of retail stores.

However, Dennis Gioia's comments about script schemas in Chapter 7 may explain why the best intentions of Cheung Shu-Hung and Bob Eckert went awry. Dennis Gioia described script schemas as the reason why experienced decision makers may overlook things that others might have considered to be obvious factors that should be assessed during decision making. Script schemas provide a cognitive framework that imposes a structure upon information, situations, and expectations, in order to facilitate understanding. They are developed from a manager's prior experience such that, once formed, they preclude the necessity for further active cognition; thus, script schemas help experienced decision makers to be more efficient. Bob Eckert and Cheung Shu-Hung both had a substantial amount of prior experience and probably had well-developed cognitive script schemas that served as templates against which incoming information was assessed. Bob Eckert and Mattel's managers had no reason to doubt Lee Der's ability to provide toys that met Mattel's specifications, based on having worked together for over 10 years, during which time there had been no problems with Lee Der's toys. Similarly, Cheung Shu-Hung had no reason to question Dongxin or its owner (his best friend), Liang Jiacheng, also based on many years of having worked together. It did not occur to either Mattel's or Lee Der's managers that Dongxin might reoutsource its production (although this may have occurred previously) or that it would bypass the third-party testing that was required. This was a difficult situation because it involved the sort of trust that we believe is an important element of supply chain management.

Because the key players trusted each other, on the basis of a long and successful relationship, they were acting on autopilot, without any suspicion or what they believed would be unnecessary questioning.

8.3 Definition of SCQM

We have described six key elements of SCQM: supply chain leadership for quality, strategic supply chain design for quality, upstream QM system, downstream QM system, internal quality integration, and product recall strategy. SCQM is a holistic management system to improve quality. Without any of these six elements, SCQM will not work effectively. We propose the definition of SCQM as *a holistic management system to improve quality in a supply chain, which includes supply chain leadership for quality, strategic supply chain design for quality, upstream quality management system, downstream quality management system, internal quality integration, and product recall strategy.*

8.4 SCQM Framework

Building on the literature in Section I, the cases described in Section II, and the definition of SCQM above, we propose a holistic SCQM framework (Figure 8.1). This framework describes an organization's decisions, from the strategic level to the operational level. At the top of the framework is supply chain leadership for quality. Companies should first make decisions about the leadership of a supply chain before even forming it. Usually, there are two critical choices: each member should be either the supply chain leader or a supply chain follower. Some companies prefer to be the leader of their supply chain, in order to increase their control and influence on the other supply chain members, which in turn can help improve the SCQM system. However, other companies are content to be the follower, in order to reduce their responsibility and shift the risk to the supply chain leader. This decision depends on the resources and capabilities possessed by each supply chain member.

At the center of the framework is strategic supply chain design for quality, which focuses on the company's consideration of quality issues when designing a supply chain. In this layer, the structure of the supply chain and the role that the organization will play in the supply chain are determined. Thus, it forms a map of the entire supply chain, which in turn will guide the practices at the operational level.

At the operational level, SCQM goals are realized to the extent that there is effective upstream and downstream QM systems and product recall strategies. These are facilitated by internal quality integration, since none of them can be achieved by a single department or function. According to contingency theory, management practices adapt with the external environment (Fisher 1997; Ketokivi

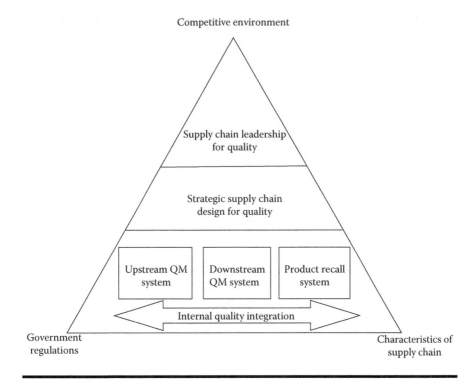

Competitive environment

Supply chain leadership
for quality

Strategic supply chain
design for quality

Upstream QM
system

Downstream
QM system

Product recall
system

Internal quality integration

Government
regulations

Characteristics of
supply chain

Figure 8.1   Framework for SCQM.

and Schroeder 2004). Contingency theory has been important in research on the success of traditional QM. For example, Zhao et al. (2004) found that the pattern of QM systems changed with the organizational context, including organizational size, international competitive hostility, environmental uncertainty, and perceived importance of quality. The results of the study of Zhang et al. (2012) showed that both internal fit (between quality practices and organizational structure) and external fit (between quality practices and environmental uncertainty) were related to the effectiveness of quality practices on performance.

Similarly, the SCQM system should also be consistent with its environmental factors. Key SCQM environmental factors (at the corners of the triangle) include the competitive environment, government regulations, and characteristics of the supply chain. The competitive environment of a supply chain is the extent of competition intensity in its market, which is determined by the number of competitors, the availability of resources, barriers to entry, etc. In a fierce competitive environment, price will be a dominating issue; therefore, supply chain members will trade off price and quality. However, in a market dominated by only a few players, supply chain members have sufficient time and resources to build up and maintain an SCQM system, which in turn will provide a substantial barrier to entry, since an effective SCQM system cannot be developed in a short period of time. For example, in the automobile industry, the competitive market is dominated by a few large manufacturers, which make substantial efforts to improve their SCQM system. In the toy industry, on the other hand, manufacturers experience fierce competition, so their major concern is cost, rather than quality.

Another external factor that can influence SCQM is government regulations on quality control, standards and their enforcement, consumer protection legislation, and the presence of regulatory agencies. The need for an overarching regulatory system that recognizes the global nature of today's business environment was described in Chapter 3 and in Bob Eckert's comments in Chapter 5. Consider the perspective of a small Chinese supplier of components to large global players in the toy industry, for example. In addition to perhaps having limited knowledge of consumer protection issues to start with, it would face a wide range of different legal standards in each of the countries of the manufacturers that it serves. Development of harmonized standards around the world would go a long way to address the sorts of problems that can ensue from this sort of situation.

SCQM should be consistent with supply chain characteristics. In a supply chain for a high-value product, for example, automobiles, tight control of quality throughout the entire supply chain is paramount due to the high internal and external failure costs. However, in a low-product-value supply chain, such as for toys or food, profit margins are narrow and cost reduction may be a higher priority than quality improvement, since higher product quality usually reflects a higher cost.

8.5 Conclusions

In this chapter, we identified the critical elements of SCQM, proposed a definition, and developed a holistic framework for SCQM based on the literature described in Chapters 1–4 and observations in the case studies described in Chapters 5–7. Compared with the existing research, the comprehensive set of elements that we identified enriches our understanding of SCQM. It also provides a foundation for future empirical research, since it will facilitate operationalization of key constructs and help to develop high-quality measurement scales. Because the critical elements were identified using case studies, future theoretical research based on it will help provide meaningful managerial insights.

References

Bowersox, D.J., D.J. Closs and T.P. Stank. 1999. *21st Century Logistics: Making Supply Chain Integration a Reality.* Oak Brook, IL: Council of Supply Chain Management Professionals.

Criteria. 2011–2012. *Criteria for Performance Excellence.* Gaithersburg, MD: Malcolm Baldrige National Quality Award.

Fawcett, S.E. and G.M. Magnan. 2002. The rhetoric and reality of supply chain integration. *Int. J. Phys. Distrib. Logist. Manag.* 32(5): 339–361.

Fisher, M.L. 1997. What is the right supply chain for your product. *Harv. Bus. Rev.* 75: 105–117.

Flynn, B.B., R.G. Schroeder and S. Sakakibara. 1994. A framework for quality management research and an associated measurement instrument. *J. Ops. Mgmt.* 11: 339–366.

Freiwald, S. 2005. *Supply Chain Design.* New York: Frankfurt/M, Peter Lang.

Hahn, C.K., C.A. Watts and K.Y. Kim. 1990. The supplier development program: A conceptual model. *J. Purch. Mat. Mgmt.* 26: 2–7.

Kabadayi, S. and D. Lerman. 2011. Made in China but sold at FAO Schwarz: Country-of-origin effect and trusting beliefs. *Int. Mktg. Rev.* 28: 102–126.

Kanter, R.M. 1994. Collaborative advantage: The art of alliances. *Harv. Bus. Rev.* 72(4): 96–112.

Ketokivi, M.A. and R.G. Schroeder. 2004. Strategic, structural contingency and institutional explanations in the adoption of innovative manufacturing performance. *Omega* 33: 63–89.

Kuman, S. and S. Schmitz. 2011. Managing recalls in a consumer product supply chain—Root cause analysis and measures to mitigate risks. *Int. J. Prod. Res.* 49: 235–253.

Lambert, D.M., J.R. Stock and L.M. Ellram. 1998. *Fundamentals of Logistics Management.* Chicago: Irwin/McGraw-Hill.

Lyles, M.A., B.B. Flynn and M.T. Frohlich. 2008. All supply chains don't flow through: Understanding supply chain issues in product recalls. *Mgmt. Org. Rev.* 4: 167–182.

Morash, E.A. and S.C. Clinton. 1997. The role of transportation capabilities in international supply chain management. *Transport. J.* 36(3): 5–17.

Richey, R.G., P.J. Daugherty, S.E. Genchev and C.W. Autry. 2004. Reverse logistics: The impact of timing and resources. *J. Bus. Log.* 25: 229–250.

Roth, A.V., A.A. Tsay, M.E. Pullman and J.V. Gray. 2008. Unraveling the food supply chain: Strategic insights from China and the 2007 recalls. *J. Supp. Chain Mgmt.* 44: 22–39.

Sabath, R. and J.M. Whipple. 2004. Using customer/product action matrix to enhance internal collaboration. *J. Bus. Logis.* 25(2): 1–9.

Sinha, K.K. and E.J. Kohnke. 2009. Health care supply chain design: Toward linking the development and delivery of care globally. *Dec. Sci.* 40: 197–212.

Soltani, E., A. Azadegan, Y.Y. Liao and P. Phillips. 2011. Quality performance in a global supply chain: Finding out the weak link. *Int. J. Prod. Res.* 49: 269–293.

Zhang, D., K. Linderman and R.G. Schroeder. 2012. The moderating role of contextual factors on quality management practices. *J. Ops. Mgmt.* 30: 12–23.

Zhang, L., S. Wang, F.C. Li, H. Wang, L. Wang and W.A. Tan. 2011. A few measures for ensuring supply chain quality. *Int. J. Prod. Res.* 49: 87–97.

Zhao, X., A.C.L. Yeung and T.S. Lee. 2004. Quality management and organizational context in selected service industries of China. *J. Ops. Mgmt.* 22: 575–587.

...

...

...

...

...

...

...

...

...

INTRODUCTION TO SECTION III: BRIGHT SIDE OF PRODUCT SAFETY: EXEMPLAR CASES

In Section III, we examine four companies whose practices provide exemplars for the management of product safety issues related to supply chain quality management. Each of these cases tells the story of a company in China that has invested in systems and prevention measures in order to ensure the quality of the products that it produces. Two of the cases are set in the automotive industry, and the other two are set in the agriculture industry. This is notable since both of these are industries where supply chain quality is known as a particular challenge, due to the length of the supply chain and strong pricing pressures in the automotive industry and due to the challenges of dealing with climate, pests, and low levels of technology in the agriculture industry. The automotive cases illustrate international joint ventures, where the international partner may present opportunities for learning, while the agriculture cases illustrate Chinese-owned and operated companies.

Chapter 9 describes the joint venture between Peugeot and Citroen, with production bases located in Wuhan and Xiangyang in Hubei province. It provides a detailed description of the quality procedures that are followed within its plants. Thus, it illustrates internal quality integration practices. Chapter 10 also describes an international joint venture between Ford and Mazda, with a plant located in Chongqing. It focuses, in particular, on systems for managing a product recall, providing a look at the planning and detailed documentation that have been developed for managing that eventuality.

Chapter 11 builds upon the foundation described in Chapter 6. Although Bright Dairy had been starting to implement a world-class manufacturing system prior to the melamine-tainted milk powder scandal, this crisis served as a call to action for improving its upstream, downstream, and internal quality management. Upstream, it has developed a number of systems for dealing with the dairy farmers who are its suppliers, both in terms of education and investments in processes to ensure that a situation like the melamine crisis can never occur again. Downstream, Bright focused on cold chain management and complete traceability of its supply chain. This chapter also illustrates the important role that the Shanghai Dairy Association has played in developing the highest quality raw milk supply in China.

In Chapter 12, we examine the CHIC Group, which is a world-class supplier of packaged fruit products to leading companies like Del Monte and Yum! Foods. It illustrates the importance and implementation of strategic supply chain design for quality, as well as the strong, but benevolent, power position that CHIC holds in its supply chains. Both the Bright and CHIC cases illustrate innovative information systems for monitoring information about their suppliers of agricultural products.

Chapter 9

Dongfeng-Peugeot-Citroen Automobile Co., Ltd.*

Xueyuan Liu

Contents

---

* From the personal communications with Mr. Lin Huang in Dongfeng-Peugeot-Citroen Automobile Co., Ltd. Some materials are adapted from "Quality of Suppliers in DPCA" slide show.

9.1 Introduction: Company Background

Dongfeng-Peugeot-Citroen Automobile Company (DPCA), founded in 1992 by Dongfeng Motor Corporation and PSA Peugeot Citroen Group, is a Sino-French joint venture and an affiliate of Dongfeng Motors Co., Ltd., the third largest automobile manufacturer in China. DPCA has two major production bases with different functional foci, located in Wuhan and Xiangyang in Hubei province. The number 1 and 2 factories in Wuhan specialize in vehicle assembly, with an annual production capacity of 450,000 vehicles, while the Xiangyang factory focuses on the production of engines and gearboxes, with an annual production capacity of 640,000 parts.

Under its policy of "one company, two brands," DPCA has two separate commercial headquarters. Dongfeng Citroen's commercial headquarters is in Shanghai, and Dongfeng Peugeot's commercial headquarters is located in Beijing. Currently, Dongfeng Citroen manufactures the C5, Triumph, C-Quatre, New Elysee, C2, and other popular models, while Dongfeng Peugeot manufactures the 508, 408, 307, and 207 as its major models. Within this structure, DPCA has established a marketing strategy with "three focus points:" products, customers, and geographical locations. This has strengthened its customer relations management and helped it to implement a precision marketing policy for continuously improving its marketing capability. Under these policies and strategies, DPCA has developed a comprehensive national distribution channel containing a network of various sales shops, including 4S (sales, spare parts, service, and survey) shops, 3S (sales, service, and spare parts) shops, and 2S+A shops, in various locations, including second- and third-tier cities and rural areas in China.

Since its founding, DPCA has had a strong reputation and corporate image. It has been awarded with many honors, including "Top Family Vehicle," "Top Environmentally Friendly Vehicle," and "Top Safe Vehicle" in China. DPCA has always adhered to its business philosophy of "Care for Every One and Concern for Each Vehicle" and has continuously provided customers with satisfying products and services. Its products have an image of being safe, reliable, environmentally friendly, comfortable, and innovative vehicles. Since 2010, the company has implemented ten new strategies, focusing on its brands, products, quality, independent research and development, cost leadership, and others.

In September 2010, DPCA released its 2011–2015 medium-term 5A business plan. According to this plan, DPCA expects to be at the top level in its product and service quality in the domestic market and have a 5% market share and annual sales of 750,000 units by 2015. Its operating margins are expected to be 5%, to achieve sustained profitable growth, launching 12 new vehicle models, six newly designed engines, and one new plant, with a production capacity of 300,000 units. Other goals include realizing vehicle exports, initiating research on self-owned brands, and implementing energy conservation and a new energy plan.

9.2 DPCA's Quality Management: Policy, Strategy, and Processes

9.2.1 "Total Organization" Quality Management

DPCA had embraced total quality management (TQM) concepts and implements them in the major sections of the company.

9.2.1.1 Design: Technology Center

The technology center employs a matrix organizational structure. It functions as both a platform center, where the project team is responsible for developing cars, parts, and process improvement, and a specialty center, where the specialized departments of technology are responsible for industrial design, manufacturing process planning, and product tracking.

9.2.1.2 Production: Wuhan and Xiangyang Plants

The Wuhan plants deal with the production of car bodies and final assembly, while the Xiangyang plant is in charge of machining engines, axles, and transmission box assemblies. The Department of Production delivers vehicles and spare parts to dealers and schedules production by developing production and supply plans. The Department of Purchasing is responsible for the purchase of industrial facilities, materials, and outsourced parts.

9.2.1.3 Commercial: Department of Commerce

The two departments of commerce (Peugeot and Citroen) develop and implement policies for vehicles, spare parts, and service. They are also responsible for managing distribution channels and dealers. The service unit in each of the two departments provides dealers with any necessary support for maintenance and service to customers' vehicles.

9.2.1.4 Support: Personnel, Public Relations, Organization and Information, and Financial Planning

DPCA's department of personnel and public relations is in charge of planning a framework to guide the implementation of human resources, provide training, and appraise employee performance. The department of financial planning is responsible for the management of finance, investments, and property management. The department of organization and information is in charge of designing, planning a framework to guide the implementation of the computer network, and providing information resources.

9.3 Quality Management Strategy

9.3.1 "Total Process" Quality Management

DPCA integrates quality management throughout its operations. Quality management is divided into five primary processes (see Figure 9.1); Process 1 through 3 are product and process oriented, while Process 4 and 5 are commercially oriented.

1. Process 1: A well-designed vehicle—design, industrialization, testing, and initial production processes.
2. Process 2: A vehicle in conformity with requirements—production process.
3. Process 3: An intensively cared for vehicle—transportation and delivery process.
4. Process 4: A well-prepared product delivery and sales network—brands and sales network are well prepared for products being put into the market successfully.
5. Process 5: A satisfied customer—process to improve the relationship between DPCA and its customers.

9.3.2 Details

The first two processes focus on internal integration of important quality concepts.

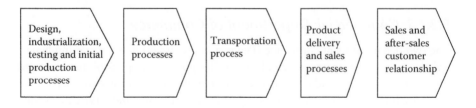

Figure 9.1 DPCA's total process quality management.

9.3.2.1 Process 1: Well-Designed Vehicle

Process 1 involves product design, development industrial design, testing, and the initial production process. It does not begin until all of the components of a vehicle and its power system have been identified and approved. Eventually, there is a detailed engineering definition of all vehicles and parts, satisfying both the brand's requirements and an industrialization process with mass production capacity. The expected results and measurement standards are as follows:

1. A vehicle that is in conformity with all laws and regulations.
2. A vehicle that satisfies customers' requirements for each brand. The vehicles' quality of performance is measured with functional indicators (power, oil consumption, etc.) and subjective evaluation criteria.
3. Production process for mass production of parts, powertrains, and vehicles.
4. Vehicle quality level. Internally, the quality of a new car is measured by indicators of appearance quality (IAQ) and indicators of functional quality (IFQ). Externally, the quality of vehicles is measured by the Quick Quality Survey. The Reliability Quality Survey is used to measure the quality of the vehicle in use.

The following methods are used to ensure the outcomes. All of the designs are undertaken simultaneously and evaluated using cross-functional quality measures. Thus, the designing of the product and process relies on the following:

1. Set a project goal.
2. Design a method to make sure the work can be done correctly the first time.
3. Control product, process, and equipment risks by designing a method chain.
4. Establish quality target curve.
5. Verify the capability of the production process.
6. Develop batch receiving methods.
7. Control product and process changes.

9.3.2.2 Process 2: Vehicle in Conformity with Requirements

Process 2 refers to the production process. Its intent is to manufacture qualified vehicles that conform to the specifications provided by the technology center. The factories must faithfully repeat the standard operations in order to consistently manufacture products at the same quality level. If all work procedures are strictly executed, the outcomes will be acceptable. The expected results and measurement standards are as follows:

1. All of the vehicles delivered to dealers must conform with the technical regulations.
2. All of the vehicles delivered to the dealers must have reached all required quality objectives. The car's overall quality standards are measured by IAQs and IFQs, which are stated in the detailed product audit standards.

3. All of the vehicles must meet the requirements of the dealers' orders.
4. Vehicles with any safety fault, internal or external instrument device failure, or quality problem must immediately be repaired and cannot be delivered to the user (failures are graded into S, P, A, and B).

Monitoring is used to prevent product failures and control production. DPCA follows predetermined monitoring-related procedures, including test methods, experimental specifications, and records. The monitoring plan asks five questions: what will be done, who will do it, where will it happen, when will it be done, and how will it be done.

The outcomes of monitoring are as follows:

1. The technology sector and support departments work together to analyze and deal with any identified defects, in order to find the cause and address the defects.
2. Guarantee that the defect will not be repeated in a similar product or process.
3. Improve the monitoring system in which the defect occurred.

9.3.2.3 Process 3: Intensively Cared for Vehicle

Process 3 refers to vehicle storage, maintenance, and transportation, addressing downstream quality management. Vehicles must be intensively cared for during the entire process in order to maintain their quality level. The expected results and measurement standards are as follows:

1. Deliver on time. Optimize the duration, quality, and cost of storage and transport.
2. Maintain the quality level of new cars and spare parts being transferred during the transportation process. Quality level is measured by IAQs before delivery to the customers.

The methods to ensure the outcomes are as follows:

1. Control techniques: Design, organize, and implement transport plans. Choose the best vehicle and spare parts storage and delivery techniques in order to contribute to the overall quality goals.
2. Maintain industry standards: Pay attention to state and industry standards related to packaging and transport requirements.
3. Create a transportation technology plan: Take the transport standards and constraints into consideration before mass production.
4. Establish suitable facilities and equipment: Establish vehicle storage garages and storage and transportation facilities to support quality requirements.

9.3.2.4 Process 4: Well-Prepared Product Delivery and Sales Network

Process 4 also deals with downstream quality management, focusing on the retail and after-sales service parts of the supply chain. This process describes the preparation work done by the commercial department and sales networks, in order to successfully launch new vehicles. Process 4 aims to provide dealers with sales- and maintenance-related methods and techniques. Expected results and measurement standards include the following:

1. Produce directories and business brochures, price lists, warranty and service cards, and car repair tooling. The sales staff must master the business methods put in place. Develop training courses for sales and repair shop technicians. Establish national and local promotional activities.
2. Define customer service standards.
3. Organize test drives. Sign business contracts with dealers.
4. Provide the dealers with demonstration vehicles, spare parts, and advertising materials.

The methods to ensure the outcomes are as follows:

1. The success of commercial activities lies in the coordination between Process 4 and Process 2. Thus, DPCA explicitly addresses the need for integration between the operations-facing (Process 2) and customer-facing (Process 4) functions. Staff from the commercial department is responsible for their coordination. Project initiation and preparation for commercial activities are simultaneous. The staff involved in commercial activities must master the necessary information in a timely manner and deal with any unanticipated situations that could jeopardize the business plan.
2. Once the industrialization and commercialization objectives have been realized, DPCA communicates with the media about it.

9.3.2.5 Process 5: Satisfied Customer

Process 5 covers the daily promotion work done by the Department of Commerce in its sales network. In order to help the dealers develop and maintain a strong relationship with their customers, the Department of Commerce does the following:

1. Ensure the necessary logistics methods. Provide dealers with the necessary vehicles, spare parts, documents, and information to meet their needs, on a daily basis.
2. Maintain the morale and expertise of staff in the network of dealers in order to ensure service quality.

Every vehicle delivered to the customers must accurately meet the customer order and be consistent with all quality standards. The expected outcomes and measurement standards are as follows:

1. There should not be any safety flaws, external or internal equipment failures, or irreparable quality problems.
2. Delivery date commitments should be met on time.
3. The service standards set by the Department of Commerce, in communication with customers, should be followed.
4. Within the prescribed period, repair and maintenance should be carried out in accordance with the commitments made by DPCA.

The methods to ensure the outcomes are as follows:

1. Control the entire new car supply chain, from taking the order to the turnkey by the customers.
2. Quality measurement standards should be consistent.
3. Train and mobilize dealers in order to achieve the results that DPCA expects.
4. The methods for measuring customer satisfaction should be in line with DPCA's objectives.
5. Before final delivery to the customers, in order to find and correct any defects, dealers should complete a final examination of the car.

Sometimes, due to unclear or unprofessional explanations by the salespersons, car owners may have failed to understand their vehicles well, which can lead to many problems during usage. It is important to remember that many Chinese consumers have not previously owned a vehicle, so it is very important that they receive a clear explanation from the salesperson.

9.4 Internal Supply Chain Quality Management

DPCA's quality management system is integrated throughout all of its sectors. Each department has its own quality task.

1. Technology Center: Design and develop automobile and parts projects and make them a success. Ensure that the design of cars and power systems conforms to the technical mission statement. The process of industrialization enables mass production of qualified cars and powertrains. The center is responsible for addressing failures; it should quickly find solutions.
2. Plants in Wuhan and Xiangyang: Implement the technical specifications provided by the Technology Center. Produce automotive products in line with the design, on the basis of cost and deadline goals. Abandon substandard products to protect the users' interest.

3. Department of Production: The commercial departments of Dongfeng Peugeot and Dongfeng Citroen consign the Department of Production to coordinate vehicle logistics to the commercial dealers. The Department of Production ensures automobile spare parts logistics to the dealers so that they can complete vehicle maintenance in the shortest period of time.
4. Department of Quality: Establish early-warning and crisis management mechanisms so that the department can respond at any time. Set high, but achievable, goals. Choose effective and reliable indicators. Work out concise and easy-to-operate standards. Review the implementation of the objectives. Effectively guide and support the product development of suppliers.
5. Commercial departments of Dongfeng Citroen and Dongfeng Peugeot: Develop and implement their business, distribution, and service policies. Provide support to the dealers in implementing their policies. The sales team must understand the products and know how to repair them. Impeccable working attitude and service quality are necessary. Correctly classify and summarize failures, then deliver this information to the Industry Division.

To further improve its quality, DPCA has implemented its PQ365 Quality Action Plan, which reviews and promotes a different action plan each year, based on the annual review of quality management issues and reality. For example, in 2011, it contained three actions to enhance quality awareness, six systematic projects to enhance quality, and five new projects to ensure quality for boosting the 5A plans. The three actions aimed at promoting quality publicity and implementation, enhancing quality awareness, promoting quality training, improving quality capacity, refining quality goals, and clarifying responsibility for quality. The six systematic projects include the quality system optimization project, improvement in reliability of product design and development project, quick response to customer quality project, improvement of vehicle and power engineering project, quality assurance of spare parts project, and service quality improvement project. The five new projects include measuring professional items, incorporating feedback into the work of the Project Approval Committee, pursuing certification plans (review approval form and product certification), and pursuing trial-production certification.

9.5 Upstream Supply Chain Quality Management

A manager responsible for quality in DPCA described the suppliers and dealers as the weakest links in its entire supply chain in terms of quality. In general, about a third of the quality problems are caused by production, another third are caused by suppliers, and another third are caused by product design, including both the manufacturer's designs and its suppliers' designs. Therefore, it is essential for DPCA to manage and collaborate with its various suppliers in terms of quality, design, and production. DPCA has a very comprehensive framework for managing its suppliers to ensure quality parts and design. Figure 9.2 illustrates DPCA's quality management framework for upstream quality management.

Figure 9.3 illustrates the details of how DPCA takes actions to manage its supplier's quality through selection, development and ratification, and quality control in mass production, during the process and after sales. These actions are undertaken through 3 phases, 19 steps, and 19 methods to fulfill DPCA's quality goals:

Phase 1: Selection of Suppliers

Objective: Choose reliable suppliers
Methods: Quality diagnosis (for new suppliers), supplier quality risk assessment,
 RETEX, AMDEC
Tools: Quality Diagnosis Guide, Guide for Quality Technical Supplier Selection,
 RETEX, ASQUE, SAGR, QUALITEX
Working model:
 – When there is a new supplier candidate, the Department of Purchasing will, according to the project requirements, host the primary selection. The Technology Center and Department of Quality will do the capacity appraisal and then issue the Quality Diagnosis Report.
 – Choose the right supplier. Do a risk assessment based on the supplier's technical offer, technology communication, and supplier quality.
Outcomes: Quality Diagnosis Report, Quality Advice of Supplier Access
 Qualification

Phase 2: Development and Certification of Suppliers

Objective: Ensure the quality of product development
Methods: AQMPP, RETEX, AMDEC, SPC, MSA, EPC
Tools: Q3P, AAQO, NSPIDIL, ASQUE, OEDIPP, SAGR, and QUALITEX
Working model: According to the AQMPP process, AAQO promotes the implementation process. According to development plans, quality plans, communication plans, risk control plans, and defect elimination plans should be made. Solve the problems in project development in a timely manner. Complete the product identification and technique process examination.
Outcomes: ATP report, Q3P document, Process Examination Report

Phase 3: Quality Control of Mass Production

Objective: Provide products with consistent quality and satisfy mass production requirements.
Methods: Objective management of supplier quality, PSF, factory test, lean management, coach–training, training for supplier's capacity, and PSA quick response process.

Currently, DPCA relies on the following organization to guarantee the supply quality

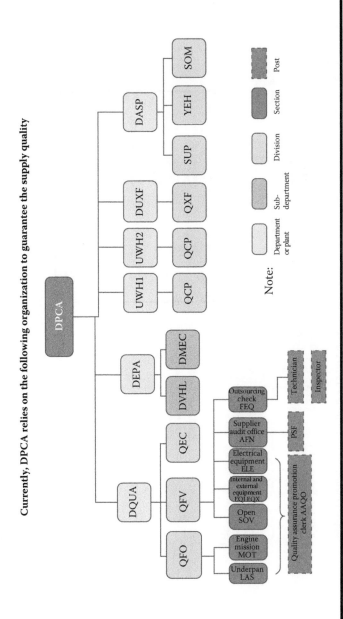

Figure 9.2   Quality framework of suppliers in DPCA. (Courtesy of DPCA.)

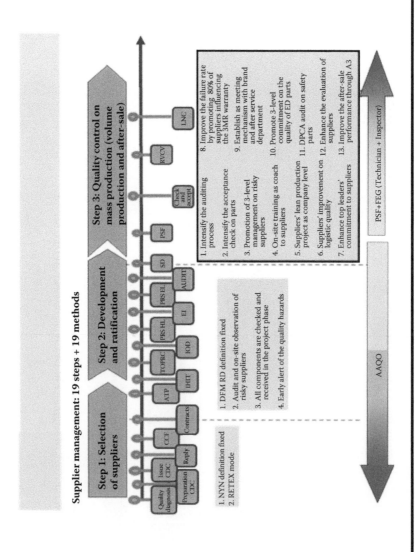

Figure 9.3 The "Three Phases, Nineteen Steps, and Nineteen Methods" of DPCA's supply chain quality management. (Courtesy of DPCA.)

Tools: Guide for risky supplier management, ASQUE, SAGR, QUALITEX

Working model: Existing production supplier quality appraisal model, PSF audit model, logistics supplier quality control model, spare parts reception model, KD parts quality promotion model, supplier manager model, coaching counseling model, lean management tutor to supplier model, promotion by the leadership model.

Outcomes: 3MR, DVT, PPM/OKM, Quality Crisis

DPCA strengthens its compliance control through strict product and process monitoring and extends its process audit to its Tier 2 suppliers. It focuses on the suppliers with the highest rate of defects and promotes its suppliers' capacity by enhancing the relationship between the management team at all levels and its suppliers and by continuous promotion of lean management of its suppliers. DPCA tries to promote coordination among factories, purchasing, technology, quality, and other areas to improve the efficiency of the relationship between DPCA and its suppliers, following 5M (man, machine, material, method, and environment) supplier management. Whenever there is a change in supplier personnel and production details, DPCA will immediately put forward a solution.

9.6 Downstream Supply Chain Quality Management

DPCA learns from its customers and searches for methods to improve its quality management. Customer feedback is a very important source of information for its quality improvement, as follows.

9.6.1 Investigations

Customers are the only ones who are qualified to evaluate the quality of the cars. Their evaluation leads largely to the decision about whether he or she will choose the same brand or another for future purchases. To assess the level of car quality and achievement of its objectives, DPCA systematically uses two types of surveys.

9.6.1.1 Quality Survey

This is carried out over the telephone, to investigate the quality of the new car 10 weeks after it was sold. DPCA carries out this investigation using representative samples. The investigation is subdivided into the following:

1. Conduct three investigations on all car models produced by DPCA each year.
2. Do a monthly continuous tracking survey when a new car model is put into the market or a model has been significantly changed or redesigned.

9.6.1.2 Reliability Survey

This survey on the quality of DPCA's cars in its primary markets is conducted by mail: Users can describe any problems that had happened during the first 1 to 3 years. Users mark a score (1–10) on the Satisfaction Scoring Sheet and deliver information back to DPCA about any problems with integrated, spare, and accessory parts. The contents include a detailed description, the cause of the problem, repair conditions, and the users' impression of the car brand (whether he or she would purchase the same brand in the future).

9.6.2 User Feedback about Quality

Information about the level of car quality also comes from several other sources:

1. Warranty feedback: Systematically analyze data from warranties conducted by the dealer network; find out what the problems are and rectify them.
2. Faults report: Through the quick information feedback system, the dealer can give information about faults found during regular maintenance and repair to DPCA.
3. Claims processing office: Every brand has an office that solves written or phone call claiming problems from unsatisfied users. It quickly takes necessary compensation measures and informs the service and production platforms of any emerging abnormal situations.

9.6.3 Quality Recovery: Product Recalls

In case there is a quality problem, DPCA has a quality control platform to follow. When the information is input, the platform analyzes the source of the quality problem (suppliers, customers, production, services, etc.) and its nature (safety, appearance). Under normal circumstances, there will be a cross-functional meeting for quality issues every Friday. For any quality emergencies, a meeting will be immediately held to discuss and resolve the problems.

Although DPCA follows a very comprehensive quality management system and process, it is inevitable that there will be some quality failures. A product recall is one of the most frequently used methods to respond to an external quality failure and customers' feedback. DPCA is fully committed to its customers' safety and initiates proactive product recall policies and measures, when needed. It has an internal quality alert system that will be set off by information about any quality problems related to a safety risk found inside the company or collected from customer feedback. This is an internal, quick response mechanism used to work out the ultimate action plan and, most importantly, to take prompt measures to reduce and resolve the risk to avoid any safety incidents to its customers. A typical recall procedure is shown in Figure 9.4.

When a recall has been initiated, the costs will include parts for replacement, service costs, and other costs, such as car replacement, etc. The major issue is how to track the car owners and the problems. It is easier to track the car owners by contacting them directly. Tracking the cause of a problem may be done one on one or as batches or lot cases.

Since 2004, DPCA has had six major product recalls. None of the safety issues caused death casualty or serious injuries. One of the latest examples of a recall incident is recorded in Figure 9.5.

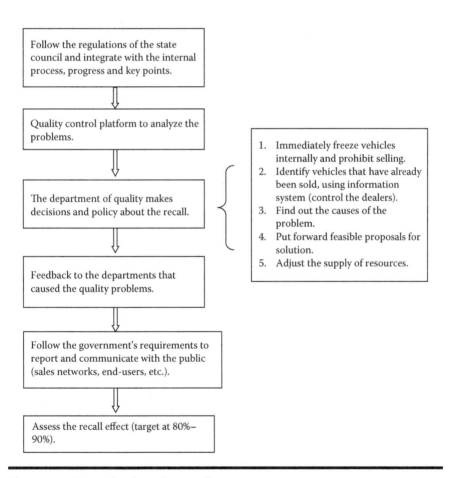

Figure 9.4   Example of recall procedure.

Manufacturer	DPCA		
Recall time	Aug 16th 2010 – Feb 16th 2011		
Quantity Involved	18,101 vehicles		
Motor Model	Specification	Year of Production	VIN range
Dongfeng Citroen C5 (2.3L)	DC7237DT		LDCA13R4092000229~ LDCA13R4XA2024669
Defects	Due to the limited space between the fuel pipe and the engine' s decorative cover, the protective cover of the fuel pipe may be abraded by the engine's decorative cover, and thus may lead to the direct contact between fuel pipe and the engine's cover.		
Possible consequence	This might cause a potential hazard safety in under extreme cases once the fuel pipe is abraded.		
Resolution	Replace the decorative covers of the engine with improved ones for free to avoid its friction with fuel pipe.		
Improvement measures	Adopt the improved decorative covers of the engine in new vehicles to avoid its contacts with fuel pipe.		
Complaints or feedback	No complaints or reports received about car accidents or people hurt.		

Figure 9.5 Example of recall incident.

9.7 Conclusion

From DPCA's practice of quality management, it is clear that product quality is the responsibility of everyone along its supply chain, from parts suppliers to the end-product dealers and customers. To provide a high-quality product to its customers, DPCA not only focuses on its internal resources and processes but also collaborates with its suppliers and customers to achieve its high-quality goals.

Chapter 10

Changan Ford Mazda Automobile Co., Ltd.

Yong Long and Junfeng Li

Contents

10.1 Introduction: Company Background*

Changan Ford Mazda Automobile Co., Ltd. (CFMA) is an automobile joint venture between China, the United States, and Japan. The main products of CFMA include the Ford Focus Hatchback, Ford Focus Sedan, Ford S-Max, Ford Mondeo-Winning, Ford Fiesta Hatchback and Sedan, Mazda 3, Mazda 2, Volvo S40, and Volvo S80.

Ford Motor Company and Changan Automobile Group invested and signed an agreement to establish Changan Ford Automobile Co., Ltd. (Changan Ford) on April 25, 2001, with each holding a 50% share. In March 2006, Mazda Automobile Company invested in Changan Ford, and the company was renamed Changan Ford Mazda Automobile Co., Ltd., with the shares distributed as Changan 50%, Ford 35%, and Mazda 15%.

On January 18, 2003, after Changan Ford had been established for only 21 months, the first product of Changan Ford (a Ford Fiesta) rolled off the assembly line. This was followed by the Ford Mondeo in February 2004, Ford Mondeo 2.5 V6 Flagship in June 2004, Ford Focus Sedan in September 2005, Ford Focus Hatchback in August 2006, Ford S-Max in March 2007, Ford Mondeo-Winning in November 2007, 2009 Ford Focus in September 2008, new Ford Fiesta in March 2009, and 2011 Ford Focus in September 2010.

On September 25, 2009, the foundation was laid for a new CFMA factory located in Chongqing. On September 25, 2010, CFMA signed a Memorandum of Understanding with the Chongqing government for investing in the construction of a production base for engines. This program would increase CFMA's engine production capability from 350,000 to 750,000 per year.

On August 27, 2012, CFMA's restructuring plan was approved by the National Development and Reform Commission. By the end of 2012, CFMA was separated according to a 50:50 equity ratio and divided into two new joint ventures, Changan Mazda and Changan Ford. Changan Ford Automobile Co., Ltd., in Chongqing now takes the responsibility for business with Ford, including developing, manufacturing,

---

* From Changan Ford Mazda Automobile Co., Ltd. Available at http://baike.baidu.com/view /1077621.htm. In order to collect materials and information on recall events in CFMA, the authors conducted out a deep survey of CFMA. The authors surveyed different departments that may be involved in recall events and interviewed managers and staff individually or during meetings with small groups of people.

selling, and servicing of Ford cars. The newly established Changan Mazda Automobile Co., Ltd., in Nanjing is responsible for business related to Mazda, such as developing, manufacturing, selling, and servicing for Mazda vehicles.

10.2 Recall Events in CFMA in Recent Years

In accordance with the Provisions on the Administration of Recalls of Defective Automobiles (The General Administration of Quality Supervision, Inspection and Quarantine of the People's Republic of China et al. 2004), CFMA submitted a recall report to the General Administration of Quality Supervision, Inspection, and Quarantine (AQSIQ) of the People's Republic of China on May 31, 2010. In this report, CFMA acknowledged that it would recall 236,643 2009 Ford Focus vehicles that had been produced from August 18, 2008, to May 28, 2010. This recall started on May 31, 2010. The reason was that, because of the effect of carbon deposition on the electronic throttle, the engine calibration software could cause the engine to stall at specific low speeds and low loads (AQSIQ 2010).

In September 2010, CFMA submitted another recall report to the AQSIQ of the People's Republic of China. In this report, CFMA recalled 14,205 Mondeo-Winning vehicles that had been produced from August 1, 2008 to April 30, 2009. It also recalled 2642 S-MAX vehicles that had been produced from July 1, 2008 to June 30, 2009. The reason for the recall was the material in the anti-lock braking system (ABS) pump motor brush, which could cause a failure of the motor control module of the ABS (DPAC 2010).

On May 7, 2011, CFMA announced a recall for 942 parts produced for the Volvo S40, which were produced from October 15, 2010 to January 28, 2011. The reason for the recall was that the cleaning pump for the vehicle headlights could interfere with the signal for the cleaning liquid level sensor. If the level of cleaning liquid fell below the set level, the driver would not receive information about liquid level from the driver information system (DIM) indicating that it was time to add the cleaning liquid (AQSIQ 2011a).

In the same month, CFMA announced an additional recall of 6599 Mondeo-Winning cars produced from February 14, 2011 to April 16, 2011. The reason for this recall was that the power wire for the air conditioning auxiliary heater could interfere with the air filter bracket, which could cause the insulating material on the power wire to wear and then short circuit (AQSIQ 2011b).

In March 2012, CFMA recalled 58,949 Mondeo-Winning cars that had been produced from October 5, 2007 to July 26, 2009. It also recalled 3496 S-MAX cars that had been produced from October 5, 2007 to June 26, 2009. The reason for this recall was the material in the ABS pump motor brush, which could cause a failure of the motor control module of the ABS (AQSIQ 2012).

It is interesting to note that the causes of all of these product recalls were all design related, including the location of various parts and the materials that were specified as part of the product design. They were not related to production defects from the Chongqing or Nanjing plants.

10.3 Program of Product Recall Management

10.3.1 Bulletins

When there is a problem detected in vehicles that are in the hands of its consumers, Changan Ford issues a service bulletin to its dealers to provide information about the vehicle technology, product information, maintenance measures, and problem solutions in the after-sales market. There are four categories of bulletin, providing information about the importance of the product problem and information about different ways to treat it, described in the following (Long and Li 2012).

10.3.1.1 General Service Information Bulletins

General service information bulletins (GSBs) provide instruction to dealers about how to diagnose and maintain procedures, solutions, and other concerning matters related to a certain system, spare part, or problems. They help to explain technical information to the customers concerning product performance and provide other information that can help dealers to diagnose and maintain vehicles. GSBs normally do not involve information about specific quality problems and detailed claim applications.

10.3.1.2 Technical Service Bulletins

Technical service bulletins (TSBs) provide dealers information about maintenance and solutions for specific product problems. TSBs include the problem description, treatment measures, spare parts information, and claim information. They include a series of procedures for vehicle diagnosis, repair, and claims, including the problem description, technical guidance, maintenance steps, spare parts supply, and claims application.

10.3.1.3 Field Service Actions

Field service actions (FSAs) target a known quality problem in CFMA's product or a product design problem that needs to be addressed due to customer complaints. FSAs provide information about the problem description, the range and detailed list of affected vehicles, maintenance guidance, spare parts supply claims, time limitation, and requirements for completion rate.

10.3.1.4 Recall Announcements

A product recall request is submitted to the Defective Product Management Center (DPMC) of the AQSIQ of the People's Republic of China. The recall announcement contains information about the problem description, range and detailed list of the affected vehicles, maintenance guidance, spare parts supply, claims information, time limits, and requirements for completion. Dealers are then responsible for contacting customers and requesting that they bring the vehicle back to the store.

10.3.2 Treatment of Defective Products

Changan Ford's treating methods for defective vehicles involve the following four categories (Long and Li 2012).

10.3.2.1 Ordinary Maintenance

Dealers diagnose and maintain a certain system, spare part, or problem or explain technical information about product performance to customers. Specific product quality problems and specific claim applications are generally not involved.

10.3.2.2 Individual Repair

Dealers repair and solve a specific product problem, focusing on a certain problem by individual users and involving claims.

10.3.2.3 Mass Maintenance

Dealers solve a known quality problem or product design problem due to customer complaints.

10.3.2.4 Product Recall

Changan Ford clarifies the range of a recall, which is restricted to the requirements of the national law and provisions that state that "due to the design, manufacturing and other reasons there prevalently exists unreasonable danger which endangers personal and property safety in a certain batch, type or class of auto products, or the products do not conform to the relevant national standards of vehicle safety" (The General Administration of Quality Supervision, Inspection and Quarantine of the People's Republic of China et al. 2004). There can be both voluntary and mandatory recalls.

10.3.3 Principles for Assessing Product Defects

There are three levels of hazard that are used for assessing a product defect (Long and Li 2012):

1. Safety performance does not conform to the relevant technical regulations and national standards for vehicle safety, after testing by an inspection agency.
2. The product has already caused personal injury and property damage to the owners or others due to problems in design and manufacturing.
3. Although the product has not yet caused personal injury or property damage to the owners or others, it is still possible to cause personal injury or property damage under particular circumstances, based on testing, experimentation, and demonstration.

These standards correspond roughly to the hazard classification levels used by the U.S. Consumer Product Safety Commission and the U.S. National Highway Safety Administration.

10.3.4 Responsible Departments

Several departments of CFMA are responsible for various aspects of a product recall (Long and Li 2012).

1. Recalls are initiated by the quality department and carried out by the after-sales service department.
2. The Executive Committee (EC) is in charge of approving the proposal and program for a vehicle recall.
3. The Critical Concern Management Group (CCMG) is responsible for organizing and coordinating the entire process of a vehicle recall. The CCMG organizes and coordinates major issues that could potentially cause a recall, drafts the 14D,* and reports to the EC.

10.3.5 Voluntary Recall Process

There are several steps in CFMA's voluntary recall process (Figure 10.1) (Long and Li 2012). The first is identification of related problems. Major problems that, based on internal and external information, are potentially critical or involve safety and have an impact on the environment or customer satisfaction are reported to the CCMG. The report describes the facts, without any assumptions, the statement of personal view and judgment, and tentative conclusion. The

---

* The structure of 14D is explained in Section 10.4.1.

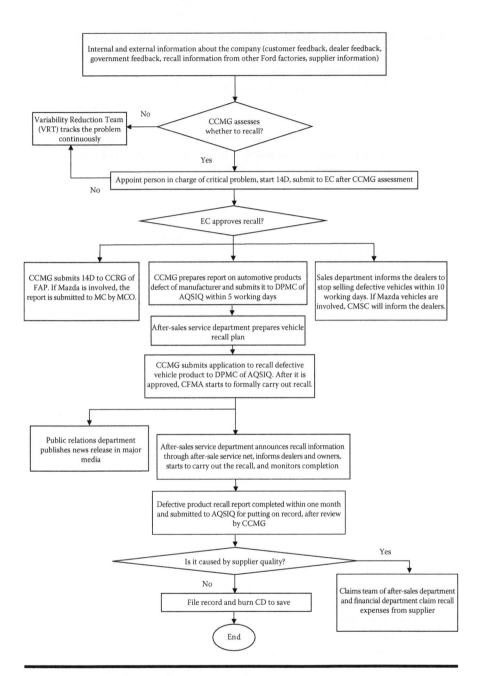

Figure 10.1   Recall procedure.

CCMG investigates any major problems and assesses their potential effect and consequences. If a vehicle recall is suggested, a person is appointed to be in charge of investigating the problem in detail.

The CCMG initiates the 14D jointly with the relevant departments and appoints specific personnel to diagnose the basic reason, analyze data, formulate corrective or preventive measures, and complete the 14D. The CCMG is responsible for submitting a report to the Critical Concern Recall Group (CCRG) of Ford Asia-Pacific (FAP). If the Mazda brand is involved, the report is submitted to the Mazda Company by the Mazda China Office.

After the EC approves a recall for the vehicle, the CCMG is responsible for preparing a "Report on Automotive Products Defect of Manufacturer," which will be submitted to the AQSIQ within five working days after it is checked by the legal consultant of CFMA. Meanwhile, the sales department informs the dealers about all related information, within 10 working days, and that they should stop selling the defective vehicles. If Mazda vehicles are involved, Changan Mazda Sales Company (CMSC) will inform the dealers.

The CCMG is then responsible for implementing the vehicle recall. With the support of the technology department, the after-sales service department is responsible for preparing the vehicle recall plan,* which usually includes the following:

1. Measures to stop producing defective automobile products
2. Measures to inform dealers to stop wholesaling and retailing related vehicles
3. Arrangements for supplying and distributing the components needed for the recall
4. Arrangements for providing explanation and training about the recall to dealers
5. Arrangements for feedback and statistics about recall completion
6. Preparation of a notice, in formal business format, for the owners, including the following:
   a. Description about measures to recall the defective vehicles
   b. After-sales service information about disposing of the defective vehicles
   c. Estimate of the time for disposing of the defective vehicles
   d. Possible consequences or potential risk if the vehicle is not recalled
   e. Plans for encouraging dealers to respond quickly (if appropriate)

Within 1 month after the Report on Automotive Products Defects of the Manufacturer is submitted, the CCMG submits the Application to Recall Defective Vehicle Product, Recall Plan, Defective Vehicle Recall Notice,† and News Release to the AQSIQ. After the recall has been approved by the Law Enforcement Supervision Division of the AQSIQ, CFMA starts to formally carry out the product recall. The

---

* An example of vehicle recall control plan is shown in Section 10.4.2.
† An example of recall notice in CFMA is shown in Section 10.4.3.

public relations department is responsible for publishing a news release in the major media. The after-sales service department announces information about the recall through the after-sales service net, informs dealers and owners, starts to carry out the recall, and monitors its completion.

After the recall has been implemented, the after-sales service department completes the Defective Vehicle Recall Report* within 1 month. If there are still vehicles that have not been returned, the report should specify the reasons why and the targeted measures that have been followed. After review by the CCMG, the report is submitted to the AQSIQ, to be put on record. The CCMG is then responsible for summarizing the recall process and initiating preventive measures. Related departments will execute the preventive measures, according to the summary.

10.3.6 Mandatory Recall Process†

After CFMA receives a notice of an Automotive Product Mandatory Recall (Long and Li 2012), the after-sales service department requires the dealers to stop selling the recalled product within five working days and informs dealers and owners about relevant information on the defective vehicles, issued by competent authorities, within 10 working days. After CFMA receives the Notice of Automotive Product Mandatory Recall, the CCMG should complete the Vehicle Recall Plan and submit it to the AQSIQ of the People's Republic of China for approval.

The AQSIQ usually informs CFMA about the results of its review of the Vehicle Recall Plan within five working days. After the plan has been approved, the after-sales service department develops an Automobile Product Recall Notice within 1 month, informs dealers and owners, and begins to implement the recall. Meanwhile, the CCMG submits an Automobile Product Recall Notice to the AQSIQ to be put on record. The public relations department is responsible for running the Defective Automobile Product Recall Notice in three consecutive issues of the newspaper designated by government authorities and for continuing to post the notice on the designated website until the end of the recall.

If the Law Enforcement Supervision Division of the AQSIQ does not approve the Vehicle Recall Plan, the CCMG will immediately make modifications, based on the opinions raised by competent authorities, and submit the revised plan to the DPMC of the AQSIQ of the People's Republic of China within ten working days. The plan will be implemented upon approval.

During the mandatory recall, the after-sales service department completes an Automobile Product Recall Progress Report every 3 months and submits it to the AQSIQ. Based on the results, the DPMC of the AQSIQ of the People's Republic of China will then decide whether or not to demand that CFMA take more effective

---

* The common structure of the Defective Vehicle Recall Report is introduced briefly in Section 10.4.4.

† From Long and Li (2012).

recall measures. Upon completion of the above, the CCMG completes the 14D and submits it to the FAP after it has been approved by the EC.

CFMA must implement a mandatory recall within the time stipulated in the Vehicle Recall Plan. If there are reasonable reasons for failing to complete the recall within that amount of time, the CCMG can submit an application to the AQSIQ for extending the duration of the recall. After the application has been approved, CFMA can extend the time of the recall.

10.4 Key Documents

10.4.1 14D

The 14D is usually structured as follows (Long and Li 2012):

1. Problem description (what/when/extent)
   a. Describe what went wrong and how it was discovered.
   b. Problem component information (part number, part name, quantity etc.).
   c. Vehicles affected.
   d. Are knock down (KD) units affected?
   e. Markets affected.
   f. Corporate product systems classification(s) affected.
   Section 1 attachments
2. Define root cause
   a. Description.
   b. Describe company system or process intended to prevent this from happening and why the system/process did not prevent this problem from happening.
   Section 2 attachments
3. Problem investigation/verification of data
   a. Lab test data
   b. Vehicle test data
   c. Plant/supplier reports data
   d. Quality indicator system data (indicate by country or region)
   e. Field reports (indicate by country or region)
   f. Part sales
   g. Number of accidents/fires and injuries attributed to this condition
   Section 3 attachments
4. Actions taken in production; interim (containment) and/or permanent
   a. Corrective actions/WERS alert number/dates
   b. Notification/WERS alert number/dates
   c. Component batch issues
   Section 4 attachments

5. Verify effectiveness of production corrective actions
   a. Measure effectiveness of actions identified
   Section 5 attachments
6. Estimated production and problem statistics
   a. Statistics (vehicle lines, model years, plants, volume, build dates)
   b. Source(s) of data for the above estimates
   Section 6 attachments
7. Service parts
   a. Service parts
   b. Notes if yes or no
8. Assessment of effect on vehicle operation
   a. Assessment of effect on vehicle operation
   Section 8 attachments
9. Description of concern solution and parts requirements
   a. Recommended concern solution, parts requirements, and verification of repair effectiveness (if different from Section 5)
      i. Does the field service action include multiple model years and/or vehicle lines?
      ii. If yes, has the repair been verified by product engineering to be an effective fix, taking into account possible design differences between the various model years and vehicle lines?
   b. Has the repair procedure been time studied and approved by the FCSD Recall/Service program department?
   c. Fix it right the first time assessment of repair procedure.
   d. Part name/WERS concern/notice no./date/production part number/ service part/FINIS number (EUROPE)/quantity required in service per vehicle/per repair.
   e. Other parts.
      i. Does the proposed fix have an effect on emissions, such that emissions levels are higher than those to which the vehicle was certified?
      ii. If yes, explain the emissions effect and confirm that a 14D or White Paper has been fully approved through the Certification Review Process.
      iii. Does corrective action affect PCM/TCM calibration changes?
   f. Analytical Warranty System (AWS)
      i. Is the remedy part currently used in service?
      ii. If yes, should vehicles repaired with the remedy part be excluded from this field service action?
   Section 9 attachments
10. Program parts sign off/availability
11. Vendor involvement
    a. Supplier contribution
    b. Supplier name and address
    c. Indicate type of condition

  d. Manufacturer site code
  e. Purchasing manager or buyer
  f. STA field engineer CDSID
 12. Financial implications
 13. Preliminary assessment of prevent action
  Preventative actions will be finalized during the Preventative Action Closure process (FAP03-171).
 14. Reference data
  a. Author's full name
  b. Author's phone number
  c. Author's CDSID
  d. Author's organization

10.4.2 Recall Control Plan

An example of a recall control plan for Ford Focus and Mondeo-Winning sunroof glass for CFMA is shown in Table 10.1 (Long and Li 2012).

10.4.3 Defective Vehicle Recall Notice

An example of a product recall notice for CFMA is shown in Table 10.2 (DPAC 2011).

10.4.4 Defective Vehicle Recall Report

According to Provisions on the Administration for the Recall of Defective Automobiles, CFMA should submit a recall report to the DPMC of the AQSIQ of the People's Republic of China. The report usually includes the following parts (The General Administration of Quality Supervision, Inspection and Quarantine of the People's Republic of China et al. 2004):

 1. The reason the defects occurred
 2. Detailed recall implementation plan, including particular actions and methods for recall
 3. Sales scope and quantity
 4. Recall effects, including the quantity of recalled vehicles in which the defect has been eliminated and the quantity of vehicles that have not been recalled
 5. Explanation for the reasons the defective vehicles have not been recalled yet and the specific actions to be taken
 6. Suggestions for the prevention of the recurrence of the same defect and for the improvements for the recall action

Table 10.1   Recall Control Plan Example

No.	Plan Description	Up to Time	Responsible Person	April	May	June	July	August
1	FSA propose to EC meeting	20xx/4/xx	XXX	√				
2	FSA part request to supplier	20xx/4/xx	XXX	√				
3	VIN arrange	20xx/4/xx	XXX	√				
4	Customer information arrange	20xx/4/xx	XXX	√				
5	Stop to sell the vehicle	20xx/4/xx	XXX	√				
6	FSA TSB	20xx/4/xx	XXX	√				
7	FSA request submit to recall department	20xx/4/xx	XXX	√				
8	Part shipped to PDC	20xx/4/xx	XXX	√				
9	Part shipped to dealers	20xx/4/xx	XXX	√				
10	FSA process training for regional RM	20xx/4/xx	XXX	√				
11	FSA GFB	20xx/4/xx	XXX	√				
12	FSA process training for dealer G—manager	20xx/4/xx	XXX	√				
13	Dealer received part confirm	20xx/4/xx	XXX	√				
14	FSA first day status follow-up	20xx/4/xx	XXX	√				

(continued)

Table 10.1   Recall Control Plan Example (Continued)

No.	Plan Description	Up to Time	Responsible Person	April	May	June	July	August
15	No customer information feedback	20xx/5/xx	XXX		√			
16	Solution for no customer information	20xx/5/xx	XXX		√			
17	Part status adjustment	20xx/5/xx	XXX		√			
18	Complete rate for first month	20xx/5/27	XXX		√			
19	Complete rate for second month	20xx/6/xx	XXX			√		
20	Complete rate for third month	20xx/7/xx	XXX				√	
21	Submit report to the recall center	20xx/8/xx	XXX					√

Table 10.2   Product Recall Notice Example

Manufacturer		CFMA	
Recall time		Apr 1, 2012–Mar 31, 2013	
Quantity Involved		62,445 vehicles	
Motor Model	*Specification*	*Year of Production*	*VIN Range*
Mondeo-Winning	CAF7203M/CAF7230A	2008–2009	From: LVSFBFAF67F000394 To: LVSHBFAF29F080479
S-Max	CAF6480A/CAF6480A1	2008–2009	From: LVSFFSAF57F004305 To: LVSHFSAFX9F011309
Defects	Because the material of electric motor and brush of ABS pump of some vehicles do not meet the requirements, ABS pump motor fails to work.		

(continued)

Table 10.2 Product Recall Notice Example (Continued)

Manufacturer	CFMA		
Recall time	Apr 1, 2012–Mar 31, 2013		
Quantity Involved	62,445 vehicles		
Motor Model	*Specification*	*Year of Production*	*VIN Range*
Possible consequence	When ABS warning light and hand brake warning light are lit permanently (if ESC is configured, ESC warning light is lit permanently too), the function of ABS and ESC will not work. The function of normal brake and EBD is not influenced.		
Resolution	Replace HCU of ABS module for free for all vehicles involved.		
Improvement measures	Adopt electric motor and brush of ABS pump that meet the requirements in Mondeo-Winning and S-Max manufactured outside the recall period. This problem has been eliminated.		
Complaints or feedback	So far, no complaints or reports received about car accidents or people hurt.		
Vehicle owner notification	The dealers authorized by CFMA contact relevant customers via letter or telephone. CFMA issues recall information via media. The customers can acquire relevant information about this recall through the official website of CFMA (www.ford.com.cn). If the customers have any questions, they can contact dealers nearby or dial the hotline of the customer service (400-887-7766,800-810-8168).		
Other information	If you want to know the details about this recall or have any questions, please log on www.qiche365.org.cn or dial Defective Product Management Center (010-65537365).		
Attachment. A diagram of failure description.			
Attachment. A list of repair stations.			

10.5 Conclusions

This chapter describes how CFMA uses a very standardized process that involves the coordination of different departments to improve the quality of its products following a product recall. In fact, CFMA uses much stricter criteria to judge whether to recall a vehicle than what is stipulated in the Administrative Regulations for the Recall of Defective Automobiles by the State Council of the People's Republic of China, which began to be implemented in 2013. CFMA divides its treatment of defective vehicles into four categories: GSB, TSB, FSA, and recall. Through these distinctions and multidepartment efforts, both internally and externally, CFMA achieves a high level of customer satisfaction with its product safety and quality.

References

AQSIQ. 2010. CFMA will recall 2009 Ford Focus. Available at http://www.aqsiq.gov.cn/zjxw/zjxw/zjftpxw/201005/t20100531_145541.htm, accessed on May 31, 2010.

AQSIQ. 2011a. CFMA will recall Volvo S40 made in China mainland. Available at http://www.aqsiq.gov.cn/zjxw/zjxw/zjftpxw/201105/t20110506_183673.htm, accessed on May 6, 2011.

AQSIQ. 2011b. CFMA will recall Mondeo-Winning vehicles. Available at http://www.aqsiq.gov.cn/zjxw/zjxw/zjftpxw/201105/t20110511_184054.htm, accessed on May 11, 2011.

AQSIQ. 2012. CFMA will recall parts of Mondeo-Winning and S-Max cars. Available at http://www.aqsiq.gov.cn/zjxw/zjxw/zjftpxw/201203/t20120331_214365.htm, accessed on March 31, 2012.

Baidu.com. Changan Ford Mazda Automobile Co., Ltd. Available at http://baike.baidu.com/view/1077621.htm.

DPAC. 2010. CFMA will recall Mondeo-Winning and S-Max vehicles. Available at http://www.dpac.gov.cn/xwzl/gnxw/201009/t20100917_115785.html, accessed on September 17, 2010.

DPAC. 2011. CFMA will recall parts of Mondeo-Winning and S-Max cars. Available at http://www.dpac.gov.cn/other/zhgg/car/201204/t20120409_118348.html, accessed on March 31, 2011.

The General Administration of Quality Supervision, Inspection and Quarantine of the People's Republic of China, National Development and Reform Commission, Ministry of Commerce of the People's Republic of China, and General Administration of Customs of the People's Republic of China. 2004. The Provisions on the Administration of Recalls of Defective Automobiles.

Chapter 11

Bright Dairy

TingTing Zhao and Xiucheng Fan

Contents

11.1 Introduction: Company Background

The Chinese melamine milk powder contamination incident, which happened in 2008, had an estimated 300,000 victims, with six infants dying from kidney stones and other kidney damage, and an estimated 54,000 babies being hospitalized.[1] The incident has been a black mark on the record of China's dairy product quality since

169

then. However, Bright Dairy rebounded from the melamine scandal and became a leader in developing approaches to ensure the safety of its products.

Founded in Shanghai as a state-owned dairy products manufacturing factory, the brand "Bright" was created in 1951. With the continuous help of the Shanghai Dairy Association (SDA), Bright Dairy has been a model of product quality and safety. As a leading enterprise in the dairy industry in China, Bright Dairy & Food Co., Ltd., has developed a diversified product line that includes pasteurized milk, fresh milk, yoghurt, ultra-high-heat pasteurized milk, milk powder, butter and cheese, and fruit juices. It is one of the largest dairy production and sales companies in China.[2]

Bright Dairy has more than 50 years' history of producing dairy products, making an effort to share an innovative and healthy life with its consumers since its inception. All of its employees share the value of providing consumers with safe, fresh, nutritious, and healthy dairy products. The company has the largest market share of fresh milk, yoghurt, and cheese in China.

11.2 Bright's World-Class Manufacturing System

Faced with declining profits in the dairy industry, Bright Dairy's top management made the decision to introduce world-class manufacturing (WCM) systems to the company in 2006. They were first launched it in its eighth factory, which produces mainly yoghurt. "We are aiming to forge the company, and help it to become a world-class manufacturer," the president of Bright Dairy, Mr. Benheng Guo, stated in an interview with *Financial Daily*. He explained that the action of introducing WCM systems is consistent with the company's mission and values since it always keeps its mission of "sharing innovative and healthy life with consumers" in mind, as well as its value "do better, and pursue excellence."[3]

World-class manufacturers are those that demonstrate industry best practice. To achieve this, a company should strive to be the best in the field at each of the competitive priorities (quality, price, delivery speed, delivery reliability, flexibility, and innovation). A company should therefore aim to maximize its performance in these areas in order to maximize competitiveness. However, as resources are unlikely to allow improvement in all areas, the company should concentrate on maintaining its performance in "qualifying" factors and improving its performance on "competitive edge" factors. Its priorities will change over time and must therefore periodically be reviewed. WCM is an advanced technology that is based on total productive maintenance, combining together elements of supply chain management, total quality management, strategic cost management, and lean manufacturing, which is very practical and effective.

The actions of Bright Dairy related to WCM had started earlier than the melamine-tainted milk powder crisis. After an intense process of understanding and discussion, the top management of Bright Dairy decided to use the WCM system. So far, Bright Dairy is the first and only company in China's dairy industry that has launched a WCM system.

Bright Dairy used its WCM system as an important way to improve its competitiveness, that is, to effectively reduce its cost based on ensuring quality, gradually reaching the status of zero defects in equipment, zero stock outs of materials, and zero complaints about its products. In 2003, Bright's complaint management system was first launched. Several years later, reporting from the producing system was launched in 2006. From late 2008 to early 2009, Bright Dairy successfully accomplished significant improvements and upgrades of its raw milk collection information system, which is very innovative and pioneering in China and even in the world.

Mr. Guo described the essence of WCM as overall optimization and continuous improvement, which guides Bright Dairy's every action. The launching of its WCM system represents a revolution of management, realizing that the "people" element was actually the greatest obstacle to launching the system. In order to overcome it, the top management of Bright Dairy made an effort to promote WCM. Even more importantly, it worked diligently to change every employee's mindset so that WCM was perceived as the norm.

To a company in the process of maturing, the WCM system plays the role of a navigator; at the same time, it is also an accelerator. As Bright's first branch to launch a WCM system, the eighth factory has developed to become an advanced and model factory among all the branches of Bright Dairy. Founded in 1984, and starting to produce dairy products in October 1988, the eighth factory of Bright Dairy has a plant with an area of over 15,366 m². It uses 23 assembly lines, which can produce diversified canned dairy products. With an annual production of approximately 200,000 tons, it is Asia's largest producer of dairy products and ranks in the top five in the world. Ninety-five percent of Bright's products in its eighth factory are yoghurt, supplying almost the entire yoghurt market in the Yangtze River Delta region of China. When we visited the factory in August 2010, the factory looked clean and well organized. The manager of the factory, Mr. Junfei Lu, told us, "We are using the regulations for pharmacy production to manage our yoghurt production," which was the most impressive comment that we heard.

Since 2007, Bright's eighth factory has been using centralized control and management systems to manage production. Most of the production processes are controlled by the computer system in order to ensure the precision of production. Bright has very strict standards about the production process, beginning with raw milk collection. The suppliers are very carefully selected by the Quality Department at Bright's headquarters. Bright's preventive measures begin at the farms of its suppliers, where their milk tank vehicles are sealed and labeled. Every tank has its own code and guard ribbon. Through the code, Bright can easily trace back to the farm if a quality issue should happen. Once the raw milk has arrived at Bright's factory, there are strict controls on its safety during each process.

Bright also has strict requirements for its employees who can the sterilized milk. The factory owns an inspection lab, with fast-detection equipment. Bright has been conducting regular internal examinations every 2 years and has also established preventive systems for dealing with a product harm crisis. The factory conducts an annual product recall simulation in July of each year. The quality director leads a group to do this, through which they must reply to consumer complaints in a timely fashion and determine what is the proper compensation for the affected consumers.

11.3 Upstream Quality Management

11.3.1 Coordination with Dairy Farms

Because of their position at the beginning of the supply chain, dairy farms play an important role in ensuring the quality of Bright Dairy's products. According to an expert from the SDA, the staff who work at each farm are all Bright Dairy employees. The company also controls 98% of the cows.

There is an independent department in Bright Dairy, called the Raw Milk Sourcing Department (RMSD), that has the responsibility for dealing with transactions with the farms. The RMSD signs contracts with the farms on behalf of Bright Dairy, ensuring what its demand will be. Bright Dairy takes the upper hand, with strict requirements on the quality of the raw milk that it produces. Every afternoon, the RMSD informs the farms about the amount of raw milk that will be needed for the next day's production, and then the farm delivers according to the expected demand. Thus, Bright is positioned as the supply chain leader. It strictly enforces standards and quantities for its raw materials, in exchange for guaranteed business for its suppliers.

11.3.2 100-Point Measurement System

Bright Dairy has been using a "100-point measurement system" to evaluate its farms, with the purpose of guaranteeing the safety of its raw milk supply. When signing a contract with a certain farm, it is clearly spelled out that the manufacturing factories of Bright Dairy and the RMSD are responsible for the evaluation of the farms. The factory checks the quality of the raw milk supplied by each farm, as well as performs regular inspections of each farm. The RMSD is in charge of the final evaluation of farms, calculating the score for each farm according to the 100-point measurement system, which includes five categories of measurement items, including feedstuffs, cow management, sewage treatment, environment, and pest management.

11.4 Internal Quality Management

11.4.1 Information Sharing

All of Bright's farms use advanced information systems to manage their cows. All of the cows have barcoded ear tags. Information about every cow (daily yield, medication, feeding, etc.) is automatically input into the information technology (IT) system for each farm. Each farm keeps the information for all its cows, which is also available for Bright Dairy whenever it wants to check or refer to it. Thus, the farm and Bright Dairy have an effective way of sharing information. Even if the farmers are poorly educated or unfamiliar with computers, using the barcode scanner allows the easy input of information.

11.4.2 Internal Quality Management

The quality department at Bright's headquarters is in charge of the group's overall quality management. Bright Dairy's quality management extends from the RMSD to the Logistics and Sales departments, then across each factory and each farm, where there is also staff belonging to Bright's quality department. Organized in a matrix organization, the quality department staff members follow daily routines in the various departments of Bright Dairy, while their performance is measured by the quality department. They have a regular meeting every month, in which they report their work to the leader of the quality department.

11.4.3 Quality Management Systems

Bright Dairy launched advanced quality control methods to ensure the safety of its products, including International Organization for Standardization (ISO) categories, hazard analysis critical control point (HCCP) categories, and SEIRI, SEITON, SEISO, SEIKETSU, and SHITSUKE (5S). Among these quality management systems, ISO 22000, 14000, and 9001 certifications are compulsory for all of Bright's factories. The ISO 22000 family of international standards addresses food safety management,[4] while the ISO 14000 family of international standards addresses various aspects of environmental management.[5] They provide practical tools for companies looking to identify and control their environmental impact and constantly improve their environmental performance. ISO 9001:2008 specifies requirements for a quality management system where an organization needs to demonstrate its ability to consistently provide products that meet customer needs and applicable statutory and regulatory requirements.[6] It aims to enhance customer satisfaction through the effective application of the system, including processes for continuous improvement of the system and the assurance of conformity to customer and applicable statutory and regulatory requirements.

In 2008, the group introduced the "1000-point system" (1000SS). Compared with other quality management systems, 1000SS has more detailed requirements for a company's quality control and management. When it comes to the quality management of Bright Dairy, the requirements are reflected in the washing of milk jars, the hygiene of factory environment, the management of insect pests, the traceability of its supply chain, staff training, repair and maintenance management, and the environment of the factory. 1000SS scores every aspect, with a specialized inspection group performing at least one annual inspection of each factory, scoring it according to its performance on the aspects that 1000SS covers.

We interviewed Mr. Jianping Duan, who is the leader of the Butter and Cheese Factory (BCF) of the Bright Dairy Group. Mr. Duan told us about the implementation of 1000SS. BCF scored 894/1000 on its most recent inspection, which helped the factory to rank second among all the departments that were inspected. He also described his thoughts on the 1000SS, stating that factories can vary in their scores for a number of reasons. Some factories have received lower scores because of the complexity of their production processes and the over-all capability of their staff. It is harder to recruit staff with good capabilities in the less developed regions of China. Another reason that could help to explain this phenomenon is that some of the factories of Bright Dairy Group were acquired to be renovated, so their foundation is much weaker. He summarized that there are five main factors that determine the extent to which the quality management (QM) implementation is done well. The five factors are the allocation of staff, raw materials, equipment, supply, and management.

11.5 Supply Chain Management

11.5.1 Cold Chain Management

The factory has the responsibility for keeping the products it provides to customers safe. Besides product safety, as a well-known brand for fresh milk products, the most important thing for Bright Dairy Group is to capture moments of truth in its supply chain to ensure the freshness of its products. There are two important routes for delivery: the pre-cold chain and the post-cold chain.

The pre-cold chain is the upstream supply chain, referring to delivery of raw milk from the farms to the factory. In order to ensure the freshness of the raw milk, it should be delivered with 12 hours of milking the cows. In delivering the raw milk, two cards (a collection card and a transportation card) and one sheet (the transportation sheet) are necessary. The transportation card contains detailed information about the truck that delivered the raw milk, including the license plate number of the truck and the names of the staff who go to the farm to accomplish the work. Every truck has GPS positioning, a sign for sealing it, and an automatic temperature recorder. Once the truck arrives at a farm, related staff inspect the quality of the raw milk for fat, protein, and antibiotics content. After that, all the rims of the containers are tightly sealed.

Once the milk arrives at the factory, the staff there note the amount of raw milk, the staff who was in charge of the transportation, the truck that carried the raw milk, whether the rims were sealed well, and whether the temperature is proper. They then break the seal and do a sampling of the raw milk in order to double check that the standards for raw milk have been met and to ensure that the raw milk characteristics are the same as the information that appeared on the transportation sheet. All of the factories of the Bright Dairy Group use 27 indexes to assess the quality of raw milk, including physical and chemical indexes, microbe index, residual urine index, and antibiotics index. Among these indexes, there are seven or eight indexes that deal with potential cheating behavior during the collection and delivery of raw milk.

Freshness is the most important characteristic of Bright Dairy's milk products and the most important thing that Bright Dairy wants to guarantee for its customers. Bright Dairy's marketing channels cover East China, West China, the middle of China, and also the northeast of China. Among the milk products of Bright Dairy, the shortest time duration for some of the products to stay fresh is only 2 days, which presents a substantial challenge in the delivery of milk products. The aim of the post-cold chain management is to confront this challenge and maintain the freshness of its milk products. The logistics department of Bright Dairy is responsible for the storage, keeping, and delivering of all the milk products that are manufactured by factories of the Bright Dairy Group. It has been making an effort to extend the coverage of its logistics channels wider and wider. Its core concept is to ensure the "professional, punctual, high-quality and meticulous milk products delivery."[7]

11.5.2 Traceability of Bright Dairy's Supply Chain

To keep its milk products safe and fresh, Bright Dairy has been enhancing the concept of "managing quality from the process of the original source to the dining table."[8] Traceability is an important aspect of its supply chain management.

As the original source for raw milk, the farms are controlled by Bright Dairy Group. Every cow on each farm has an ear tag with a barcode and number. During the feeding of the cows, the staff at the farm record the feed ingredients and do daily checks for every cow. They record detailed information about its medication use, which enables both the farm and Bright Dairy Group to have a good understanding of the situation of every cow. In case that there is product safety problem, they can trace the problem at the level of a single cow.

At each farm, the cows are milked three times each day (morning, noon, and evening). Once the raw milk arrives at the factory, before mixing it together, Bright keeps the milk from each cow in a separate jar and does sampling of each jar. Before the raw milk is mixed together, the last thing done is to check the indexes. If there is a quality problem in a particular milk jar, Bright knows which jar the raw milk is from, and it can give the feedback to the farm. The farm can identify which cow the milk is from, since it is required to keep a sample from each cow for 24 hours. There are professional staff that judge the smell and taste of the raw milk. Furthermore, there is monthly sampling on each farm to check and compare the results with the results of the factory's inspection.

Following the production process, the factory continues sampling of the end product during its entire quality guarantee period. Process management maintains a detailed record of the original source and the route of delivery. In case a product safety problem is found by customers, they will first contact the sales department of Bright Dairy Group, which clarifies the problem and gives feedback to the involved factory. The factory then tracks the product batch and clarifies responsibility for the problem. If the problem was caused by the original source of the milk, Bright will give feedback to the involved farm.

11.6 Role of the SDA

As the intermediary between the government and dairy producers and between a dairy producer and other dairy producers, the SDA plays a very important role in enhancing the development of the dairy industry in Shanghai. Through its leadership, it has pushed the dairy farms and dairy producers in the Shanghai region to have the highest quality dairy products in China. Thus, the SDA has been an important catalyst for improving supply chain quality management in the Shanghai region.

11.6.1 About the Association

The SDA is composed of committees: the experts committee, the production committee, the manufacturing committee, and the farm engineering committee. The SDA provides some of the public affairs services that the government cannot provide. It participates in the drawing up of official regulations and works with dairy producers to implement and achieve the standards. It also provides solutions to dairy farmers when they confront a problem that they are not able to solve by themselves.

11.6.2 Dairy Industry in Shanghai

We interviewed the vice president of the SDA, Mr. Mingshi Cao, and an expert named Mrs. Linmei Gong, who had worked at Bright Dairy as a professional quality manager for many years before joining the SDA. They gave us detailed information about the dairy industry in Shanghai. Shanghai began the process of terminating individual cow feeding and raw milk collection stations in 2004; this process was completed by 2006. Raw milk has been collected by the dairy producers since then, which was a significant contributor to the good performance of dairy producers in the Shanghai region during the 2008 melamine scandal, relative to dairy producers in other parts of China.

Bright works with a total of 123 dairy farms in Shanghai, plus those that it acquired in other parts of China, for a total of 150. Most of the farms are state owned, with amounts of raw milk production that account for two-thirds of the total production in Shanghai; the rest are privately operated. The standards for the quality of raw milk collection are higher in Shanghai than in the rest of China. The quality of the raw milk is determined by a third party, which is the Shanghai Milk Products Inspection Center. The cost of inspection is shared half and half between the farm owner and the dairy producer. This mechanism for raw milk inspection has been operating in Shanghai for 15 years, working well to ensure the overall quality of milk products.

11.6.3 Efforts of the SDA

Since the end of 2006, the SDA considered using international standards for milk products to regulate its dairy enterprises. This would further shorten the distance between China's milk products and those from Europe and the United States. The SDA has been trying to change dairy producers' thinking about quality management, so that they understand that product quality is not improved through inspection, but, rather, by controlling every element of the production process. Post-cold chain management is an important part of the SDA's Three-Year Plan for Improving Product Quality. The goal of post-cold chain management is to keep the milk products fresh through the entire delivery route, from the manufacturing factory to the hands of customers. The temperatures for chilling milk and for milk transportation are strictly controlled. The processes of milk product delivery from the manufacturing factory to the milk delivery station and from the milk delivery station to the customer are smoothly connected. All of these efforts are made to ensure the safety and freshness of milk products.

With the goal of keeping milk products safe and freshness always in mind, the SDA also started to develop rules for implementation of pre-cold chain management in 2008. The key route of pre-cold chain management is delivery from the milk transportation truck to the manufacturing factory. Even though each dairy producer establishes its own contract with its farms, the SDA has set uniform standards and processes with which they must conform, which are an ongoing element of the participation of farms and dairy enterprises.

References

1. Xinhua News Agency. Death toll rises to four in tainted baby formula scandal in China, September 18th, 2008.
2. Bright Dairy Group. About Bright Dairy. Available at http://www.brightfood.com/cn/about.aspx?Class_ID=11, accessed January 3, 2011.
3. Q. Liu. Interview on Guo Benheng: Reshape the Image of Local Dairy Brand. Available at http://www.yicai.com/news/2011/12/1313077.html, accessed February 15, 2012.
4. ISO. Introduction to ISO 22000. Available at http://www.iso.org/iso/home/standards/management-standards/iso22000.html, accessed November 13, 2012.

5. ISO. Introduction to ISO 14000. Available at http://www.iso.org/iso/home/standards/management-standards/iso14000.html, accessed November 13, 2012.
6. ISO. Introduction to ISO 9000. Available at http://www.iso.org/iso/iso_9000, accessed November 13, 2012.
7. Bright Dairy Group. Cold Chain Management System of Bright Dairy. Available at http://www.brightdairy.com/quality-cold.php, accessed November 13, 2012.
8. J. Li. The Construction of Bright Dairy's Food Safety Management System. Available at http://www.cqn.com.cn/news/zjpd/wpbm/814251.html, accessed November 8, 2012.

Chapter 12

CHIC Group Global Co., Ltd.

Li Luo, Xiande Zhao, and Barbara B. Flynn

Contents

12.1 Introduction: Company Background

CHIC Group Global Co., Ltd., was founded in Shanghai in 1997. It branched out from its original base in distribution logistics to establish and invest in completely new businesses related to fruit canning and processing, orthopedic medical products distribution, supply chain management, information systems and technology, and marketing and business design. In each of these sectors, the CHIC Group has achieved remarkable success, with an excellent track record.

It has done this under the umbrella of supply chain management. The CHIC Group defines itself as an integrated value creation-based one-stop shop for supply chain management services, expertise, and resources for businesses in the food, agriculture, merchant banking, home & orchard, manufacturing, and medical devices industries, with innovative products and services. Consider, for example, CHIC Foods, which is one of the divisions of the CHIC Group. CHIC Foods has a total of 400 full-time employees and annual sales of over 10,000 containers, with a vision and mission to be the number one international brand of choice. CHIC Foods owns over 1700 acres of orchards and nurseries and has five processing plants, located throughout China. As the largest exporter and processor of acidic fruit in China, its annual export amounts to 50,000 tons, accounting for about 20% of the export volume of similar products in China, its processed citrus products account for 45% market share in the United States and 75% in Britain.[1]

12.2 Fresh Fruit Industry in China

China is the largest fruit-producing country in the world and the place of origin of fruit trees, with the most varieties in the world. Since its reform and opening up, China has implemented a policy of open pricing and multiple channels of operation for fruit, which has led to the rapid development of its fruit production. With its expansion of industrial scale, especially after joining the World Trade Organization, the export of fruit products in China has increased year on year. The fruit processing industry in China started relatively late and developed slowly. Processing is relatively backward, and the export of fresh fruit has been the primary way of trading for many years. Fruit processing constitutes less than 10% of total fruit production in China. International fruit processing is mainly in the form of fruit juice, wines, jams, and canned fruit, among which juice processing has developed the fastest, particularly frozen pure juice.

Processed fruit in China is generally characterized by poor flavor and uneven appearance, with high or over-the-limit residues of fertilizers, pesticides, and other harmful substances and weak commercial processing after fruit picking. Compared with fruit processing in other countries, there is quite a big difference with respect to ideas, technology, equipment, and other issues among fruit processors. The export of fruit products with good quality varieties is quite limited, as well as the bulk export of high-quality fruit.[2]

The industrialization level of the Chinese fruit industry, which is fragmented and lacks overall industrial collaboration, is relatively low. At present, most fruit orchards in China are owned by individual operators. Cultivation, planting, and sales are scattered, with a small amount of investment, and are of small scale. In addition, the education level of the farmers, standardized management, and intensive operation levels are low; many of the farmers are illiterate, which makes the use of state-of-the art techniques challenging. Without unified fruit industry associations, most market production organizers do not provide farmers with detailed market information, production information, technical guidance, or other preproduction services, due to their own limited capacity. As a result of limited industry coordination, information is transmitted slowly or is blocked; farmers often all rush to plant the same variety of fruit, which leads to oversupply for some types of fruit and short supply for others. This results in disorderly distribution channels for fruit products, sales difficulties, poorly organized market operations, and nonstandardized market behaviors. Many fruit farmers do not understand the control standards for pesticide residues and use inappropriate pesticides to control the spread of plant diseases and pests, then blindly launch their products into the market, resulting in residues of harmful substances in fruit that severely exceed standards.

Due to the short shelf life and perishability of fruit, vegetables, and other agricultural products, there are strict requirements for transport and insurance. However, the Chinese logistics infrastructure for agriculture is backward. Transportation of agricultural products is mainly at normal temperatures and in their natural form, lacking refrigeration equipment and technology, which results in substantial wastage during the logistics process. The wastage of Chinese fruit, vegetables, and other agricultural products during picking, transport, storage, and other logistics links amounts to 25% to 30%, for a total of $12.25 billion perished and wasted agricultural products during transport each year. In contrast, the wastage rate for fruit and vegetables in developed countries is less than 5%; in the United States, it is only 1% to 2%.[3] In addition, quality and safety systems for Chinese agricultural products were developed relatively late, with an absence of systems for agricultural product standards, food inspection and testing systems, and evaluation indicators for food quality and safety. Over the past few years, fruit has been polluted by pesticides, fertilizers, wastewater, waste gas, and industrial residues to differing extents during the planting process. This has been exacerbated by additives and preservatives that are misused by underground factories during the fruit processing link, which poses the potential for substantial danger to people's physical health.

With the appearance of supermarket chains, the construction of wholesale markets for agricultural products, technology innovation, and changes in the rules for international trade in agricultural products, China's fruit supply chain has been gradually developing.[4] The fruit supply chain can be simply described as the chain along which fruit moves from farmers, processing companies, distribution centers, wholesalers, and retailers to consumers. Compared with traditional industrial products, fruit has a natural cycle and is susceptible to being affected by biology, season, climate, and other natural conditions. As a result, the fruit supply chain has its own relatively unique aspects. However, China's fruit supply chain is still developing, with many problems and shortcomings.

The links in China's fruit supply chain have loose connections, which can be easily disrupted, in a number of ways. First, the Chinese fruit supply chain is composed of a large number of entities with a low level of organization in every link. Moreover, information is not communicated smoothly. The external environment is becoming more complicated. As a result, the fruit supply chain is relatively weak. Second, because of the absence of core companies with leadership and authority, the links in the fruit supply chain are lacking in strategic cooperation. Third, due to the complexity and uncertainty of transactions, fruit farmers' transactions costs and risk have been increasing, while their returns have been decreasing. Once the expected returns do not compensate for their cost, the farmers give up the production of fruit, which disrupts the production process and affects the operations of the fruit supply chain.[4] Fourth, fruit processing companies do not analyze, evaluate, compare, or investigate their suppliers and do not build up long-term cooperative partnerships with them. In addition, most supermarkets do not have fixed long-term fruit suppliers and instead search for partners in transport, packing, loading, unloading, and other logistic links on a transactional basis. The connection between these links is very fragile, susceptible to risk, and difficult to recover. Normally, the value of goods and services is created by different participants in the supply chain. Since an ideal supply chain for fruit production has not been formed, however, the cost of producing fruit products is high, leaving minimal profits for operators and price, quality, freshness, varieties, and other aspects that fall under minimal standards.

CHIC set out to address these problems and create a world-class fruit supply chain in China. In the following, we describe how this was accomplished.

12.3 CHIC's Supply Chain Strategy for Quality

In the CHIC Group, quality management is not merely about operations management, it is a strategic issue dealing with planning and operating the entire supply chain. The quality improvement process not only is a process for production control but is also considered to be a continuous improvement process related to the competitiveness of the entire supply chain. Specifically, CHIC established a comprehensive supply chain quality assurance system. Through the clear strategic supply chain positioning, strategic design of its supply chain structure, excellent supply chain integration, and close alignment among these three critical components, CHIC provides an outstanding example of effective supply chain quality management.

12.3.1 Supply Chain Strategy for Quality

In the fruit supply chain, seeds, fertilizers, pesticides, picking, storage, transport, processing, and other links are typically all performed by different service providers, including tens of thousands of individual agricultural operators. In addition, unpredictable weather changes bring changes in quality. Without sophisticated supply chain management tools, it is nearly impossible to ensure food safety in China, and management and control of the entire fruit supply chain are the only ways to ensure quality. Because of this, CHIC developed a supply chain strategy for quality.

12.3.2 Strategic Positioning in the Supply Chain

CHIC defines itself as a management company for the entire fruit supply chain, as well as its integrator and leader. It determined that its focus was not only to complete the functions of certain links in the supply chain but also to ensure the successful operation of the entire chain. From its investment in the development and selection of varieties, seeding, fertilizers, pesticides, growing, planting, harvesting, transporting, processing in factories, entering into the market and marketing, CHIC is involved in different links of the fruit supply chain. By managing the entire supply chain of "farmers–orchards–fruit processing companies–customers,"[5] CHIC creatively realizes corporate value in its supply chain integration. Because of the importance of safety in the food industry, CHIC considers high quality as the core target of its supply chain management, around which the operations of all other aspects are carried out.

12.4 CHIC's Strategic Resources and Capabilities

As the supply chain leader, CHIC always holds the three most important resources and capabilities that determine the quality of its supply chain: continuous technological innovation capability, quality market resources, and a wide range of social resources. The effective use of these strategic resources and constant value innovation equip CHIC's supply chain with unique core competitive advantages in its supply chain, which puts CHIC in an invincible position in the fierce competition of the market.

12.4.1 Continuous Technological Innovation Capability

CHIC always considers the pursuit of food preservation and quality assurance as its top priority in technological innovation. CHIC developed a unique fruit preservation technology, after 8 years' research, which changed the packaging materials from tin cans and glass bottles to plastic cups, extending the preservation period for fresh cut fruit to 12 months without adding any preservatives or any other sub-stances.[5] This was a revolutionary technology in traditional food processing, which helped CHIC to establish a leading position in the industry. CHIC set up a global R&D center in Jia Ding, with an investment of $70 million, to build the world's top fruit technology R&D center, in order to further enhance the strength of its research and innovation and bring more high value-added products and technology to its customers.[6]

12.4.2 Stable Quality Market Resources

CHIC has quality global resources for orders and leverages them into the ability to provide long-term stable orders to the farmers and downstream companies in its supply chain. As the largest exporter and processor of acidic fruit in China, CHIC occupies a considerable market share in the United States and United Kingdom fruit processing market; it is the core supplier of several global major food brands, including Del Monte, Heinz, Yum!, etc. It is the exclusive supplier of citrus prod-ucts to Del Monte Foods, the largest food processing conglomerate in the United States.[5]

12.4.3 Social Resources

CHIC has developed a huge support system of social resources. It integrates numerous resources that are closely related to quality, to provide strong support for continuous improvement in product quality. CHIC is not only a supply chain integrator but also an integrator of industrial resources, government resources, and even global resources. In addition to its partners in the food supply chain, CHIC's partners also include local governments, industry associations, research institu-tions, UNESCO, etc. In this open system, CHIC has established a strong motive for its sustained development.

12.5 CHIC's Strategic Supply Chain Design for Quality

Implementation of any kind of strategy requires structural support. The design of CHIC's supply chain governance structure is based on its supply chain inte-gration strategy for quality. CHIC's supply chain governance structure defines transaction arrangements among its supply chain members. It ensures that its goals of high quality, control, and stability are the key principles of the design of its supply chain governance structure. Therefore, the main characteristics of CHIC's supply chain structure are high centralization of authority during the decision making process and high standardization of process and standards dur-ing the production process. As the leader of its supply chain, CHIC is able to enforce these.

12.5.1 CHIC's Current Supply Chain Structure

The design of CHIC's supply chain network is built upon its strategic focus on high quality. The basic idea is to integrate the entire supply chain to provide products and services of the best quality for world-class customers. CHIC has established strategic alliances with Heinz, Yum!, Del Monte Foods, Coca Cola, and other world-class companies that attach great importance to food safety and are willing to pay a premium for it. Strategic alliances with downstream partners with high standards and strict requirements, such as Del Monte Foods, which constitutes 30% to 40% of the global market share for fruit processing, have been instrumental in CHIC's strategic supply chain design for high quality from the beginning.[5]

Because of the small-scale peasant economy in China's agricultural industry, CHIC's current supply chain structure is relatively complex. In order to ensure food quality and safety, CHIC set up a dozen holding companies or joint ventures to strengthen its control of its supply chain, among which it has a holding of 51% in most orchards and processing plants, while its R&D and supply chain management are 100% wholly owned by CHIC.[5] The key advantage of this centralized structure lies in its orderliness and economics of scale. For these investment projects, CHIC not only invests money but also invests in the involvement of teams of several hundred people. Through developing a keen understanding of its markets, operations, lean agriculture, and other advanced concepts, CHIC has integrated technology and management into its investment projects and company operating teams, to help them avoid risks and support them in problem solving.

CHIC regards the construction of its raw materials base as a core project for the development and expansion of the company, which relies on expanding the raw materials base by farmers. Due to the complex environment for investment in agriculture in China, CHIC has adopted a diversified management model, based on the farmers' cultural level and quality, variety of plants, soil conditions, geographic and geomorphic conditions, and other specific local circumstances. It follows several different models.[5]

1. Self-cultivation model: CHIC buys the land and plants fruit, operates, and controls the growth of citrus products on its own. After the harvest, CHIC exports the products or the processed products.
2. Lease-back and contracting model: CHIC rents the land and builds the orchards. It then divides these into small portions and rents these back to farmers, providing them with planting technology and other training and a guarantee that it will purchase the products from the farmers at the market price.
3. Cooperative model: CHIC operates in cooperation with farmers. Farmers provide the land and labor, while CHIC provides the technology and varieties and is responsible for market operations and the purchase of the farmers' products.

Cooperatives are the organizers and represent farmers' interests in production and sales, enjoying both CHIC's resources and independent legal representation. Cooperatives provide farmers with "five unified" services, namely, unified technical services, unified agricultural materials supply, unified production loans, unified certification, and unified product sales, which improve the organization level of farmers. CHIC developed "Pollution-Free Citrus Cultivation Practices of CHIC," "Technical Specification of Organic Citrus Cultivation in the Demonstration Field of Citrus Raw Material Base for Food Export of CHIC," and a series of technical standards, which form a complete technical system. CHIC's power, as its supply chain leader, allows it to enforce these standards. For fruit farmers producing strictly in accordance with its standard requirements, CHIC gives their fruit priority for purchasing, at a higher price, and provides recognition and rewards. For operators that are not in line with these practices, CHIC rejects their fruit, recovers the lease rights, and terminates the contract.

In the process of supply network construction, CHIC provides a series of measures to guarantee the interests of the farmers, orchards, processing companies, and other partners, in order to achieve a win–win situation with its supply chain partners. The upstream supply chain obtains the global orders received by CHIC and high-quality supply chain services for its products. Investments in technology and its guaranteed orders help CHIC to become the farmers' partner, instead of their adversary, despite CHIC's power. Because of this win–win cooperation, opportunistic behaviors by supply chain members are minimized. CHIC signs a contract with each fruit farmer, specifying the principles and measures of interest, as well as specific provisions for the farmers' income, so that they have clear income expectations. CHIC's practices demonstrate that designing a fine supply chain structure with strong supply chain leadership and centralized control over the entire process of planting, manufacturing, and marketing is an effective approach for supply chain quality management.

12.5.2 CHIC's Future Supply Chain Structure

CHIC's current supply chain structure has not truly covered the entire fruit industry supply chain. Some of the fruit used by CHIC is collected from individual fruit operators, who sign a cooperation agreement with CHIC. Ensuring food safety remains a priority in this segment of CHIC's supply chain. In order to fundamentally solve the product quality problem, the most secure way is to cover the entire supply chain. However, since Chinese agriculture still takes place in what is primarily a small-scale peasant economy, food safety systems are difficult to implement among millions of small, often illiterate, farmers in different places. The fundamental problem of food safety lies in the Chinese agricultural system. After years of struggling to explore solutions, CHIC finally found the tipping point in 2010, namely, to cooperate with the government to achieve economies of scale through CHIC's integrated rural urbanization projects.[7] In these projects, CHIC centralizes the land and performs unified management, essentially making farmers industrial workers and fundamentally solving the low efficiency of cultivation and planting by hundreds of millions of farmers. With further promotion of this integrated rural urbanization, CHIC will optimize the supply chain structure, eliminating quality problems through solve the three rural issues (agriculture, rural areas and farmers).

In May 2010, CHIC signed a comprehensive integrated rural urbanization project agreement with the Chongqing government, with a total project investment of $1.8 billion. This project will use about 7000 acres of land to construct a base for integrated rural urbanization, including a citrus processing factory and logistics base with a capacity of 100,000 tons.[1] In the lands grown and managed by CHIC, farmers will become the masters of the farm. An individual farmer can manage a little over 100 acres of farmland. In addition, CHIC has signed an agreement with the Suzhou government in Anhui province to use 25,000 acres of land in the suburban area of Xiaoxian County as an experimental zone for comprehensive agricultural reform. In the future, this area will be built as a comprehensive demonstration zone for cultivation and planting, production, product processing, logistics, and ecological tourism for yellow peaches and organic agricultural products. The goal is to process deciduous fruit (e.g., yellow peaches), with an annual capacity of 400,000 tons.[5] This demonstration zone will become the largest base for growing, producing, and processing peaches in the world. At present, CHIC has five agriculture bases in China: it grows citrus in Hunan, Chongqing and Jiangxi, peaches and other deciduous fruit in Anhui, and blueberries and other berry products in Qingdao, Shandong.[5] This base provides a good foundation for CHIC's strategic design of large-scale production. By reducing the number of upstream individual agricultural operators, CHIC's design of large-scale production will profoundly reduce the complexity of the entire supply chain structure.

12.6 CHIC's Supply Chain Integration for Quality

Building on its clear strategic positioning and strategic supply network structure design, and capitalizing on its position as the supply chain leader, CHIC integrated the product flow, information flow, and capital flow in its supply chain. CHIC is involved in every link of food production, from raw materials cultivation and planting, application of fertilizers, pesticide management, and control of food quality to final preservation, packaging, and logistics. Different from the practices of many other companies, CHIC's fruit supply chain does not start with breeding and seed-rearing, but from conducting a detailed "check-up" on the local environment. The check-up covers a very wide range of scope, including the condition of the soil, water, the surrounding buildings, factories, and other layout and even the air, climate, and wind direction in previous years.[8] CHIC grows different varieties, based on different soil conditions, and establishes corresponding agricultural irrigation management systems to standardize its agricultural operations. CHIC manages the farmers' orchards in its upstream supply chain as the first link in the supply chain and strictly controls and manages the product flow, information flow, and funds flow of its supply chain.

12.6.1 Product Flow

The orchards in CHIC's upstream supply chain are managed as the first link in its supply chain. CHIC has established a close cooperative relationship with a number of research institutes and has formed an expert service team composed of senior professional technical personnel. CHIC regularly invites foreign experts from Japan, Israel, and other countries to provide on-the-spot guidance and staff training, strengthening technical services for farmers. A technical services team is assigned to each base, forming an integrated technical service system from seed breeding, cultivation and management, fertilizers and pesticides application, picking and storage, preservation, to transport and others, providing fruit farmers with "point-to-point" preproduction, production, and postproduction all-around technical guidance services.

In 2006, CHIC took the initiative to destroy a million dollars' worth of products due to pesticide residues in raw fruit that exceeded its standards.[1] From then on, it determined to control quality from the source and began regarding its raw materials base as the first link in its supply chain. It managed farmers as workers in a plant would be managed, strictly cultivating and managing orchards according to its technical standards and strictly controlling the link of raw materials production. The product flow control in CHIC's supply chain starts with the seeds for its products. CHIC sticks to breed seedlings for their own orchards, in order to strictly control quality at the source. CHIC invested more than a half million dollars to build a seedling base of "three zones, two orchards, one field," covering an area of 60 acres: the seeding zone, the resource reserve zone, the container seedling zone, the parent orchard, the monitoring orchard and the cutting field, reserving more than 50 mother plants and breeding eight new quality varieties. This base has provided fruit farmers with more than 1 million virus-free container seedlings accumulatively.[5]

Following its technical specifications for production, CHIC implements quality management in its orchard planning, planting, soil management, fertilizer application, water management, tree management, flower and fruit management, pest control, fruit harvesting, transport, storage, and all production processes. A detailed record card and attached images or files are set up for each orchard, each farmer, and each production process. Daily inspection and monitoring mechanisms are established, implementing digital management of the entire process, in order to ensure that each process is in accordance with CHIC's pollution-free standards. During the cultivation period, CHIC conducts random checks on farmers on an irregular basis. Each random check is recorded in the testing center at

CHIC's headquarters. If a farmer fails a random check, the computer records indicate red. Even if this farmer then passes a second check, the land will be indicated as yellow in the computer. For lands that have passed both checks, the computer will indicate green. CHIC purchases fruit from the lands indicated in green, as a priority.[8] The CHIC SGS certification food safety laboratory, set up by CHIC and Société Générale de Surveillance (SGS) cooperatively, performs pesticide residue and heavy metal detection on all of CHIC's products.[5] Testing items includes heavy metal and element testing, microbiological testing, toxin testing, antibiotics residue testing, pesticide residue detection, and pesticide residue scanning, ensuring that each bottle or cup of fruit juice is in line with the stringent standards for food quality and safety in Europe and the United States. Only after many strict screenings can the mature and qualified fruit be transported to the fruit processing factory.

12.6.2 Information Flow

With its powerful information technology, CHIC achieved traceability and transparency of the entire process of the production and sales of its products. When a consumer buys a CHIC product and inputs its barcode into the computer, the customer can see which farmer in China, in which area, the product came from. Each tree in an orchard that is under CHIC's management has a barcode, recording the growth, fertilizer, and pesticide applications of the tree. At the same time, fruit transport, processing and packaging, and other links all have corresponding barcodes, recording the entire process of the products' release, so as to ensure that CHIC's fruit products are safe and sound in every link, from the orchard to the table. CHIC issues a certified farmer card to each farmer, which includes photos, basic information about the farmer, and land information. The first thing for the certified farmer to do is to walk around his farm holding communication equipment fitted with a GPS, 3G that can withstand temperature, humidity, and other working conditions. CHIC's headquarters in Shanghai will receive specific land area information from the farmer on Google maps. After that, the land and the soil in the land, trees, and fruit will be under monitoring by CHIC.[8] The company performs remote monitoring and tracking of each farmer's planting situation, so as to effectively control quality problems in all supply chain links.

12.6.3 Funds Flow

As an investment company, CHIC has strong capital operations ability. Over the past 15 years, CHIC has achieved an astounding track record of 100% ROA annually using investment strategies such as zero-debt growth and no-cost acquisitions.[9] Its founder, Edward Zhu, is known as China's Warren Buffett.[9] Through effective capital management, CHIC has the ability to always put quality first in the trade-off between quality and cost and will not sacrifice the quality of its products because of a money shortage. Since CHIC has owned proprietary technology for fresh fruit preservation for more than 10 years, it has been able to acquire companies in China mostly with the investment of technology, achieving its "zero-capital-investment" miracle.[9] Under its vision of supply chain integration, funds as the lifeblood of company operation always flow to the links of the most importance in the supply chain, such as research, food safety, and land and fruit orchard construction.

CHIC learned from the loan model followed by small immigration banks in Bangladesh and established an investment mechanism of a joint guarantee and supply chain loans by four parties: "company + professional cooperative + farmer + bank." For the fruit farmers of professional cooperatives who need loans, the bank will uniformly allocate loans to the account of the cooperative, with a guarantee by CHIC. The cooperative distributes the loans to its farmers, according to their needs, for production and operations. The loans of farmers are paid in installments, from the payment for citrus that is sold. Since 2007, this model has provided loans totaling $7 million for the production and operations of farmers, benefiting more than 8200 households of farmers. For fruit farmers with large capital gaps in their production and operations, in addition to helping them secure the loans, CHIC pays on their behalf by providing fertilizers, pesticides, and other agricultural materials, the payment of which will be deducted from their payment for citrus sold in installments. Over recent years, CHIC has provided capital for production and operations for 3700 households of farmers, for a total of more than $2 million, and set the lowest protective price for collecting citrus.[5]

CHIC also provides farmers with contracting support. For farmers contracting CHIC's orchards, the company supports them with free rent for 5 years and then charges rent and a management fee of $16 per mu (0.16 acre) from the sixth year after the production amount has been reached. At the same time, considering the output efficiency rate, the contracting area of each fruit farmer is between 30 and 100 mu. Moderately controlling the scale contributes to the lowest risk, highest efficiency, and best results. CHIC signs a contract for production and sales with the farmers, in which it will purchase the citrus from the fruit farmers at the minimum purchase price or at the market price, when the market price is higher than the minimum purchase price, reducing the market risk for the farmers. It supports the fruit farmers in interplanting watermelon and other economic products before citrus is grown and provides a corresponding subsidy, realizing supporting orchards with orchards. CHIC has established a system of regular visits to fruit farmers, discovering and solving any difficulties in production and the life of the fruit farmers. Even for a small matter, as long as the farmer asks for help, CHIC will treat it in a serious manner. Over recent years, CHIC has provided a total of $1 million for helping fruit farmers with various difficulties that they may encounter.[5] CHIC has set up a special fund to make up for the losses to farmers due to natural disasters, helping fruit farmers overcome their difficulties. Through genuine humanistic care, it lets fruit farmers enjoy their treatment as employees and enhances their master consciousness.

12.7 Case Summary

The case of CHIC is a successful model of improving product quality through excellent supply chain management and strong supply chain leadership. While most companies were fighting with each other for even a small market share, CHIC chose a unique development model for the entire supply chain management and created a blue ocean strategy to grow healthily and rapidly. CHIC has explored a new road, with Chinese characteristics, for food quality and safety assurance. Compared with traditional companies that focus only on internal quality management, CHIC extended its product quality management to the entire supply chain, breaking through the narrow scope of traditional quality management and showing a systematic way to conduct supply chain quality management. The major characteristic of CHIC's operation is to "do agricultural business beyond agriculture" (跳出农业做农业).[1] CHIC accurately understands agricultural mechanisms and other fundamental factors affecting food quality. Through cooperating with the local government and establishing a control-oriented supply chain structure to ensure supply chain integration, CHIC has achieved the ideal state of "performing quality management beyond quality management" (跳出质量管理做质量管理),[1] ultimately solving the problem of quality management at the source.

CHIC's successful experiences show that supply chain integration is an effective approach to supply chain quality management. Supply chain quality management, which involves multiple supply chain members, is a huge systematic project. High quality standards cannot be met merely through the control of production process. A company must have a clear strategic positioning in its supply chain and an overall plan for the supply chain, from a strategic point of view, to ensure that the resources in the entire supply chain are utilized effectively. Only in this way can the passive situation of "treat the head when the head aches and treat the feet when the feet ache" (头痛医头、脚痛医脚)[1] be avoided. At the same time, CHIC has formed an efficient supply chain network in alignment with its overall supply chain strategy through the strategic design of its supply chain structure. The consistency of strategy and structure is the precondition for ensuring the smooth integration of CHIC's supply chain. Only with strong guidance by its strategic supply chain design and strategic supply chain structure can supply chain quality integration be developed in an effective manner and in the right direction. When the entire supply chain operates in an efficient and integrated manner, high-quality products will become the certain result, which is the secret of the success of CHIC's supply chain quality management.

In view of the unique characteristics of the Chinese supply chain for agricultural products, CHIC made a strategic choice to manage the entire supply chain and strategically designed its supply chain with the goal of integrating the supply chain to serve customers with world-class food brands. Selected world-class companies in its downstream supply chain determine the high quality standards for the entire supply chain, from the demand side. In order to meet such high quality standards,

CHIC adopted a centralized supply chain structure, laying out the upstream supply network structure by investment in shares, cooperatives, and other means. The combination and application of these helped CHIC to realize effective control of its supply chain and, at the same time, maintain sufficient flexibility to adapt to market changes. The success of the "company + farmer" model implemented by CHIC is largely because CHIC never pursues temporary profit at the expense of the interests of farmers but instead guarantees the farmers' income through its fine system design. Thus, CHIC exemplifies strong, but benevolent, supply chain leadership.

You Lu, a Chinese poet of the ancient Southern Song Dynasty, was once asked by his son to impart the secret of poetry. In reply, he said, "You must do more things beyond poems, if you want to learn to write them" (汝果欲学诗, 功夫在诗外). Thus, CHIC's ultimate success richly illustrates the meaning of the phrase "Do more things beyond poems" (功夫在诗外). Just as poetry is a form of literature, which requires gradual intrinsic accumulation, good product quality reflects the long-term accumulation of management, technology, and other aspects of a company. CHIC's success in quality management benefits from its in-depth understanding of food quality problems in the context of China's small-scale peasant economy, continuous investment in technical innovation, and more than 10 years of unremitting effort to solve the three rural issues (agriculture, rural areas and farmers). The superlative quality of CHIC's effort was not realized in the course of a single day. Instead, it was attained through the consistent, deliberate practice of a concept, which is "to be well prepared so as to be able to succeed" (厚积薄发, 水到渠成). When a company considers building a solid foundation and benefiting society as its ultimate pursuit, success is not a destination but the inevitable outcome.

References

1. Bingxin Yang, The Legend of Mandarin Orange. *Global Entrepreneur*, January 5, 2012:162–166.
2. Hancheng Liu, Fahai Yi, Fruits Exporting Features and International Competitiveness in China. *Research of Agricultural Modernization*, Vol. 28, No. 4, 2007:450–453.
3. Junmiao Deng, Pengjun Dai, Fresh Agricultural Product Circulation Under Supply Chain Management. *Commercial Research*, Vol. 23, 2006:185–187.
4. Junrong Deng, Chunjie Qi, Our Country Fruit Farmer in Fruit Supply Chain Present Situation and Countermeasures Analysis—Take the Citrus Fruits as an Example. *Rural Economy*, Vol. 9, 2009:19–22.
5. CHIC Group, Available at http://www.chicgroup.cn/zh/.
6. Fengling Zhao, Jiankang Cui, Boundless Innovation System. *21st Century Business Herald- World Economic Forum in Dalian*, Special Issue, September 14, 2011.
7. David Dal Molin, Fixing China's Food Prices. *Shanghai Business Review*, January Issue, 2012:30–31.
8. Xiao Ning, The Ambition of the King of the Fruits. *Business Value*, December 5, 2011: 92–95.
9. Echo Zhou, China's Warren Buffett. *The Link (CEIBS)*, Issue 1, 2011:18–27.

INTRODUCTION TO SECTION IV: FINANCIAL PERSPECTIVE ON PRODUCT RECALLS

IV

Section IV contains examples of recent research about product recalls from the financial perspective. The impact of a product recall announcement can be devastating to a company's brand equity and reputation, which can lead to revenue and market share losses. Although estimating the long-term damage of a product recall on brand equity and company reputation is difficult, if not impossible, the short-term impact on stock market reaction is readily estimable using event study methodology. Event study methodology is based on the assumption that, in an efficient market, the financial impact of any unanticipated event will be immediately reflected in the stock price (Fama 1970).

Event study methodology is well established and has been used by researchers to measure the financial impact of events such as chief executive officer succession (Davidson et al. 1992), supply chain glitches (Hendricks and Singhal 2003), supply chain disruptions (Hendricks and Singhal 2009a,b), ISO 9000 certification (Corbett et al. 2005), winning a quality award (Hendricks and Singhal 1996), implementation of an environmental management program (Klassen and McLoughlin 1996), and medical device recall announcements (Thirumalai and Sinha 2011). The objective is to examine the stock market's response to a well-defined event, such as a recall announcement, through the observation of security prices around the event (Peterson 1989). We use the approaches described by Brown and Warner (1985),

MacKinlay (1997), Kothari and Warner (2007), and McWilliams and Siegel (1997), which examine patterns of cumulative returns. If the cumulative returns are significantly different following an event like the announcement of a product recall, they are considered "abnormal" and reflect the market's reaction to this information.

Three time windows are critical in event study methodology: the estimation window, the event window, and the postevent window, where Day 0 is the day that the event occurs. The estimation window is used to derive ordinary least squares (OLS) estimates of market model parameters, which reflect the "normal" return. Among the models for estimating expected returns, the market model has performed as well as or better than other models (Chen et al. 2009; Hendricks and Singhal 2003; Thirumalai and Sinha 2011). The event window is the time period over which the abnormal return is estimated by subtracting the expected normal return from the actual ex post return of the sample firm. Many previous event studies on product recalls have used long event windows. For instance, Hoffer et al. (1987) specified an 11-day event window (Day –5 through 5) in their study of automotive recall announcements. However, using a long event window severely reduces the power of test statistics, leading to false inferences about the significance of the event (McWilliams and Siegel 1997). Moreover, it is much more difficult to control for confounding effects when a longer event window is used. Therefore, a short event window is more appropriate for recall event studies. Monitoring the change in stock price over a relatively short event window effectively captures the financial impact of the event on firm performance (MacKinlay 1997; McWilliams and Siegel 1997).

The abnormal return reflects the stock market's reaction to the arrival of new information (McWilliams and Siegel 1997), such as a product recall announcement. It is estimated as

$$AR_{it} = R_{it} - (\hat{\alpha}_i + \hat{\beta}_i R_{mt}),$$

where

R_{it} = Return on the share price of firm i on day t,
R_{mt} = Return on the market portfolio of stocks on day t, and
$\hat{\alpha}_i, \hat{\beta}_i$ = OLS parameter estimates obtained from the regression of R_{it} on R_{mt} over the estimation period.

The parameter estimates α_i and β_i are based on the assumption that stock returns are linearly correlated with returns on the market portfolio over the estimation window:

$$R_{it} = \alpha_i + \beta_i R_{mt} + \varepsilon_{it},$$

where
α_i = intercept term,
β_i = systematic risk of stock i, and
ε_{it} = error term with $E(\varepsilon_{it}) = 0$.

The daily mean abnormal return on day t, $\overline{AR_t}$, is the average of the abnormal returns across the sample firms. The cumulative abnormal return over the event window (t_1, t_2), $AR(t_1, t_2)$, is the sum of the daily mean abnormal returns:

$$CAR(t_1, t_2) = \sum_{t=t_1}^{t_2} \overline{AR_t}.$$

The test statistic is the ratio of Day 0's mean abnormal return to its estimated standard deviation (Brown and Warner 1985):

$$\frac{\overline{AR_t}}{\hat{S}(\overline{AR_t})},$$

where

$$\overline{AR_t} = \frac{1}{N_t} \sum_{i=1}^{N_t} AR_{it},$$

$$\hat{S}(\overline{AR_t}) = \sqrt{\frac{\sum_{t=T_0}^{T_1} (\overline{AR_t} - \overline{AR})^2}{T_1 - T_0}}, \text{ and}$$

$$\overline{AR} = \frac{\sum_{t=T_0}^{T_1} \overline{AR_t}}{T_1 - T_0 + 1}.$$

The estimates α_i, β_i, and S_i^2 obtained above are then used to compute the normal return of stock i on each day t of the event period.

$$E(R_{it}) = \alpha_i + \beta_i \cdot R_{mt}$$

A t test is used to determine the statistical significance of the average cumulative abnormal return:

$$t = \sum_{i=1}^{N} \frac{\sum_{t=t_1}^{t=t_2} CAR_{it}}{\sqrt{\sum_{t=t_1}^{t=t_2} SD_{tt}^2}} \Big/ \sqrt{N}.$$

In Chapters 13, 14, and 15, event study methodology is applied to product recall announcements in several industries in China, recall announcements in the

U.S. toy industry, and recall announcements by retailers in the United States. The methodology described above is applied in all three chapters, in order to determine the reaction of the stock market to the announcement of a product recall. In this way, we examine the way that investors perceive the impact of a product recall on a company's future earnings potential.

References

Brown, S.J. and Warner, J.B. 1985. Using daily stock returns: The case of event studies. *Journal of Financial Economics*, 14(1), 3–31.

Chen, Y., Ganesan, S. and Liu, Y. 2009. Does a firm's product-recall strategy affect its financial value? An examination of strategic alternatives during product-harm crises. *Journal of Marketing*, 73(6), 214–226.

Corbett, C.J., Montes-Sancho, M.J. and Kirsch, D.A. 2005. The financial impact of ISO9000 certification in the United States: An empirical analysis. *Management Science*, 5(7), 1046–1059.

Davidson, W.N. and Worrell, D.L. 1992. The effect of product recall announcements on shareholder wealth. *Strategic Management Journal*, 13(6), 467–473.

Fama, E.F. 1970. Efficient capital markets: A review of theory and empirical work. *The Journal of Finance*, 25(2), 383–417.

Hendricks, K.B. and Singhal, V.R. 1996. Quality awards and the market value of the firm: An empirical investigation. *Management Science*, 42(3), 415–436.

Hendricks, K.B. and Singhal, V.R. 2003. The effect of supply chain glitches on shareholder wealth. *Journal of Operations Management*, 21(5), 501–522.

Hendricks, K.B. and Singhal, V.G. 2009a. Demand-supply mismatches and stock market reaction: Evidence from excess inventory announcements. *Manufacturing and Service Operations Management*, 11(3), 509–524.

Hendricks, K.B. and Singhal, V.G. 2009b. The effect of operational slack, diversification, and vertical relatedness on the stock market reaction to supply chain disruptions. *Journal of Operations Management*, 27(3), 233–242.

Hoffer, G.E., Pruitt, S.W. and Reilly, R.J. 1987. Automotive recalls and informational efficiency. *Financial Review*, 22(4), 433.

Klassen, R.D. and McLaughlin, C.P. 1996. The impact of environmental management on firm performance. *Management Science*, 42(8), 1199–1214.

Kothari, S.P. and Warner, J.B. 2007. *Econometrics of Event Studies*. North-Holland, Amsterdam: Elsevier.

MacKinlay, A.C. 1997. Event studies in economics and finance. *Journal of Economic Literature*, 35(1), 13–39.

McWilliams, A. and Siegel, D. 1997. Event studies in management research: Theoretical and empirical issues. *Academy of Management Journal*, 40(3), 626–657.

Peterson, P.P. 1989. Event studies: A review of issues and methodology. *Quarterly Journal of Business and Economics*, 28(3), 36.

Thirumalai, S. and Sinha, K.K. 2011. Product recalls in the medical device industry: An empirical exploration of the sources and financial consequences. *Management Science*, 57(2), 376–392.

Chapter 13

Impact of Product Recall Announcements on Shareholder Wealth in China*

Xiande Zhao, Yina Li, Barbara B. Flynn, and Stephen Ng

Contents

---

* Part of the content of this chapter comes from "Zhao, X., Li, Y. and Flynn, B. 2013. The financial impact of product recall announcements in China. *International Journal of Production Economics*. 142(1): 115–123."

13.1 Introduction: Background

Numerous researchers have examined the effect of a product recall announcement on shareholder wealth in the United States (Jarrell and Peltzman 1985; Pruitt and Peterson 1986; Hoffer et al. 1988; Bromiley and Marcus 1989; Chu et al. 2005). However, little research has been done on shareholder wealth effects of a product recall announcement in China. To bridge this gap, we collected secondary data from Chinese major security newspapers and websites and used event study methodology to unravel the financial impact of a product recall announcement on the shareholder wealth of the affected companies. We then compared the shareholder wealth effect of product recall announcements in China and the United States, examining the differential impact of product recall announcements in different industries. Finally, we investigated the possibility of a spillover effect to competitors, using the case of the melamine-tainted milk as an example.

13.2 Product Recall Announcements and Shareholder Wealth

A product recall announcement, like other types of negative publicity, can severely damage a firm's image and destroy investors' confidence, which will be reflected in the decline of its stock price. Table 13.1 summarizes the existing event study literature about product recall announcements in the United States. It reveals that a significant decline in shareholder wealth generally corresponds to a product recall announcement, although there are mixed results. For example, Jarrell and Peltzman (1985) found that the shareholders of firms producing recalled drugs and automobiles experienced losses that exceeded the direct cost of recalling the products; similarly, Pruitt and Peterson (1986) found a negative financial impact for nonautomobile product recalls. Chu et al. (2005) found that the drug and cosmetics industries suffered greater losses, while the rubber and automotive industries were less affected, and Hoffer et al. (1988) found "little evidence" of significant effects, after correcting some methodological problems and reanalyzing the data of Jarrell and Peltzman (1985). Bromiley and Marcus (1989) found that the negative returns associated with an automobile recall announcement were too small to prevent producers from providing defective automobiles, relative to the expected gains from doing so.

Another stream of research argues that the shareholder wealth effect might vary with the differing information content of announcements, including the severity of the safety issue (Reilly et al. 1983). For example, Thomsen and McKenzie (2001) found that a recall announcement of a product with a more serious hazard was associated

Table 13.1 Event Study Results for U.S. Product Recall Announcements

Author	Analysis Period	Sample Size	Industry	Abnormal Return on Day −1	Abnormal Return on Day 0
Jarrell and Peltzman (1985)	1967–1981	116	Automobile	−0.81%*** (−1, 1)	–
Pruitt and Peterson (1986)	1968–1983	156	Nonautomobile	−0.4%***	−0.363%***
Hoffer et al. (1987)	1970–1984	46	Severe automobile recall	−0.565%***	−0.093%
Bromiley and Marcus (1989)	1967–1983	119	Automobile	−0.32%*	−0.32%*
Davidson and Worrell (1992)	1968–1987	133	Nonautomobile	−0.36%***	−0.12%
Thomsen and McKenzie (2001)[a]	1992–1998	252 (Class 1) 189 (Class 2)	Meat and poultry	–	−0.4%** (Class 1) 0.2% (Class 2)
Chu et al. (2005)	1984–2003	269	Nonautomobile	−1.1%***	−0.6%*
Chen et al. (2009)[b]	1996–2007	24 (proactive recall) 65 (passive recall)	Consumer products	–	−0.6%** (proactive recall) 0.38% (passive recall)

[a] The samples for this study came from the Food Safety and Inspection Service. Hence, Day 0 is the announcement day.
[b] The samples for this study came from the Consumer Product Safety Commission. Hence, Day 0 is the announcement day.
*p < .10; **p < .05; ***p < .01.

with a significant loss, while that for products with less serious hazards had no negative impact. Davidson and Worrell (1992) found more significantly negative abnormal returns for recall announcements related to replacing or returning products, rather than repairing or checking them. They also found that government-ordered (passive) recalls were associated with greater losses than voluntary (proactive) recalls were (Rupp 2001). Passive recalls were not associated with greater shareholder losses; similarly, Chen et al. (2009) found that a proactive product recall announcement had a more negative effect on a firm's financial value than a passive recall announcement did. They explained their results in terms of the signaling effect of the recall announcement, with investors viewing a proactive recall announcement as a signal of larger impending future losses.

Whether a recall triggers a spillover effect to the shareholder wealth of competitors was another focus of previous studies. A spillover effect (Balachander and Ghose 2003) is the extent to which external information (e.g., a product recall announcement by a firm producing a similar product) changes attitudes about brands that were not directly involved. In other words, are consumers able to differentiate between brands, or do their concerns about one brand spill over (a negative spillover effect) to unaffected brands? On the other hand, might competitors benefit (a positive spillover effect) by becoming the substitute for a competitor's recalled product? The effect seems to be industry dependent, with a negative spillover effect in the drug and food industries (Jarrell and Peltzman 1985; Dowdell et al. 1992), but a positive spillover effect in the tire industry (Govindaraj et al. 2004).

As seen from the prior research, many studies have discussed and examined the short-term impact of product recall announcements on shareholder wealth in a Western context. However, little is known about the impact of a product recall announcement in the Chinese stock market. In order to advance the knowledge about the impact of product recalls, we studied Chinese product recall announcements using event study methodology and compared our findings with previous studies in Western stock markets.

13.3 Approach

We selected product recall announcements from companies whose common stock was publicly listed on either the Shenzhen or Shanghai A Share Stock Exchange. We searched for product recall announcements, using "recall," "return," "replace," and "take off the shelf" as key words. The sources included four Chinese major security newspapers designated by the China Securities Regulatory Commission (CSRC) to release news about Chinese publicly traded companies: *China Security Journal, Shanghai Securities News, Securities Daily*, and *Secutimes*. We also collected product recall announcements from the China Infobank database, which archives basic materials, important decisions, announcements, and reports of Chinese publicly traded companies in the Shenzhen and Shanghai stock exchanges, and the official website designated by the CSRC for releasing news about Chinese publicly traded companies (http://www.cninfo.com.cn). Information about automobile

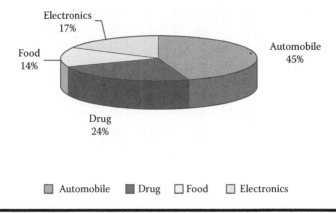

Figure 13.1   Industry distribution of product recall announcements.

Table 13.2   Descriptive Statistics

	Sales (Million RMB)	Total Assets (Million RMB)	Net Profit (Million RMB)	Employees
Mean	6,405.59	6,026.03	175.74	5101
Median	4,077.48	4,161.50	58.45	4244
SD	6,975.83	5,736.47	362.48	3957
Maximum	25,675.34	23,232.14	1,450.68	16,688
Minimum	178.79	569.42	−587.60	563

recall announcements was obtained from the official website of Chinese automobile recall administration (http://www.qiche365.org.cn/), which releases automobile recall news as part of the system mandated by the Chinese government in 2004.

We collected a total of 29 product recall announcements, covering the 2002–2008 time period, among which 13 were in the automobile industry, 7 were in the pharmaceutical industry, 5 were in the electronics industry, and 4 were in the food industry. The distribution of announcements by industry is shown in Figure 13.1, and descriptive statistics are contained in Table 13.2, based on the most recent fiscal year completed before the announcement was made.

13.4 Findings

13.4.1 Short-Term Event Study Results

Table 13.3 reveals that, on the announcement day (Day 0), there was a mean abnormal return of −0.22%, which was not statistically different from 0. Similarly, there

Table 13.3 Event Study Results for Chinese Publicly Traded Companies

Day	Abnormal Return			Cumulative Abnormal Return		
	Mean	Median	% Negative	Mean	Median	% Negative
−5	−0.15% (0.08)	−0.76% (−1.160)	58.62% (0.928)	–	–	–
−4	0.81% (1.00)	0.73% (−1.290)	34.48% (−1.671)	–	–	–
−3	0.50% (1.05)	−0.24% (−0.550)	55.17% (0.557)	–	–	–
−2	0.79% (1.32)	0.50% (−1.690*)	37.93% (−1.300)	–	–	–
−1	−0.39% (−0.83)	−1.00% (−0.465)	51.72% (0.186)	–	–	–
0	−0.22% (−0.73)	0.02% (−0.390)	46.15% (−0.392)	−0.22% (−0.076)	0.02% (−0.39)	46.15% (−0.392)
1	−2.81% (−5.20***)	−2.58% (−4.020***)	89.66% (4.271***)	−3.01% (−4.256***)	−2.60% (−3.644***)	82.76% (3.528***)

Note: t statistic for mean abnormal return, Wilcoxon signed-rank test Z statistic for the median abnormal return, and binomial sign test Z statistic for the % negative abnormal return are reported in parentheses.

* *p* < .10; *** *p* < .01.

were no statistically significant results for the median abnormal return and percentage of negative abnormal returns on Day 0. However, there were significant results on the day following the announcement day. The mean abnormal return on Day 1 was –2.81%, the median abnormal return was –2.58%, and the percentage of negative abnormal returns was 89.66%. The statistics in parentheses in Table 13.3 indicate that the probability of obtaining such a negative abnormal return by chance is less than 1%, supporting the idea that the negative abnormal return reflected a market reaction to the recall announcement. During the days before the announcement day (Day –5 to –1), the abnormal returns varied without statistical significance, driven by chance rather than economic factors (Wright et al. 1995). This suggests that the negative abnormal return on Day 1 can be attributed to the recall announcement, which was unanticipated by the stock market. Thus, a product recall announcement was associated with a negative stock price change; investors perceive a product recall announcement as a signal of looming financial losses for the firm. The cumulative abnormal returns provide further support for this finding.

13.4.2 Comparison of Shareholder Wealth Effects between China and the United States

Comparing Table 13.1 with Table 13.3, we can see that most previous research on product recall announcements in the United States found a significant negative abnormal return on Day –1, and some found significant negative abnormal returns on Day 0. In the case of China, however, we found a significant negative abnormal return only on Day 1. The reason for this may be that previous research set Day 0 to be the *Wall Street Journal* (*WSJ*) announcement date. However, recall announcements are often released to the public in the United States by the official websites* described in Chapter 1 on the day prior to their publication in *WSJ*, that is, Day –1. Therefore, investors would be expected to react on Day –1 or on Day 0 in cases where the announcement was released near, or after, the stock market close. In this situation, we would expect to see significant negative abnormal returns on both Day –1 and Day 0, since some announcements are reacted to on Day –1, while others are reacted to on Day 0 (Chu et al. 2005).

We set Day 0 to be the date on which the public first knew about the product harm crisis. For example, for the melamine-tainted milk crisis, we set September 16, 2008, to be Day 0, since this was the day that it was announced to the public on CCTV. However, investors had to wait until the next trading day, Day 1, to act on the news, since the stock market had already closed when the china central

---

* In the United States, all the recall announcements are released to the public first on the official websites of different agencies, including the National Highway Traffic Safety Administration (http://www.nhtsa.gov), Food and Drug Administration (http://www.fda.gov), Food Safety and Inspection Service (http://www.fsis.usda.gov), and Consumer Product Safety Commission (http://www.cpsc.gov).

television (CCTV) announcement was made. Thus, investors were unable to place a trade on Day 0.

Comparing Tables 13.1 and 13.3, we see that a recall announcement is related to greater financial losses in China compared with a recall announcement in the United States. One possible explanation is that, in the United States, the first product recalls occurred back in 1966, which is much earlier than the first product recalls in China. The U.S. infrastructure for product recalls is more mature, and its consumers are more accustomed to product recalls. Product recall announcements in the United States are almost always proactive, initiated by the company even though there have been no accidents, illnesses, or injuries; hence, consumers and investors may perceive these recalls as a signal of socially responsible action to proactively prevent potential hazards in the hands of consumers, rather than as potentially leading to substantial financial losses for the affected companies (Chen et al. 2009). Recalls are often for very minor safety issues, which consumers may perceive as trivial. Thus, a product recall announcement in the United States may be perceived as a signal of a firm's sincerity and diligence in attending to consumer safety issues, and socially responsible firms may be perceived as more likely to produce high-quality products (Siegel and Vitaliano 2007). This enhances consumer confidence in the firm's products, resulting in increases in future sales, which helps to alleviate the negative impact of the stock market reaction (Margolis et al. 2007; Chen et al. 2009).

Although it seemed that there were new stories in the United States about defective products and recalls practically every day in 2007–2008, all leading back to Chinese facilities (Lyles et al. 2008), there was very little news about product recalls in China during the same time period. For example, on March 12, 2009, the U.S. Department of Agriculture's Food Safety and Inspection Service released a recall announcement for a Class II hazard in drink products manufactured by the Khong Guan Corporation for products that did not meet product inspection or exemption requirements, even though no reports of illness had been received. However, in China, the products of the Khong Guan Corporation were not recalled. Thus, because product recalls are so unusual in China, consumers and investors may assume that there must be a severe product hazard that will result in substantial financial losses to the company. This causes the Chinese stock market to react more negatively to a product recall announcement.

13.4.3 Industry Effects

Another important question is whether recall announcements have a differential impact in different industries. Table 13.4 lists the mean standardized abnormal returns that were found in China on Day 1, by industry. It reveals that the food industry suffered more severe effects, while the automobile industry suffered less. This may be because defective food products can lead to serious and immediate health issues, while automotive defects, which are often due to minor issues like a

Table 13.4   Mean SAR on Day 1 by Industry

Industry	Mean SAR on Day 1
Automobile (*n* = 13)	−0.685
Drugs (*n* = 7)	−0.992
Electronics (*n* = 5)	−1.091
Food (*n* = 4)	−1.677

defective radio or window switch, seldom do. Also, because food is ubiquitous, the perception is that everybody is affected by tainted food products. Hence, a product recall announcement in the food industry has a greater negative impact. For example, after the announcement of the melamine-tainted milk powder crisis, many Chinese people stopped purchasing Chinese dairy products entirely. In contrast, automobiles were still a luxury good in China, where only 38 of every 1000 people owned an automobile in 2008 (Cui 2009). Thus, the impact of an automobile recall announcement in China would not be as substantial as it would be for a food product. Many Chinese automobile recalls were made proactively; thus, the perception of socially responsible action and diligence may mitigate the negative consequences of a product recall announcement on stock returns. However, all food product recalls in China were passive, in response to health-related incidents; thus, investors perceive a food recall announcement as a signal of a serious impending financial loss. Figure 13.2 illustrates the impact of product recall announcements in the food and automobile industries.

Another explanation for the industry effects may be the extent of global exposure by various industries in China. The entire network of organizations within which a firm is embedded is a social network (McFarland et al. 2008) that it is likely to imitate (Henisz and Delios 2001). Galaskiewicz and Wasserman (1989) found that firms not only imitate those organizations that they perceive to be successful in their own industry but are also likely imitate the organizations with which they have social ties, known as mimetic isomorphism in institutional theory. The social network for many Chinese automobile companies is composed of cooperative arrangements with foreign companies, as described in Chapters 9 and 10. For example, First Automotive Group Corporation works with international leaders, such as Volkswagen AG, Toyota, and Mazda, to establish strategic, long-term cooperative relationships. Chana Auto Co. Ltd. has joint ventures with Ford, Mazda, and Suzuki and has established several joint ventures in China. As a result of such cooperative activities, Chinese companies learn many things from their international partners, including corporate social responsibility. This may cause Chinese automobile companies to be more proactive in handling product defects than companies in other industries.

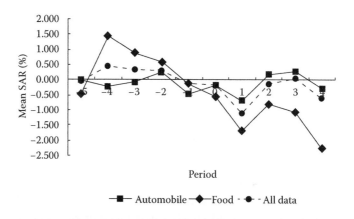

Figure 13.2 Mean standardized abnormal returns (SAR) by industry.

Researchers have long recognized the importance of institutional theory in explaining firm behavior. Government regulation drives coercive isomorphism (DiMaggio and Powell 1983; Ketokivi and Schroeder 2004; McFarland et al. 2008). Chinese government legislation of the automobile industry has led it to take a more proactive stance about product safety and consumer protection. In contrast, almost all food recalls in China have been passive, initiated only in response to consumer complaints or incidents.

Barriers to entry are relatively high in China's automobile industry. Most automobile companies are large, as are their suppliers. "Their supply-network structure will take on a more formalized face that comes with the more standardized configuration of the work procedures of ERP" (Choi and Hong 2002, p. 490). Because of this, traceability and process control are relatively easier in the automobile industry, with its well-established information systems. Furthermore, because each automobile is discrete and has a unique identity vehicle identification number (VIN), it is easier to recall a particular set of automobiles. Because of this, automobile companies may be more willing to employ a proactive recall strategy.

However, the situation in the food industry is quite different. There are many tiers in the food supply chain, "from farm to fork." Food is usually traced by batches, instead of as discrete items (Jansen-Vullers et al. 2003). As described in Chapter 6, raw material batches from different suppliers are often mixed together, making it impossible to trace a quality problem back to its source (Wang et al. 2009). Hence, it is very difficult to use top-down quality control to "trace and follow food, feed and ingredients through all stages of production, processing and distribution" (Wang et al. 2009, p. 2), which increases the number of potentially recalled products.

13.4.4 Recall Strategy Effects

Investors may react differently to a product recall announcement, depending on the actions and strategies followed by a company in releasing the announcement (Chen et al. 2009). Siomkos and Kurzbard (1994) divided company responses into four types: denial, involuntary recall, voluntary recall, and super-effort. Chen et al. (2009) identified proactive and passive recall strategies and identified antecedents that influence a firm's choice of recall strategy, including firm size, reputation, and the volume of recalled product.

We define a proactive recall announcement as one that is initiated by a firm that takes initial action without receiving any complaint from consumers or mandate from a government agency. Otherwise, we define the recall strategy as passive. When we examined product recall announcements in China, we found that most automobile industry recalls had been proactive, while other industries almost always followed a passive recall strategy. Figure 13.3 shows the frequency distribution of recall strategies by industry. As Table 13.5 and Figure 13.4 illustrate, companies following a passive recall strategy suffered significantly greater negative abnormal returns. Thus, investors were more concerned about a product recall announcement that followed a passive strategy.

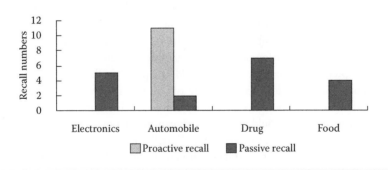

Figure 13.3 Frequency distribution recall strategy by industry.

Table 13.5 Mean SAR on Day 1 by Recall Strategy

Recall Strategy	Mean SAR on Day 1
Proactive ($n = 11$)	−0.569
Passive ($n = 18$)	−1.208

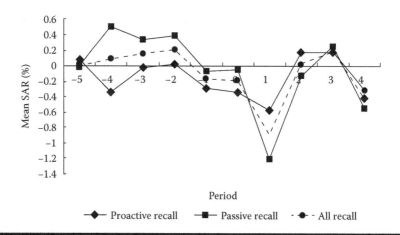

Figure 13.4 Mean standardized abnormal returns (SAR) for different recall strategies.

13.5 Melamine-Tainted Dairy Product Recalls

During the melamine-tainted dairy product recall, it was evident that the market performance of the companies producing tainted milk products was negatively affected. Mengniu Dairy's stock price plummeted from HK$20.00 to HK$7.95 (60.25%) in a single day, on September 23, 2008, upon initial reporting of the tainted milk powder, and the stock price of Synutra International Inc. (SYUT) plummeted from $33.61 to $15.29 (54.51%) on September 16, 2008. The expected market reaction to the stock prices of competitors not found to have melamine in their milk, however, was more difficult to predict. On one hand, there could be a positive effect on the stock prices of competitors, which would reap the benefit of customers' switching to their products. On the other hand, the public could lose confidence in the entire dairy products industry, and the government could put more stringent regulations on it; hence, there could be a negative spillover effect to competitors (Jarrell and Peltzman 1985).

We studied the six publicly traded Chinese dairy product companies,* including Yili, Bright Dairy Group, and Sanyuan, which are listed on the China A Share Stock Exchange; Mengniu, which is listed on the Hong Kong Stock Exchange; and SYUT and American Dairy, Inc., which are listed on the New York Stock Exchange. Yili, Bright Dairy Group, Mengniu, and SYUT were found to have melamine in their milk, while Sanyuan and American Dairy were not. Since the Chinese government released the melamine investigation results on September 16, 2008, we selected this date to be Day 0. Because SYUT and American Dairy are listed in the United States, we set September 15, 2008, to be Day 0 for them, due to the time difference between

---

* Although the Sanlu group is at the heart of the tainted milk scandal and its products were found to contain the highest level of melamine contamination, it is not a publically traded company, so its stock price information was not available.

Table 13.6 Abnormal Returns of Chinese Dairy Companies[a]

	Abnormal Returns					
	Affected Companies				Competitors	
Day	Yili	Mengniu	Bright Dairy	SYUT	Sanyuan	ADY
-5	2.12%	-1.60%	-2.61%	1.72%	-5.49%	1.08%
-4	2.12%	0.10%	2.66%	-4.73%	2.16%	3.19%
-3	-0.47%	2.97%	1.47%	0.46%	0.59%	-2.48%
-2	2.22%	-3.87%*	3.22%	-1.99%	0.63%	-4.12%
-1	-1.24%	-3.64%*	-2.86%	-1.84%	0.09%	-12.31%***
0	-1.79%	5.11%**	-2.04%	-23.21%***	-6.03%	-6.52%
1	-7.36%***	-56.28%***	-6.23%**	-56.51%***	5.50%	28.02%***
2	-8.55%***	2.06%	-1.29%	-1.02%	11.44%***	1.41%
3	-6.50%***	3.06%	0.07%	-8.49%**	5.69%	6.56%
4	-8.67%***	-0.53%	-7.99%***	10.12%***	6.40%	0.94%
5	-9.98%***	-2.52%	9.07%***	32.62%***	11.20%***	4.10%

[a] Since these companies are listed in different stock markets, we used different market indexes as market returns to control systematic risk and compute the abnormal returns for different companies. We used the Shanghai composite index for Yili, Bright Dairy, and Sanyuan; the Hang Seng China Enterprises (HSCE) index for Mengniu; the Nasdaq index for SYUT; and the Dow Jones Industrial Average (DJS) index for ADY.

* $p < .10$; ** $p < .05$; *** $p < .01$.

Table 13.7 60-Day Cumulative Abnormal Returns of Chinese Dairy Companies

| | Cumulative Abnormal Returns | | | | | |
| | Affected Companies | | | | Competitors | |
Day	Yili	Mengniu	Bright Dairy	SYUT	Sanyuan[a]	ADY
0	-1.79%	5.11%**	-2.04%	-23.21%***	-6.03%	-6.52%
1	-9.15%***	-51.17%***	-8.27%**	-79.72%***	-0.53%	21.50%***
2	-17.70%***	-49.11%***	-9.56%**	-80.73%***	10.92%	22.92%***
3	-24.21%***	-46.05%***	-9.49%*	-89.23%***	16.60%*	29.48%***
4	-32.88%***	-46.58%***	-17.48%***	-79.11%***	23.00%**	30.42%***
5	-42.87%***	-49.10%***	-8.41%	-46.49%***	34.21%***	34.52%***
6	-40.18%***	-46.85%***	-3.14%	-31.39%***	44.22%***	34.84%***
7	-29.56%***	-45.26%***	-3.30%	-40.61%***	52.81%***	29.00%**
8	-34.98%***	-37.85%***	3.09%	-47.61%***	–	26.90%**
9	-38.08%***	-27.55%***	-0.68%	-47.17%***	–	23.22%*
10	-45.43%***	-28.50%***	-4.10%	-37.41%***	–	33.21%**
11	-52.16%***	-26.17%***	-5.55%	-44.00%***	–	34.87%***

12	−39.73%***	−27.37%***	−5.24%	−38.68%***	–	52.44%***
13	−45.55%***	−34.11%***	8.38%	−28.66%***	–	56.18%***
14	−46.21%***	−36.59%***	4.15%	−26.44%**	–	56.65%***
15	−43.68%***	−33.44%***	4.59%	−21.94%	–	57.80%***
……						
51	−34.73%**	−29.17%*	21.30%	−47.48%*	–	99.47%***
52	−36.46%**	−28.37%*	22.30%	−48.29%*	–	102.15%***
53	−29.81%*	−27.98%*	22.68%	−47.47%*	–	105.17%***
54	−32.66%*	−20.52%	26.35%	−57.24%**	–	103.03%***
55	−34.57%**	−23.95%	25.36%	−55.35%**	–	102.97%***
56	−34.86%**	−29.79%*	24.40%	−60.09%**	–	105.95%***
57	−33.80%*	−27.24%*	22.51%	−61.57%**	–	103.82%***
58	−34.13%*	−27.48%*	25.04%	−59.50%**	–	101.93%***
59	−36.30%**	−25.36%	26.82%	−54.85%**	–	94.40%***

[a] Sanyuan experienced a trading halt on September 26, 2008, after getting six days continuous raising limits. Then it considered to acquire the Sanlu group.

$*p < .10$; $**p < .05$; $***p < .01$.

China and the United States. The results of the analysis of abnormal returns and the post-announcement stock price performance of the 60-day cumulative abnormal returns for these six companies are provided in Tables 13.6 and 13.7.

13.5.1 Effects on the Companies with Tainted Milk

The abnormal returns before the announcement day (Day –5 to –1) varied randomly and without statistical significance, indicating that they were driven by chance. Thus, the melamine-tainted milk incident was unanticipated before the recall announcement. Table 13.6 shows that, on Day 1, all of the dairy companies with melamine contamination experienced a highly significant negative abnormal return, especially Mengniu and SYUT, which had a negative abnormal return that exceeded 50%. Due to the 10% up-and-down price limit policy in the Chinese stock market,* we did not capture as great a negative abnormal return for Yili and Bright, which are listed on the China A Share Stock Exchange, compared with Mengniu, which is listed on the Hong Kong Stock Exchange, or SYUT, which is listed on the New York Stock Exchange. However, from the cumulative abnormal return results in Table 13.7, we can see that, for a 60-day event window, Yili suffered a more negative abnormal return than Mengniu did. This indicates that the limited stock price fluctuations in 1 day were reflected in the following trading days.

13.5.2 Spillover Effect to Competitors

Tables 13.6 and 13.7 also show the results for the competitors. The stock prices of American Dairy and Sanyuan, which were not involved in the melamine scandal, experienced significant positive abnormal returns on Days 1 and 2. The positive cumulative abnormal returns of the Sanyuan group on Day 7 was more than 50%, after which a trade halt was imposed due to its pending merger with and acquisition of the Sanlu group. The 60-day cumulative abnormal returns for American Dairy doubled, providing strong evidence that competitor firms benefitted from the recall.

Figure 13.5 shows the 60-day cumulative abnormal returns. From Table 13.7 and Figure 13.5, we can see that, in the 60-day event window, the affected companies, other than Bright Dairy, experienced significant negative cumulative abnormal returns.

---

* Since December 16, 1996, the stock price fluctuations of all the stocks traded in Shenzhen and Shanghai stock exchanges have been limited into ±10% per day.

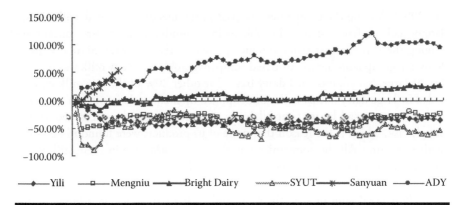

Figure 13.5   60-Day cumulative abnormal returns of Chinese dairy companies.

13.5.3 Strategic Supply Chain Design

The speed of recovery for Bright Dairy was much quicker than for the other affected dairy companies (see the last column of Table 13.2). From Table 13.3 and Figure 13.1, we can see that, in the 60-day event window, the affected companies, other than Bright Dairy, experienced significant negative cumulative abnormal returns. While Bright's stock price recovered from Day 5 until Day 59, its cumulative abnormal return was 26.82%. Although this was not significantly different from zero, it shows that Bright Dairy had recovered from the melamine-tainted milk crisis, to some extent. There are two possible explanations for this. The first is related to Bright Dairy's strategic supply chain design. Bright Dairy purchased only 5% of its raw milk from small-scale independent farmers in the spot market, while the other 95% was supplied by vertically integrated and closely related suppliers. Hence, the fewest detected problems were found in Bright Dairy's products. After the melamine scandal, Bright Dairy refused to accept any raw milk from small-scale independent farmers. The second reason for Bright's relatively speedy recovery is related to its quality assurance system. Bright Dairy had invested substantially in establishing a quality assurance system that ensured quality and traceability, as described in Chapter 11. By doing these things, Bright Dairy enhanced its customers' confidence in its products, thus helping it to recover more quickly from the product harm crisis.

Different types of dairy companies have different raw milk supply modes. More than 80% of the raw milk used by the resource-based companies was provided by small-scale farmers scattered across the country and gathered through independent milk collection stations (Ding 2009). In contrast, 95% of the raw milk used by Bright (an urban-based company) was provided by Bright-owned large dairy farms and small dairy farm complexes; only 5% of the raw milk was provided by small-scale farmers

(Li 2008). Among the companies involved in the melamine-tainted milk scandal, Bright had the fewest detected problems in its products; most were concentrated among the three largest dairy product producers (Ding 2009). Similarly, in the Sanyuan group (another urban-based company), 80% of the raw milk was provided by the large, Sanyuan-owned dairy base. The other 20% of the raw milk was provided by large dairy farms, with none supplied by small-scale farmers (Yang 2009). Thus, Sanyuan had better controllability of its raw material sources, reducing its supply risk, which is the reason that none of its products were found to be tainted with melamine. All the companies found to have melamine in their milk experienced a significant abnormal return, and each of them

1. Purchased some or all of their raw milk from small-scale independent farmers
2. Had less vertical integration
3. Did not have a close relationship with outside suppliers in their supply chain governance structure
4. Invested less in prevention cost
5. Invested less in appraisal cost

The situation was quite different for the companies that did not experience melamine contamination, American Dairy and the Sanyuan Group. All of the raw milk for American Dairy and the Sanyuan Group is supplied by cooperative dairy farms and corporate-owned dairy farms. The more vertical integration and the closer the relationship with a few large outside suppliers is, the more information about quality the company will know. This means that it will invest more in in interorganization and intraorganization quality assurance systems designed to prevent and appraise quality risks, which will reduce potential quality risks and reduce failure costs and thus improve the bottom line. The stock prices for American Dairy and Sanyuan had significant positive abnormal returns, providing strong evidence that competitor firms benefited from the recall and that dairy products are perceived as substitutable and replaceable by the products of competitors. Thus, there was a positive spillover effect for the competitors of the affected companies, indicating that investors and customers could differentiate between the companies and that they were confident that the unaffected companies would continue to produce high-quality, safe dairy products.

13.6 Conclusions

This study investigates the shareholder wealth effects of a product recall announcement in China. We found significant negative abnormal returns on the day following the announcement, which indicates that the stock market reacts quickly and efficiently to a recall announcement. Our findings further revealed that the negative abnormal returns in the China market are generally larger than those in the United States. The use of different recall strategies and actions between the United States and China provides a possible explanation for the results.

Our results also reveal that companies in the food industry experience a more severe reaction to a recall announcement and that food recalls in China have always been a result of consumer illnesses. Thus, companies in the Chinese food industry employ a passive recall strategy. In contrast, companies in the automobile industry are more likely to recall a car proactively, before there have been any accidents. In the case of the melamine-tainted milk recall incidents in China, while all of the affected companies suffered from significant negative financial losses, we found that there was a positive spillover effect occurring for competitors, such that their sales benefitted from the recalls.

A limitation of our study is the relatively small sample size of 29 recall announcements, which was necessary because recalls are such a recent phenomenon in China, and consumer protection systems are relatively immature. Although additional product recalls have occurred in nonpublicly traded companies in China, there is no stock price information available for them. However, the use of small sample sizes is common in the literature on the relationship between recall announcements and stock prices. For example, 28 pharmaceutical recall cases were used by Dowdell et al. (1992) in their examination of the spillover effect of the Tylenol recall. Govindaraj et al. (2004) used the case of Firestone Tires and Ford Explorer's product recall and two competitors, and ten pharmaceutical recall cases in the United Kingdom were used in the study of Cheah et al. (2007).

There are a number of relevant directions for future research. First, while this study addresses the recall issue from the shareholder perspective, it may be fruitful to examine this issue from a customer perspective. Without the availability of secondary data, different methodologies, such as experiments and surveys, may be helpful. Second, some in-depth matched case studies for the same industries in China and the United States should be conducted to determine differing reactions of customers, government, and the stock market during a product harm crisis, exploring the underpinning of these differences between China and the United States. Finally, development of an effective supply chain quality management system, in order to prevent the recurrence of product recalls, is becoming increasingly imperative.

Acknowledgments

This study was supported by the Centre for Supply Chain Management & Logistics, Li & Fung Institute of Supply Chain Management & Logistics.

References

Balachander, S. and S. Ghose. 2003. Reciprocal spillover effects: A strategic benefit of brand extensions. *J. Mktg.* 67(1): 4–13.

Bromiley, P. and A. Marcus. 1989. The deterrent to dubious corporate behavior: Profitability, probability and safety recalls. *Strat. Mgmt. J.* 10(3): 233–250.

Cheah, E.T., W.L. Chan, and C.L. Chieng. 2007. The corporate social responsibility of pharmaceutical product recalls: An empirical examination of U.S. and U.K. markets. *J. Bus. Ethics* 76(4): 427–449.

Chen, Y., S. Ganesan, and Y. Liu. 2009. Does a firm's product recall strategy affect its financial value? An examination of strategic alternatives during product-harm crises. *J. Mktg.* 73(6): 214–226.

Choi, T.Y. and Y. Hong. 2002. Unveiling the structure of supply networks: Case studies in Honda, Acura, and Daimler Chrysler. *J. Ops. Mgmt.* 20(5): 469–493.

Chu, T.H., C.C. Lin, and L.J. Prather. 2005. An extension of security price reactions around product recall announcements. *Q. J. Bus. Econ.* 44(3/4): 33–48.

Cui, J. 2009. The owned automobile per 1000 people in China is much lower than developed countries [online]. Available from: http://news.xinhuanet.com/video/2009-03/06/content_10956617.htm (Accessed March 6, 2009).

Davidson, W.N. and D.L. Worrell. 1992. The effect of product recall announcements on shareholder wealth. *Strat. Mgmt. J.* 13(6): 467–473.

DiMaggio, P.J. and W.W. Powell. 1983. The iron cage revisited: Institutional isomorphism and collective rationality in organizaitonal fields. *Am. Soc. Rev.* 48(2): 147–160.

Ding, L. 2009. Bright Dairy should have a turnaround [online]. Available from://finance.jrj.com.cn/2009/01/214503391111.shtml (Accessed January 20, 2009).

Dowdell, T.D., S. Govindaraj, and P.C. Jain. 1992. The Tylenol incident, ensuing regulation, and stock prices. *J. Fin. Quant. Anal.* 27(2): 283–301.

Galaskiewicz, J. and S. Wasserman. 1989. Mimetic processes within an interorganizational field: An empirical test. *Adm. Sci. Q.* 34(3): 454–479.

Govindaraj, S., B. Jaggi, and B. Lin. 2004. Market overreaction to product recall revisited— The case of Firestone tires and the Ford Explorer. *Rev. Quant. Fin. Acctg.* 23(1): 31–54.

Henisz, W.J. and A. Delios. 2001. Uncertainty, imitation, and plant location: Japanese multinational corporations, 1990–1996. *Adm. Sci. Q.* 46(3): 443–475.

Hoffer, G.E., S.W. Pruitt, and R.J. Reilly. 1987. Automotive recalls and informational efficiency. *Fin. Rev.* 22(4): 433–442.

Hoffer, G.E., S.W. Pruitt, and R.J. Reilly. 1988. The impact of product recalls on the wealth of sellers: A reexamination. *J. Pol. Econ.* 96(3): 663–670.

Jansen-Vullers, M.H., C.Q. Van Dorp, and A.J. Beulens. 2003. Managing traceability information in manufacture. *Int. J. Info. Mgmt.* 23(5): 395–413.

Jarrell, G. and S. Peltzman. 1985. The impact of product recalls on the wealth of sellers. *J. Pol. Econ.* 93(3): 512–536.

Ketokivi, M.A. and R.G. Schroeder. 2004. Strategic, structural contingency and institutional explanations in the adoption of innovative manufacturing practices. *J. Op. Mgmt.* 22(1): 63–89.

Li, R. 2008. Bright Dairy: Neither building new factory nor expanding the scale of production without qualified milk sources [online]. Available from: http://jjckb.xinhuanet.com/gnyw/2008-10/30/content_125338.htm (Accessed October 30, 2008).

Lyles, M.A., B.B. Flynn, and M.T. Frohlich. 2008. All supply chains don't flow through: Understanding supply chain issues in product recalls. *Mgmt. Ops. Rev.* 4(2): 167–182.

Margolis, J.D., H. Elfenbein, and J. Walsh. 2007. Does it pay to be good? A meta-analysis and redirection of research on corporate social and financial performance. Working paper.

McFarland, R.G., J.M. Bloodgood, and J.M. Payan. 2008. Supply chain contagion. *J. Mktg.* 72(2): 63–79.

Pruitt, S.W. and D.R. Peterson. 1986. Security price reactions around product recall announcements. *J. Fin. Res.* 9(2): 113–122.

Reilly, R.J., G.E. Hoffer, and E. George. 1983. Will retarding the information flow on automobile recalls affect consumer demand? *Econ. Inquiry* 21(3): 444–447.

Rupp, N.G. 2001. Are government initiated recalls more damaging for shareholders? Evidence from automotive recalls, 1973–1998. *Econ. Lett.* 71(2): 265–270.

Siegel, D.S. and D.F. Vitaliano. 2007. An empirical analysis of the strategic use of corporate social responsibility. *J. Econ. Mgmt. Strat.* 16(3): 773–792.

Siomkos, G.J. and G. Kurzbard. 1994. The hidden crisis in product-harm crisis management. *Eur. J. Mktg.* 28(2): 30–41.

Thomsen, M.R. and A.M. McKenzie. 2001. Market incentives for safe foods: An examination of shareholder losses from meat and poultry recalls. *Am. J. Agri. Econ.* 83(3): 526–538.

Wang, X., D. Li, and C. O'Brien. 2009. Optimisation of traceability and operations planning: An integrated model for perishable food production. *Int. J. Prod. Res.* 47(11): 2865–2886.

Yang, S.J. 2009. Sanyuan: Keep on "Sanyuan Mode," control product quality strictly [online]. Available from: http://www.bj.xinhuanet.com/bjpd-wq/2009-03/04/content_16505202.htm (Accessed March 4, 2009).

Wright, P., S.P. Ferris, J.S. Hiller, and M. Kroll. 1995. Competitiveness through management of diversity: Effects on stock price valuation. *Acad. Mgmt. J.* 38(1): 272–287.

Chapter 14

Impact of Toy Product Recalls on Shareholder Wealth in the United States

John Z. Ni, Barbara B. Flynn, and F. Robert Jacobs

Contents

14.1 Introduction: Background

This chapter examines the effect of a toy recall announcement on shareholder wealth. Toys are an especially interesting product to study because toy consumers are usually not the ultimate customers. Parents and other adults typically purchase toys, acting as agents for their children. Toy product safety issues loom large in the minds of adult customers, while having little or no impact on the perception of the consumers (children).

We apply event study methodology to compute the abnormal returns around the date when a toy product recall was announced, using data from the Consumer Product Safety Commission (CPSC). To explain the difference in abnormal returns, we use regression analysis to examine a number of firm- and recall-related characteristics. We provide a theoretical explanation for these phenomena, developing new insights about the factors associated with the effect of a product recall announcement.

14.2 Factors in the Impact of a Toy Recall Announcement

14.2.1 Effect of Brand

Major toymakers like Mattel manage a vast collection of brands, such as Barbie, Hot Wheels, Fisher-Price, and Matchbox (Johnson 2001). In addition, many of their products use licensed characters, such as Winnie the Pooh, Barney, or the Muppets (Clark 2007). The proliferation of these licensing arrangements can obscure the link between a toy's brand (Winnie the Pooh) and the company that owns the brand (Mattel). This may affect purchasing behavior. For example, if there is a recall of Barbie dolls, customers may stop buying Barbie dolls but would probably not stop buying other Mattel dolls, such as American Girl dolls. Therefore, the stock performance of a company that announces a toy product recall may not fluctuate as much as the stock performance for an automobile company, where the link between an automaker (Toyota) and its brands is highly evident.

Brand loyalty may be an important factor in customer behavior following a recall announcement, building on the brand and brand equity literature (Aaker 1991, 1996; Dawar and Lei 2009; Keller 1993, 2003; Leone et al. 2006; Smith et al. 1996). Brand loyalty is at the core of a brand's equity because the presence of loyal customers reduces the risk of competitive actions by rival companies. In the case of a product recall, however, customers' purchase habits are broken, resulting in their need to purchase a different brand as a replacement. Therefore, established brand loyalty may crumble as a result of a recall, which would affect the company's future revenue. On the other hand, children (the consumers of toys) may not be willing to accept a substitute for a toy with a strong brand, such as Barbie or Hot Wheels.

A product recall announcement can also change customer perceptions about brand quality. Because customers do not have all the information necessary to make a rational, objective judgment about product quality, they tend to rely on a few salient cues that they associate with quality. The perceived quality of a brand provides them with a reason for deciding which brands to consider. However, a product recall provides a strong negative cue about brand quality. Perceived quality is also meaningful to retailers, distributors, and other supply chain members. To minimize damage to their own brand equity, retailers and distributors may disassociate themselves from the manufacturer and its brand by reducing future ordering, which further reduces the future revenues for the manufacturer.

Thus, a recall announcement devaluates a company's brand equity by decreasing brand loyalty and perceived quality, thereby reducing future revenues. The reduced future cash flow caused by a product recall announcement is reflected in its stock price (Fama 1970; Ross 1983). Thus, our first hypothesis is as follows:

H_1: The announcement of a toy recall will be associated with a negative stock market reaction.

14.2.2 Effect of Source Transparency

Attribution theory posits that people look for the causes of events (Weiner 1989), especially unexpected and negative events like a product recall announcement (Coombs 2007). When product performance fails to meet customers' expectations, they try to assign attribution for the product failure. During a product recall, the manufacturer has more information about the magnitude and nature of the problem than investors do, resulting in information asymmetry between them. However, investors can influence the stock price through their buying or selling behavior, rewarding or penalizing the company.

Agency theory (Laffont and Martimort 2002) provides an explanation for the way that asymmetric information impacts the shareholder wealth of a company that has announced a product recall. According to agency theory, a principal–agent relationship is present whenever one party (the principal) depends on another party (the agent) to undertake some action on the principal's behalf (Bergen et al. 1992). In a financial market, stockholders (the principal), who are the firm's owners, delegate day-to-day management to the manager (the agent), who has better information about actual business conditions (Laffont and Martimort 2002). Information is asymmetric to the extent that the principal is unable to observe and verify the actions that the agent has taken (Bergen et al. 1992; Eisenhardt 1989). This causes the principal to have uncertainty about the agent. To reduce it, the principal can induce the agent to exert greater effort by providing rewards, such as the stock market's pricing structure. The magnitude of incentives is in proportion to the principal's level of uncertainty about the agent (Laffont and Martimort 2002). Since financial market incentives are usually expressed as the change in abnormal returns, the uncertainty associated with a product recall announcement influences how investors react. For example, they may be uncertain about which company ultimately manufactured a branded product (Mattel? Winnie the Pooh? a Chinese subcontractor?) and its reputation. Disclosure of information about the manufacturing source can help mitigate this uncertainty, and, indeed, customers and government agencies have begun to be more demanding about requiring details about the sources (New 2010).

We define source transparency as the amount of information about the manufacturing source that is available to customers and investors. Investors typically obtain their information about publicly traded manufacturers through quarterly or annual reports. However, for a privately held or overseas manufacturer, such information is sparse, unless the company voluntarily discloses it. As a result, source transparency is higher (uncertainty is lower) for a publicly traded manufacturer than it is for privately held or overseas manufacturers. On the basis of these arguments, we make the following hypothesis:

H_2: The stock market's reaction to a product recall announcement will be more negative for toys made by privately held or overseas manufacturers than for those made by publicly traded manufacturers.

14.2.3 Effect of Firm Size

Firm size is often used as an explanatory variable in operations management research (Hendricks and Singhal 2001, 2003, 2005a; Hendricks et al. 1995; Klassen and McLaughlin 1996). The relationship between firm size and innovation is especially relevant to this research. Damanpour's (1992) meta-analysis of 53 studies revealed a consistently positive relationship between firm size and innovation; larger firms have an R&D advantage because of the larger output over which they can spread the high fixed costs of their R&D (Cohen and Klepper 1996). Through innovation, larger firms are able to develop diversified product offerings and better production technology. Therefore, we posit that the negative impact of a product recall announcement will be more severe for smaller firms, which are likely to be more focused, with profitability that is critically dependent on the quality of their limited set of products (Hendricks and Singhal 2003).

The more negative effect of a product recall announcement on smaller firms may also be related to distribution factors. Managing a product recall relies on the seamless operation of a firm's supply chain network, including retailers, distribution centers, transportation carriers, and suppliers (Tibben-Lembke and Rogers 2002). The costs of the reverse distribution channels used in a product recall are higher than for forward distribution (Jayaraman et al. 2003) due to the smaller quantities, fluctuating and uncertain demand, and the urgency with which the channels must operate during a product safety crisis (Min 1989).

There are also information systems explanations for the size effect. Previous studies have shown that firm size is highly correlated with the sophistication of information technology (Hill and Scudder 2002). Smaller firms are expected to incur higher recall costs because their supply chain networks are less well integrated. In addition, smaller firms have less clout to influence and change the behavior of their supply chain partners, which could help them recover, following a product recall (Hendricks and Singhal 2003). Thus, our first hypothesis regarding firm size is as follows:

H_{3a}: The stock market's reaction to a product recall announcement will be more negative for smaller firms than for larger firms.

There may also be a source transparency effect related to size. Transaction cost economics (TCE) theory suggests that firm size is associated with source transparency (Williamson 1985, 1996). Because they may lack supporting resources and economies of scale, smaller firms experience higher transaction costs, in the form of search and contracting costs, as they search for supply chain partners. Unlike larger firms, which have specialized staff for marketing, supply chain, and legal affairs, smaller firms may have greater difficulty finding capable suppliers. In addition, smaller firms are less likely to command a volume discount due to their lower sales volumes. Opportunistic behavior provides an additional reason why transaction costs are higher for smaller firms (Brown et al. 2000). Because larger firms deal with a wider set of suppliers, they are better able to deal with the opportunistic behavior of a supplier, since it can be compensated for by transactions with other partners; this also contributes to lower transaction costs (Nooteboom 1993). Thus, we suggest that larger firms are more likely to outsource their production to overseas or privately held manufacturers because of their lower transactions costs, reducing source transparency. Our second hypothesis about firm size is as follows:

H_{3b}: Source transparency mediates the effect of firm size on the stock market's reaction to a product recall announcement.

14.2.4 Effect of Degree of Product Hazard

Previous researchers have shown that customers and investors may react differently to an announcement of a product recall, based on the hazard level of the safety issue that precipitated the announcement. Hoffer et al. (1994) found that owners of vehicles recalled for more severe defects were more likely to respond to a recall announcement, while the cumulative abnormal returns following a pharmaceutical product recall increased as the level of hazard increased (Cheah et al. 2007). Prospect theory (Kahneman and Tversky 1979) provides an explanation, describing how the response to loss is more extreme than the response to gain, due to loss aversion, where a change for the worse looms larger than an equivalent change for the better (Novemsky and Kahneman 2005; Tversky and Kahneman 1991). When there is a product recall announcement, investors' disutility increases rapidly as the severity of product hazard worsens, due to their loss aversion.

An alternative explanation is that a recall announcement for a higher level of product hazard will receive substantially more media attention because the media pays selective attention to news (Hoffman and Ocasio 2001). An important criterion in its selection of which stories to publicize is the amount of attention the stories are likely to attract (Rhee and Haunschild 2006); an attention-grabbing event is more likely to be reported in the news (Barber and Odean 2008). A recall of a product for a more severe hazard is more likely to be reported, not only because it is newsworthy but also because it promptly alerts a large number of consumers to stop using the recalled product. Several news stories about product recall announcements illustrate this. Mattel's recall of Polly Pocket toys in 2006 for a severe hazard was reported 38 times in major public media, including CNN, NBC, ABC, and the *Washington Post*, within 2 days of the initial announcement. In contrast, Wal-Mart's recall of stuffed Christmas beagles for a minor hazard around the same time was mentioned only once in the mass media. Greater media coverage reduces customer confidence about the product, making them more hesitant to buy toys from the company in the future. Investors note this, and the loss in future revenue will be reflected by a drop in stock price. Thus, we hypothesize the following:

H_4: The greater the degree of hazard of the recalled product, the more negative the stock market's reaction to a product recall announcement will be.

Our conceptual model showing the impact of product recalls is depicted in Figure 14.1.

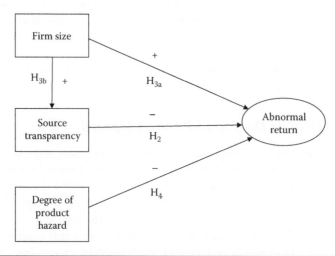

Figure 14.1   Conceptual model of the impact of a product recall announcement.

14.3 Approach

14.3.1 Recall Announcement Data

We searched for announcement dates (Day 0 in event time) between 2000 and 2009 on the CPSC website, as well as the earliest reporting date and time by major public media such as Dow Jones Newswire, *Wall Street Journal*, and the Associated Press. We focused on companies whose common stock was listed on either the New York or American Stock Exchange, permitting the use of the Center for Research in Security Prices (CRSP; at the University of Chicago) stock return data. We used an estimation window of 210 trading days, from Day –255 through Day –46, to estimate the normal return. If the media reported a recall before the market closed on the day of the CPSC announcement, we had a 1-day event window. However, if the report was made after the market closed, the next trading day was included in the event window, and thus, we would have a 2-day event window (0, +1) (Figure 14.2).

In order to ensure that the event windows for the announcements did not overlap in calendar time (MacKinlay 1997), we randomly selected one announcement to include. If multiple product recalls were announced by the same company on the same day, we aggregated their quantities and dollar values. We excluded any announcement where the company experienced other contemporaneous newsworthy events within the event window.

Our initial sample was 141 announcements. After exclusion of companies that did not have data prior to the recall date or were missing data in Compustat, the final sample size for the regression analysis was 127. For the postannouncement performance analysis, we excluded any announcement that was followed by another recall by the same company in less than 60 trading days, in order to control for potential confounding effects. Thus, the final sample for the postannouncement analysis was 117.

Table 14.1 presents the descriptive statistics for the companies in the sample announcements. The median manufacturer had a market value of equity of $3.7 million, sales of $4.2 million, total debt of $2.3 million, and total shareholder's equity of $1.5 million, while the median retailer had a market value of equity of $3.2 million, sales of $3.7 million, total debt of $1.6 million, and total shareholder's equity of $10.5 million. Thus, the typical retailer (e.g., Wal-Mart) was much larger than the typical manufacturer.

14.3.2 Analysis

We tested the hypotheses using cross-sectional regression analysis to address possible Type I errors, the portfolio approach to estimate long-term postannouncement effects and examine the relationship between stock price effects and firm characteristics, and mediation analysis to test the role of source transparency. The

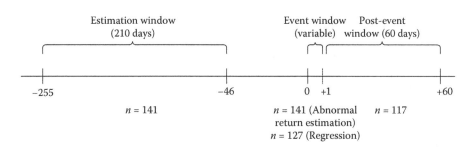

Figure 14.2   Timeline for event study.

Table 14.1   Description of Sample Measures

	Mean	*Median*	*SD*	*Maximum*	*Minimum*
Manufacturers (*n* = 65)					
Market size (million US$)	6878.04	3659.74	13,034.01	95,526.56	2.54
Sales (million US$)	5399.99	4232.26	8946.19	66,775.01	21.58
Total debt (million US$)	3886.03	2315.00	8363.48	61,601.52	10.17
Total shareholder's equity (million US$)	1943.12	1548.48	3422.33	26,770.55	−560.00
Retailers (*n* = 76)					
Market size (million US$)	63,247.42	32,244.53	80,776.10	250,000.00	108.66
Sales (million US$)	90,574.02	36,903.00	130,000.00	400,000.00	241.19
Total debt (million US$)	25,925.79	16,485.00	31,431.97	96,967.00	45.03
Total shareholder's equity (million US$)	17,896.73	10,527.10	21,125.86	65,285.00	−887.52

t test for the significance of the mean abnormal return takes into account cross-sectional dependence in security-specific abnormal returns (Brown and Warner 1985); however, it assumes that abnormal return estimators have identical variances across companies. To reduce the effect of stocks with large variances, we reported the Patell Z statistic. The technical details of the analysis are contained in Appendix 14.1.

14.4 Results

14.4.1 Stock Market Reaction to a Toy Recall Announcement

Table 14.2 presents the mean cumulative abnormal returns. On average, the announcement of a toy recall was associated with a significant loss by shareholders, supporting H_1. The results of the standardized cross-sectional test provide further support for H_1.

To provide a perspective on the significance of the stock market response to a toy recall announcement, Table 14.3 compares our results with a sample of similar research on product recalls in other industries. Although these studies used various event windows, they typically included the recall day and the day before the

Table 14.2 Abnormal Returns Associated with Toy Recalls

No. of Recalls	Mean Cumulative Abnormal Return	t	Patell Z	BMP t
141	−0.55%	−2.069*	−2.578**	−2.196*

$^*p < .05; ^{**}p < .01.$

Table 14.3 Results of Selected Prior Event Studies on Product Recalls

Author	Recall Period	Industry	Sample Size	Event Window	Mean Cumulative Abnormal Return
Jarrell and Peltzman (1985)	1967–1981	Automobile	116	(−1, 1)	−0.81%
Hoffer et al. (1987)	1970–1984	Automobile	46	(−1, 0)	−0.649%
Bromiley and Marcus (1989)	1967–1983	Automobile	91	(−1, 0)	−0.64%
Davidson and Worrell (1992)	1968–1987	Nonautomobile	133	(−1, 1)	−0.68%
Barber and Darrough (1996)	1973–1992	Automobile	573	(−1, 0)	−0.32% (United States) −0.69% (Japan)
Rupp (2001)	1973–1998	Automobile	494	(−1, 0)	−0.28%

announcement. The magnitude of the stock market reaction to a recall announcement ranged from roughly –0.5% to –1%. Our research adds to the consistent evidence that a product recall announcement is associated with a wealth loss by the shareholders of a company. Our results further suggest that the negative impact of a toy recall announcement is less severe than that of an automobile recall announcement.

14.4.2 Postannouncement Performance

Table 14.4 contains the regression estimates for the average daily abnormal returns for the portfolio of toy companies over the 60-day period. Table 14.5 displays the mean abnormal returns and associated test statistics for the 60 days subsequent to the recall announcement. The most significant drop in stock price occurred on the announcement day (Day 0), with a mean abnormal return of –0.69%. Consistent with the findings of Hendricks and Singhal (2003), the market captured most of the wealth effects of a product recall announcement very close to the announcement date.

Figure 14.3 presents the 60-day postannouncement cumulative performance by product hazard class. The stock prices for all hazard levels initially dropped within the event window (0, +1); however, their subsequent performance diverged. For toys with a Class C hazard, the downward pattern stopped around 20 days. A similar pattern was observed for toys with a Class B hazard, although the nadir was roughly 2.5 times lower and recovery took 10 days longer than for a Class C hazard. A significant difference was noted in the stock performance of toy companies whose products were recalled for a Class A hazard. While the average decline was

Table 14.4 Time Portfolio Regression

	Average Day in (–0, +59)	t	Heteroskedasticity Constant t
Intercept (abnormal return)	0.0006	1.79*	1.78*
b(p)	0.82000	33.42***	21.72***
s(p)	0.2113	3.90***	2.88**
h(p)	0.1201	2.50**	1.74*
R^2	32.31%		
Adjusted R^2	32.23%		
$F(3, 2373)$	377.65***		

$*p < .05;\ **p < .01;\ ***p < .001.$

Table 14.5 Mean Abnormal Returns over 60 Days

Day	Mean Abnormal Return %	Positive: Negative	Patell Z	StdCsect C	Day	Mean Abnormal Return %	Positive: Negative	Patell Z	StdCsect C
0	−0.69	52:65	−2.83**	−2.30*	+31	0.00	56:60	0.08	0.08
+1	−0.03	50:67	−0.51	−0.46	+32	0.05	60:56	−0.11	−0.12
+2	0.09	54:63	−1.38	−1.23	+33	0.34	66:50	1.63	1.59
+3	0.22	62:55	2.17*	2.08*	+34	0.31	64:52	1.91	1.94
+4	0.19	56:61	0.43	0.35	+35	−0.14	57:59	−0.62	−0.36
+5	0.28	58:59	1.09	1.02	+36	−0.03	51:65	−0.18	−0.15
+6	−0.19	59:58	−0.79	−0.93	+37	0.50	66:50	2.84**	2.66**
+7	0.02	59:58	−0.98	−0.84	+38	−0.04	61:55	−0.33	0.30
+8	0.22	57:60	1.93	1.51	+39	0.15	61:55	0.06	0.06
+9	0.10	51:66	0.20	0.19	+40	0.21	59:57	1.30	−0.97
+10	0.07	57:60	0.69	0.72	+41	−0.25	58:58	−0.21	−0.15
+11	−0.15	51:66	−1.19	−1.11	+42	0.01	55:61	0.66	0.69
+12	−0.44	55:62	−0.12	−0.10	+43	−0.39	52:64	−1.85	−1.73
+13	0.13	56:61	0.60	0.60	+44	−0.32	46:70	−1.99*	−2.32*

(continued)

Table 14.5   Mean Abnormal Returns over 60 Days (Continued)

Day	Mean Abnormal Return %	Positive: Negative	Patell Z	StdCsect C
+14	0.42	54:63	−0.55	−0.39
+15	−0.10	56:61	−0.65	−0.58
+16	−0.53	50:67	−1.59	−1.59
+17	−0.13	58:59	−0.09	−0.11
+18	0.30	55:62	0.71	−0.59
+19	−0.03	47:70	−0.80	−0.69
+20	0.55	65:52	2.28*	2.01*
+21	0.00	58:59	−0.04	−0.03
+45	−0.04	57:59	0.33	0.42
+46	−0.30	55:61	−1.22	−0.89
+47	−0.03	56:60	−0.47	−0.32
+48	0.23	59:57	1.38	1.31
+49	0.23	56:60	0.10	0.10
+50	0.43	68:48	2.04*	2.09*
+51	−0.01	60:56	1.54	1.40
+52	0.38	52:64	1.01	0.74

+22	-0.08	57:60	0.47	0.51	+53	-0.06	55:61	0.22	0.21
+23	0.56	60:57	0.92	0.88	+54	-0.09	56:60	0.14	0.12
+24	0.02	53:64	0.10	0.09	+55	0.17	59:57	0.98	0.91
+25	0.53	61:56	0.20	0.17	+56	0.66	71:45	2.49*	2.60*
+26	-0.43	51:66	-1.24	-1.10	+57	0.12	56:60	0.68	0.52
+27	0.24	56:61	-0.67	-0.63	+58	-0.18	55:61	-0.55	-0.42
+28	-0.02	58:59	-0.56	-0.06	+59	0.00	53:63	-1.59	-1.53
+29	0.04	44:73	-1.55	-1.55	+60	0.06	57:58	0.63	0.68
+30	0.68	59:58	1.64	1.49					

*$p < .05$; **$p < .01$; ***$p < .001$.

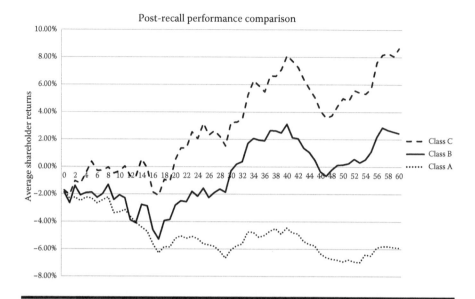

Figure 14.3 Average market-adjusted cumulative shareholder loss.

approximately the same magnitude as it was for a Class B hazard, the stock prices for toy companies with a Class A hazard did not rebound, even 60 days after the initial announcement of the recall. This provides preliminary support for H_4.

14.4.3 Effect of Firm Size, Source Transparency, and Degree of Product Hazard

Model 1 in Table 14.6 presents the regression analysis results, which support our last three hypotheses. As predicted by H_{3a}, the estimated coefficient for firm size was positive and highly significant. Thus, toy companies with greater revenues had smaller negative abnormal returns following a product recall announcement than did toy companies with lower revenues. The estimated coefficient for source transparency was also negative, indicating that the negative consequences for a toy company were more severe when products for which the source was not transparent (manufactured by nonpublicly traded or overseas manufacturers were recalled), as predicted by H_2. The negative and highly significant coefficient for hazard Class A shows that the severity of the hazard had a significant impact on how investors responded, supporting H_4.

There was no support for a relationship between growth potential (market-to-book ratio) and abnormal returns. Thus, when hazard level is included in the regression model, the growth potential is no longer significant. This prompted us to examine whether the degree of product hazard moderated the effect of growth potential on the abnormal returns. As shown in Model 2 in Table 14.6, the addition

Table 14.6   Results of Cross-Sectional Regression of Abnormal Returns

Variable	Model 1 (No Interaction Term)		Model 2 (Including Interaction Term)	
	Parameter Estimate	*Standard Error*	*Parameter Estimate*	*Standard Error*
Intercept	−3.30**	1.37	−2.99**	1.37
Size	0.54***	0.15	0.56***	0.15
Growth potential	−0.05	0.07	−0.16*	0.10
Debt: equity	−1.79	1.70	−2.45	1.73
Fatality	−1.69	2.07	−1.66	2.06
Recall size	−0.06	0.13	−0.09	0.13
Strategy	0.82	0.69	0.95	0.69
Source transparency	−1.55**	0.72	−1.62**	0.71
Hazard A	−1.92***	0.70	−2.89***	0.80
Hazard B	−0.92	0.77	−0.89	0.76
Growth potential × hazard A	–	–	0.23	0.13
Number of observations	127		127	
F	3.05***		3.08***	
R^2	.19		.21	
Adjusted R^2	.13		.14	

$*p < .05; **p < .01; ***p < .001.$

of the interaction term increased the explanatory power of the observed variance in the abnormal returns to 20%, with $F(10, 117) = 3.082$. The R^2 increase associated with the interaction term was .02 ($F = 2.9567$). The unstandardized regression coefficient for the interaction term was .23 ($p = .0882$), indicating the possible moderating role of degree of toy product hazard on the effect of growth potential.

To fully understand the form of this interaction, we used the MODPROBE macro (Hayes and Matthes 2009), based on the pick-a-point approach. It estimates the effect of a predictor variable at various values of the moderator variable. Figure 14.4 shows that the effect of growth potential on abnormal returns depended on the degree of product hazard described in the recall announcement.

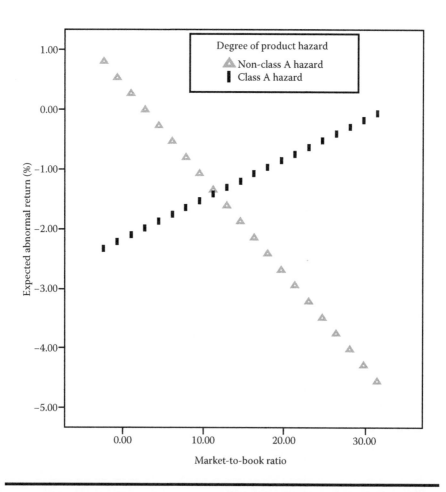

Figure 14.4   Interaction between growth potential and degree of product hazard.

For toys with a Class A hazard, investors punish toy companies with lower growth potential more than those with higher growth potential. On the other hand, when there is a recall announcement for a toy with a Class B or C hazard, toy companies with higher growth potential experience a more negative stock market reaction than do their competitors with lower growth potential. This suggests that investors are more forgiving when a toy company with higher growth potential issues a recall announcement for a toy with a severe hazard than they are with a company with lower growth potential.

The estimated coefficient for recall size was negative but insignificant. Thus, the market did not react differently to recall announcements associated with larger or smaller revenue losses, contradicting the conventional wisdom that a larger recall would be viewed more negatively. The insignificant coefficient for strategy is counter to the claim of Chen et al. (2009) that a proactive recall strategy would be more negatively related to the company's financial value than a passive recall strategy will be. Given the perspectives of the signaling theory and the corporate social responsibility literature, this lack of impact of recall strategy on abnormal return was expected for the toy industry. The overall fit of Model 1 was significant at the .01 level. Compared with other similar recent studies on product recalls with comparable sample sizes and numbers of variables (Chen et al. 2009; Hendricks and Singhal 2003), our hypothetical model showed a good fit with the data.

14.4.4 Mediating Effect of Source Transparency

The results of our logistic regression are presented in Model 1 in Table 14.7. Consistent with our prediction in H_{3b}, the estimated coefficient for company size was positive and highly significant. This suggests that toy companies with greater revenue are more likely to purchase from nonpublicly traded or overseas manufacturers. Considering that our sample contains large retailers like Wal-Mart and

Table 14.7 Results of Mediation Test

Variables	Model 1 (Logit on Transparency)	Model 2 (Excluding Transparency)
Intercept	−5.585***	−3.111**
Size	1.156 ****	0.319**
Growth potential	−0.290	0.022
Debt: equity	−6.741***	0.316
Fatality	2.166	−2.270
Recall size	−0.560***	0.063
Strategy	−1.161	1.407**
Hazard A	−1.314	−2.098***
Hazard B	−0.056	−1.450
Number of observations	127	127
−2 Log likelihood		3.235***
Model F value	81.152	
R^2		.179
Adjusted R^2		.123

Note: Significance levels (two-tailed tests): **$p < .05$; *** $p < .01$; ****$p < .001$.

Table 14.8 Results of Sobel (1982) Test

Comparable Coefficient	Parameter Estimate
a'	0.784019
b'	−0.41872
S'_a	0.157346
S'_b	0.171293
Sobel test	−2.1946**
Aroian test	−2.1598**
Goodman test	−2.2311**

Note: Independent variable: firm size, mediator: source transparency.

$*p < .05; **p < .01; ***p < .001$.

Target, this finding is not surprising. In order to reduce their operating costs, many large retailers use privately held or overseas toy manufacturers as suppliers, at least to some extent. The regression results are shown in Model 2 of Table 14.7. Without the mediator, the significantly positive coefficient for company size indicates partial mediation. Using Kenny et al.'s (1998) transformation method, we computed the comparable coefficients used in the Sobel Test, as shown in Table 14.8. The Sobel test statistic was −2.19458, implying that transparency indeed mediates the influence of toy company size on the abnormal returns.

14.5 Summary and Conclusions

We examined the impact of a toy product recall announcement on shareholder wealth. Using a sample of 141 toy product recall announcements, we found that the shareholders of toy companies that announced a recall experienced a significant wealth loss. The 2-day mean cumulative abnormal return was −0.55%, which is about the same magnitude as has been reported in other industries. Thus, our research complements the previous research, which has been focused primarily on automotive recalls, by providing confirming evidence from the toy industry.

This research contributes to the recall literature by providing a theoretical explanation for the impact of several firm- and recall-related characteristics for this loss of shareholder wealth. Applying agency theory, we posited and found that toys made by privately held and overseas manufacturers were associated with a greater loss in financial value, compared with toys made by publicly traded manufacturers. Our cross-sectional regression implied that larger companies were shielded from the negative impact of a recall announcement due to their economies of scale, diverse product offerings, and leverage over suppliers. On the other hand, through the lens of TCE, our results suggest that larger toy companies are more likely to outsource their production to privately held or overseas suppliers; thus, they may inadvertently induce lower source transparency in their supply chains. Through the mediating effect of source transparency, larger toy companies are also likely to experience more negative abnormal returns. The countervailing forces of the direct and indirect effects may explain why previous researchers have failed to find a significant impact of firm size. Drawing upon prospect theory, we also showed why the level of hazard is negatively correlated with abnormal returns.

Our findings have strong academic and managerial implications. Supply chain risk is an important topic that has gained considerable attention from both academics and practitioners (Wagner and Bode 2008), as described in Chapter 4. The importance of supply chain risk will likely increase with the growth of global sourcing, whose complexity can cause severe supply chain disruptions (Blackhurst et al. 2005). Our results provide evidence about the detrimental financial effects of supply chain disruptions, since a product recall is a risk that originates from the supply side (Wagner and Bode 2008).

The important role of source transparency calls into question the conventional wisdom of outsourcing (Craighead et al. 2007). While we do not challenge the strategic advantages associated with global outsourcing, we do raise concerns about the negative impact that the accompanying source opaqueness might have on the severity of supply chain disruptions. In the event of a product recall, the greater financial loss caused by using unknown or overseas suppliers may outweigh potential savings in production costs. To cope with this, it is important to improve transparency across deep supply chains, so that supply chain partners can better monitor and control the actions of their upstream and downstream partners (Lyles et al. 2008). Our empirical evidence illustrates the benefits of improving supply chain transparency. That is, increased source transparency helps a company to minimize the potential negative impact of a product recall announcement.

From a managerial perspective, outsourcing to a reputable publicly traded manufacturer is preferable to privately held or overseas manufacturers. If a privately held or overseas manufacturer is used as a supplier, voluntary disclosure of supplier information can increase source transparency. Such information disclosure puts the supplier under public scrutiny, thereby deterring it from opportunistic behavior and reducing the possibility of a supply chain disruption, such as a product recall.

There are a number of opportunities for future research on this interesting topic. We focused mainly on the short-term effects of a recall announcement on toy company value. However, recent empirical research suggests that the stock market reaction to new information is not fully reflected in stock price at the announcement date; rather, the stock market adjusts slowly to new information, resulting in abnormal stock price behavior after the announcement (Hendricks and Singhal 2005b). To fully estimate the impact of a product recall announcement, it would be worthwhile to more completely examine the associated long-run stock price effects. Another interesting research direction would be to estimate whether there is a spillover effect to a toy company's competitors. Current studies provide mixed evidence on this subject, suggesting that competitors may either benefit or suffer from a recall (Bromiley and Marcus 1989; Dowdell et al. 1992). The strength of a toy's brand may be important in this research, as stronger brands deter substitutability. If other firms are expected to gain market share at the expense of the manufacturer, then their stock prices will increase if their products can be substituted for the recalled products (Barber and Darrough 1996; Dowdell et al. 1992; Govindaraj et al. 2004; Reilly and Hoffer 1983). On the other hand, some firms may suffer because of the possible decline in overall demand for the recalled product (Freedman et al. 2009; Jarrell and Peltzman 1985), exemplified by the recent spinach recalls, or because of costs imposed by expected stringent regulations. Because customers did not differentiate between spinach brands, due to lack of strong branding, sales declined for all brands of spinach, including those that were uncontaminated. Further empirical evidence from both recall companies and their competitors could help to resolve the debate in this area. Brand strength may be an important factor in this research.

Because of their negative impact, companies will ultimately seek to minimize the occurrence of a product recall, especially those for the most severe product hazards. Thus, future research should also examine the impact of various measures to prevent hazards that could lead to a product recall. Such measures could include increasing investment in new product research, improved information exchange among supply chain partners, statistical process control, and proactive defect detection. Instead of using abnormal returns as the dependent variable, researchers could use other objective measures, such as the number of recalls within a year or the average time duration between similar recalls. Significant correlations would signal whether these measures were effective.

Appendix 14.1 Technical Details of the Data Analysis

Prior research has found that with even minor increases in variance, most commonly used methods will often reject the null hypothesis of zero average abnormal returns even when it is true, resulting in a Type I error (Boehmer et al. 1991). Thus, we followed the approach of Boehmer et al. (1991) of standardizing the event-period abnormal returns by the estimation-period standard deviation (adjusted for forecast error) in order to eliminate such misspecification problems. The test statistic was then calculated by dividing the average event-period standardized abnormal returns by their contemporaneous cross-sectional standard error.

In order to examine postannouncement effects, we measured the 60-day long-run abnormal stock performance after a recall announcement using the calendar time portfolio approach (Jaffe 1974; Mandelker 1974; Lyon et al. 1999), which provides several advantages over tests that employ buy-and-hold abnormal returns (Lyon et al. 1999). First, it eliminates the problem of cross-sectional dependence among sample firms because the returns for sample firms are aggregated into a single portfolio. In addition, it yields more robust test statistics in random samples.

We estimated the portfolio excess returns over the 60-day period subsequent to the recall announcement. For each day, we calculated the returns for a portfolio composed of toy companies that had a product recall within the last 60 days. The excess returns for the portfolio were regressed on three of the factors of Fama and French (1993), shown in Equation 14.1 (Kothari and Warner 2007; Lyon et al. 1999; Mitchell and Stafford 2000):

$$R_{pt} - R_{ft} = \alpha_i + \beta_i(R_{mt} - R_{ft}) + s_i SMB_t + h_i HML_t + \varepsilon_{it} \tag{14.1}$$

where:

R_{pt} = Equal or value-weighted return for calendar day t for the portfolio of event firms

R_{ft} = Risk-free interest rate

R_{mt} = Return on the CRSP value-weighted market portfolio

SMB_t = Difference between the return on the portfolio of "small" and "big" stocks

HML_t = Difference between the return on the portfolio of "high" and "low" book-to-market stocks

The intercept, α_i, measures the average daily return on the portfolio of companies, which is zero under the null hypothesis of no abnormal performance.

We used cross-sectional regression of the abnormal returns for the variables of interest in order to examine how the stock price effects of a recall announcement are related to firm characteristics (Kothari and Warner 2007). We estimated the following regression model:

$$\text{Abreturn}_i = \beta_0 + \beta_1 \text{Size}_i + \beta_2 \text{Market-to-book}_i + \beta_3 \text{Debt-equity}_i + \beta_4 \text{Fatality}_i + \beta_5 \text{RecallSize}_i + \beta_6 \text{Strategy}_i + \beta_7 \text{Transparency}_i + \beta_8 \text{Hazard}_i + \varepsilon_i. \tag{14.2}$$

Abreturn$_i$ is the abnormal returns for company i during the event period. Size$_i$, market-to-book$_i$, and debt-equity$_i$ measure company characteristics, based on Hendricks and Singhal (2003). Size$_i$ is the natural logarithm of the company's sales in the most recent fiscal year ending prior to the announcement date; we used the logarithmic transformation to address the right skewness that is typical of a revenue distribution. Market-to-book$_i$ is a proxy for the company's growth potential, calculated as the ratio of the market value of equity to the book value of equity. Market value was calculated using financial data from the ten trading days prior to the announcement date, and book equity was obtained from the company's annual report at the most recent fiscal year-end. Debt-equity$_i$ is the ratio of the book value of the debt to the sum of the book value of debt and the market value of equity. The binary indicator fatality$_i$ is 1 if the hazard resulted in any deaths and 0 otherwise. Strategy$_i$ is a dichotomous variable that denotes whether the recall was initiated by the company (initiation$_i$ = 1) or mandated by a government agency (initiation$_i$ = 0). RecallSize$_i$ is the natural logarithm of sales revenue, which was calculated as the recalled quantity times the maximum retail price. The value of the binary variable transparency$_i$ is 0 if the manufacturer of the recalled product is publicly traded or 1 if it is not publicly traded or is located overseas. Hazard$_i$ indicates the severity of the recall, based CPSC hazard classifications. Class A is for hazards where the risk of death, grievous injury, or illness is likely. Class B is when death, grievous injury, or illness is possible, and Class C is when only moderate injury or illness is possible.

Hypothesis H_{3b} postulates that the effect of company size on abnormal returns is partially mediated by the transparency of the product's source. A variable functions as a mediator when (Baron and Kenny 1986; Judd and Kenny 1981; Kenny et al. 1998) (1) the total effect of the independent variable on the outcome (Path c) is different from zero, (2) variations in the level of the independent variable account for variations in the presumed mediator (Path a), (3) variations in the mediator account for variations in the dependent variable (Path b), and (4) when Paths a and b are controlled, a previously significant relationship between the independent and dependent variables (Path c') is no longer significant. If the last condition is not met, then partial mediation is indicated. Based on these principles, our preliminary mediation test was composed of two-stage multiple regressions; in the first stage, we established whether the independent variables were correlated with the mediator, by treating the mediator as if it were an outcome variable (Kenny et al. 1998). Due the dichotomous nature of our mediator, we used the following logistic regression model:

$$\ln\left(\frac{\text{Prob}(\text{Transparency}_i = 1)}{1 - \text{Prob}(\text{Transparency}_i = 1)}\right) = \beta_0 + \sum \beta_i X_i, \qquad (14.3)$$

where $\dfrac{\text{Prob}(\text{Transparency}_i = 1)}{1 - \text{Prob}(\text{Transparency}_i = 1)}$ is the odds ratio.

The significance of the intercept β_0 and coefficient of the variable X_i β_i indicates whether the variables are correlated with the mediator. To complete the mediation test, we regressed the abnormal returns on the independent variables, excluding the proposed mediator. We performed a Sobel test to statistically establish whether the indirect effect differed significantly from zero (Judd and Kenny 2010).

References

Aaker, D.A. 1991. *Managing Brand Equity: Capitalizing on the Value of a Brand Name*. New York, Free Press.

Aaker, D.A. 1996. *Building Strong Brands*. New York, Free Press.

Barber, B.M. and M.N. Darrough. 1996. Product reliability and firm value: The experience of American and Japanese automakers, 1973–1992. *J. Pol. Econ.* 104(5): 1084–1099.

Barber, B.M. and T. Odean. 2008. All that glitters: The effect of attention and news on the buying behavior of individual and institutional investors. *Rev. Fin. Stud.* 21(2): 785–818.

Baron, R.M. and D.A. Kenny. 1986. The moderator–mediator variable distinction in social psychological research: Conceptual, strategic, and statistical considerations. *J. Pers. Soc. Psych.* 51(6): 1173–1182.

Berg, B. and A. Stylianou. 2009. Factors considered when outsourcing an IS system: An empirical examination of the impacts of organizational size, strategy and the object of a decision. *Eur. J. Info. Sys.* 18(3): 235–248.

Bergen, M., S. Dutta, and O.C. Walker Jr. 1992. Agency relationships in marketing: A review of the implications and applications of agency and related theories. *J. Mktg.* 56(3): 1–24.

Blackhurst, J., C.W. Craighead, D. Elkins, and R.B. Handfield. 2005. An empirically derived agenda of critical research issues for managing supply-chain disruptions. *Int. J. Prod. Res.* 43(19): 4067–4081.

Boehmer, E., J. Masumeci, and A. B. Poulsen. 1991. Event-study methodology under conditions of event-induced variance. *J. Fin. Econ.* 30(2): 253–272.

Boyer, K.K. and M.L. Swink. 2008. Empirical elephants—Why multiple methods are essential to quality research in operations and supply chain management. *J. Ops. Mgmt.* 26(3): 338–344.

Bromiley, P. and A. Marcus. 1989. The deterrent to dubious corporate behavior: Profitability, probability and safety recalls. *Strat. Mgmt. J.* 10(3): 233–250.

Brown, J.R., C.S. Dev, and D.J. Lee. 2000. Managing marketing channel opportunism: The efficacy of alternative governance mechanisms. *J. Mktg.* 64(2): 51–65.

Brown, S.J. and J.B. Warner. 1985. Using daily stock returns: The case of event studies. *J. Fin. Econ.* 14(1): 3–31.

Cheah, E., W. Chan, and C. Chieng. 2007. The corporate social responsibility of pharmaceutical product recalls: An empirical examination of U.S. and U.K. markets. *J. Bus. Ethics* 76(4): 427–449.

Chen, Y., S. Ganesan, and Y. Liu. 2009. Does a firm's product-recall strategy affect its financial value? An examination of strategic alternatives during product-harm crises. *J. Mktg.* 3(6): 214–226.

Clark, E. 2007. *The Real Toy Story: Inside the Ruthless Battle for America's Youngest Consumers*. New York, Free Press.

Cohen, W.M. and S. Klepper. 1996. Firm size and the nature of innovation within industries: The case of process and product R&D. *Rev. Econ. Stat.* 78(2): 232–243.

Coombs, W.T. 2007. Attribution theory as a guide for post-crisis communication research. *Pub. Rel. Rev.* 33(2): 135–139.

Craighead, C.W., J. Blackhurst, M.J. Rungtusanatham, and R.B. Handfield. 2007. The severity of supply chain disruptions: Design characteristics and mitigation capabilities. *Dec. Sci.* 38(1): 131–156.

Damanpour, F. 1992. Organizational size and innovation. *Org. Stud.* 13(3): 375–402.

Davidson, W.N. III and D.L. Worrell. 1992. The effect of product recall announcements on shareholder wealth. *Strat. Mgmt. J.* 13(6): 467–473.

Dawar, N. and J. Lei. 2009. Brand crises: The roles of brand familiarity and crisis relevance in determining the impact on brand evaluations. *J. Bus. Res.* 62(4): 509–516.

Dowdell, T.D., S. Govindaraj, and P.C. Jain. 1992. The Tylenol incident, ensuing regulation, and stock prices. *J. Fin. Quant. Anal.* 27(2): 283–301.

Eisenhardt, K.M. 1989. Agency theory: An assessment and review. *Acad. Mgmt. Rev.* 14(1): 57–74.

Fama, E.F. 1970. Efficient capital markets: A review of theory and empirical work. *J. Fin.* 25(2): 383–417.

Fama, E.F. and K.R. French. 1993. Common risk factors in the returns on stocks and bonds. *J. Fin. Econ.* 33(1): 3–56.

Freedman, S., M.S. Kearney, and M. Lederman. 2009. Product recalls, imperfect information, and spillover effects: Lessons from the consumer response to the 2007 toy recalls. NBER Working Paper Series, w15183.

Govindaraj, S., B. Jaggi, and B. Lin. 2004. Market overreaction to product recall revisited— The case of Firestone tires and the Ford Explorer. *Rev. Quant. Fin. Acctg.* 23(1): 31–54.

Hayes, A.F. and J. Matthes. 2009. Computational procedures for probing interactions in OLS and logistic regression: SPSS and SAS implementations. *Beh. Res. Meth.* 41(3): 924–936.

Hendricks, K.B. and V.R. Singhal. 2001. Firm characteristics, total quality management, and financial performance. *J. Ops. Mgmt.* 19(3): 269–285.

Hendricks, K.B. and V.R. Singhal. 2003. The effect of supply chain glitches on shareholder wealth. *J. Ops. Mgmt.* 21(5): 501–522.

Hendricks, K.B. and V.R. Singhal. 2005a. Association between supply chain glitches and operating performance. *Mgmt. Sci.* 51(5): 695–711.

Hendricks, K.B. and V.R. Singhal. 2005b. An empirical analysis of the effect of supply chain disruptions on long-run stock: Price performance and equity risk of the firm. *Prod. Ops. Mgmt.* 14(1): 35–52.

Hendricks, K.B., V.R. Singhal, and C.I. Wiedman. 1995. The impact of capacity expansion on the market value of the firm. *J. Ops. Mgmt.* 12(3–4): 259–272.

Hill, C.A. and G.D. Scudder. 2002. The use of electronic data interchange for supply chain coordination in the food industry. *J. Ops. Mgmt.* 20(4): 375–387.

Hoffer, G.E., S.W. Pruitt, and R.J. Reilly. 1987. Automotive recalls and informational efficiency. *Fin. Rev.* 22(4): 433.

Hoffer, G.E., S.W. Pruitt, and R.J. Reilly. 1994. When recalls matter: Factors affecting owner response to automotive recalls. *J. Cons. Affairs* 28(1): 96–106.

Hoffman, A.J. and W. Ocasio. 2001. Not all events are attended equally: Toward a middle-range theory of industry attention to external events. *Org. Sci.* 12(4): 414–434.

Jaffe, J.F. 1974. Special information and insider trading. *J. Bus.* 47(3): 410–428.

Jarrell, G. and S. Peltzman. 1985. The impact of product recalls on the wealth of sellers. *J. Pol. Econ.* 93(3): 512–536.

Jayaraman, V., R.A. Patterson, and E. Rolland. 2003. The design of reverse distribution networks: Models and solution procedures. *Eur. J. Oper. Res.* 150(1): 128–149.

Johnson, M.E. 2001. Learning from toys: Lessons in managing supply chain risk from the toy industry. *Cal. Mgmt. Rev.* 43(3): 106–124.

Judd, C.M. and D.A. Kenny. 1981. Process analysis. *Eval. Rev.* 5(5): 602–619.

Judd, C.M. and D.A. Kenny. 2010. Data analysis in social psychology: Recent and recurring issues. In Fiske, S.T., D.T. Gilbert, and G. Lindzey (Eds.), *Handbook of Social Psychology*. Hoboken, NJ, John Wiley.

Kahneman, D. and A. Tversky. 1979. Prospect theory: An analysis of decision under risk. *Econometrica* 47(2): 263–291.

Keller, K.L. 1993. Conceptualizing, measuring, and managing customer-based brand equity. *J. Mktg.* 57(1): 1–22.

Keller, K.L. 2003. *Strategic Brand Management: Building, Measuring, and Managing Brand Equity* (2nd ed.). Upper Saddle River, NJ, Prentice-Hall.

Kenny, D.A., D.A. Kashy, and N. Bolger. 1998. Data analysis in social psychology. In Gilbert, D.T., S.T. Fiske, and G. Lindzey (Eds.), *The Handbook of Social Psychology* (4th ed., Vol. 1). Boston, McGraw-Hill: 233–265.

Klassen, R.D. and C.P. McLaughlin. 1996. The impact of environmental management on firm performance. *Mgmt. Sci.* 42(8): 1199–1214.

Kothari, S.P. and J.B. Warner. 2007. Econometrics of event studies. In Eckbo, B.E. (Ed.), *Handbook of Corporate Finance: Empirical Corporate Finance* (Vol. 1). Boston, Elsevier/North-Holland.

Laffont, J.J. and D. Martimort. 2002. *The Theory of Incentives: The Principal–Agent Model*. Princeton, NJ, Princeton University Press.

Leone, R.P., V.R. Rao, K.L. Keller, and A.M. Luo. 2006. Linking brand equity to customer equity. *J. Serv. Res.* 9(2): 125.

Lyles, M.A., B.B. Flynn, and M.T. Frohlich. 2008. All supply chains don't flow through: Understanding supply chain issues in product recalls. *Mgmt. Org. Rev.* 4(2): 167–182.

Lyon, J.D., B.M. Barber, and C.L. Tsai. 1999. Improved methods for tests of long-run abnormal stock returns. *J. Fin.* 54(1): 165–201.

MacKinlay, A.C. 1997. Event studies in economics and finance. *J. Econ. Lit.* 35(1): 13–39.

Mandelker, G. 1974. Risk and return: The case of merging firms. *J. Fin. Econ.* 1(4): 303–335.

Min, H. 1989. A bicriterion reverse distribution model for product recall. *Omega* 17(5): 483–490.

Mitchell, M.L. and E. Stafford. 2000. Managerial decisions and long-term stock price performance. *J. Bus.* 73(3): 287–329.

New, S. 2010. The transparent supply chain. *Harv. Bus. Rev.* 88(10): 76–82.

Nooteboom, B. 1993. Firm size effects on transaction costs. *Small Bus. Econ.* 5(4): 283–295.

Novemsky, N. and D. Kahneman. 2005. The boundaries of loss aversion. *J. Mktg. Res.* 42(2): 119–128.

Reilly, R.J. and G.E. Hoffer. 1983. Will retarding the information flow on automobile recalls affect consumer demand? *Econ. Inquiry* 21(3): 444–447.

Rhee, M. and P.R. Haunschild. 2006. The liability of good reputation: A study of product recalls in the U.S. automobile industry. *Org. Sci.* 17(1): 101–117.

Ross, S.A. 1983. Accounting and economics. *Acctg. Rev.* 58(2): 375–380.

Rupp, N.G. 2001. Are government initiated recalls more damaging for shareholders? Evidence from automotive recalls, 1973–1998. *Econ. Lett.* 71(2): 265–270.

Smith, N.C., R.J. Thomas, and J.A. Quelch. 1996. A strategic approach to managing product recalls. *Harv. Bus. Rev.* 74(5): 102–112.

Sobel, M.E. 1982. Asymptotic confidence intervals for indirect effects in structural equation models. *Soc. Meth.* 13: 290–312.

Tibben-Lembke, R.S. and D.S. Rogers. 2002. Differences between forward and reverse logistics in a retail environment. *Supp. Chain Mgmt.* 7(5): 271–282.

Tversky, A. and D. Kahneman. 1991. Loss aversion in riskless choice: A reference-dependent model. *Q. J. Econ.* 106(4): 1039–1061.

Wagner, S.M. and C. Bode. 2008. An empirical examination of supply chain performance along several dimensions of risk. *J. Bus. Log.* 29(1): 307–325.

Weiner, B. 1989. *Human Motivation.* Hillsdale, NJ, Erlbaum.

Williamson, O.E. 1985. *The Economic Institutions of Capitalism: Firms, Markets, Relational Contracting.* New York, Free Press.

Williamson, O.E. 1996. *The Mechanisms of Governance.* New York, Oxford University Press.

Chapter 15

Impact of Recalls on Retailer Shareholder Wealth in the United States

John Z. Ni, F. Robert Jacobs, and Barbara B. Flynn

Contents

15.1 Introduction: Importance of Studying Retailers

Customer product recalls are a particularly insidious problem because they occur relatively frequently and can have potentially disastrous consequences. The recent surge in the number of high-profile product recalls has shaken public confidence in the ability of manufacturers, retailers, and the government to ensure product safety. This analysis investigates how product brand, remedy strategy, and degree of product hazard affect the stock market reaction to a product recall announcement by a retailer.

Although there has been a substantial amount of research on the cost of a product recall to a manufacturer or brand owner, there has been little research done in the context of retailers. This is an important omission in light of the increasing number of product recalls and the amount of publicity that some have received. It is important to understand product recalls from the perspective of retailers because they are the final link in the supply chain between manufacturers and customers. Although the products that retailers sell are produced by manufacturers, customers purchase these from retailers and return any defective products to them. Thus, retailers serve as the "gatekeeper" between customers and the manufacturer. While product quality issues that result in a product recall may be due to a number of issues, including design flaws, manufacturing problems, issues with transportation, and other reasons, it is the retailer where customers ultimately take possession of a product and return defective products.

In order for a retailer to be willing to sell a product, it must believe that it will be able to make a profit, and significant retailer costs associated with a product recall announcement can impact its profitability. While most product quality problems that occur in the hands of customers are easily rectified, in the instance where a product is recalled due to a potential safety issue, the retailer becomes the intermediary between the customer and the manufacturer in reclaiming the product. The cost to the manufacturer in such an instance has been well established; however, there may be potential costs for the retailer, including loss of profitability due to reduced customer trust and goodwill. In the case where the retailer is also the manufacturer (a privately branded product), there is no intermediary, and the retailer bears the full cost of the product recall. It is expected that the cost to a retailer of a recall of a privately branded product will be significantly more than for a nationally branded product.

We begin by extending the prior research on product recalls by manufacturers to retailers, focusing on their gatekeeper role in a supply chain. Building on attribution theory, we develop hypotheses about the role of private vs. nationally branded products in the cost of a product recall for a retailer. We use information asymmetry to examine the role of remedy strategy and build on prospect theory to hypothesize about the role of product hazard in the cost to a retailer of a product recall. These hypotheses are tested using event study methodology with objective archival data on product recalls recently announced by the Customer Product Safety Commission (CPSC).

15.2 Background

15.2.1 Importance of Extending Recalls Research to Retailers

Research questions related to the effect of a product recall announcement on a retailer have been by and large ignored in the existing literature. Regardless of the supply chain entity that owns the brand, a recalled product is generally returned to the point from which it was originally purchased; in many instances, this is a retailer (Petersen and Kumar 2009). If the recalled product is a privately branded product, customers may lay the blame for product defect on the retailer. However, even if the recalled product is a nationally branded product, the retailer is still actively involved in the reverse logistics process, by which it collects defective items and returns them to the manufacturer. Thus, the direct costs of a product recall can be substantial for a retailer. Retailers may be reluctant to spend time on recall-related returns because they detract from their sales objective (Mollenkopf et al. 2011), creating operational and profitability concerns. In addition, selling products whose quality is questionable can potentially shrink retailer sales or margins (Mollenkopf et al. 2011), due to the loss of customer loyalty.

In addition to the direct costs associated with a product recall, a retailer may also find that a product recall may affect its sales of other products. Retailers typically stock similar products with competing brands in order to cope with demand variability (Kraiselburd et al. 2004; Kulp et al. 2004). When a retailer stocks out of a particular brand of item, customers who had hoped to find it are likely to switch to a substitute product with a different brand at the same retail outlet. Thus, the lost sales from a recalled product may be offset by revenues associated with selling substitute products of competing brands. Conversely, however, we could also conjecture a negative spillover effect through which customers would stop buying all products similar to the one being recalled, for example, all brands of raw spinach, thereby leading to a greater loss in revenue for the retailer. Clearly, a better understanding of the potential costs of a product recall for retailers is needed.

We address these unresolved issues by extending the manufacturing-based research on product recalls to retailers, focusing on the effect of a product recall announcement on a retailer's shareholder wealth. We include the role of product brand, which is unique to retailers, as well as the effect of two variables that have been largely overlooked by the manufacturing recalls research: remedy strategy and degree of hazard.

15.2.2 Product Brand

The first decade of the 21st century has witnessed rapid development of privately branded products for customer products, particularly in developed countries, where their market share has steadily increased (Lamey et al. 2007). Privately branded products, such as Kenmore (Sears) and Insignia (Best Buy), now account for more than 20% of the U.S. retail market (Kumar and Steenkamp 2007). Their success has been attributed to factors such as the growing concentration of the retail sector (Hoch and Banerji 1993), improvement in the quality of privately branded products (Steenkamp and Dekimpe 1997), and the increasing efforts that retailers have put into their privately branded products (Hoch 1996). Introducing a privately branded product enables a retailer to enjoy lower wholesale prices (Ailawadi and Harlam 2004), compared with nationally branded products. Privately branded products also help retailers improve their store image and develop store loyalty (Ailawadi 2001; Steenkamp and Dekimpe 1997). However, the growth in privately branded products may also influence how investors respond to a product recall announcement by retailers.

Using attribution theory, as described in Chapter 14, we postulate that, compared with a nationally branded product, the recall of a privately branded product will be associated with a greater reduction in financial value for the retailer. When a nationally branded product is recalled, it is natural that investors would attribute its cause to the manufacturer, such as Mattel or Alpo. In contrast, in the recall of a privately branded product, the retailer may receive some portion of the blame for providing the hazardous product. In addition, retailers have more responsibility for their private brand supply chains, including sourcing, warehousing, merchandising, and marketing (Hoch and Banerji 1993), than they have for national brands. By placing its name or a name that is known to be associated with it prominently on a product, the relationship of a privately branded product to the retailer is transparent (Dhar and Hoch 1997). Therefore, in the eyes of its customers, a retailer assumes greater ownership and accountability for its privately branded products.

The attribution of responsibility influences customer equity and anger reactions (Folkes 1984) when there are safety problems with a privately branded product. Because defects in a privately branded product may be attributed to controllable actions by the retailer in its sourcing, warehousing, merchandising, and manufacturing, the inequity of the marketplace exchange upsets the relationship between the customer and retailer. This may cause customers to stop buying products from the retailer. Thus, a significant reduction in future revenues would be expected for a retailer that issues a recall announcement for a privately branded product. In addition, customers' anger reaction may cause them to engage in disapproving behaviors, such as negative word of mouth or boycotting, which further increase the negative publicity about the retailer and lead to more lost sales. In contrast, when there is a safety problem in a nationally branded product, we expect customers to react in the same way; however, the target of their market equity and anger reactions will be the manufacturer, not the retailer.

The factors discussed above lead to greater uncertainty in the minds of investors about the impact of a product recall announcement on a retailer's current and future earnings potential for a privately branded product, compared with a nationally branded product. Therefore, we posit that differences in the attribution of blame by customers will lead to an expected decrease in future cash flows in the minds of investors. Because financial market incentives are usually expressed as the abnormal change in stock performance, the uncertainty associated with a product recall announcement for a private vs. nationally branded product influences how investors react to a recall announcement. Thus,

H_1: The stock market's reaction to a product recall announcement by a retailer will be more negative for a privately branded product than for a nationally branded product.

15.2.3 Remedy Strategy

When a product defect is discovered after a product is in the hands of its customers, a retailer can offer several remedies: Customers may be asked to discard the product, receive a repair kit, return the product for repair, return the product for replacement, or return the product for a refund of the purchase price. Along this "company response continuum" (Siomkos and Kurzbard 1994), the remedies are progressively more socially responsible, showing more compassion for customers by removing potentially hazardous products from their hands. Research on crisis management suggests that companies that are perceived as more compassionate in their response will have a stronger organizational reputation (Coombs 1999).

Manufacturers may face substantial penalties levied by government agencies and lawsuits by injured customers. When a product defect results in injury or death, the courts may find that more could have been done more to recall the product more expeditiously (Ross 2009). Thus, an effective remedy strategy will reduce the number of potentially harmful products in the field, encouraging the legal system and government agencies to conclude that the manufacturer's conduct was not negligent. On the other hand, failing to take adequate remedial action can result in substantial liability, including punitive damages, if there are numerous injured customers (Ross and Prince 2009). Although these arguments are based on research with manufacturers, the same logic applies to retailers. Thus, implementing an effective remedy strategy should be associated with investors perceiving greater future cash flows, compared with implementation of a remedy strategy that is expected to be less effective.

Provision of an incentive that is sufficient to motivate customers to return the product is critical to the effectiveness of a recall initiative (Bapuji 2011). Prior research has found that returning a product for repair or replacement is a less appealing option for customers, whose confidence in the quality of the product has already been diminished, compared with receiving a refund of the purchase price. The negative psychological impact of a product recall is persistent, lingering in the minds of customers into the future (Van Heerde et al. 2007), who may be uncertain about whether the root cause of the product failure was fully addressed, even after a product was repaired or replaced. On the other hand, a refund allows customers to overcome their apprehension about a future product failure, since it is no longer in their hands. Therefore, a refund is the most effective remedy strategy for motivating customers to return a recalled product. Because of its strong incentive, offering a refund enables a retailer to retrieve the greatest number of units; thus, the potential for product harm is more substantially reduced. Thus, it is reasonable to assume that retailers offering a refund will be viewed more favorably by customers than those providing repair or replacement.

However, prior research on remedy strategy has dealt only with customer reactions. The issue of how remedy strategy influences investors' reactions has not been examined. Investor reactions to a product recall announcement may be very different from customer reactions Investors are concerned with the retailer's future earnings potential, rather than with potential harm to themselves or their families. Investors may prefer a less costly remedy, such as repair or replacement, rather than a refund. When a retailer offers a refund, it foregoes all previous profits, in addition to the cost of administering the recall (Bapuji 2011). On the other hand, if the remedy strategy is a repair kit (Felcher 2003), rather than a refund, this may be preferred by investors because it has less impact on the retailer's future earnings.

The information asymmetry between the retailer and the stock market (Dierkens 1991) is intensified when the retailer recalls a privately branded product, because the investors have greater uncertainty about its source. Therefore, investors have greater difficulty in assessing the future impact of a product recall announcement when it is for a privately branded product. The more that information asymmetry and ambiguity characterize the interaction between a retailer and investors, the more likely investors are to search for information signals about the retailer (Shrum and Wuthnow 1988). The choice of remedy strategy can provide a potent signal about how well the retailer expects to be able to contain the impact of the product defect. Investors observing that a retailer has offered a refund may speculate that the likelihood of product harm and penalties are so high that the retailer was forced to retrieve the defective product, in order to contain the damage. In contrast, a repair or replacement remedy may signal that the retailer is confident about the quality of the recalled product and that the possibility of future product harm will be minimal. Therefore, we propose that remedy strategy is viewed by investors as a signal of the retailer's belief about its ability to contain and rectify the product defect.

H_2: The stock market's reaction to a product recall announcement will be more negative for retailers offering a refund than for those offering replacement or repair as the remedy strategy.

15.2.4 Degree of Product Hazard

We also postulate that the degree of product hazard associated with a recalled product triggers differential responses from investors, following the logic previously described in Chapter 14. Thus,

H_3: The higher the hazard level of a product recalled by a retailer, the more negative the stock market's reaction to a product recall announcement will be.

15.3 Approach

15.3.1 Recall Announcement Data

We searched the CPSC website's recall announcements between 2000 and 2009 for those by retailers whose common stock was listed on either the New York or American Stock Exchange (Davidson and Worrell 1992). We gathered the earliest reporting date and time in the major public media by searching the Dow Jones Newswire, *Wall Street Journal*, and the Associated Press. The announcement day on the CPSC website was denoted as Day 0 in event time, and the trading day preceding the announcement day was Day –1. The initial sample was composed of 251 announcements.

Company information was obtained from Compustat. The companies were all primarily engaged in retail operations and carried nationally branded products supplied by customer product manufacturers and/or their own privately branded products. To ensure that the companies met these criteria, we searched Dun & Bradstreet's Million Dollar Database, Hoovers.com, and the companies' websites for evidence.

To avoid overlapping events (MacKinlay 1997), we excluded recall announcements for products that were sold by more than one company. If multiple products were recalled by the same retailer on the same day, we aggregated their quantities and dollar values. We excluded any announcement where the retailer experienced other contemporaneous events, such as earnings announcements, within the event window. We searched Factiva for information about safety issues related to the retailer prior to the recall announcement and excluded any such recall announcements. After excluding all such announcements, the final sample consisted of 164 product recall announcements, described in Table 15.1.

15.3.2 Analysis

The data were analyzed using hierarchical regression analysis to test the importance of various retailer and recall announcement characteristics. We used supplementary robustness analysis and endogeneity selection bias correction. The details of these approaches are described in Appendix 15.1.

Table 15.1 Descriptive Statistics and Frequencies

	Mean	Median	SD	Maximum	Minimum
Descriptive Statistics					
Annual sales ($ million)	142,814	69,948	138,289	402,298	573
Recall size[a] ($ million)	11.67	1.45	36.75	360	0.0025
Recall Frequencies					
Year	n	Remedy Strategy	n	Degree of Hazard	n
2000	11	Repair	31	Class A	40
2001	10	Replacement	41	Class B	75
2002	12	Refund	92	Class C	49
2003	9				
2004	10				
2005	22				
2006	20				
2007	18				
2008	19				
2009	33				

[a] Recall size = maximum price × total number of products recalled.

15.4 Results

15.4.1 Hypothesis Testing

Table 15.2 provides the means, standard deviations, and correlations for all variables. The results of the comparison of the abnormal returns associated with recall announcements for nationally vs. privately branded products are summarized in Table 15.3. Recall announcements for privately branded products were significantly associated with a significant wealth loss by shareholders. In contrast, the abnormal returns for recall announcements for nationally branded products were not significantly different from zero. These results support H_1, which stated that a more significant loss in shareholder wealth would be expected for the announcement of

Table 15.2 Descriptive Statistics and Correlation Coefficients

Variables	1	2	3	4	5	6	7	8	9	10	11	12	13	14
1. Company size	1.000													
2. Recall size	0.136 (0.083)	1.000												
3. Product brand	−0.342 (0.000)	−0.153 (0.050)	1.000											
4. Repair (remedy = 0)	−0.084 (0.285)	0.277 (0.000)	−0.145 (0.064)	1.000										
5. Replacement (remedy = 1)	0.140 (0.074)	0.255 (0.001)	−0.380 (0.000)	−0.279 (0.000)	1.000									
6. Refund (remedy = 2)	−0.056 (0.478)	−0.441 (0.000)	0.446 (0.000)	−0.546 (0.000)	−0.653 (0.000)	1.000								
7. Class C (hazard = 0)	−0.024 (0.757)	−0.106 (0.178)	0.129 (0.100)	0.127 (0.105)	−0.100 (0.203)	−0.013 (0.868)	1.000							
8. Class B (hazard = 1)	−0.095 (0.225)	−0.044 (0.575)	−0.030 (0.704)	−0.131 (0.096)	0.148 (0.058)	−0.026 (0.737)	−0.599 (0.000)	1.000						

(continued)

Table 15.2 Descriptive Statistics and Correlation Coefficients (Continued)

Variables	1	2	3	4	5	6	7	8	9	10	11	12	13	14
9. Class A (hazard = 2)	0.137 (0.081)	0.164 (0.036)	-0.103 (0.191)	0.016 (0.840)	-0.066 (0.404)	0.045 (0.570)	-0.371 (0.000)	-0.521 (0.000)	1.000					
10. Household products	-0.004 (0.964)	0.070 (0.375)	0.184 (0.018)	-0.011 (0.888)	0.000 (10.000)	0.009 (0.912)	0.057 (0.466)	0.014 (0.856)	-0.078 (.323)	1.000				
11. Infant/child products	-0.029 (0.710)	0.069 (0.378)	-0.063 (0.422)	0.169 (0.030)	-0.025 (0.753)	-0.112 (0.154)	-0.114 (0.145)	-0.024 (0.760)	0.150 (0.056)	-0.424 (0.000)	1.000			
12. Outdoor products	0.003 (0.966)	0.096 (0.221)	-0.107 (0.173)	-0.037 (0.637)	0.043 (0.584)	-0.008 (0.917)	0.001 (0.990)	-0.005 (0.945)	0.005 (0.946)	-0.283 (0.000)	-0.208 (0.007)	1.000		
13. Sports and recreation	0.043 (0.581)	0.090 (0.250)	-0.181 (0.021)	0.063 (0.423)	0.061 (0.437)	-0.103 (0.190)	0.024 (0.761)	0.006 (0.940)	-0.032 (0.680)	-0.241 (0.002)	-0.177 (0.023)	-0.118 (0.132)	1.000	
14. Toys	0.001 (0.986)	-0.312 (0.000)	0.065 (0.410)	-0.188 (0.016)	-0.055 (0.487)	0.196 (0.012)	0.036 (0.650)	0.009 (0.910)	-0.048 (0.538)	-0.359 (0.000)	-0.264 (0.001)	-0.176 (0.024)	-0.150 (0.055)	1.000
Mean	-0.002	-0.028	0.335	0.189	0.250	0.561	0.299	0.457	0.244	0.366	0.238	0.122	0.091	0.183
SD	-1.366	-2.208	0.474	0.393	0.434	0.498	0.459	0.500	0.431	0.483	0.427	0.328	0.289	0.388

Note: p values are in parentheses.

Table 15.3   Abnormal Returns*

	n	Mean CAR	t	Patell Z	t-BMP	Diff.	t	Z
Privately branded products	55	−1.17%	−2.99*	−3.49***	−3.74***	−1.50%	−3.80****	−3.07***
Nationally branded products	109	0.33%	1.51	0.84	0.96			

*$p < 0.10$; **$p < 0.05$; ***$p < 0.01$; ****$p < 0.0001$.

a recall of a privately branded product, compared with a nationally branded product. Similarly, the *t* test and Wilcoxon-Mann-Whitney test results indicated that there was a significant difference in the cumulative abnormal returns (CARs) for privately vs. nationally branded product recall announcements.

The results of the hierarchical regression analysis are presented in Table 15.4. The variance inflation factor (VIF) values indicate that multicollinearity was not a problem. Model 1 includes only the control variables, in order to provide a baseline. The significant change in R^2 for Model 2 indicates that the addition of product brand, remedy strategy, and the degree of product hazard contributed significantly to the predictive power of the model.

The evidence from Model 2 strongly supports the hypothesis that the market reaction is more severe for the announcement of a recall of a privately branded product than for a nationally branded product. H_2 predicted that the stock market's reaction to a product recall announcement would be more negative for a refund, rather than replacement or repair, remedy strategy, which was supported by the results. Compared with repair, an offer of a refund or replacement was associated with a decrease in abnormal returns. H_3 posited that the higher the hazard level of the recalled product, the more negative the stock market's reaction to the product recall announcement would be. The coefficients for Class B and Class A hazards were both significant and negative; compared with a recall announcement for a product with a Class C hazard (the least severe), recalls for products with a more severe hazard were associated with a greater financial penalty from the stock market. These results provide support for H_3. Thus, all three hypotheses were supported by the hierarchical regression analysis.

Table 15.4   Results of Hierarchical Regression Analysis*

Independent Variable	Model 1 Coefficient	SE	Model 2 Coefficient	SE	VIF (Model 2)
Intercept	−0.403	0.309	2.176****	0.527	
Company size	−0.069	0.139	−0.171	0.137	1.22
Recall size	0.111	0.090	0.057	0.092	1.45
Infant/child products	−0.283	0.492	−0.440	0.457	1.33
Outdoor products	1.167*	0.618	0.927	0.570	1.22
Sports and recreation	1.525**	0.692	0.893	0.641	1.20
Toys	−0.006	0.555	0.035	0.504	1.34
Product brand			−1.437***	0.452	1.60
Replacement			−1.043**	0.537	1.90
Refund			−1.265**	0.534	2.47
Class B			−1.275***	0.409	1.46
Class A			−1.757****	0.487	1.54
F	2.12		5.11		
p	0.0539		0.0000		
R^2	0.0749		0.2701		
Adjusted R^2	0.0396		0.2173		
ΔR^2	–		0.1952		

* $p < 0.10$; ** $p < 0.05$; *** $p < 0.01$; **** $p < 0.001$.

15.4.2 Selection Bias Correction

Table 15.5 contains the results of the selection bias correction. As shown in the last three columns, the coefficients of inverse Mills ratios for the three subgroups were not significantly different from zero. Therefore, selection bias is not a concern in the empirical model, and our conclusions based on the hierarchical regression analysis are robust.

Table 15.5 Two-Stage Selection Bias Correction*

Independent Variables	Multinomial Logistic Regression of Remedy Strategy[a]		OLS Regression of Abnormal Returns[a]		
	Repair	Replacement	Repair	Replacement	Refund
Intercept	0.536 (0.650)	0.502 (0.695)	0.734 (2.005)	0.566 (1.080)	−0.223 (0.932)
Company size	−0.496 (0.181)***	−0.128 (0.195)	−1.386 (0.491)**	0.065 (0.284)	0.109 (0.202)
Recall size	0.622 (0.174)****	0.542 (0.135)****			
Infant/child products	0.644 (0.626)	−0.294 (0.611)	0.419 (1.348)	−0.218 (0.635)	−0.160 (0.921)
Outdoor products	−1.204 (1.098)	−0.786 (0.736)	−2.262 (2.404)	1.490 (0.740)*	1.720 (0.669)**
Sports and recreation products	−0.185 (0.870)	−0.604 (0.807)	0.853 (1.806)	0.435 (0.795)	1.506 (1.084)
Toys	−1.323 (1.107)	−0.271 (0.730)	−2.367 (1.627)	0.522 (0.707)	0.503 (0.757)
Product brand	−2.648 (0.626)****	−4.297 (1.168)****	−5.021 (2.140)	−0.794 (1.707)	−0.639 (0.700)
Replacement (remedy = 1)					

(continued)

Table 15.5 Two-Stage Selection Bias Correction* (Continued)

Independent Variables	Multinomial Logistic Regression of Remedy Strategy[a]		OLS Regression of Abnormal Returns[a]		
	Repair	Replacement	Repair	Replacement	Refund
Refund (remedy = 2)					
Class B (hazard = 1)	−1.256 (0.590)**	0.128 (0.571)	−2.462 (1.250)*	−0.891 (0.698)	−1.426 (0.570)**
Class A (hazard = 2)	−1.469 (0.668)**	−1.148 (0.700)	−1.692 (1.553)	−1.346 (0.705)*	−1.757 (0.782)**
Inverse mills ratio			2.094 (1.571)	0.082 (0.893)	1.020 (0.613)
R^2			0.3338	0.2785	0.2530
n			31	41	92

Note: OLS, ordinary least squares.

[a] Estimated coefficients reported (robust standard errors in parentheses).

*$p < 0.10$; **$p < 0.05$; ***$p < 0.01$; ****$p < 0.001$.

15.5 Discussion

Our findings indicate that retailers suffer a significantly higher financial penalty from the stock market for recalling a privately branded product, compared with a nationally branded product. While privately branded products provide retailers with higher gross margins than nationally branded products do, our findings point to an important drawback. The introduction of a privately branded product is associated with greater responsibility for the retailer, which is no longer a mere gatekeeper in the supply chain. Rather, the retailer may be perceived as bearing at least some responsibility for the quality and safety of the products carrying its brand (Ailawadi and Keller 2004; Chan Choi and Coughlan 2006; Steenkamp and Dekimpe 1997). As manifested by the downward adjustment in the stock price after a recall of a privately branded product, investors may attribute some of the blame for the product defect to the retailer. In contrast, when a nationally branded product was recalled, the change in the retailer's stock price was not significant. In combination with the findings of the prior literature, we can posit that the manufacturer of a nationally branded product will experience a greater loss in financial value than its retailers will when a product recall is announced. This important finding may explain the inconsistent results in the limited prior research on recall announcements by retailers. Thus, as privately branded products continue to show strong growth in customer product markets (Kumar and Steenkamp 2007), retailers should have heightened concerns about ensuring their quality.

Our results also suggest that, contrary to conventional wisdom, a refund remedy strategy is associated with a more negative reaction from the stock market than an exchange or repair strategy. This suggests that investors perceive the selection of remedy strategy differently from customers. Investors are more concerned with a remedy's cash flow implications. Compared with repair, a refund of the purchase price is more costly, thereby more negatively impacting the retailer's future earnings. In an unexpected event like a product recall announcement, investors rely on signals to assess the potential financial consequences of the event. Remedy strategy is one of those signals, providing a clue about how well the retailer expects to be able to contain the damage associated with the product defect. Investors associate a refund remedy with a high possibility of harm or greater difficulty for the retailer to rectify. In contrast, repair or replacement signals that the damage will be minimal. Thus, the capital market penalty is greater for a retailer that offers a refund, compared with a replacement or repair remedy. This finding emphasizes the importance of moving beyond experimental studies based on customer reactions to event studies of investors' reactions, when studying the impact of remedy strategies.

We also found that the stock market reaction is more negative as the degree of product hazard increases. Although unsurprising, this important factor has been left out of much of the prior research on product recall announcements by both manufacturers and retailers. Due to their loss aversion, investors react more strongly to recall announcements for more hazardous products, which translates into a greater decrease in market value. Customers are more apprehensive about buying from a retailer that has recently announced a product recall, leading to a greater loss of future revenue, which further drives down the retailer's stock price. In addition, the variation in media attention given to recall announcements associated with different levels of product hazard is important. Because a recall announcement for a severely hazardous product receives more media coverage, it is more likely to be considered by investors as a signal of serious problems.

15.5.1 Academic Contribution

The contribution of this research to the literature on product recalls and product safety is fourfold. First, it expands the domain of product recall research from manufacturers to retailers. This is important because of the increasing influence of retailers in supply chains and their rising number of product recalls. Second, using attribution theory, we identified the differing effects of recalls of privately and nationally branded products on the shareholder wealth of a retailer announcing a product recall. Our findings are consistent with the view that product quality, in addition to price, is an important contributor to privately branded product success (Kumar and Steenkamp 2007).

Third, our findings on the effect of remedies enrich the study of product harm crisis management strategies for both manufacturers and retailers. The negative impact of a refund remedy indicates that investors perceive recall remedies differently than customers do. This reveals the unintended signaling effect provided by a recall strategy, as investors gather information to assess the expected impact of an unexpected product recall. Fourth, this study provides a theoretical explanation for the effect of product hazard level on firm value when a recall is announced, for both manufacturers and retailers. It will help to advance theory building in the product recalls and supply chain risk management literature.

15.5.2 Managerial Implications

Our findings have strong managerial implications. While it is undeniable that privately branded products increase retailer profitability, retailers should also recognize the potential risk of placing their name or associated brand on a product. As customers increasingly seek privately branded products (Kumar and Steenkamp 2007), retailers should strive to take an active role in monitoring and improving the quality of these products (Hoch and Banerji 1993). For example, establishing a collaborative relationship with suppliers of privately branded products will give retailers more direct control of the manufacturing process and establish trust among supply chain partners. Implementation of advanced design tools, such as quality function deployment and prevention through design, will better enable the integration of product safety objectives with design requirements.

In addition, our results suggest that when a retailer offers a refund remedy, it should be aware of the different interpretation of this strategy by customers and investors. While customers interpret a refund positively, investors interpret it negatively. It is important that retailers communicate clearly to their shareholders about why a refund has been offered; if the refund was intended to enhance customers' convenience, it should not be interpreted as a signal of a looming severe product hazard. The retailer should also explain to its investors the way in which the direct costs of the recall will be shared between itself and the manufacturer, which typically bears all of most of the direct cost, in order to alleviate investor concerns.

15.5.3 Limitations and Future Research

While this study makes a significant contribution to the research on product recalls, several limitations should be noted. First, we focused our assessment of the consequences of product recalls upon the loss in shareholder value by retailers. It is unclear whether these losses are caused by the investors' assessment of the impact of recalls on retailers' performance or by stock market sensitivity to the negative information about these companies. Thus, it would be fruitful for future research to study how a product recall negatively affects retailers' actual performance, including operating income, sales, costs, assets, and inventories.

Second, by examining recall remedy strategies, our intent was to develop an understanding of how retailers manage product recalls. A better approach, however, would be for retailers to focus on the development of capabilities to prevent or reduce the occurrence of product recalls. This can be accomplished by explicitly considering product safety and traceability during new product development, proactively coordinating recall management with supplier relationship management, and providing for rapid notification of product defects (Rogers et al. 2002; Smith et al. 1996). Future research should examine the impact of preventive measures on mitigating the negative consequence of product recalls.

There may be other variables that could influence the impact of a product recall announcement but were not included in the model. Future research should examine how the perceived quality product (Kumar and Steenkamp 2007; Zeithaml 1988) of a privately branded product influences customer and investor reactions to a retailer's recall announcement. Biases due to prior beliefs about a firm may also be important; they have previously been shown to influence customer judgments of a product recall (Dawar and Pillutla 2000; Klein and Dawar 2004). Similarly, positive perceptions of the product quality of a privately branded product may reduce the risk of damage to brand evaluation and thus moderate the negative consequences of a product recall announcement.

Second, there is an ongoing debate about how retailers maintain a balance between private brands and national brands in their product offerings (Ailawadi and Harlam 2004). Future studies on the role of privately branded products in the context of a product recall may provide new insights on this issue. Third, future research should examine how adopting a proactive vs. reactive recall strategy impacts retailers. Recent research with manufacturers has found that, while applauded as more socially responsible, a proactive recall strategy is associated with more negative stock market reaction.

Another important direction is to examine the impact of a retailer's product recall announcement on the financial value of its competitors. Previous research with manufacturers has suggested that there is either a substitution effect, by which competitors benefit from the recall by taking over customers (Barber and Darrough 1996; Dowdell et al. 1992), or a spillover effect, by which competitors also suffer from the recall (Freedman et al. 2009). Last, we have shown that the fundamental reason for the differential interpretation of a refund remedy by customers and investors is the information asymmetry between retailers and the stock market. Future research should explore methods for resolving this, such as mandatory disclosure of manufacturing sources for both privately branded and nationally branded products.

Appendix 15.1 Technical Details of the Data Analysis

Hierarchical regression was used to examine how the stock price effects of a recall announcement were related to various retailer and recall characteristics (Kothari and Warner 2007). We tested the effect of product brand (H_1), remedy strategy (H_2), and degree of product hazard (H_3) on the abnormal returns using the following model:

$$Abret_i = \beta_0 + \beta_1 Company\_size_i + \beta_2 Recall\_size_i + \beta_3 Product\_label_i$$
$$+ \beta_4 Remedy_i + \beta_5 Hazard_i + \beta_6 Product\_cat_i + \varepsilon_i \qquad (15.1)$$

where $Abret_i$ is the abnormal return for firm i, based on the CAR over the event period. $Company\_size_i$ is the natural logarithm of sales in the most recent fiscal year ending prior to the recall date; the logarithmic transformation addressed the right skewness that is typical of distributions of revenue. $Recall\_size_i$ is the natural logarithm of the product of the maximum unit price and total quantity recalled. In order to make the first-order coefficient and the intercept more interpretable (Aguinis 2004; Aiken and West 1991), $Company\_size_i$ and $Recall\_size_i$ were centered. $Product\_label_i$ had a value of 1 if the recalled product was a privately branded product and 0 if it was a nationally branded product. There were several categorical variables that were coded as dummy variables, summarized in Table 15.A1. Hazard categories were based on the CPSC's classification. A Class A hazard exists when the risk of death or grievous injury or illness is likely or very likely or serious injury

Table 15.A1   Coding Scheme for Categorical Variables

	Remedy 1	Remedy 2		Hazard 1	Hazard 2
Repair	0	0	Class A	0	0
Replacement	1	0	Class B	1	0
Refund	0	1	Class C	0	1

	Prod_cat1	Prod_cat2	Prod_cat3	Prod_cat4
Household products	0	0	0	0
Infant/child products	1	0	0	0
Outdoor products	0	1	0	0
Sports and recreation products	0	0	1	0
Toys	0	0	0	1

or illness is very likely. A Class B hazard exists when the risk of death or grievous injury or illness is not likely but is possible or when serious injury or illness is likely or moderate injury or illness is very likely. A Class C hazard exists when the risk of serious injury or illness is not likely but is possible or when moderate injury or illness is not likely but is possible.

To measure the difference in abnormal returns associated with a recall of a privately branded vs. nationally branded product, we conducted a two-sample *t* test and a Wilcoxon–Mann–Whitney rank-sum test. The nonparametric Wilcoxon–Mann–Whitney test allows testing the difference between sample means without assuming that the abnormal returns are normally distributed.

Heckman's (1979) two-step estimation procedure is often used (Hamilton and Nickerson 2003) to correct potential endogeneity and self-selection bias in event study research (Chen et al. 2009; Gaspar et al. 2005). However, a major limitation to the Heckman two-step procedure is that the choice variable must be dichotomous. We instead followed Lee's (1982, 1983) generalization of Heckman's approach, which allows for more than two choices. We first estimated a reduced form multinomial logit model for the choice of remedy strategy, which has a closed form solution:

$$\Pr\left(Remedy_i = n\right) = \frac{\exp(X_i\beta_n + Z_i\delta_n)}{\sum \exp(X_i\beta_j + Z_i\delta_n)} = P_{in} \quad (n = 0, 1, 2). \quad (15.2)$$

X_i includes the intercept and all exogenous variables that jointly influence CARs and the remedy strategy. Lee (1982, 1983) suggests that there should be one or more instrumental variables Z_i that affect remedy choice but do not directly impact abnormal returns (Hamilton and Nickerson 2003). As shown in the hierarchical regression analysis, the size of a recall did not significantly influence the stock market reaction. However, it could be argued that the size of a recall is directly related to a retailer's choice of remedy strategy. For instance, for a large recall, a retailer might prefer to minimize potential revenue losses by offering repair or replacement, rather than a refund remedy strategy. Thus, we excluded recall size from the second stage of the hierarchical regression. To correct for heteroscedasticity, robust standard errors were used in our model estimation. We defined $J_{ik} = \Phi^{-1}(P_{ik})$, where $\Phi^{-1}(.)$ is the inverse normal distribution function and $k = 0, 1, 2$, then computed the inverse Mills ratio by $\lambda_{ik} = \phi(J_{ik})/P_{ik}$. $\phi(.)$ as the probability density function of the standard normal distribution. The second-stage selection-corrected performance equations are as follows:

$$Abret_i(Remedy_i = n) = X_i\beta_n - \sigma_{\lambda n}\lambda_{in} + \varepsilon_{ni} \ (n = 0, 1, 2). \tag{15.3}$$

These equations were estimated via ordinary least squares using the subset of observations for each remedy choice. If the parameters $\lambda_{i0} = \lambda_{i1} = \lambda_{i2} = 0$, the remedy choice is exogenous, and self-selection bias is not an issue.

References

Aguinis, H. 2004. *Regression Analysis for Categorical Moderators*. New York, Guilford Press.
Aiken, L.S. and West, S.G. 1991. *Multiple Regression: Testing and Interpreting Interactions*. Newbury Park, CA, Sage Publications.
Ailawadi, K.L. 2001. The retail power–performance conundrum: What have we learned? *J. Retail.* 77(3): 299–318.
Ailawadi, K.L. and Harlam, B. 2004. An empirical analysis of the determinants of retail margins: The role of store-brand share. *J. Mktg.* 68(1): 147–165.
Ailawadi, K.L. and Keller, K.L. 2004. Understanding retail branding: Conceptual insights and research priorities. *J. Retail.* 80(4): 331–342.
Bapuji, H. 2011. *Not Just China: The Rise of Recalls in the Age of Global Business*. New York, Palgrave Macmillan.
Barber, B.M. and Darrough, M.N. 1996. Product reliability and firm value: The experience of American and Japanese automakers, 1973–1992. *J. Pol. Econ.* 104(5): 1084–1099.
Chan Choi, S. and Coughlan, A.T. 2006. Private label positioning: Quality versus feature differentiation from the national brand. *J. Retail.* 82(2): 79–93.
Chen, Y., Ganesan, S. and Liu, Y. 2009. Does a firm's product-recall strategy affect its financial value? An examination of strategic alternatives during product-harm crises. *J. Mktg.* 73(6): 214–226.
Coombs, W.T. 1999. Information and compassion in crisis responses: A test of their effects. *J. Pub. Rel. Res.* 11(2): 125–142.

Davidson, W.N. and Worrell, D.L. 1992. The effect of product recall announcements on shareholder wealth. *Strat. Mgmt. J.* 13(6): 467–473.

Dawar, N. and Pillutla, M.M. 2000. Impact of product-harm crises on brand equity: The moderating role of customer expectations. *J. Mktg. Res.* 37(2): 215–226.

Dhar, S.K. and Hoch, S.J. 1997. Why store brand penetration varies by retailer. *Mktg. Sci.* 16(3): 208–227.

Dierkens, N. 1991. Information asymmetry and equity issues. *J. Fin. Quant. Anal.* 26(2): 181–199.

Dowdell, T.D., Govindaraj, S. and Jain, P.C. 1992. The Tylenol incident, ensuing regulation, and stock prices. *J. Fin. Quant. Anal.* 27(2): 283–301.

Felcher, E.M. 2003. Product recalls: Gaping holes in the nation's product safety net. *J. Cons. Affairs* 37(1): 170–179.

Folkes, V.S. 1984. Customer reactions to product failure: An attributional approach. *J. Customer Res.* 10(4): 398–409.

Freedman, S., Kearney, M.S. and Lederman, M. 2009. Product recalls, imperfect information, and spillover effects: Lessons from the customer response to the 2007 toy recalls. NBER Working Paper Series, w15183, July.

Gaspar, J.-M., Massa, M. and Matos, P. 2005. Shareholder investment horizons and the market for corporate control. *J. Fin. Econ.* 76(1): 135–165.

Hamilton, B.H. and Nickerson, J.A. 2003. Correcting for endogeneity in strategic management research. *Strat. Org.* 1(1): 51–78.

Heckman, J.J. 1979. Sample selection bias as a specification error. *Econometrica* 47(1): 153–161.

Hoch, S.J. 1996. How should national brands think about private labels? *Sloan Mgmt. Rev.* 37(2): 89–102.

Hoch, S.J. and Banerji, S. 1993. When do private labels succeed? *Sloan Mgmt. Rev.* 34(4): 57–68.

Klein, J. and Dawar, N. 2004. Corporate social responsibility and customers' attributions and brand evaluations in a product-harm crisis. *Int. J. Res. Mktg.* 21(3): 203–217.

Kothari, S.P. and Warner, J.B. 2007. *Econometrics of Event Studies.* Amsterdam, North-Holland, Elsevier.

Kraiselburd, S., Narayanan, V.G. and Raman, A. 2004. Contracting in a supply chain with stochastic demand and substitute products. *Prod. Ops. Mgmt.* 13(1): 46–62.

Kulp, S.C., Lee, H.L. and Ofek, E. 2004. Manufacturer benefits from information integration with retail customers. *Mgmt. Sci.* 50(4): 431–444.

Kumar, N. and Steenkamp, J.-B.E.M. 2007. *Private Label Strategy: How to Meet the Store Brand Challenge.* Boston, Harvard Business School Press.

Lamey, L., Deleersnyder, B., Dekimpe, M.G. and Steenkamp, J.-B.E.M. 2007. How business cycles contribute to private-label success: Evidence from the United States and Europe. *J. Mktg.* 71(1): 1–15.

Lee, L.-F. 1982. Some approaches to the correction of selectivity bias. *Rev. Econ. Stud.* 49(3): 355–372.

Lee, L.-F. 1983. Generalized econometric models with selectivity. *Econometrica* 51(2): 507–512.

MacKinlay, A.C. 1997. Event studies in economics and finance. *J. Econ. Lit.* 35(1): 13–39.

Mollenkopf, D.A., Frankel, R. and Russo, I. 2011. Creating value through returns management: Exploring the marketing–operations interface. *J. Ops. Mgmt.* 29(5): 391–403.

Petersen, J.A. and Kumar, V. 2009. Are product returns a necessary evil? Antecedents and consequences. *J. Mktg.* 73(3): 35–51.

Rogers, D.S., Lambert, D.M., Croxton, K.L. and García-Dastugue, S.J. 2002. The returns management process. *Int. J. Log. Mgmt.* 13(2): 1–18.

Ross, K. 2009. Recall effectiveness: A hot topic. *Product Liability Committee Newsletter.*

Ross, K. and Prince, J.D. 2009. Post-sale duties—The most expansive theory in product liability. *Brooklyn Law Rev.* 74(3): 963–986.

Shrum, W. and Wuthnow, R. 1988. Reputational status of organizations in technical systems. *Am. J. Soc.* 93(4): 882–912.

Siomkos, G. and Kurzbard, G. 1994. The hidden crisis in product-harm crisis management. *Eur. J. Mktg.* 28(2): 30–41.

Smith, N.C., Thomas, R.J. and Quelch, J.A. 1996. A strategic approach to managing product recalls. *Harv. Bus. Rev.* 74(5): 102–112.

Steenkamp, J.-B.E.M. and Dekimpe, M.G. 1997. The increasing power of store brands: Building loyalty and market share. *Long Range Plann.* 30(6): 917–930.

Van Heerde, H., Helsen, K. and Dekimpe, M.G. 2007. The impact of a product-harm crisis on marketing effectiveness. *Mktg. Sci.* 26(2): 230–245.

Zeithaml, V.A. 1988. Customer perceptions of price, quality, and value: A means-end model and synthesis of evidence. *J. Mktg.* 52(3): 2–22.

INTRODUCTION TO SECTION V: CONSUMER PERSPECTIVE ON PRODUCT RECALLS

V

In Section V, we examine product recalls from the perspective of consumers, using scenario experiments. In a scenario experiment, a story about a hypothetical product (a scenario) is developed. Within the story, there are several variables that can be manipulated. For example, in Chapter 16, one of the manipulated variables is recall proactiveness. In one version of the story, the hypothetical company recalls the product immediately, as soon as it has detected the problem. In the other version of the story, the hypothetical company waits to recall the product until a recall is mandated. The manipulation levels are tested statistically in order to make sure that the respondents perceive the difference between the levels of the manipulated variables.

There are typically two or three manipulated variables within a scenario. If there are three manipulated variables, each with a high level and a low level, there can be eight different versions of the scenario that are developed. A set of consumers who would be appropriate for the hypothetical product are each given a copy of one of the scenarios to read. They are then asked questions about the scenario. For example, in Chapter 16, the respondents are asked about their perception of the fairness of the recall strategy and their perception of the organizational legitimacy of the hypothetical company. The data that are collected are statistically analyzed in order to determine where the significant differences occurred.

Chapter 16 focuses on recall strategies. The respondents are students, who would be typical consumers of the orange juice drink that is the topic of the scenario they are presented with. There are two manipulated variables: the level of compensation that was provided to customers who previously purchased a bottle of the orange juice drink and the proactiveness with which it was recalled, once it was discovered to have a safety issue.

In Chapter 17, the role of the respondents both direct consumers and bystanders is examined. Three experiments manipulate the role of the respondents (consumer vs. bystander who simply reads a news story about a product recall) and the familiarity of the bystanders with the consumers (an acquaintance vs. someone described in a news story), in order to develop an understanding of the role of panic in evaluating a product recall announcement.

Chapter 16

Effectiveness of Recall Strategies on Customer Perceptions

Haiju Hu, Xiande Zhao, and Barbara B. Flynn

Contents

16.1 Introduction: Importance of the Customers' Perspective

In this chapter, we investigate the effectiveness of recall strategies from the perspective of the very end of the downstream supply chain: customers. This is an important perspective because customers, as the direct target and beneficiaries of a product recall, are in the best position to evaluate the way in which it was designed and administered. Our research provides important insights for companies as they structure a product recall announcement and consider remedies, strategies, and incentives for customers. The perception and reaction of customers may also be related to the company's financial performance in the future, so there are also important implications for investors.

Previous research about product recalls from the customers' perspective has focused on topics such as perceived danger (Siomkos and Kurzbard 1994), future purchase intention (Siomkos and Kurzbard 1994; Vassilikopoulou et al. 2009), and attitude toward the company (Dean 2004). However, the results have been mixed. For instance, Mowen (1979) argued that customers' intention to purchase a replacement product made by the company following a recall is significantly influenced by the length of time the company took before issuing the recall announcement, while Siomkos and Kurzbard (1994) found that the intensity of the company response (denial, involuntary recall, voluntary recall, super-effort) had no significant effect on customers' future purchase intention.

We believe that one of the main reasons for the conflicting results is that prior research has treated product recall management as a single dimension. In reality, there are two critical decisions faced by companies dealing with a product recall: when to issue the recall announcement (recall proactiveness) and how to compensate the affected customers (recall compensation). We deal with both of these dimensions in this research.

The setting for this research is mainland China. The prior literature about the effectiveness of recall strategies is based in Western cultures. However, product safety issues and the product recalls that result from them are issues that are faced by customers in most regions of the world. In particular, the number of recent product recalls in China has increased as customer protection has become a higher priority. Yet, Chinese customers may react differently than Western customers, for whom product recalls are a more common occurrence. Thus, we test how Chinese customers react to different recall strategies.

We investigate the effects of recall strategy on Chinese customers' reactions, differentiating between the dimensions of recall proactiveness and compensation. This study is framed in the perspective of service recovery and the theoretical foundations provided by service-dominant logic, the organizational legitimacy theory, and the two-factor theory.

In Section 16.2, we introduce service-dominant logic as an explanation for why we address this issue from the service recovery perspective, even though product recalls deal with tangible products. We then develop the theoretical background for the hypotheses, focusing on organizational legitimacy, fairness, and the two-factor theory. In Section 16.3, the experimental method that we used to test the hypotheses is described. Section 16.4 presents the results of the data analysis, and Section 16.5 presents our conclusions and discussion of the implications of this research for academics and managers.

16.2 Theoretical Background and Research Hypotheses

In the following, we lay the theoretical foundation for this research, which builds on some of the key premises of service-dominant logic. The framework for customer perceptions of an organization is described by the literature on organizational legitimacy. Alternative explanations for customer perceptions of organizational legitimacy following a product recall are provided by the fairness theory and the two-factor theory.

16.2.1 Service-Dominant Logic

Service-dominant logic was first proposed by Vargo and Lusch (2004) in "Evolving to a New Dominant Logic for Marketing." It has attracted a substantial amount of interest, and it has induced a rethinking of marketing logic. Service-dominant logic provides a potent explanation for why we can study product recalls from the service recovery perspective.

First, service-dominant logic is explicitly customer oriented (Lusch and Vargo 2006). It emphasizes the importance of customers' perceptions because the main purpose of a company is to provide value for its customers. Therefore, companies should focus on not only the provision of high-quality products but also the entire lifecycle of its products. Consider, for example, superior after-sales service. The responsibilities of a company should not end with the sale of the product. Rather, these should be extended to the end of the product's useful life. Thus, when a product is found to be unsafe, the company should take action, such as issuing a product recall announcement, to minimize its loss of customers and maximize the value of the product, which in turn will influence customers' perceptions.

Second, one of the fundamental premises of service-dominant logic is that goods are the distribution mechanism for the provision of a service (Lusch et al. 2007). Therefore, we can draw the conclusion that goods are a part of a service. If a product is found to be unsafe, there is a kind of service failure. Service recovery is an important way of dealing with a service failure, in order to turn a service mishap into a positive experience in the minds of customers. With strong service recovery, customers' perception of the company can actually be improved. We suggest that a well-handled product recall can have the same effect. Thus, the design of a product recall strategy is akin to service recovery.

16.2.2 Organizational Legitimacy

Organizational legitimacy is a social judgment that is ultimately accorded to an organization by its constituents (Ashforth 1990). An organization is perceived as legitimate when its values and actions are congruent with its audience's values and expectations (Dowling and Pfeffer 1975) or its audience accepts or endorses the organization's means and ends as valid, reasonable, and rational (Suchman 1995). In the context of a product recall, we examine how customers perceive organizational legitimacy following a recall announcement.

Suchman (1995) described three types of organizational legitimacy: pragmatic legitimacy, moral legitimacy, and cognitive legitimacy. Pragmatic legitimacy is based on the self-interested calculations of an organization's immediate audience, such as customers whose purchases have been recalled. Moral legitimacy rests on the audience's judgment about whether a given activity is "the right thing to do." It is assessed in terms of evaluation of outputs (consequential legitimacy), procedures (procedural legitimacy), structures (structural legitimacy), and leaders (personal legitimacy). Cognitive legitimacy based on cognition. It is assessed in terms of legitimacy based on comprehensibility and taken-for-grantedness.

Organizational legitimacy is very important to companies (Dowling and Pfeffer 1975; Meyer and Rowan 1977; Perrow 1970) because it can help to attract economic resources and gain the social and political support necessary for continued successful operations (Ogden and Clarke 2005). Organizational legitimacy affects not only how people act toward a company but also how they understand it (Suchman 1995). The audience will perceive a legitimate organization as more worthy, meaningful, predictable, and trustworthy. All kinds of organizational decisions require legitimation; otherwise, they cannot be justified.

However, in the operations management research, the importance of organizational legitimacy has been overlooked, even though it has been an integral part of the marketing and management literatures. During a product recall, it is very important that the company establish the legitimacy of its reaction to the safety hazard and its decisions related to the product recall. By demonstrating that it has its customer's best interests and safety at heart, it demonstrates that it is trustworthy and deserving of their business. Administering a recall with clear procedures increases organizational legitimacy by demonstrating that the company is predictable and fair. Thus, we use customers' perceived organizational legitimacy as a measure of the effectiveness of a recall strategy.

16.2.3 Fairness in Service Recovery

During the service recovery process, customers expect to be treated fairly, in terms of both the process and the outcomes. They expect the process to be fair, in terms of its policies, rules, timeliness, whether the company allows the affected customers to express their concerns, whether it follows suggestions from customers, and whether it answers their questions in a timely manner. These concerns all apply to a product recall. Customers expect the process to be timely, with hazardous products removed as quickly as possible, and they expect to receive fair compensation. They expect that the rules and procedures for returning the product are clearly spelled out and easy to follow. If they have questions or concerns, they expect to be able to express these. Furthermore, customers will perceive the procedure as more fair if the company is proactive in recalling the product with the safety issue than if the recall is passive. Customers also expect the outcome of the recall (compensation) to match the level of their dissatisfaction; if it does, they perceive it to be fair. If the compensation matches their perception of the losses caused by the product safety issue, they will believe that the company was fair.

In organizational legitimacy theory, organizational legitimacy is endorsed based on either process or output or both (Dowling and Pfeffer 1975). Therefore, customers will perceive the company as more legitimate if it is fair and open with procedures and outcomes.

H_{1a}: During a product recall, customers will perceive a company that is proactive in announcing a recall as more legitimate than one that is passive in its announcement.

H_{2a}: During a product recall, customers will perceive a company that provides a higher level of compensation as more legitimate than one that provides a lower level of compensation as they remedy.

A second measure of the success of a product recall is the intention of customers to make future purchases from the company even though it has issued a product recall. Since customers will support companies that meet their fairness expectations, they will be more likely to purchase products from a company that issues a proactive recall announcement or offers higher compensation, in the event of a product safety issue.

H_{1b}: Customers will have a higher intention of making future purchases from a company that is proactive in making a recall announcement than one that is passive.

H_{2b}: Customers will have a higher intention of making future purchases from a company that compensates them more than one that compensates them less during a product recall.

16.2.4 Two-Factor Theory

An alternative view of product recall effectiveness is provided by two-factor theory. Thus, we test competing hypotheses based on both the fairness theory and the two-factor theory.

The two-factor theory proposes that service attributes can be categorized into one of two categories: qualifying or vantage factors. Vantage factors significantly affect satisfaction only when qualifying factors meet or exceed customer expectations (Johnston 1995). Financial outcomes are usually considered as a qualifying factor. This logic can also be applied to product recalls. It suggests that recall proactiveness is important to customers only if the level of compensation meets or exceeds their expectations. Thus, we hypothesize that compensation following a product recall operates as a qualifying factor. Therefore, according to the two-factor theory, we predict the following:

H_{3a}: Recall proactiveness will not influence perceived legitimacy when compensation is low, while recall proactiveness will increase perceived organizational legitimacy when compensation is high.

H_{3b}: Recall proactiveness will not influence repurchase intention when compensation is low, while recall proactiveness will increase repurchase intention when compensation is high.

In a crisis, there is a positive relationship between attitude and behavior (Coombs 2007; McDonald et al. 2010). Negative emotion will lead to negative behavior, while positive emotion can increase customer support for a company, in terms of repurchase intention (Coombs 2007). Therefore, if customers perceive the company to have greater organizational legitimacy, they are more likely to make future purchases from it.

H_{4a}: Perceived organizational legitimacy will mediate the relationship between recall proactiveness and repurchase intention.

H_{4b}: Perceived organizational legitimacy will mediate the relationship between compensation and repurchase intention.

Figure 16.1 presents the conceptual model that will be tested in this chapter.

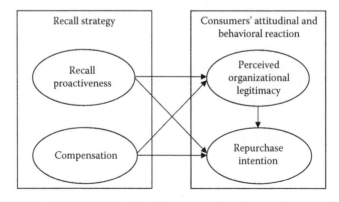

Figure 16.1 Experimental model.

16.3 Research Method

16.3.1 Participants and Experimental Design

A scenario experiment with two levels of compensation (high vs. low) and two levels of recall strategy (proactive vs. passive) was conducted to test the hypotheses. The participants were 172 undergraduate student volunteers enrolled in Nankai University in mainland China. Their average age was 19.52 years (ranging from 17 to 23 years). To ensure that the participants were familiar with the stimulus, we chose a fruit juice company as the context. We gave the company a fictional name (ABC), in order to minimize any preconceived biases that the participants might have about an existing company.

16.3.2 Procedure

Questionnaires were administered to the participants in their classrooms. The experimenter started by providing the following explanation:

> This is a study about customer behavior. Your responses will be kept confidential, and the data will be analyzed only at the aggregate level. The results will be used for academic research only and not for any other purpose. In this study, you will be asked to carefully read a short scenario as if it were real and then respond to the questionnaire following the scenario. This will take you about 15 minutes. You are not required to participate in this study. You may drop out after you have started if you do not wish to continue participating.

After the participants indicated their willingness to participate, the experimenter randomly distributed different questionnaire packets among the participants.

The first page of the questionnaire contained a brief introduction, reinforcing what the experimenter had verbally instructed. Following that, there was a one-page questionnaire where participants were asked questions about their frequency of drinking fruit juice, their knowledge about product recalls in general, and other demographic information.

This was followed by a short scenario. All of the scenarios began with the same background information about the company:

> Imagine that you are a customer of the ABC group, a company which produces an orange juice drink. You have been drinking this juice drink for several years and really love it. Yesterday, ABC announced that it would recall 300,000 bottles of its orange juice drink (production code 091206-01). The company reported that an additive

used in these products was tainted, due to the company's production process, and that consumption of the juice drink could lead to health problems.

The next statement described either high or low compensation. The participants in the high-compensation group were shown the information that is underlined, while those in the low compensation condition saw the information that is included in parentheses:

> ABC officially recalled the tainted products and *offered a refund of five times the purchase price to all affected parties. In addition, ABC offered to cover the medical expenses for a physical check-up and any associated treatment* (ABC offered a refund of the purchase price to all affected parties. No additional compensation was provided to the affected customers).

The next statement described either a proactive or passive recall. In the proactive recall scenario, the company was described as follows (underlined), while the participants in the passive recall condition were shown the information that is included in parentheses.

> A trusted media source reported that ABC found the defect through its own internal inspection *and decided to recall the product immediately* (but didn't recall the products until ordered by the government to do so).

Thus, there were four different scenarios containing different combinations of two levels of compensation and two levels of proactiveness.

After reading the entire scenario, participants rated ABC's response to the product safety issue on proactiveness and compensation as manipulation checks. Finally, all the participants completed the questionnaire, responding to questions about their perceptions of organizational legitimacy and future purchase intention from ABC.

16.4 Analysis and Results

16.4.1 Manipulation Checks

There were two manipulation checks, one for each independent variable. The results are shown in Tables 16.1 and 16.2.

16.4.1.1 Compensation

As shown in Table 16.1, participants in the high-compensation group perceived that they were provided with higher compensation than those in the low compensation

Table 16.1   Group Means

Variable	Manipulation	Mean	SD
Perceived compensation	Low	2.32	1.41
	High	3.99	1.28
Perceived proactiveness	Passive	2.02	1.08
	Proactive	5.09	1.27

Table 16.2   Univariate ANOVA for Manipulation Check

	Dependent Variable			
	Perceived Compensation		Perceived Proactiveness	
Independent Variable	F	p	F	p
Perceived compensation	61.92	.00	3.57	.06
Perceived proactiveness	1.51	.22	254.28	.00
Interaction	1.17	.28	0.27	.60

group [$F(1,161) = 62.21$, $p < .001$]. This perceived compensation was not affected by the company's recall proactiveness (Table 16.2). Therefore, the manipulation of compensation was successful.

16.4.1.2 Recall Proactiveness

The second manipulation check indicated that participants in the proactive recall group believed that ABC's response was more proactive than did those in the passive group did [$F(1,149) = 255.39$, $p < .001$]. In addition, this perception was not affected by the compensation manipulation. Therefore, the respondents perceived that there were differences in the level of proactiveness between the two conditions; therefore, the manipulation of recall proactiveness (Table 16.2) was successful.

16.4.2 Hypothesis Tests

The data were analyzed using multivariate analysis of variance (ANOVA), which is a more powerful way to test for differences when there is more than one dependent variable and the dependent variables are correlated with each other. The

Table 16.3   Results of Multivariate Analysis

	F	p
Gender	5.14	.007
Age	3.75	.026
Drink fruit juice?	0.15	.865
Heard of recall?	1.37	.256
Experienced any recalls?	0.26	.769
Compensation	9.54	.000
Proactiveness	10.68	.000
Compensation × proactiveness	4.05	.019

results (Table 16.3) revealed a significant multivariate main effect for compensation [Wilks' Λ = .889, $F(2,153)$ = 9.54] and recall proactiveness [Wilks' Λ = .877, $F(2,153)$ = 10.68]. Moreover, in the univariate analysis, in the proactive group, participants' perceived organizational legitimacy was higher than that in the passive group [proactive group: $\bar{X}$ = 4.23, SD = 1.17; passive group: $\bar{X}$ = 3.56, SD = 1.02; $F(1,154)$ = 14.46, p < .001]. Therefore, H_{1a} was supported. We also observed that the perceived organizational legitimacy in the high-compensation group ($\bar{X}$ = 4.26, SD = 1.08) was significantly higher than that in the low-compensation group [$\bar{X}$ = 3.54, SD = 1.11; $F(1,154)$ = 18.04, p < .001]. Thus, H_{2a} was supported.

In the proactive group, participants' repurchase intention was higher than that in the passive group [proactive group: $\bar{X}$ = 3.71, SD = 1.56; passive group: $\bar{X}$ = 2.78, SD = 1.30; $F(1,154)$ = 16.74, p < .001]. Therefore, H_{1b} was supported. The repurchase intention in the high-compensation group ($\bar{X}$ = 3.59, SD = 1.49) was significantly higher than that in the low-compensation group [$\bar{X}$ = 2.92, SD = 1.45; $F(1,154)$ = 8.33, p < .01]. Thus, H_{2b} was supported.

There was a significant multivariate interaction effect [Wilks' Λ = .950, $F(2,153)$ = 4.05, p < .05] and two univariate interaction effects for perceived organizational legitimacy [$F(1,154)$ = 7.14, p <.01] and repurchase intention [$F(1,154)$ = 4.46, p < .05). To test H_{3a}, the simple main effect for recall proactiveness was tested at each compensation level. The results showed that when the company provides low compensation, perceived organizational legitimacy is not influenced by recall proactiveness [passive recall: $\bar{X}$ = 3.43, SD = 1.09; proactive recall: $\bar{X}$ = 3.65, SD = 1.11; $F(1,81)$ = 1.01, p > .10], while under high compensation, perceived organizational legitimacy increases with recall proactiveness [passive recall: $\bar{X}$ = 3.69,

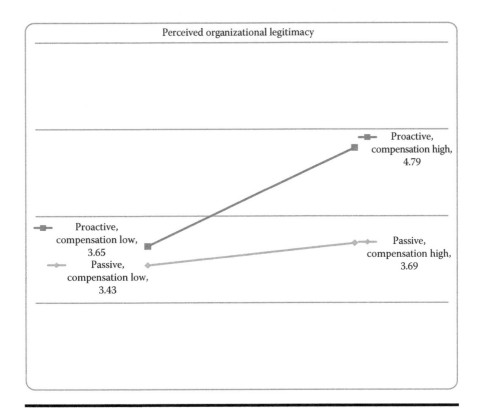

Figure 16.2 Interaction effect of recall proactiveness and compensation on perceived organizational legitimacy.

SD = 0.93; proactive recall: $\bar{X}$ = 4.79, SD = 0.94; $F(1,80)$ = 28.25, $p < .001$]. Therefore, we can conclude that H_{3a} was supported (Figure 16.2).

Similarly, we found that when the compensation is lower, repurchase intention is not influenced by recall proactiveness [passive recall: $\bar{X}$ = 2.64, SD = 1.38; proactive recall: $\bar{X}$ = 3.19, SD = 1.49; $F(1,66)$ = 2.31; $p > .10$], while when compensation is lower, repurchase intention is positively influenced by recall proactiveness [passive recall: $\bar{X}$ = 2.92, SD = 1.21; proactive recall: $\bar{X}$ = 4.20, SD = 1.47; $F(1,70)$ = 18.71, $p < .01$]. Therefore, H_{3b} was supported (Figure 16.3).

We tested the mediation effect of organizational legitimacy following the three steps suggested by Baron and Kenny (1986). The results are listed in Tables 16.4 and 16.5. From these two tables, we can conclude that perceived organizational legitimacy fully mediates the relationship between compensation and repurchase intention. However, it only partially mediates the relationship between recall proactiveness and repurchase intention. Therefore, H_{4a} is supported, while H_{4b} is partially supported.

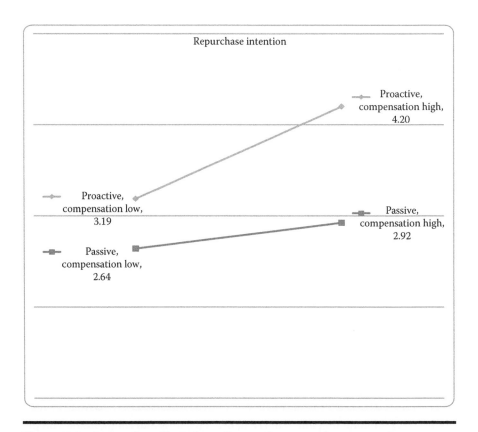

Figure 16.3 Interaction effect of recall proactiveness and compensation on repurchase intention.

Table 16.4 Regression Coefficients: Mediating Effect of Perceived Organizational Legitimacy for Compensation and Repurchase Intention

	Organizational Legitimacy	Repurchase Intention	Repurchase Intention
Compensation	.30***	.23***	.06[n.s.]
Legitimacy	–	–	.52***
R^2	.09***	.05**	.35***
ΔR^2		–	.29***

Note: n.s., not significant.

$*p < .05; **p < .01; ***p < .005.$

Table 16.5 Regression Coefficients: Mediating Effect of Perceived Organizational Legitimacy for Recall Proactiveness and Repurchase Intention

	Perceived Organizational Legitimacy	Repurchase Intention	Repurchase Intention
Recall proactiveness	.36***	.31***	.16*
Perceived organizational legitimacy	–	–	.49***
R^2	.13***	.09***	.31***
ΔR^2	–	–	.22***

*$p < .05$; **$p < .01$; ***$p < .005$.

16.5 Conclusions and Discussion

In this chapter, we strived to test the effectiveness of different recall strategies from the customers' perspective. Through the results of our scenario experiments, we can draw a number of conclusions. First, the significant main effects of compensation and recall proactiveness on purchase intention and perceived legitimacy indicate that both procedure and outcome are related to customers' attitudinal and behavioral reactions, as expected by the service recovery perspective. Second, the significant interaction effect predicted by the two-factor theory implies that when a company does not provide a favorable outcome (low compensation) following a product recall, it will not benefit from using a desirable procedure (proactiveness). However, when a company provides a favorable outcome (high compensation) following a product recall, customers perceive the company as more legitimate and will express a higher repurchase intention. Finally, the outcome (compensation) only had an indirect effect on repurchase intention; that is, the outcome changes customers' behavior (repurchase intention) only by changing their attitude (perceived organizational legitimacy). Moreover, the procedure (recall proactiveness) has both direct and indirect effect on repurchase intention.

This study also provides some insights for managers who have to manage a product recall. First, to recover from the nightmare of a product recall more quickly, higher levels of compensation and a proactive recall strategy are more effective. If compensation is not at an appropriate level, the effectiveness of the recall strategy will be discounted by the customers. Second, customers' attitude about a company plays a very important role in their future purchasing behavior. Therefore, when there is a product recall, the company should take measures to placate customers by offering both higher levels of compensation and taking a proactive stance.

This research contributes to the literature on product recalls by providing more evidence about how Chinese customers react to different recall strategies and provides insight about how Chinese firms can effectively manage a product recall when it becomes necessary. Future research should test these hypotheses in non-Chinese contexts, to determine whether the findings are generalizable.

References

Ashforth, B. E. (1990). "The double-edge of organizational legitimation." *Organization Science* **1**(2): 177–194.

Baron, R. M. and D. A. Kenny (1986). "The moderator–mediator variable distinction in social psychological research: Conceptual, strategic, and statistical considerations." *Journal of Personality and Social Psychology* **51**(6): 1173–1182.

Coombs, W. T. (2007). "Protecting organization reputation during a crisis: The development and application of Situational Crisis Communication Theory." *Corporate Reputation Review* **10**: 163–176.

Dean, D. (2004). "Consumer reaction to negative publicity." *Journal of Business Communication* **41**(2): 192–211.

Dowling, J. and J. Pfeffer (1975). "Organizational legitimacy: Social values and organizational behavior." *Pacific Sociological Review* **18**(1): 122–136.

Johnston, R. 1995. "The determinants of service quality: Satisfiers and dissatisfiers." *International Journal of Service Industry Management* **6**(5): 53–71.

Lusch, R. F. and S. L. Vargo (2006). "Service-dominant logic: Reactions, reflections and refinements." *Marketing Theory* **6**(3): 281–288.

Lusch, R. F., S. L. Vargo and M. O'Brien (2007). "Competing through service: Insights from service-dominant logic." *Journal of Retailing* **83**(1): 5–18.

McDonald, L. M., B. Sparks and A. I. Glendon (2010). "Stakeholder reactions to company crisis communication and causes." *Public Relations Review* **36**(3): 263–271.

Meyer, J. W. and B. Rowan (1977). "Institutionalized organizations: Formal structure as myth and ceremony." *American Journal of Sociology* **83**(2): 340–363.

Mowen, J. (1979). *Consumer Reactions to Product Recalls: An Empirical and Theoretical Examination.* Department of Marketing, Oklahoma State University.

Ogden, S. and J. Clarke (2005). "Customer disclosures, impression management and the construction of legitimacy corporate reports in the UK privatised water industry." *Accounting, Auditing and Accountability Journal* **18**(3): 313–345.

Perrow, C. (1970). *Organizational Analysis: A Sociological View.* Taylor & Francis, London.

Siomkos, G. and G. Kurzbard (1994). "The hidden crisis in product-harm crisis management." *European Journal of Marketing* **28**(2): 30–41.

Suchman, M. C. (1995). "Managing legitimacy: Strategic and institutional approaches." *Academy of Management Review* **20**(3): 571–610.

Vargo, S. L. and R. F. Lusch (2004). "Evolving to a new dominant logic for marketing." *Journal of Marketing* **68**(1): 1–17.

Vassilikopoulou, A., G. Siomkos, K. Chatzipanagiotou and A. Pantouvakis (2009). "Product-harm crisis management: Time heals all wounds?" *Journal of Retailing and Consumer Services* **16**(3): 174–180.

Chapter 17

Customer Perceptions of a Product Recall: The Role of Panic

Jiangang Du

Contents

17.1 Introduction: Background and Research Objectives

In reviewing the research on product harm crises, there is an important theme that has not been addressed. Although some scholars have studied the impact of a product harm crisis on customers' subjective risk (Siomkos and Kurzbard 1994), there has been no discussion of the impact of customers' panic on their risk perception after a product harm crisis. This is an important omission because panic can influence their willingness to make future purchases from the company.

A panic reaction is common when there is a product recall announcement. Customers who have already purchased a product may wonder whether they own a defective product. Worse yet, if the product is something that they have ingested, they wonder whether it may have already done damage to their health. However, bystanders who have not purchased the product may also experience panic, particularly if they have a relationship with those who have purchased it.

We use the risk-as-feelings hypothesis and affect heuristic theory to speculate about whether customers' panic will affect their risk perception, that is, whether the likelihood of harm subjectively perceived by a customer will expand its objective probability. We put forward a number of important research questions, as follows.

First, most of the authors of the existing research have focused on the expansion of customer's subjective risk under cognitive judgment, after a product harm crisis (Siomkos and Kurzbard 1994), while ignoring the role of emotions. However, we argue that emotions, particularly panic, can color customers' reaction to a product harm crisis. Do emotions play a mediation role between harm degree and perceived risk? Under the impact of panic, will customers' subjective assessment and perceived risk expand?

Second, while the vast majority of scholars have paid attention to customer's risk perception and their behavioral intention as potential victims, few have examined the third-party perspective. What are the feelings and risk perception of customers who sit on the sidelines and have not touched the product that has been recalled? It is important to focus on those who are directly affected by a product harm crisis as well as bystanders since both groups represent potential future customers. How do bystanders look at the harm of products? How do they estimate the risk to the potential victims? If the potential victims are our acquaintances, do we perceive the risk of harm differently? On the other hand, if they are strangers, how do we perceive the risk of harm?

Third, the intensity of the harm can affect people's judgment of risk (Slovic and Peters 2006). Faced with different degrees of the products' probability of harm (Dawar and Pillutla 2000), what are the differences in intensity of feelings and risk perception between customers who were victims and those who are bystanders?

A product harm crisis is precipitated by the presence of a product defect. However, not all defective products are associated with a product harm crisis; many defects are benign and many are avoidable. Thus, we divide product defects into four types, illustrated in Figure 17.1.

The horizontal axis of Figure 17.1 (whether it does harm to human body) represents that when customers use the product in question, will it do harm to their bodies? The vertical axis (whether it can be avoided) deals with whether customers are able to avoid the damage caused by the product.

For a Type 1 defect, the product does not harm the human body, and its impact can be avoided after purchase. For example, for the HP laptop cooling pad, customers could eliminate the impact of its overheating by simply stopping their use of it or replacing it with a new one. A product with a Type 2 defect does not do any harm to the human body, but its impact cannot be avoided after purchase. For example, KFC's use of soybean powder in its milk did not hurt the body; however, it was not up to the pure milk standard that was advertised. There was no way to avoid this kind of defect once KFC's milk had been ingested.

A Type 3 defect does harm to the body, but its impact can be avoided after purchase. For example, in the example of the children's tents produced by IKEA,

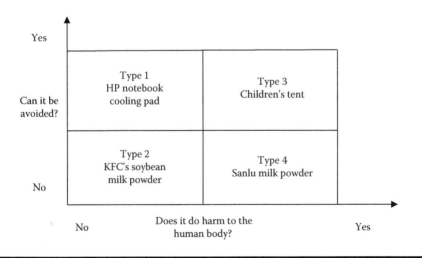

Figure 17.1 Types of product defects.

the wire frame could break and cause stabbing wounds. However, customers could eliminate the potential for such harm by stopping use of the product, repairing it, or replacing it with a new tent. The most serious type of defect is Type 4, where the product does harm to the body, and its impact cannot be avoided. For example, the melamine in Sanlu's milk powder could cause kidney stones in infants and even death. Once ingested, the impact could not be avoided.

As seen above, the fourth type of defect is the most serious; harmful substances contained in these products will be taken into the body and can do damage, which cannot be avoided after ingestion. When such serious consequences occur, they can cause panic among a great number of customers and potential customers. This chapter focuses on the fourth type of damage and its potential for causing customer panic.

17.2 Literature Review

17.2.1 Risk-as-Feelings Theory

Since the time of the ancient Greeks, rationalists have assumed that emotions, like an unexpected robber, can hijack advanced human cognitive activities, such as judgment, reasoning, and decision making. This point of view has dominated the decision making under risk research field. Psychologists who have studied decision-making problems over the years have avoided studying the impact of feelings on decision-making behavior under risk because of this assumption.

In contrast, expected utility theory is at the opposite extreme. Since the early research on Game Theory was published, expected utility theory has been the mainstream of the decision making under risk research field (Becker 1974). Expected utility theory assumes that decision makers are completely rational, that people assess the likelihood of the possible outcomes of choice alternatives and integrate that information to arrive at a decision. This theory completely excludes the influence of emotions, focusing on a mathematical model of rational decision making (Harless and Camerer 1994; Luce and von Winterfeldt 1994). In more recent studies, scholars have introduced new factors into the model in order to explain phenomena that expected utility theory cannot.

Loewenstein et al. (2001) put forward the risk-as-feelings hypothesis, as shown in Figure 17.2. This theory holds the view that, in decision making, people take actions not only through evaluating risky alternatives at a cognitive level but also through affective reactions. In addition, cognitive evaluation of risk and affective reactions interact with each other.

Loewenstein et al. (2001) described how evaluation of alternatives and affective reactions work hand-in-hand (see Figure 17.2). Through cognitive evaluation, people evaluate the severity and probability of outcomes of the alternatives, then integrate the information, through some calculation based

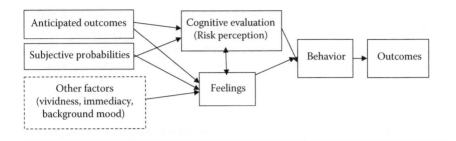

Figure 17.2   Risk-as-feelings hypothesis.

on expectation, and arrive at a decision (Slovic et al. 2004). Feelings represent the immediate emotions that diverge from cognitive evaluations and directly influence decision making. For example, a reaction to a dangerous situation is partly a result of the emotional impact, such as worry, fear, dread, or anxiety. The antecedents in our model include the customers' anticipated outcomes and subjective assessments.

17.2.2 Affect Heuristic Theory

Risk in real life is perceived and acted upon in two fundamental ways: (1) "risk as feelings," which refers to our instinctive and intuitive reactions to danger, and (2) "risk as analysis," which brings logic, reason, and scientific deliberation to bear on our risk assessment and decision making. In most cases, risk in daily life is handled quickly and automatically by feelings arising from what is known as the "experiential" mode of thinking.

On the basis of a large number of studies on the impact of feelings on decision making, Slovic et al. (2002) found out that in the decision-making process, feelings often occur before cognition and can directly affect decision making or influence it through interaction with cognition. They put forward the concept of the affect heuristic, which they described as a shortcut in decision making. When people face a judgment or decision, they usually make decisions based on their own intuition or common sense. During the decision-making process, the affect heuristic is a shortcut that people take in order to skip tedious rational analysis, similar to what Gioia described as a script schema in Chapter 7. The affect heuristic proposed by Slovic et al. (2002) focuses on how feelings affect judgment and decision making. "Affect" refers to the specific quality of "goodness" or "badness" experienced as a feeling state (with or without consciousness) and demarcating a positive or negative quality of a stimulus. On the basis of a large amount of research, they found that external events are linked with the appearance of positive or negative affect in people's minds, and these emotions guide or directly influence their judgment and decision making. This entire process is called the affect heuristic.

Slovic et al. (2002) described the affect heuristic's impact on decision making as follows. In the long-term, learning and strengthening for people, objects, and events in real life will form corresponding images in people's minds. All of the images are tagged to varying degrees with affect, and a large amount of this affect forms an "affect pool" in the brain. During the process of making a judgment or decision, the exposure to external events will automatically activate the corresponding images, as well as the emotions linked to the images, causing people to develop such emotional experiences, such as like/dislike and good/bad. In the decision-making process, the positive or negative affect linked to a task's mental representation will influence decisions (the process that people follow to refer to affect to make decisions is sometimes conscious and sometimes unconscious). If feeling pleasant (positive feelings), people tend to show the trended behaviors; however, if feeling unpleasant (negative feelings), people tend to avoid showing their feelings in behavior. Reliance on affect is generally the easiest way to navigate an unfamiliar or complex circumstance.

Standard economic theory suggests that risk and benefit should be positively correlated; that is, high risk is associated with high benefit, while low risk is associated with low benefit. However, in earlier studies of the affect heuristic, researchers found that perceptions of risk and benefit were negatively correlated (high risk was associated with low benefit, while low risk was associated with high benefit). In many cases, the greater the perceived benefit, the lower the risk will be, and the greater the perceived risk, the lower the benefit will be. Slovic et al. (2007) implied that the inverse relationship between perceived risk and benefit of an activity was linked to the strength of positive or negative affect associated with that activity, that is, whether people like it or not. If they like the activity, people tend to make a low-risk, high-benefit judgment; if they do not like it, they tend to make the opposite judgment.

In summary, on one hand, these studies show that the affect heuristics exists in the process of decision making, and in many cases, people make decisions based on feeling good (positive affect) or bad (negative affect). On the other hand, they also demonstrate that the affect heuristic has the following characteristics: Emotions influence individual perceived risk and benefits, and positive affect guides the perception of high benefits, while negative affect guides the perception of high risk.

17.3 Hypothesis Development

Through the literature review, we have established the important role of feelings in decision making, as well as the mechanism of emotion, which has an impact on customers' cognitive analysis and behavioral judgment. On this basis, we position feelings as an antecedent factor in cognitive analysis and decision making, discussing the role and impact of panic on risk perception. We propose theoretical hypotheses according to the relationships between these variables.

17.3.1 Involved Customers' Subjective and Objective Probability

On the basis of the research described above, this study uses affect heuristic theory as its foundation, using it to analyze a product harm crisis (Siomkos and Shrivastava 1993) and further explore the risk-as-feelings hypothesis (see Figure 17.3). There are a number of important constructs in Figure 17.3. Harm degree is the degree of physical and psychological harm to customers that was caused by a product harm crisis, which is associated with an objective probability. Panic is a negative emotion of customers, such as fear and dread, that is stimulated by a product harm crisis. Subjective assessment refers to the probability of a product causing harm to the human body and the extent to which it is subjectively perceived by customers. We refer to the customers who have used the products affected by a product harm crisis as the "involved customers."

According to affect heuristic theory, positive events will stimulate positive feelings, therefore causing an individual to have a positive risk evaluation and make a positive decision. In contrast, negative events will stimulate negative feelings, therefore causing an individual to have a negative risk evaluation and make a negative decision (Slovic and Peters 2006). People judge risk and make decisions not by what they think about it but by how they feel about it.

Accordingly, we place panic at the forefront of perceived risk as a mediating variable between harm degree and subjective assessment. Because a product involved in a product harm crisis can do harm to the human body, it provides negative information, which stimulates panic in the involved customers. Due to the impact of their panic, involved customers will make negative judgments; that is, their subjective assessment of the probability of the product causing harm will increase and their perceived risk will increase as well. On this basis, we propose the following hypotheses:

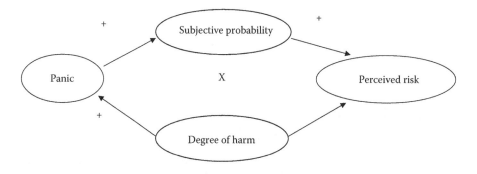

Figure 17.3   Further explanation of risk-as-feelings hypothesis.

H_1: After a product harm crisis, involved customers' subjective assessment of a product's harm is higher than its objective probability.

H_2: Panic plays a mediation role between harm degree and subjective assessment for noninvolved customers.

17.3.2 Noninvolved Customers' Subjective and Objective Probability

In H_1 and H_2, we considered the involved customers (potential victims) and proposed that their subjective assessment of the probability of the product causing harm was greater than the objective probability. In the following, we take the perspective of a third-party group to discuss the panic reaction of noninvolved customers who are bystanders and what they think about the product's risk of harm to involved customers.

A product harm crisis can have a substantial psychological impact on third-party customers who have never used the affected product (Folkes 1988; Laurent and Kapferer 1985). Thus, this is a group that cannot be neglected. It may include both relatives and friends and other stakeholders of the involved customers and the future potential customers of the affected product. In either case, they have a close relationship with the affected product (Hisrich et al. 1972; Knox and Walker 2003; Richins et al. 1992; Venkatraman 1989) and can have a substantial and immeasurable impact on word of mouth about the product.

According to the affect heuristic theory, negative events stimulate negative feelings, therefore causing people to make a negative risk evaluation and a negative decision (Slovic and Peters 2006). Although a product harm crisis does not cause direct physical harm to noninvolved customers who have never used the product, they are still psychologically influenced and can experience panic; therefore, they will have a negative risk perception. Accordingly, we propose the following hypotheses:

H_3: After a product harm crisis, noninvolved customers' subjective assessment of the product's harm is higher than the objective probability.

H_4: Panic plays a mediation role between harm degree and subjective assessment for noninvolved customers.

17.3.3 Different Familiarity Groups' Subjective and Objective Probability

If a person is in danger or suffers harm, the level of familiarity that another party has with them can stimulate different levels of emotion. The intensity of the non-involved person's emotions can affect his or her perceived risk. The stronger the emotions stimulated by decision-making circumstances, the more their negative risk perception will be (Lastovicka and Gardner 1979). Thus, the more familiar they are with the customers who are involved, the stronger the bystanders' emotions will be. On the other hand, if strangers suffer harm, the emotions of bystanders are much weaker. Different intensity of emotions will lead to different levels of risk perception (Bauer 1960; Tuck 1981); the more negative the emotions, the higher the perceived risk will be. Accordingly, we propose the following hypotheses:

H_5: After a product harm crisis, the panic of noninvolved customers who are familiar with involved customers is higher than that of those who are not familiar with involved customers.

H_6: After a product harm crisis, the amplification effect of subjective assessment on objective probability, caused by noninvolved customers who are familiar with involved customers, is higher than that of those who are not familiar with involved customers.

17.3.4 Involved Customers' Subjective Perception of Different Objective Probabilities

In the hypotheses above, we discussed actual and prospective customers' subjective assessment perception when faced with the same objective probability. In fact, when the objective probability changes (when the likelihood of harm changes), customers' risk perception will change as well. According to the social cognitive theory, the rationality of products and emotional knowledge owned by customers, which is known as product involvement, will have an important impact on their product cognition, customer loyalty, and perceived risk (Hisrich et al. 1972; Venkatraman 1989). Therefore, we distinguish between different levels of customers' product involvement and discuss the changes in their risk perception when differently involved customers face different objective probabilities.

When the objective probability of an event is lower and there is better cognitive understanding and more user experience and brand emotion before the event (Too et al. 2001), highly involved customers' trust and emotion about a product cannot be easily shaken. Thus, their probability assessment of the product's damage to their own body is lower; they will have less panic and more perceived risk (Bauer 1960; Tuck 1981). Conversely, when there is less cognitive understanding and lower user experience and brand emotions before the event, less involved customers' trust and emotion of the product can be easily shaken, and they will have stronger panic (Buck 1985) and higher perceived risk (Dowling and Staelin 1994).

When the objective probability of a crisis is greater and there is more user experience before the recall, highly involved customers will be more worried that the product will do harm to their bodies (Too et al. 2001); thus, a strong sense of panic will arise and the perceived risk will be high (Bauer 1960; Tuck 1981). Conversely, when there is less user experience before a product is recalled, less involved customers will have less panic and lower perceived risk (Buck 1985; Dowling and Staelin 1994). Accordingly, we propose the following hypotheses:

H_{7a}: In the condition of low objective probability, highly involved customers' panic is less than that of less involved customers.

H_{7b}: In the condition of low objective probability, the amplification effect of highly involved customers' subjective assessment on objective probability is less than that of less involved customers.

H_{8a}: In the condition of high objective probability, highly involved customers' panic is stronger than that of less involved customers.

H_{8b}: In the condition of high objective probability, the amplification effect of highly involved customers' subjective assessment on objective probability is more than that of less involved customers.

17.4 Experimental Design

This section will describe the three experiments in detail, including their purpose and experimental design.

17.4.1 Overview of the Experiments

Three experiments were conducted to test different combinations of customers' risk perception under the impact of panic after a product harm crisis. Experiment 1 tests the amplification effect of involved customers' subjective assessment of a product's harm to their own bodies on their objective probability. Experiment 2 tests the amplification effect of noninvolved customers' subjective assessment of a product's harm to their own bodies on their objective probability. For noninvolved customers who have a different level of familiarity with the involved customers, it tests the amplification effect of their subjective assessment of a product's harm to their bodies on their objective probability. Experiment 3 will test whether, when differently involved customers face different objective probabilities, there are differences between their subjective assessments.

17.4.2 Choice of Tested Products

The tested products used in this study all had hypothetical brands, for the following reasons. First, we can control factors such as brand familiarity, brand influence, customer involvement, and the quality of the relationship between the customer and the brand. These factors' influence on different customers will be excluded; thus, they will not affect the accuracy of the experimental results. Second, this will ensure that the customers have no familiarity or prior experience with the brands.

In order to ensure the validity of the study, we selected different products for the three experiments as the experimental stimuli. Experiment 1 uses tea bags and packaged coffee as the tested products, while Experiment 2 uses milk tea and a vitamin drink, and Experiment 3 uses toothpaste as the tested product. All the tested products were specially prepared before the experiment, and the old labels were replaced with new labels for the hypothetical brands.

17.4.3 Setting

We selected an empty classroom to use as a temporary laboratory. The volunteers were brought into the classroom by lab assistants and asked to sit down as a group. In order to ensure that the volunteers could not communicate with each other, there was a three-meter distance between groups and a two-meter distance between volunteers. To improve the internal validity of the experiment, the two lab assistants were trained in advance to use standardized language and processes for dealing with each volunteer.

The descriptions of the product harm crisis events were all based on real news reports found on the Internet, adapted to the hypothetical products, in order to highlight the credibility of the reports.

17.5 Experiments and Results

17.5.1 Experiment 1

17.5.1.1 Purpose

The purpose of Experiment 1 was to test whether there was a difference between involved customers' subjective assessment of product harm and its objective probability, due to the mediation impact of panic. The experiment tests H_1 and H_2.

17.5.1.2 Design

This experiment divided the volunteers into two groups. The first group's tested product was tea bags, and the second group's tested product was packaged instant coffee. The volunteers consisted of 60 students from a university's business school, who were randomly divided into the two groups, the tea group and the coffee group. The description of product harm crisis for the tea group is as follows:

> A website recently revealed that a certain brand of tea bags contained level one carcinogens, such as industrial additives, benzopyrene, etc.,

which can cause serious harm to humans' stomach, liver, and kidneys. It has been reported that, after using this brand of tea bags, about 100 out of 10,000 residents in a certain area experienced diarrhea, vomiting, kidney failure, and other symptoms.

The description of product harm crisis for the coffee group is as follows:

A website recently revealed that a certain brand of packaged coffee contained level one carcinogens, such as industrial additives, benzopyrene, etc., which can cause serious harm to humans' stomach, liver, and kidneys. It has been reported that, after using this brand of packaged coffee, about 100 out of 10,000 residents in a certain area experienced diarrhea, vomiting, kidney failure, and other symptoms.

After reading the descriptions, the two groups of volunteers were asked to judge the probability of the harm to their bodies as a result of using this product.

17.5.1.3 Results

The results of Experiment 1 are shown in Figure 17.4. When the product was tea, involved customers' subjective assessment was much higher than the objective probability of the event occurring; the result was the same when the product was coffee. Therefore, after a product harm crisis, involved customers' subjective assessment amplified the objective probability of harm, due to the mediation role of panic.

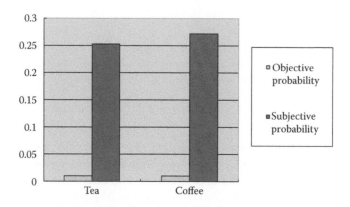

Figure 17.4 Difference between subjective and objective probability of involved customers.

17.5.2 Experiment 2

17.5.2.1 Purpose

The purpose of Experiment 2 was to determine whether there was a difference between bystanders' (noninvolved customers) subjective assessment of product harm and its objective probability, due to the mediation role of panic. It also tested whether there was a difference between bystanders' subjective assessment of product harm to the involved customers when they had different levels of familiarity with the involved customers and there were different objective probabilities of harm. This experiment tests H_3, H_4, H_5, and H_6.

17.5.2.2 Design

This experiment used a 2 (milk tea, vitamin drink) × 2 (involved, noninvolved) × 2 (familiar, not familiar) group design. The tested products were milk tea and a vitamin drink, which were familiar products to the volunteers. The volunteers consisted of 180 students from a university's business school, who were divided into eight groups. The groups were the involved/familiar milk tea group, noninvolved/familiar vitamin drink group, involved/not familiar milk tea group, noninvolved/not familiar vitamin drink group, involved/familiar vitamin drink group, noninvolved/familiar milk tea group, involved/not familiar vitamin drink group, and noninvolved/not familiar milk tea group.

The description of the product harm crisis read by the involved/familiar milk tea group, noninvolved/familiar vitamin drink group, involved/not familiar milk tea group, and noninvolved/not familiar vitamin drink group is as follows:

> A website recently revealed that a certain brand of packaged milk tea contained level one carcinogens, such as industrial additives, plasticizer, etc., which can cause serious harm to humans' stomach, liver, and kidneys. It has been reported that, after using this brand of packaged milk tea, about 100 out of 10,000 residents in a certain area experienced diarrhea, vomiting, kidney failure, and other symptoms.

At this point, the involved/familiar milk tea group and the noninvolved/familiar vitamin drink group became a pairing combination. The involved/familiar milk tea group (the involved customers) was asked to judge the probability of harm by the packaged milk tea to themselves. Meanwhile, the noninvolved/familiar vitamin drink group (the familiar bystanders) was asked to judge the probability of harm by the packaged milk tea to the involved/familiar milk tea group. Similarly, the involved/not familiar milk tea group and noninvolved/not familiar vitamin drink group became a pairing combination, and the involved/not familiar milk tea group (the involved customers) was asked to judge the probability of harm by packaged milk tea to themselves. The noninvolved/not familiar vitamin drink group (the not familiar bystanders) was asked to assess the probability of harm from the packaged milk tea to the involved/not familiar milk tea group.

The description of product harm crisis seen by the involved/familiar vitamin drink group, noninvolved/familiar milk tea group, involved/not familiar vitamin drink group, and noninvolved/not familiar milk tea group was as follows:

> A website recently revealed that a certain brand of vitamin drinks contained synthetic colors, such as carmine, which are banned by the national government, and level one carcinogens, such as industrial additives, which can cause serious harm to humans' stomach, liver, and kidneys. It has been reported that, after using this brand of vitamin drinks, about 100 out of 10,000 residents in a certain area experienced diarrhea, vomiting, kidney failure, and other symptoms.

At this point, the involved/familiar vitamin drink group and noninvolved/familiar milk tea group became a pairing combination, and the involved/familiar vitamin drink group (the involved customers) was asked to judge the probability of harm by the vitamin drink to themselves. Meanwhile, the noninvolved/familiar milk tea group (the familiar bystanders) was asked to judge the probability of harm from the critical vitamin drink to the involved/familiar vitamin drink group. Similarly, the involved/not familiar vitamin drink group and the noninvolved/not familiar milk tea group became a pairing combination. The involved/not familiar vitamin drink group (the involved customers) was asked to assess the probability of harm from the vitamin drink to themselves. The noninvolved/not familiar milk tea group (the not familiar bystanders) was asked to assess the probability of harm from the vitamin drink to the involved/not familiar vitamin drink group.

The specific design is as follows (see Table 17.1).

17.5.2.3 Results

Figure 17.5 shows that when the product was milk tea, the noninvolved customers' subjective assessment was much higher than the objective probability of the event occurring; the result was the same when the product was vitamin drinks. Therefore, after a product harm crisis, noninvolved customers' subjective assessment of harm had an amplification effect on the objective probability of harm, due to the mediation role of panic.

Second, as illustrated in Figures 17.6 and 17.7, when the product was milk tea, the panic of the noninvolved customers (bystanders) who were familiar with the involved customers was higher than it was for those who were not familiar with the

Table 17.1   Design of Experiment 2

Experimental Product	Product in the Questionnaire	Whether Involved or Not	Familiarity
Milk tea	Milk tea	Yes	Familiar
Vitamin drink	Milk tea	No	Familiar
Milk tea	Milk tea	Yes	Not familiar
Vitamin drink	Milk tea	No	Not familiar
Vitamin drink	Vitamin drink	Yes	Familiar
Milk tea	Vitamin drink	No	Familiar
Vitamin drink	Vitamin drink	Yes	Not familiar
Milk tea	Vitamin drink	No	Not familiar

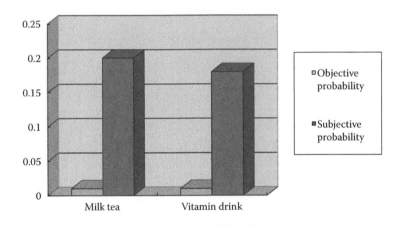

Figure 17.5   Difference between subjective and objective probability of non-involved customers.

involved customers. Their subjective assessment of harm was higher than it was for those who were not familiar with the involved customers. The result was the same when the product was the vitamin drink. Therefore, the more familiar the bystanders are with the involved customers, the higher their panic will be. Thus, due to the mediation role of panic, their subjective assessment of harm was greater. That is, when bystanders are more familiar with the involved customers, the amplification effect for the noninvolved customers' subjective assessment of the objective probability will be greater.

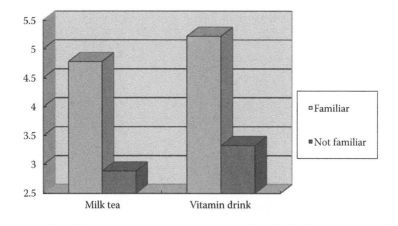

Figure 17.6 Different levels of panic of noninvolved customers in different familiarity.

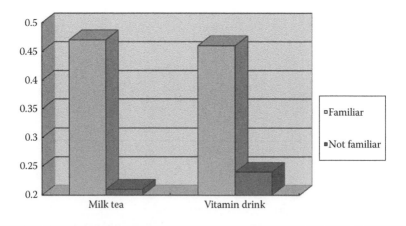

Figure 17.7 Perceived probability of noninvolved customers in different familiarity.

17.5.3 Experiment 3

17.5.3.1 Purpose

The purpose of Experiment 3 was to determine the difference between involved customers' and bystanders' subjective assessment of different levels of objective probability of harm, due to the mediation role of panic. It tests H_{7a}, H_{7b}, H_{8a}, and H_{8b}.

17.5.3.2 Design

This experiment used a 2 (low objective probability, high objective probability) × 2 (low involvement, high involvement) group design. The tested product was toothpaste. The volunteers consisted of 120 students from a university's business school, who were randomly divided into four groups: the low objective probability/low involvement group, the low objective probability/high involvement group, the high objective probability/low involvement group, and the high objective probability/ high involvement group. The description of the product harm crisis presented to the low objective probability/low involvement group is as follows:

> A website recently revealed that a certain brand of toothpaste contained triclosan and other chemicals that can produce level one carcinogens from contact with chlorinated water, which can cause serious harm to humans' stomach, liver, and kidneys. It has been reported that about 1% of the users experienced arrhythmia, renal failure, hepatomegaly, and other symptoms. If you bought this brand of toothpaste for the first time and only used one tube, there should not be any adverse reaction.

The description of the product harm crisis presented to the low objective probability/high involvement group is as follows:

> A website recently revealed that a certain brand of toothpaste contained triclosan and other chemicals that can produce level one carcinogens from contact with chlorinated water, which can cause serious harm to humans' stomach, liver, and kidneys. It has been reported that about 1% of the users experienced arrhythmia, renal failure, hepatomegaly, and other symptoms. If you have used this brand of toothpaste for a year or less, there should not be any adverse reaction.

The description of product harm crisis seen by the high objective probability/ low involvement group is as follows:

> A website recently revealed that a certain brand of toothpaste contained triclosan and other chemicals that can produce level one carcinogens from contact with chlorinated water, which can cause serious harm to humans' stomach, liver, and kidneys. It has been reported that about 20% of the users experienced arrhythmia, renal failure, hepatomegaly, and other symptoms. If you bought this brand of toothpaste for the first time and only used one tube, there should not be any adverse reaction.

The description of product harm crisis seen by the high objective probability/ high involvement group is as follows:

> A website recently revealed that a certain brand of toothpaste contained triclosan and other chemicals that can produce level one carcinogens from contact with chlorinated water, which can cause serious harm to humans' stomach, liver, and kidneys. It has been reported that about 20% of the users experienced arrhythmia, renal failure, hepatomegaly, and other symptoms. If you have used this brand of toothpaste for a year or less, there should not be any adverse reaction.

After reading the descriptions above, the four groups of volunteers were asked to assess the probability of harm to themselves.

17.5.3.3 Results

The results of Experiment 3 are shown in Figures 17.8 and 17.9. When the objective probability of harm was low, less involved customers' (bought the toothpaste only once) panic was higher than that of highly involved (used the toothpaste for a year or less) customers. The results for their subjective assessment were the same. Therefore, the lower the involvement of customers, the more panic they will experience. Thus, due to the mediation role of panic, their subjective assessment of harm

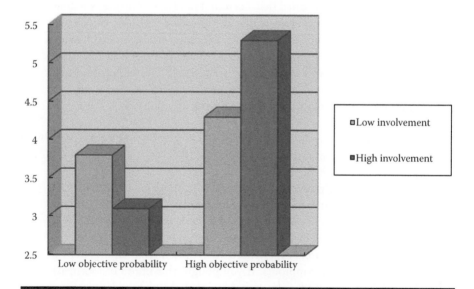

Figure 17.8 Panic of differently involved customers in different objective probability.

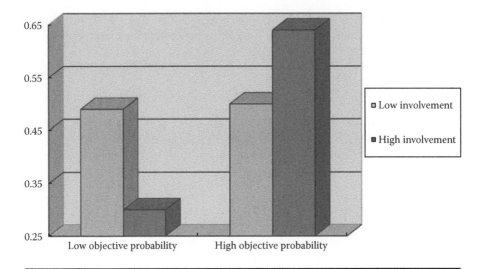

0.65

0.55

0.45

0.35

0.25

Low objective probability   High objective probability

□ Low involvement

■ High involvement

Figure 17.9 Subjective assessment of differently involved customers in different objective probability.

to themselves was greater. When the objective probability of harm was relatively low, the lower the involvement of customers, the more obvious the amplification effect of their subjective assessment on the objective probability will be.

Figures 17.8 and 17.9 demonstrate that when the objective probability was high, highly involved customers' panic was higher than it was for less involved customers. The results for their subjective assessment were the same. Therefore, the higher the involvement of customers, the more panic they will have. Thus, due to the mediation role of panic, their subjective assessment of harm to themselves is greater. When the objective probability of a product harm crisis is relatively high and the involvement of customers is high, the more obvious the amplification effect of their subjective assessment on the objective probability will be.

References

Bauer, R.A. 1960. Customer behavior as risk taking. In *Dynamic Marketing for a Changing World.* Hancock, R.S., ed. Chicago, American Marketing Association: 389–398.

Becker, M.H. 1974. The health belief model and personal health behavior. *Health Ed. Monogr.* 2: 324–508.

Buck, R. 1985. Prime theory: An integrated view of motivation and emotion. *Psych. Rev.* 92(3): 389–413.

Dawar, N. and Pillutla, M.M. 2000. Impact of product-harm crises on brand equity: The moderating role of customer expectations. *J. Mktg.* 37(2): 215–226.

Dowling, G.R. and Staelin, R. 1994. A model of perceived risk and intended risk-handling activity. *J. Cons. Res.* 21(June): 119–134.

Folkes, V.S. 1988. The availability heuristic and perceived risk. *J. Cons. Res.* 15(June): 13–23.

Harless, D.W. and Camerer, C.F. 1994. The predictive utility of generalized expected utility theories. *Econometrica* 62: 1251–1289.

Hisrich, R.D., Dornoff, R.J. and Kernan, J.B. 1972. Perceived risk in store selection. *J. Mktg. Res.* 4(4): 435–439.

Knox, S. and Walker, D. 2003. Empirical development in the measurement of involvement— Brand loyalty and their relationship in grocery markets. *J. Strat. Mktg.* 2(4): 271–286.

Lastovicka, J.L. and Gardner, D.M. 1979. *Components of Involvement Attitude Research Plays for High Stakes.* Chicago, American Marketing Association: 53–73.

Laurent, G. and Kapferer, J. 1985. Measuring customer involvement profiles. *J. Mktg. Res.* 22(2): 42–53.

Loewenstein, G.F., Weber, E., Hsee, C.K. and Welch, N. 2001. Risk as feelings. *Psych. Bull.* 127(2): 267–286.

Luce, R.D. and von Winterfeldt, D. 1994. What common ground exists for descriptive, prescriptive and normative theories? *Mgt. Sci.,* 40(2): 263–279.

Richins, M.L., Bloch, P.H. and McQuarrie, E.F. 1992. How enduring and situational involvement combine to create involvement responses. *J. Cons. Psych.* 1(2): 143–153.

Siomkos, G. and Kurzbard, G. 1994. The hidden crisis in product-harm crisis management. *Eur. J. Mktg.* 28(2): 30–41.

Siomkos, G. and Shrivastava, P. 1993. Responding to product liability crises. *Long Range Plann.* 26(5): 72–79.

Slovic, R., Finueane, M., Peters, E. and MacGregor, D. 2002. The affect heuristic. In *Heuristic and Biases: The Psychology of Intuitive Judgement.* Gilovieh, T., Griffin, D. and Kahneman, D., eds. NY, Cambridge University Press.

Slovic, P., Finueane, M., Peters, E. and MacGregor, D.G. 2004. Risk as analysis and risk as feelings: Some thoughts about affect, reason, risk, and rationality. *Risk Anal.* 24: 1–12.

Slovic, P., Finueane, M., Peters, E. and MacGregor, D. 2007. The affect heuristic. *Eur. J. Op. Res.* 177: 1333–1352.

Slovic, P. and Peters, E. 2006. Risk perception and affect. *Psych. Sci.* 15: 321–325.

Too, L.H.Y., Souchon, A.L. and Thirkell, P.C. 2001. Relationship marketing and customer loyalty in a retail setting: A dyadic exploration. *J. Mktg. Mgmt.* 17(4): 287–319.

Tuck, D.M. 1981. Lateral brain function, emotion and conceptualization. *Psych. Bull.* 89: 19–46.

Venkatraman, M. 1989. Involvement and risk. *Psych. Mktg.* 6(3): 229–247.

INTRODUCTION TO SECTION VI: SUPPLY CHAIN QUALITY MANAGEMENT AND PERFORMANCE

VI

In Section VI, we describe research that tests the relationship between various factors related to supply chain quality management and performance. These studies all use empirical surveys as the means for collecting data. Based on the factors of interest, questionnaires were developed and administered to company managers. Their responses were statistically analyzed in order to develop an understanding of the relationship between the factors.

Chapter 18 examines some of the key factors related to supply chain quality integration, including internal quality integration, customer quality integration, and supplier quality integration, testing whether internal quality integration sets the stage for external (customer and supplier) quality integration. It also tested the role of the competitive intensity of the industry and organization-wide approach as drivers of supply chain quality integration. The factors of interest were tested using a sample of managers in 10 countries.

Chapter 19 focuses primarily on downstream quality management, describing the important role of customer orientation as an element of supply chain quality integration. It tests whether customer orientation provides the foundation for the development of process management capabilities related to product quality and innovation and how these capabilities are related to company performance. The respondents were a set of 560 managers from brand manufacturers in China.

In Chapter 20, we return to the framework for supply chain quality management that was developed in Chapter 8. The sample of 400 managers in the toys, food, automobile, and pharmaceuticals industries was located in three regions of China, representing different stages of economic development. The relationships that were tested dealt with supply chain leadership for quality, strategic supply chain design for quality, internal quality integration, product recall systems, upstream quality management, downstream quality management, and product recall systems. The data analysis led to developing a better understanding of the relationships between these factors and how they were related to company performance.

Chapter 18

Relationship between Supply Chain Quality Integration and Performance

Baofeng Huo, Xiande Zhao, and Fujun Lai

Contents

18.1 Introduction: Supply Chain Quality Integration

In this chapter, we focus on supply chain quality integration (SCQI), which is a way of preventing quality defects through the development of supply chain relationships. We focus on the question of how a company can design and implement effective quality management systems for today's complex global supply chain competitive environment in order to avoid quality catastrophes.

Because most products are designed, produced, and delivered to final consumers through a complex network of companies in different countries, it is important to extend quality management to a global supply chain context (Flynn and Flynn 2005; Kannan and Tan 2005; Kaynak and Hartley 2008; Robinson and Malhotra 2005; Sila et al. 2006; Zhu et al. 2007). Quality managers cannot just focus their quality management efforts within their company's boundaries; rather they must extend their quality vision and improvements into their supply chains (Foster and Ogden 2008; Kaynak and Hartley 2008; Lin et al. 2005). This is made challenging by globalization, which has significantly increased the number of suppliers and customers located outside national boundaries. Many companies in different parts of the world collaborate with each other in the design, production, and delivery processes of a typical supply chain. As a result, quality management has become both more global oriented and more supply chain oriented (Jiang et al. 2007; Zhao et al. 2007).

Although scholars have recognized the importance of addressing quality issues from the perspective of a global supply chain and have proposed the need for supply chain quality management systems (Foster and Ogden 2008; Wang et al. 2009), prior research is primarily conceptual. Our research fills this gap by empirically examining quality management from the perspective of supply chain integration (SCI). We develop the concept of SCQI, which includes internal quality integration (within a company), upstream quality integration with suppliers, and downstream quality integration with customers (Foster 2008).

SCQI builds on the foundation of SCI. SCI is "the degree to which a company strategically collaborates with its supply chain partners and manages its intra- and inter-organization processes to achieve effective and efficient flows of products, services, information, money and decisions, with the objective of providing maximum value to its customers" (Zhao et al. 2008, p. 374). Conceptually, SCI is the across-the-board process integration of the internal functions of a company, including marketing, inventory management, manufacturing, R&D, purchasing, quality management, planning, technology, human resource, logistics, accounting and finance, and its supply chain partners, including both upstream suppliers and downstream customers. Thus, quality management is an important element of supply chain quality integration. Although SCI has been studied from various perspectives (Devaraj et al. 2007; Grover and Saeed 2007; Harland et al. 2007; Koufteros et al. 2002, 2005, 2007; Krajewski and Wei 2001; Kulp et al. 2004; Seggie et al. 2006; Stank et al. 2001a; Stock and Tatikonda 2004, 2008; Swink et al. 2007; Themistocleous et al. 2004; Wei and Krajewski 2000; Zeng and Pathak 2003), it has not yet been examined from the specific perspective of quality management.

We define SCQI as the degree to which a company strategically collaborates with its supply chain partners and manages intraorganization and interorganization quality-related processes to produce high-quality products and services. As with SCI, there are three dimensions of SCQI: internal quality integration, supplier quality integration, and customer quality integration. We propose that competitive intensity and organization-wide commitment to quality are two key drivers of SCQI. Competitive intensity pushes a company to develop an organization-wide commitment to quality management, develop its internal functions, and work with its supply chain partners to collaborate in their approach to quality management. An organization-wide approach to quality management helps that company collaborate, both within its internal functions and with its external supply chain partners, to improve quality performance.

However, there is no extant research on SCQI. Although the impact of quality management practices on company performance has been investigated by various authors (e.g., Adam et al. 1997; Dow et al. 1999; Kaynak 2003; Kaynak and Hartley 2008; Samson and Terziovski 1999), previous studies have not examined SCQI and its relationship with performance measures, such as product quality, delivery, and the cost of quality. Therefore, this study focuses on SCQI, investigating its drivers and outcomes in a global context.

We propose that SCQI is an organizational capability. Organizational capabilities are related to the resource-based view of the firm, which addresses how resources and capabilities are used to achieve a competitive advantage (Armstrong and Shimizu 2007; Bharadwaj 2000; Collis 1994; Mahoney 1995; Newbert 2007; Peng et al. 2008). We view SCQI as a set of internal and external integrative capabilities that lead, directly or indirectly, to quality performance. Specifically, we address three research questions: (1) How are competitive intensity and organization-wide approach related to internal, supplier, and customer quality integration? (2) How is internal quality integration related to supplier and customer quality integration? (3) How are the three dimensions of SCQI related to quality performance? We propose a conceptual model specifying relationships among the antecedents, dimensions, and outcomes of SCQI and empirically test this model using a global dataset. This study makes a significant contribution to both the literature on SCI and quality management literature, as well as lays the foundation for future research on SCQI.

18.2 Theoretical Background and Research Hypotheses

18.2.1 SCI and Quality Management

Understanding and effectively implementing quality management in a supply chain context are critical in today's highly competitive and global markets. Although there is limited literature on SCQI per se, there is an abundance of prior literature on its building blocks: SCI and quality management. The literature on SCI (Devaraj et al. 2007; Koufteros et al. 2002, 2005, 2007; Rosenzweig et al. 2003; Swink et al. 2007) has reported mixed findings about the relationship between SCI and various types of performance. After analyzing 38 papers, Fabbe-Costes and Jahre (2008) concluded that SCI was not always associated with improved performance because the definitions and measures of SCI and performance are too diverse. They called for more empirical SCI research with clear definitions and good measures, especially in a more focused context (e.g., quality performance rather than overall business performance). Previous studies on quality management suggest a positive impact of cooperative supply chain relationships on quality performance (Kannan and Tan 2005; Nair 2006; Sila et al. 2006; Singer et al. 2003; Sroufe and Curkovic 2008; Stanley and Wisner 2001; Zu et al. 2008).

We limit our research to the more focused context of the relationship between SCQI and quality performance. We focus on three quality-related performance measures (product quality, delivery, and the cost of quality) (Kaynak and Hartley 2008; Srivastava 2008). In our extensive literature review and interviews with executives, we found that these three performance measures are perceived as crucial to the success of quality management initiatives (cf. Kuei et al. 2008).

18.2.2 Supply Chain Quality Integration

There are three dimensions of SCQI: internal quality integration, supplier quality integration, and customer quality integration. Supplier quality integration and customer quality integration are forms of external quality integration, which is the degree to which a company integrates with its external partners to structure interorganizational strategies, practices, and processes into collaborative, synchronized quality-related processes in order to fulfill customers' quality requirements (Flynn et al. 2009; Stank et al. 2001b). Supplier quality integration integrates core quality competencies derived from the coordination with critical suppliers, whereas customer quality integration integrates core quality competencies related to coordination with critical customers (Bowersox et al. 1999). In contrast, internal quality integration focuses on integrative quality-related activities of a company's own internal functions. It is the degree to which a company structures its organizational strategies, practices, and processes into collaborative, synchronized quality-related processes in order to fulfill its customers' quality requirements (Flynn et al. 2009; Stank et al. 2001b). Internal quality integration includes cross-functional quality management and teamwork for managing quality activities and solving quality problems.

While internal quality integration recognizes that the departments and functions within a company should be integrated and coordinated to manage quality together and develop teams to solve quality problems, external quality integration recognizes the importance of establishing close, interactive relationships with customers and suppliers, involving them in product design and process improvement and working with them to solve quality problems. Both internal SCQI and external SCQI are important in ensuring that supply chain members act in a concerted way, to maximize supply chain quality. The classification of SCQI into internal and external dimensions is consistent with the taxonomy of quality management proposed by Sila et al. (2006, p. 328), which includes "(i) intra-organizational coordination (or traditional quality management) within an internal supply chain context and focus and, (ii) inter-organizational integration interfacing supply chain and quality methodologies from an external supply chain context and focus."

The three dimensions of SCQI are consistent with recent supply chain management studies on such topics as supplier relations, supplier selection, supplier participation, supply quality management, customer focus, customer relationships, and process management practices (Foster 2008; Kaynak and Hartley 2008; Kuei et al. 2001, 2008; Robinson and Malhotra 2005; Sroufe and Curkovic 2008). They are also consistent with the components of traditional quality management, such as those described by Kaynak and Hartley (2008), ISO 9000 (Sroufe and Curkovic 2008), Lo and Yeung (2004), Mehra et al. (2001), Nair (2006), Flynn et al. (1994), and Anderson et al. (1995). Thus, the dimensions of SCQI draw heavily upon prior research in supply chain management and quality management, extending the synergies between them to the perspective of supply chain quality management.

Organizational capability is the "ability to perform repeatedly a productive task which relates, either directly or indirectly, to a company's capacity for creating value through effecting the transformation of inputs into outputs" (Grant 1996, p. 377). Dynamic capability is the ability to integrate, build, structure, and reconfigure internal and external competencies to meet the requirements of a changing environment, in order to generate multiple sustained competitive capabilities simultaneously (Andrew et al. 2001; Gianni and Andrea 1999; Grant 1996; Huh et al. 2008; Peng et al. 2008; Schreyögg and Kliesch-Eberl 2007; Teece et al. 1997; Verona 1999; Wade and Hulland 2004). We view SCQI as a dynamic organizational capability. Internal and external quality integration builds upon a company's internal and external dynamic capabilities, respectively (Grant 1996; Teece et al. 1997).

18.2.3 Drivers of SCQI

18.2.3.1 Competitive Intensity

Global competition pushes companies to change their quality and supply chain strategies, processes, and practices, and a substantial amount of recent research has examined the role of the competitive environment in operations and supply chain management performance (Pagell and Krause 2004; Ward and Duray 2000; Ward et al. 1995; Zhou and Benton 2007). In the context of SCQI, the competitive environment affects upstream and downstream relationships and the ability to develop quality management systems that transcend individual organization boundaries. It is complicated by the fact that the organizations within a supply chain may be embedded in different competitive environments. The competitive environment is characterized by its competitive intensity (Ward et al. 1995), which refers to the level of competition within an industry (Miller 1987).

18.2.3.2 Organization-Wide Approach to Quality

People play an important role in quality management (Beer 2003; Bou and Beltran 2005; Flynn and Saladin 2001; Flynn et al. 1994; Foster 2008), both within an organization and across a supply chain. An organization-wide approach to quality forms the foundation for SCQI; if an organization does not follow a consistent approach to quality management internally, it will be difficult for it to function as part of a supply chain–wide approach. In an organization-wide approach to quality, managers and frontline employees in all functional areas accept their responsibility for quality improvement. A highly competitive environment intensifies the need for high quality and encourages all levels and functional areas within in a company to take responsibility for quality management. Therefore, we hypothesize the following:

H_1: Competitive intensity is positively related to an organization-wide approach to quality.

18.2.3.3 Impact on SCQI

Transaction cost theory (TCT) helps to explain the relationship between competitive intensity and SCQI. One of the important assumptions underlying TCT is that of opportunism (Williamson 1985), which is the self-serving behavior of a company at the expense of another. The potential for opportunism increases transaction costs, as contracts or other governance mechanisms are needed to safeguard against opportunism (Williamson 1985).

SCQI provides a mechanism for coordinating with supply chain partners and reducing their potential for opportunism (Zhao et al. 2008). For example, close relationships and communication with suppliers and customers enhance a company's understanding of its suppliers' and customers' businesses and develop trust between them, which reduces opportunism. The involvement of suppliers and customers in quality improvement efforts also helps a company to identify the risks and potential for opportunism in its relationships. As competition intensifies, there may be greater pressure for lead time reduction to respond more quickly to customer demands (Cao and Dowlatshahi 2005). These challenges provide a powerful incentive for integrating quality efforts, both internally and with suppliers and customers. Quality integration between a company and its customers allows it to react more promptly to its customers' changing needs, reduce lead times and inventory costs, offer more customized products, and improve product quality and delivery reliability. Therefore, we hypothesize the following:

H_{2a}: Competitive intensity is positively related to supplier quality integration.

H_{2b}: Competitive intensity is positively related to internal quality integration.

H_{2c}: Competitive intensity is positively related to customer quality integration.

The traditional quality management literature establishes the importance of the relationship between top management's leadership for quality and the development of close relationships with suppliers and customers (Ahire and Ravichandran 2001; Anderson et al. 1995; Flynn et al. 1995, 1997; Kaynak 2003; Kaynak and Hartley 2008; Lin et al. 2005; Robinson and Malhotra 2005; Rungtusanatham et al. 1998, 2003; Theodorakioglou et al. 2006; Zu et al. 2008). When the leaders of different functions take responsibility for quality management, the internal functions of a company must work together in order to achieve common goals. With the help of department leaders, especially marketing and purchasing managers, customer integration and supplier integration develop through the cooperation of internal functions and external supply chain partners. Managers develop policies and structures that enable internal functions and their external supply chain partners to focus on quality management. Employees will have a good understanding of the company's quality priorities, causing them to actively and promptly respond to quality-related signals from top management about the integration of quality management processes. Leadership thus drives the formation of a culture of communication and cooperation among internal functions and throughout the supply chain (Zhao et al. 2008, 2009). Therefore, we hypothesize the following:

H_{3a}: An organization-wide approach to quality is positively related to supplier quality integration.

H_{3b}: An organization-wide approach to quality is positively related to internal quality integration.

H_{3c}: An organization-wide approach to quality is positively related to customer quality integration.

18.2.3.4 Relationship between Dimensions of SCQI

We view internal quality integration as the foundation for custom and supplier integration, as described above. This is supported by the stage theory, which suggests that internal integration is a prerequisite to external integration (e.g., King and Teo 1997; Morash and Clinton 1998), allowing external uncertainty to be absorbed into the proper places within a company's internal structure. Without a foundation of internal quality cooperation, it would be difficult for a company to achieve a high level of external quality integration. A company with better internal communication and coordination capabilities will be more capable of achieving a high level of external (customer and supplier) quality integration, as it learns from its external partners and better understands their businesses. Thus, internal quality integration provides absorptive capacity for learning from external partners (e.g., Hillebrand and Biemans 2003; Lane et al. 2006), as well as developing a foundation for internal coordination capability that makes external coordination easier (Takeishi 2001). This leads to the following hypotheses:

H_{4a}: Internal quality integration is positively related to supplier quality integration.

H_{4b}: Internal quality integration is positively related to customer quality integration.

18.2.4 Impact of SCQI on Quality Performance

The literature on integrative capabilities, in general, suggests that they drive company performance (e.g., Andrew et al. 2001; Schroeder et al. 2002). Verona (1999) proposed that internal and external integrative capabilities improve both process efficiency and product effectiveness. Andrew et al. (2001) found that both knowledge infrastructure and process capabilities were related to improved organizational effectiveness, and Schroeder et al. (2002) found that internal and external learning capabilities improved manufacturing performance. We extend the findings on the relationship between integrative capabilities and performance to supplier, internal, and customer quality integration.

18.2.4.1 Supplier Quality Integration

Previous studies in the supply chain management literature have suggested a positive relationship between supplier management and performance (Kaynak and Hartley 2008; Lin et al. 2005; Paulraj and Chen 2005; Prajogo et al. 2008; Tan et al. 1999; Victor and Alice 2006). Extending their findings to quality in supply chains, we propose that supplier quality integration is related to quality performance. Supplier quality integration reduces supply chain risk and enhances supply chain members' understanding of quality requirements and specifications. A close relationship and communication with suppliers facilitate a company's delivery and product design processes, which leads to higher product quality and a lower cost of quality. A company's involvement in its suppliers' quality improvement efforts helps suppliers reduce their cost of quality and improve delivery performance, which in turn lowers the cost of quality, increases product quality, and speeds delivery. Involving suppliers in product development helps a company to improve its quality performance. Therefore, we hypothesize the following:

H_{5a}: Supplier quality integration is positively related to product quality.

H_{5b}: Supplier quality integration is positively related to delivery performance.

H_{5c}: Supplier quality integration is positively related to the cost of quality.

18.2.4.2 Internal Quality Integration

We also propose that internal integration drives quality performance. Traditional departmentalization and specialization foster the development of functional silos that hinder cooperation among employees from different functions. Internal quality integration breaks down functional barriers, encouraging employees from different functions to work together to solve conflicts and work collaboratively to meet quality requirements. For example, cooperation among the marketing, planning, manufacturing, inventory, and logistics functions enhances the speed of delivery to customers (Sroufe and Curkovic 2008). At a more fundamental level, internal integration gives everyone in the company the responsibility for quality management and pushes functions to work cooperatively under the same quality criteria. Therefore, we hypothesize the following:

H_{6a}: Internal quality integration is positively related to product quality.

H_{6b}: Internal quality integration is positively related to delivery performance.

H_{6c}: Internal quality integration is positively related to the cost of quality.

18.2.4.3 Customer Quality Integration

The importance of customer quality integration is consistent with the principles of ISO 9000:2000 (Sroufe and Curkovic 2008) and the findings of traditional quality

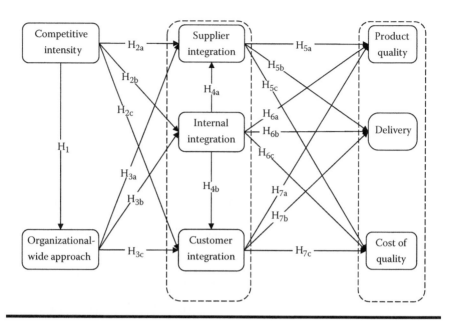

Figure 18.1 Conceptual model.

management research (Kaynak and Hartley 2008; Prajogo et al. 2008; Tan et al. 1999). A company that has a good understanding of its customer requirements can better provide high-quality products and reliable, speedy delivery in a cost-effective way. Therefore, we hypothesize the following:

H_{7a}: Customer quality integration is positively related to product quality.

H_{7b}: Customer quality integration is positively related to delivery performance.

H_{7c}: Customer quality integration is positively related to the cost of quality.

The conceptual framework described by these hypotheses is shown in Figure 18.1.

18.3 Research Method

18.3.1 Sample

The unit of analysis in this study is a manufacturing plant. The data were from the third round of a high-performance manufacturing project, which was conducted by a team of researchers in the United States, Europe, and Asia (Bozarth et al. 2009; Huang et al. 2008). The dataset contains a total of 291 plant-level responses, aggregated from individual respondents in each plant. The plants are located in 10 countries and three industries, providing a global perspective of quality management.

Table 18.1 Demographics of the Sample

Country	Industry			Total
	Electronics	Machinery	Transportation Components	
Austria	10	4	4	18
Finland	14	6	10	30
Germany	9	13	18	40
Italy	10	10	7	27
Japan	10	12	13	35
South Korea	7	8	7	22
Sweden	7	10	7	24
United States	5	9	9	23
Spain	8	9	10	27
China	19	15	11	45
Total	99	96	96	291

Each plant has at least 100 employees. The response rate was about 65% of the plants contacted in each country. A profile of the participating plants is shown in Table 18.1.

18.3.2 Questionnaire Design

The questionnaire items and scales were developed based on the literature and have undergone rigorous pilot testing and revision (cf. Flynn and Saladin 2006). There were 12 different questionnaires completed in each plant by various managers, containing items targeted at different respondents. The questionnaire was originally developed in English and then translated into the local language in each country by a local member of the research team. It was then back-translated into English by a different local team member and the translation was checked against the original English version for accuracy. The constructs and measurement items used in this study are shown in Appendix 18.1.

18.3.3 Variables

The variables were measured using perceptual items and a 7-point Likert scale, ranging from strongly disagree (1) to strongly agree (7). Competitive intensity was measured as the degree to which a plant competes with its peers in its industry. Organization-wide approach to quality was measured as the extent to which responsibility for quality is assumed by managers and other employees. Supplier quality integration was measured as the extent of cooperative supplier relationships, supplier communication, supplier involvement in product design, and supplier certification. Similarly, customer quality integration was measured as the extent of cooperative customer relationships, customer communication, and customer involvement in product design. Internal quality integration was measured as a second-order construct, composed of two first-order dimensions: cross-functional quality management and teamwork. Cross-functional quality management was measured as the extent of working together and coordination across functions, while quality management teamwork was measured by four items about the degree to which the company used teamwork to solve quality problems.

Product quality was measured by eight items about product quality performance, relative to competitors. Delivery was measured as on-time delivery, fast delivery, and cycle time, relative to competitors. The cost of quality was measured using objective measures of the percentage of scrapped, reworked, and returned items. Company size and country were included in the model as control variables.

18.3.4 Analysis

18.3.4.1 Unidimensionality, Reliability, and Validity

Technical details about the assessment of the unidimensionality, reliability, and validity of the measurement scales are contained in Appendix 18.2.

18.3.4.2 Partial Least Squares

Partial least squares (PLS-Graph 3.00) software was used to assess the measurement and structural models. A bootstrapping estimation procedure examined the significance of the factor loadings of the scales in the measurement model and the significance of the path coefficients in the structural model (Gefen and Straub 2005).

18.4 Results

The standardized path coefficients of the final model are shown in Figure 18.2. Among the 18 hypotheses, 14 were supported and 4 were rejected. The results indicate that competitive intensity was positively related to organization-wide approach to quality and internal quality integration but was not related to external quality integration, supporting H_1 and H_{2b} and rejecting H_{2a} and H_{2c}. The path coefficients from organization-wide approach to quality to all three dimensions of SCQI were

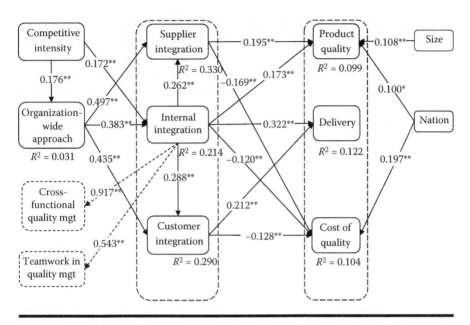

Figure 18.2 PLS results. **p < 0.01; *p < 0.05; no link as hypothesized: not significant at the 0.05 level; ------, second order.

significant, supporting H_{3a}, H_{3b}, and H_{3c}. As hypothesized, internal quality integration was related to quality integration, supporting H_{4a} and H_{4b}.

All three dimensions of SCQI were negatively related to the cost of quality, supporting H_{5c}, H_{6c}, and H_{7c}. While internal quality integration and supplier quality integration were related to product quality, internal quality integration and customer quality integration were related to delivery performance. Supplier quality integration was not related to delivery, and customer quality integration was not related to product quality. These results support H_{6a}, H_{5a}, H_{6b}, and H_{7b} but not H_{5b} or H_{7a}. The second-order structure of internal quality integration was also supported, indicated by the significant and large path coefficients for cross-functional quality management and teamwork.

18.5 Discussion

18.5.1 Drivers of SCQI

Our results show that competitive intensity is an antecedent to an organization-wide approach to quality management, which, in turn, is related to SCQI. This indicates that an organization-wide approach to quality mediates the relationship between competitive intensity and supplier, internal, and customer quality integration. This not only confirms the importance of employee involvement and leadership in internal quality management (e.g., Bou and Beltran 2005; Wilson and Collier 2000) but also indicates that an organization-wide approach to quality is a strong driving force for quality integration with customers and suppliers. In other words, leadership and employee involvement are crucial to the implementation of SCQI activities.

Our results also indicate that competitive intensity has both direct and indirect effects on internal quality integration but only indirectly affects supplier and customer quality integration. Competitive intensity was a stronger driver of internal quality integration than customer or supplier quality integration. The results also indicate that internal integration is strongly related to both supplier and customer quality integration. This suggests a central role for internal quality integration, which lays the foundation for external integration. Both competitive intensity and organization-wide approach to quality were related to supplier and customer quality integration through internal integration.

Companies that are faced with an intense competitive environment should strive to develop internal quality integration capabilities to meet the requirements of their global competition. However, managers should not rely on external suppliers and customers to directly cope with competitive intensity. Rather, employees should work to cope with their competitive environment; this organization-wide approach to quality will also help a company to develop SCQI. In developing its SCQI capabilities, a company should develop its internal quality integrative capabilities first and then develop external supplier and customer quality integration capabilities, leveraging its internal quality integration capability.

18.5.2 Improving Quality Performance through SCQI

Our results reveal differential effects of the dimensions of SCQI on quality performance. Internal quality integration was the most influential dimension of SCQI, associated with better product quality, delivery, and cost of quality performance, both directly and indirectly. Through cross-functional quality management and teamwork, companies can simultaneously improve quality and reduce costs. Furthermore, improvements in the design of products and processes and better control of processes will prevent quality problems from occurring, shorten lead times, and avoid delays in the delivery of the products to customers, thus enhancing delivery performance.

While supplier quality integration was related to product quality and reduced cost of quality, it was not related to delivery performance. Because a close collaboration with suppliers in designing products and working together with suppliers may help to prevent quality-related problems, reduce defects, and improve the efficiency of processes, supplier quality integration can help to enhance quality and reduce quality-related costs. Since the supplier is further away from the customer, it is understandable that supplier integration was not significantly related to delivery performance.

Customer integration was significantly related to both delivery performance and reduced cost of quality. Getting feedback from customers and involving them in product design and quality improvement help a company to prevent quality problems and avoid delays in delivery. By understanding customer requirements and incorporating them, early in the design stage, companies can reduce defects and rework and thus reduce the cost of quality. At the same time, they can also improve delivery performance. Our results indicate that customer integration was not related to product quality.

Companies that seek to improve product quality should strive to integrate both internally and with their suppliers. For improvements in delivery, integrating internally and with customers is critical, and all three dimensions of SCQI are important in keeping the cost of quality down. This contingent method can help companies to pursue a particular quality target through a targeted investment in one of the three dimensions of SCQI. This will improve the effectiveness and efficiency of supply chain quality management.

18.6 Conclusions

This study contributes to the literature and practices of SCI and supply chain quality management in several ways. First, it is one of the first empirical studies of SCQI and its impact on quality performance. We found that internal quality integration was related to product quality, delivery, and cost of quality. Furthermore, it was related to quality integration with suppliers and customers. Considering both direct and indirect effects, internal quality integration is the most powerful dimension of SCQI in improving the quality, delivery, and cost performance of a company. We also found that supplier quality integration and customer quality integration help to improve quality-related performance. While customer quality integration is more effective in improving cost and delivery performance, supplier quality integration is more effective in reducing the cost of quality. Our findings enrich the SCI and quality management literature by empirically testing the relationships between different dimensions of SCQI and quality performance.

Second, this study enriches both the SCI and quality management literature by empirically testing the relationship among the competitive intensity of the business environment, the company's quality orientation, and the dimensions of SCQI. We found that competitive intensity supports an organization-wide approach to quality, which is related to all three dimensions of SCQI. This provides empirical evidence for the linkage among the environment, strategy, and practices with regards to SCQI.

While this study contributes to both the literature and business practice, there are several limitations that open up avenues for future research. First, we limited our investigation to the impact of competitive intensity in the business environment and organization-wide quality management approach on SCQI. Future studies should include other dimensions of the business environment, such as uncertainty and dynamism, and other organizational factors, such as organization culture. Second, in addition to environmental and organizational variables, other factors, such as interorganizational relationships, may also have an impact on SCQI. Future research should explore other enablers of SCQI and examine their impact. Third, we performed an aggregate analysis of the data collected from three industries in 10 countries. Another interesting venue of research would be to investigate the cross-industry, cross-national, and cultural differences in the relationships among environment, quality orientation, SCQI, and performance. Future studies should also collect data from companies and their suppliers and customers, examining triadic relationships.

SCQI and quality performance are rich concepts. This study is one of the first to examine SCQI and its enablers and outcomes from the perspective of quality integration activities and quality performance. Future studies should include more SCQI activities and more dimensions of quality performance.

Appendix 18.1 Measurement Scales

Competitive Intensity

Please indicate the extent to which you agree or disagree with each of these statements (1 = strongly disagree, 7 = strongly agree).

1. CMP01 We are in a highly competitive industry.
2. CMP02 Our competitive pressures are extremely high.
3. CMP03 We don't pay much attention to our competitors. (Reversed)

Respondent: plant manager

Organization-Wide Approach

Please indicate the extent to which you agree or disagree with each of these statements (1 = strongly disagree, 7 = strongly agree).

1. OWA01 All major department heads within the plant accept their responsibility for quality.

2. OWA02 Our plant management creates and communicates a vision focused on quality improvement.
3. OWA03 We believe that quality should be the responsibility of everyone in the organization.
4. OWA04 Everyone in this organization has been made accountable for quality.

Respondent: quality manager

Supplier Integration

Please indicate the extent to which you agree or disagree with each of these statements (1 = strongly disagree, 7 = strongly agree).

1. SQI01 We maintain cooperative relationships with our suppliers.
2. SQI02 We help our suppliers to improve their quality.
3. SQI03 We maintain close communications with suppliers about quality considerations and design changes.
4. SQI04 Our key suppliers provide input into our product development projects.
5. SQI05 Our suppliers are actively involved in our new product development process.
6. SQI06 We use mostly suppliers that we have certified.
7. SQI07 We actively engage suppliers in our quality improvement efforts.

Respondent: quality manager

Internal Integration (2nd Order Construct)

Please indicate the extent to which you agree or disagree with each of these statements (1 = strongly disagree, 7 = strongly agree).

Cross-Functional Quality Management

1. CFI01 The functions in our plant work well together.
2. CFI02 The functions in our plant cooperate to solve conflicts between them, when they arise.
3. CFI03 Our plant's functions coordinate their activities.
4. CFI04 Our plant's functions work interactively with each other.

Respondent: plant manager

Teamwork

1. TMW01 During problem-solving sessions, we make an effort to get all team members' opinions and ideas before making a decision.
2. TMW02 Our plant forms teams to solve problems.
3. TMW03 In the past three years, many problems have been solved through small group sessions.
4. TMW04 Problem-solving teams have helped improve manufacturing processes at this plant.

Respondent: quality manager

Customer Integration

Please indicate the extent to which you agree or disagree with each of these statements (1 = strongly disagree, 7 = strongly agree).

1. CQI01 We frequently are in close contact with our customers.
2. CQI02 Our customers give us feedback on our quality and delivery performance.
3. CQI03 Our customers are actively involved in our product design process.
4. CQI04 Our processes are certified, or qualified, by our customers.
5. CQI05 Our customers involve us in their quality improvement efforts.

Respondent: quality manager

Product Quality

How does the quality of your products compare to your competitors' products? (1 = significantly worse, 7 = significantly better).

1. PQT01 Primary product performance characteristics.
2. PQT02 Secondary options or features; characteristics that supplement the basic functioning of the product.
3. PQT03 Reliability of the product; probability of failure in a specified time.
4. PQT04 Conformance to established standards.
5. PQT05 Durability; amount of use before the product deteriorates or needs to be replaced.
6. PQT06 Serviceability; ease of repair.
7. PQT07 Aesthetics; how the product looks, feels, sounds, tastes or smells.
8. PQT08 Overall product quality perceived by customers.

Respondent: quality manager

Delivery

Please circle the number that indicates your opinion about how your plant compares to its competition in your industry, on a global basis (1 = significantly lower, 7 = significantly higher).

1. DLV01 On-time delivery performance.
2. DLV02 Fast delivery.
3. DLV03 Cycle time (from raw materials to delivery).

Respondent: plant manager

Cost of Quality

1. CQT01 What percent of the products pass final inspection without rework? [Reversed]
2. CQT02 What is the percentage of internal scrap and rework?
3. CQT03 What is the percentage of products returned which are defective?
4. CQT04 What percent of the products require warranty work?

Respondent: quality manager

Appendix 18.2 Technical Details of the Measurement Analysis

An exploratory factor analysis (EFA) was used to assess the unidimensionality of the scales. The final results of the EFA analysis are shown in Tables 18.A2.1 and 18.A2.2. The measurement items all had strong loadings on the construct that they were supposed to measure and lower loadings on the constructs that they were not supposed to measure, indicating unidimensionality.

Confirmatory factor analysis (CFA) was then conducted using PLS. The composite reliabilities in the measurement model were all above the recommended threshold value of 0.70 (Nunnally and Bernstein 1994), suggesting adequate reliability. We assessed convergent validity in terms of average variance extracted (AVE), which explains the variance that is measured by a construct in relation to the measurement error. Table 18.A2.3 shows that all AVE values were above the recommended value of 0.50 (Fornell and Larcker 1981), demonstrating adequate convergent validity. Discriminant validity was assessed by comparing the square root of the AVE for each construct with the correlation between the focal construct and each other construct. Table 18.A2.4 shows the comparison of the correlations and square roots of the AVEs on the diagonal, indicating adequate discriminant validity.

Table 18.A2.1   EFA for SCQI

	Supplier Integration	*Cross-Functional Quality Management*	*Teamwork*	*Customer Integration*
SQI01	0.617	0.006	0.245	0.127
SQI02	0.751	−0.040	0.221	0.068
SQI04	0.698	−0.066	0.285	0.278
SQI05	0.786	0.182	0.016	0.058
SQI06	0.707	0.175	0.002	0.138
SQI07	0.794	0.177	0.241	0.071
CQI01	0.184	0.073	0.191	0.697
CQI02	0.025	0.142	0.249	0.551
CQI03	0.042	−0.004	0.159	0.645
CQI04	0.146	0.076	0.087	0.752
CQI05	0.355	0.019	0.067	0.680
TMW01	0.295	0.120	0.636	0.142
TMW02	0.209	0.038	0.765	0.181
TMW03	0.226	0.136	0.763	0.206
TMW04	0.169	0.049	0.806	0.254
CFI01	0.041	0.781	0.122	0.071
CFI02	0.008	0.798	0.040	0.102
CFI03	0.105	0.781	0.070	−0.016
CFI04	0.135	0.841	0.040	0.101
Eigenvalue	3.881	2.735	2.675	2.575
% of variance explained	19.41	13.68	13.37	12.88

Table 18.A2.2   EFA of Competitive Intensity, Organization-Wide Approach to Quality, and Quality Performance

	Product Quality	Organization-Wide Approach to Quality	Cost of Quality	Delivery	Competitive Intensity
OWA01	0.112	0.690	−0.068	−0.031	0.103
OWA02	0.111	0.716	0.000	0.188	0.044
OWA03	0.084	0.647	−0.218	−0.060	0.117
OWA04	0.064	0.750	0.031	0.018	−0.105
CMP01	−0.112	0.112	0.038	0.048	0.865
CMP02	−0.125	0.229	0.045	0.100	0.749
CMP03	−0.042	−0.118	0.087	0.068	0.523
DLV01	−0.052	0.106	−0.264	0.743	0.228
DLV02	−0.063	−0.043	−0.030	0.841	0.028
DLV03	−0.014	0.051	0.032	0.714	0.032
PQT01	0.918	0.048	0.016	−0.067	−0.036
PQT02	0.891	0.084	0.028	−0.083	−0.050
PQT03	0.924	0.049	−0.014	−0.046	−0.004
PQT04	0.898	0.049	0.044	−0.015	−0.026
PQT05	0.901	−0.026	0.066	0.011	−0.076
PQT06	0.791	0.191	0.011	0.016	−0.157
PQT07	0.825	0.129	0.017	−0.014	−0.070
PQT08	0.919	0.082	−0.020	−0.022	−0.049
CQT01	0.013	−0.262	0.834	0.020	0.030
CQT02	−0.046	−0.171	0.809	0.026	−0.014
CQT03	0.053	0.045	0.606	−0.032	0.121
CQT04	0.057	0.068	0.577	−0.168	0.040
Eigenvalue	6.340	2.243	2.195	1.870	1.733
% of variance explained	28.82	10.20	9.98	8.50	7.88

Table 18.A2.3 CFA Results

	Item	Loading	SE	t	Composite Reliability	AVE
Supplier integration	SQI01	0.671	0.040	16.783	0.892	0.543
	SQI02	0.775	0.022	34.883		
	SQI03	0.792	0.025	31.655		
	SQI04	0.765	0.032	24.232		
	SQI05	0.714	0.037	19.355		
	SQI06	0.590	0.056	10.578		
	SQI07	0.825	0.022	36.908		
Customer integration	CQI01	0.776	0.032	24.062	0.837	0.509
	CQI02	0.651	0.046	14.221		
	CQI03	0.672	0.046	14.669		
	CQI04	0.740	0.026	28.904		
	CQI05	0.719	0.031	23.528		
Teamwork	TMW01	0.703	0.037	19.253	0.878	0.644
	TMW02	0.811	0.028	28.506		
	TMW03	0.828	0.022	37.408		
	TMW04	0.860	0.014	59.937		
Cross-functional quality management	CFI01	0.810	0.026	31.255	0.890	0.669
	CFI02	0.812	0.030	27.004		
	CFI03	0.786	0.029	26.896		
	CFI04	0.86	0.020	43.729		

(continued)

Table 18.A2.3   CFA Results (Continued)

	Item	Loading	SE	t	Composite Reliability	AVE
Product quality	PQT01	0.901	0.012	77.413	0.960	0.748
	PQT02	0.868	0.013	66.179		
	PQT03	0.891	0.012	71.659		
	PQT04	0.875	0.014	62.942		
	PQT05	0.878	0.016	55.304		
	PQT06	0.793	0.024	33.653		
	PQT07	0.809	0.019	42.186		
	PQT08	0.899	0.011	81.203		
Delivery	DLV01	0.853	0.018	46.694	0.828	0.621
	DLV02	0.859	0.019	45.631		
	DLV03	0.631	0.050	12.569		
Cost of quality	CQT01	0.825	0.028	29.754	0.798	0.501
	CQT02	0.813	0.033	24.962		
	CQT03	0.667	0.085	7.850		
	CQT04	0.571	0.089	6.442		
Competitive intensity	CMP01	0.903	0.013	71.121	0.798	0.585
	CMP02	0.851	0.023	37.742		
	CMP03	0.465	0.079	5.866		
Organization-wide approach to quality	OWA01	0.764	0.037	20.428	0.815	0.525
	OWA02	0.753	0.029	25.853		
	OWA03	0.659	0.049	13.562		
	OWA04	0.718	0.047	15.170		

Table 18.A2.4 Correlation Matrix

	X1	X2	X3	X4	X5	X6	X7	X8	X9	X10	X11	X12
Supplier integration (X1)	.737											
Customer integration (X2)	.461	.713										
Teamwork (X3)	.532	.482	.802									
Cross-functional quality management (X4)	.306	.279	.215	.818								
Product quality (X5)	.246	.108	.252	.338	.865							
Delivery (X6)	.163	.228	.246	.396	.350	.788						
Cost of quality (X7)	-.181	-.151	-.188	-.286	.046	-.170	.708					
Competitive intensity (X8)	.083	.094	.181	.204	.025	.188	-.004	.765				
Organization-wide approach (X9)	.593	.549	.578	.320	.197	.233	-.189	.231	.725			
Country (X10)	.150	.132	.122	-.067	.003	.053	-.283	-.026	.133	NA		
Industry (X11)	.000	.177	.044	-.044	-.025	.049	-.041	.142	-.026	.039	NA	
Firm size (X12)	.035	-.043	.062	.056	.150	.024	.040	.020	.091	.112	-.027	NA

Note: Square root of AVE shown on the diagonal of the matrix. Interconstruct correlations are shown off the diagonal. NA, not applicable for single-item construct.

References

Adam, E.E., Corbett, L.M., Flores, B.E., Harrison, N.J., Lee, T.S., Rho, B.-H., Ribera, J., Samson, D. and Westbrook, R. 1997. An international study of quality improvement approach and firm performance. *Int. J. Ops. Prod. Mgmt.* 17(9): 842–873.

Ahire, S.L. and Ravichandran, T. 2001. An innovation diffusion model of TQM implementation. *IEEE Trans. Eng. Mgmt.* 48(4): 445–464.

Anderson, J.C., Rungtusanatham, M., Schroeder, R.G. and Devaraj, S. 1995. A path analytic model of a theory of quality management underlying the Deming management method: Preliminary empirical findings. *Dec. Sci.* 26(5): 637–658.

Andrew, H.G., Arvind, M. and Albert, H.S. 2001. Knowledge management: An organizational capabilities perspective. *J. Mgmt. Info. Sys.* 18(1): 185–214.

Armstrong, C. and Shimizu, K. 2007. A review of approaches to empirical research on the resource-based view of the firm. *J. Manage.* 33(6): 959–986.

Beer, M. 2003. Why total quality management programs do not persist: The role of management quality and implications for leading a TQM transformation. *Dec. Sci.* 34(4): 623–642.

Bharadwaj, A.S. 2000. A resource-based perspective on information technology capability and firm performance: An empirical investigation. *MIS Qly.* 24(1): 169–196.

Bou, J.C. and Beltran, I. 2005. Total quality management, high commitment human resource strategy and firm performance: An empirical study. *TQM Bus. Excell.* 16(1): 71–86.

Bowersox, D.J., Closs, D.J. and Stank, T.P. 1999. *21st Century Logistics: Making Supply Chain Integration a Reality.* Michigan State University, Council of Logistics Management, Oak Book, IL.

Bozarth, C.C., Warsing, D.P., Flynn, B.B. and Flynn, E.J. 2009. The impact of supply chain complexity on manufacturing plant performance. *J. Ops. Mgmt.* 27(1): 78–93.

Cao, Q. and Dowlatshah, S. 2005. The impact of alignment between virtual enterprise and information technology on business performance in an agile manufacturing environment. *J. Ops. Mgmt.* 23(5): 531–550.

Collis, D.J. 1994. How valuable are organisational capabilities? *Strat. Mgmt. J.* 15 (winter): 143–152.

Devaraj, S., Krajewski, L. and Wei, J.C. 2007. Impact of ebusiness technologies on operational performance: The role of production information integration in the supply chain. *J. Ops. Mgmt.* 25(6): 1199–1216.

Dow, D., Samson, D. and Ford, S. 1999. Exploding the myth: Do all quality management practices contribute to superior quality performance? *Prod. Ops. Mgmt.* 8(1): 1–27.

Fabbe-Costes, N. and Jahre, M. 2008. Supply chain integration and performance: A review of the evidence. *Int. J. Log. Mgmt.* 19(2): 130–154.

Flynn, B., Huo, B. and Zhao, X. 2009. The impact of supply chain integration on performance: A contingency and configuration approach. Chinese University of Hong Kong, working paper.

Flynn, B.B. and Flynn, E.J. 2005. Synergies between supply chain management and quality management: Emerging implications. *Int. J. Prod. Res.* 43: 3421–3436.

Flynn, B.B. and Saladin, B. 2001. Further evidence on the validity of the theoretical models underlying the Baldrige criteria. *J. Ops. Mgmt.* 19(6): 617–652.

Flynn, B.B. and Saladin, B. 2006. Relevance of Baldrige constructs in an international context: A study of national culture. *J. Ops. Mgmt.* 24(5): 583–603.

Flynn, B.B., Schroeder, R.G., Flynn, E.J., Sakakibara, S. and Bates, K.A. 1997. World-class manufacturing project: Overview and selected results. *Int. J. Ops. Prod. Mgmt.* 17(7): 671–685.

Flynn, B.B., Schroeder, R.G. and Sakakibara, S. 1994. A framework for quality management research and an associated measurement instrument. *J. Ops. Mgmt.* 11(4): 339–366.

Flynn, B.B., Schroeder, R.G. and Sakakibara, S. 1995. The impact of quality management practices on performance and competitive advantage. *Dec. Sci.* 26(5): 659–691.

Fornell, C. and Larcker, D.F. 1981. Evaluating structural equation models with unobservable variables and measurement error. *J. Mktg Res.* 18(1): 39–50.

Foster, S.T. 2008. Towards an understanding of supply chain quality management. *J. Ops. Mgmt.* 26(4): 461–467.

Foster, S.T. and Ogden, J. 2008. On differences in how operations and supply chain managers approach quality management. *Int. J. Prod. Res.* 46(24): 6945–6961.

Gefen, D. and Straub, D. 2005. A practical guide to factorial validity using PLS-graph: Tutorial and annotated example. *Comm. AIS* 16: 91–109.

Gianni, L. and Andrea, L. 1999. The leveraging of interfirm relationships as a distinctive organizational capability: A longitudinal study. *Strat. Mgmt. J.* 20(4): 317–338.

Grant, R.M. 1996. Prospering in dynamically-competitive environments: Organizational capability as knowledge integration. *Org. Sci.* 7(4): 375–387.

Grover, V. and Saeed, K.A. 2007. The impact of product, market, and relationship characteristics on interorganizational system integration in manufacturer–supplier dyads. *J. Mgmt. Info. Sys.* 23(4): 185–216.

Harland, C.M., Caldwell, N.D., Powell, P. and Zheng, J. 2007. Barriers to supply chain information integration: SMEs adrift of eLands. *J. Ops. Mgmt.* 25(6): 1234–1254.

Hillebrand, B. and Biemans, W.G. 2003. The relationship between internal and external cooperation: Literature review and propositions. *J. Bus. Res.* 56(9): 735–743.

Huang, X., Kristal, M.M. and Schroeder, R.G. 2008. Linking learning and effective process implementation to mass customization capability. *J. Ops. Mgmt.* 26(6): 714–729.

Huh, S., Yook, K. and Kim, I. 2008. Relationship between organizational capabilities and performance of target costing: An empirical study of Japanese companies. *J. Int. Bus. Res.* 7(1): 91–107.

Jiang, B., Frazier, G.V. and Heiser, D. 2007. China-related POM research: A literature review and suggestions for future research. *Int. J. Ops. Prod. Mgmt.* 27(7): 662–684.

Kannan, V.R. and Tan, K.C. 2005. Just in time, total quality management, and supply chain management: Understanding their linkages and impact on business performance. *Omega* 33(2): 153–162.

Kaynak, H. 2003. The relationship between total quality management practices and their effects on firm performance. *J. Ops. Mgmt.* 21(4): 405–435.

Kaynak, H. and Hartley, J.L. 2008. A replication and extension of quality management into the supply chain. *J. Ops. Mgmt.* 26(4): 468–489.

King, W.R. and Teo, T.S.H. 1997. Integration between business planning and information systems planning: Validating a stage hypothesis. *Dec. Sci.* 28(2): 279–308.

Koufteros, X.A., Cheng, T.C.E. and Lai, K.H. 2007. "Black-box" and "gray-box" supplier integration in product development: Antecedents, consequences and the moderating role of firm size. *J. Ops. Mgmt.* 25(4): 847–870.

Koufteros, X.A., Vonderembse, M.A. and Doll, W.J. 2002. Integrated product development practices and competitive capabilities: The effects of uncertainty, equivocality, and platform strategy. *J. Ops. Mgmt.* 20(4): 331–355.

Koufteros, X., Vonderembse, M. and Jayaram, J. 2005. Internal and external integration for product development: The contingency effect of uncertainty, equivocality, and platform strategy. *Dec. Sci.* 36(1): 97–133.

Krajewski, L. and Wei, J.C. 2001. The value of production schedule integration in supply chains. *Dec. Sci.* 32(4): 601–634.

Kuei, C.-H., Madu, C.N. and Lin, C. 2001. The relationship between supply chain quality management practices and organizational performance. *Int. J. Qual. Rel. Mgmt.* 18(8/9): 864–872.

Kuei, C.-H., Madu, C.N. and Lin, C. 2008. Implementing supply chain quality management. *TQM Bus. Excell.* 19(11): 1127–1141.

Kulp, S.C., Lee, H.L. and Ofek, E. 2004. Manufacturer benefits from information integration with retail customers. *Mgmt. Sci.* 50(4): 431–444.

Lane, P., Koka, B. and Pathak, S. 2006. The reification of absorptive capacity: A critical review and rejuvenation of the construct. *Acad. Manage. Rev.* 31(4): 833–863.

Lin, C., Chow, W.S., Madu, C.N., Kuei, C.H. and Yu, P.P. 2005. A structural equation model of supply chain quality management and organizational performance. *Int. J. Prod. Econ.* 96(3): 355–365.

Lo, V.H.Y. and Yeung, A.H.W. 2004. Practical framework for strategic alliance in Pearl River Delta manufacturing supply chain: A total quality approach. *Int. J. Prod. Econ.* 87(3): 231–240.

Mahoney, J.T. 1995. The management of resources and resource of management. *J. Bus. Res.* 33: 91–101.

Mehra, S., Hoffman, J.M. and Sirias, D. 2001. TQM as a management strategy for the next millennia. *Int. J. Ops. Prod. Mgmt.* 21(5/6): 855–876.

Miller, D. 1987. The structural and environmental correlates of business strategy. *Strat. Mgmt. J.* 8(1): 55–76.

Morash, E.A. and Clinton, S.R. 1998. Supply chain integration: Customer value through collaborative closeness versus operational excellence. *J. Mktg. Theory Prac.* 6(4): 104–120.

Nair, A. 2006. Meta-analysis of the relationship between quality management practices and firm performance—implications for quality management theory development. *J. Ops. Mgmt.* 24(6): 948–975.

Newbert, S.L. 2007. Empirical research on the resource based view of the firm: An assessment and suggestions for future research. *Strat. Mgmt. J.* 28(2): 121–146.

Nunnally, J.C. and Bernstein, I.H. 1994. *Psychometric Theory*, 3rd ed. New York, McGraw-Hill.

Pagell, M. and Krause, D.R. 2004. Re-exploring the relationship between flexibility and the external environment. *J. Ops. Mgmt.* 21(6): 629–649.

Paulraj, A. and Chen, I.J. 2005. Strategic supply management and dyadic quality performance: A path analytical model. *J. Supp. Chain. Mgmt.* 41(3): 4–18.

Peng, D.X., Schroeder, R.G. and Shah, R. 2008. Linking routines to operations capabilities: A new perspective. *J. Ops. Mgmt.* 26(6): 730–748.

Prajogo, D.I., McDermott, P. and Goh, M. 2008. Impact of value chain activities on quality and innovation. *Int. J. Ops. Prod. Mgmt.* 28(7): 615–635.

Robinson, C.J. and Malhotra, M.K. 2005. Defining the concept of supply chain quality management and its relevance to academic and industrial practice. *Int. J. Prod. Econ.* 96(3): 315–337.

Rosenzweig, E.D., Roth, A.V. and Dean Jr., J.W. 2003. The influence of an integration strategy on competitive capabilities and business performance: An exploratory study of consumer products manufacturers. *J. Ops. Mgmt.* 21(4): 437–456.

Rungtusanatham, M., Forza, C., Filippini, R. and Anderson, J.C. 1998. A replication study of a theory of quality management underlying the Deming management method: Insights from an Italian context. *J. Ops. Mgmt.* 17(1): 77–95.

Rungtusanatham, M., Ogden, J.A. and Wu, B. 2003. Advancing theory development in total quality management: A "Deming management method" perspective. *Int. J. Ops. Prod. Mgmt.* 23(7/8): 918–936.

Samson, D. and Terziovski, M. 1999. The relationship between total quality management practices and operational performance. *J. Ops. Mgmt.* 17(4): 393–409.

Schreyögg, G. and Kliesch-Eberl, M. 2007. How dynamic can organizational capabilities be? Towards a dual-process model of capability dynamization. *Strat. Mgmt. J.* 28(9): 913–933.

Schroeder, R.G., Bates, K.A. and Junttila, M.A. 2002. A resource-based view of manufacturing strategy and the relationship to manufacturing performance. *Strat. Mgmt. J.* 23(2): 105–117.

Seggie, S.H., Kim, D. and Cavusgil, S.T. 2006. Do supply chain IT alignment and supply chain interfirm system integration impact upon brand equity and firm performance? *J. Bus. Res.* 59(8): 887–895.

Sila, I., Ebrahimpour, M. and Birkholz, C. 2006. Quality in supply chains: An empirical analysis. *Supp. Chain Mgmt.* 11(6): 491–502.

Singer, M., Donoso, P. and Traverso, P. 2003. Quality strategies in supply chain alliances of disposable items. *Omega* 31(6): 499–509.

Srivastava, S.K. 2008. Towards estimating cost of quality in supply chains. *TQM Bus. Excel.* 19(3): 193–208.

Sroufe, R. and Curkovic, S. 2008. An examination of ISO 9000:2000 and supply chain quality assurance. *J. Ops. Mgmt.* 26(4): 503–520.

Stank, T.P., Keller, S.B. and Closs, D.J. 2001a. Performance benefits of supply chain logistical integration. *Trans. J.* 41(2–3): 32–46.

Stank, T.P., Keller, S.B. and Daugherty, P.J. 2001b. Supply chain collaboration and logistical service performance. *J. Bus. Log.* 22(1): 29–48.

Stanley, L.L. and Wisner, J.D. 2001. Service quality along the supply chain: Implications for purchasing. *J. Ops. Mgmt.* 19(3): 287–306.

Stock, G.N. and Tatikonda, M.V. 2004. External technology integration in product and process development. *Int. J. Ops. Prod. Mgmt.* 24(7): 642–665.

Stock, G.N. and Tatikonda, M.V. 2008. The joint influence of technology uncertainty and interorganizational interaction on external technology integration success. *J. Ops. Mgmt.* 26(1): 65–80.

Swink, M., Narasimhan, R. and Wang, C. 2007. Managing beyond the factory walls: Effects of four types of strategic integration on manufacturing plant performance. *J. Ops. Mgmt.* 25(1): 148–164.

Takeishi, A. 2001. Bridging inter- and intra-firm boundaries: Management of supplier involvement in automobile product development. *Strat. Mgmt. J.* 22(5): 403–433.

Tan, K.-C., Kannan, V.R., Handfield, R.B. and Ghosh, S. 1999. Supply chain management: An empirical study of its impact on performance. *Int. J. Ops. Prod. Mgmt.* 19(10): 1034–1052.

Teece, D., Pisano, G. and Shuen, A. 1997. Dynamic capabilities and strategic management. *Strat. Mgmt. J.* 18(7): 509–533.

Themistocleous, M., Irani, Z. and Love, P.E.D. 2004. Evaluating the integration of supply chain information systems: A case study. *Eur. J. Op. Res.* 159(2): 393–405.

Theodorakioglou, Y., Gotzamani, K. and Tsiolvas, G. 2006. Supplier management and its relationship to buyers' quality management. *Supp. Chain Mgmt.* 11(2): 148–159.

Verona, G. 1999. A resource based view of product development. *Acad. Manage. Rev.* 24(1): 132–142.

Victor, H.Y.L. and Alice, Y. 2006. Managing quality effectively in supply chain: A preliminary study. *Supp. Chain Mgmt.* 11(3): 208–215.

Wade, M. and Hulland, J. 2004. Review: The resource based view and information systems research: Review, extension, and suggestions for future research. *MIS Qly.* 28(1): 107–142.

Wang, X., Li, D. and O'Brien, C. 2009. Optimisation of traceability and operations planning: An integrated model for perishable food production. *Int. J. Prod. Res.* 47(11): 2865–2886.

Ward, P.T. and Duray, R. 2000. Manufacturing strategy in context: Environment, competitive strategy and manufacturing strategy. *J. Ops. Mgmt.* 18(2): 123–138.

Ward, P.T., Duray, R., Leong, G.K. and Sum, C.C. 1995. Business environment, operations strategy, and performance: An empirical study of Singapore manufacturers. *J. Ops. Mgmt.* 13(2): 99–115.

Wei, J. and Krajewski, L. 2000. A model for comparing supply chain schedule integration approaches. *Int. J. Prod. Res.* 38(9): 2099–2123.

Williamson, O.E. 1985. *The Economic Institutions of Capitalism.* New York, Free Press.

Wilson, D.D. and Collier, D.A. 2000. An empirical investigation of the Malcolm Baldrige National Quality Award causal model. *Dec. Sci.* 31(2): 361–390.

Zeng, A.Z. and Pathak, H.K. 2003. Achieving information integration in supply chain management through B2B e-hubs: Concepts and analyses. *Ind. Mgmt. Data Sys.* 103(8–9): 657–665.

Zhao, X., Flynn, B.B. and Roth, A.V. 2007. Decision sciences research in China: Current status, opportunities, and propositions for research in supply chain management, logistics, and quality management. *Dec. Sci.* 38(1): 39–80.

Zhao, X., Huo, B., Selen, W. and Yeung, J. 2009. The impact of relationship commitment and internal integration on external integration. Chinese University of Hong Kong, working paper.

Zhao, X.D., Huo, B.F., Flynn, B.B. and Yeung, J.H.Y. 2008. The impact of power and relationship commitment on the integration between manufacturers and customers in a supply chain. *J. Ops. Mgmt.* 26(3): 368–388.

Zhou, H. and Benton, W.H. 2007. Supply chain practice and information sharing. *J. Ops. Mgmt.* 25(6): 1348–1365.

Zhu, K., Zhang, R.Q. and Tsung, F. 2007. Pushing quality improvement along supply chains. *Mgmt. Sci.* 53(3): 421–436.

Zu, X., Fredendall, L.D. and Douglas, T.J. 2008. The evolving theory of quality management: The role of six sigma. *J. Ops. Mgmt.* 26(5): 630–650.

Chapter 19

Effect of Supply Chain Integration on Product Quality and Innovation

Bochao Zhuang, Xiande Zhao, and Stephen Ng

Contents

19.1 Introduction: Customer Orientation

Customer orientation is a company-level orientation that focuses on satisfying or exceeding customers' requirements (Sitkin et al. 1994). It drives a company to assess and meet customer expectations, manage customer relationships, and commit to serving customers (Dean and Bowen 1994). However, the existing literature on the relationship between customer orientation and company performance is inconsistent and sometimes conflicting. On the positive side, customer orientation is associated with a greater positional advantage (meaningful marketing programs and new products), which leads to market and financial performance (Im and Workman 2004) and improved organizational performance. On the negative side, however, Christensen and Bower (1996) found that a company that is too customer oriented may fail to develop breakthrough innovations and may be surpassed in product development by its competitors. Voss and Voss (2000) found that customer orientation is negatively related to company performance in professional theaters, and it was found that customer orientation was not related to return on sales (ROS) or return on assets. This inconsistent relationship between customer orientation and performance motivated us to rethink this scenario from an operations management perspective and explore the process by which customer orientation influences performance.

The resource-based view (RBV) argues that company resources or capabilities with certain characteristics are a source of competitive advantage for a company (Barney 1991; Eisenhardt and Martin 2000; Peteraf 1993; Teece et al. 1997; Wernerfelt 1984). Recently, more and more scholars have studied RBV in terms of the organizational mechanisms that influence the acquisition of resources and the development of organizational capabilities (Newbert 2007; Sinkovics and Roath 2004). However, existing research on RBV has focused less on the role of company-level orientation and capabilities in the development of a competitive advantage. Thus, we focus on customer orientation as a company-level orientation that leads to the development of internal capabilities, such as process management, and external capabilities, such as supply chain integration.

To fill this research gap, we synthesize the literature on customer orientation and RBV, proposing a framework that describes how customer orientation influences two types of organizational capability described in the operations management literature, process management capability and external supply chain integration, and how these two types of organizational capability influence product quality and product innovativeness. We also examine how product quality and product innovativeness, combined, influence financial performance.

19.2 Theoretical Background and Research Hypotheses

We begin by describing the theoretical foundation provided by the RBV of the firm and how it describes the development of capabilities that are the source of a competitive advantage that is valuable, rare, inimitable, and nonsubstitutable (VRIN). We propose that customer orientation is a company-level orientation that nurtures the development of these capabilities and propose hypotheses related to their antecedents and relationship with performance.

19.2.1 Resource-Based View

The RBV argues that company resources, consisting of its physical capital resources, human capital resources, and organizational capital resources, have the potential for achieving a sustainable competitive advantage when they are VRIN (Barney 1991). Peteraf (1993) describes resource heterogeneity as the basic condition for a company to enjoy a sustainable competitive advantage, while four conditions must be met to achieve a sustainable competitive advantage: resource heterogeneity, ex post limits to competition, imperfect resource mobility, and ex ante limits to competition. The early arguments on RBV linked resource attributes (value, rarity, appropriability, inimitability, nonsubstitutability, imperfect mobility) to sustainable competitive advantage (Wade and Hulland 2004).

In addition to the VRIN model, there have been two other important developments in RBV. Besides possessing special resource attributes, a company must be organized to exploit its resources and capabilities, in order to fully realize its potential. The valuable, rare, inimitable, nonsubstitutable framework was proposed, where a company is envisioned as providing organizing mechanisms for exploiting the potential of resources that are VRIN. Company-level orientation, strategy, and context are important characteristics of a company because they encourage a general and unified approach to the utilization of resources (Newbert 2007). Customer orientation is a company-level orientation that mobilizes resources, across a company, toward a common goal of understanding and serving customers.

Another development in RBV is the capability approach, which tries to answer the question, why do companies perform differently? (Zott 2003). Kogut and Zander (1992) proposed the concept of combinative capability as synthesizing and applying current and acquired knowledge. Capability is defined as a company's capacity to deploy resources, usually in combination, using organizational processes, to effect a desired end. They emphasize that capabilities can be information-based, tangible or intangible processes that are company specific and are developed over time through complex interactions among a company's resources. Another important capability term is architectural competence (Henderson and Cockburn 1994), which refers to the ability to use component competencies and integrate them effectively in order to develop fresh competencies as they are required. A company's ability to integrate knowledge is positively associated with its research productivity (Henderson and Cockburn 1994).

Dynamic capabilities have been proposed by several strategic management scholars (Eisenhardt and Martin 2000; Helfat and Peteraf 2003; Teece 2007; Teece et al. 1997; Wang and Ahmed 2007; Winter 2003) as a company's ability to integrate, build, and reconfigure internal and external competencies to address rapidly changing environments (Teese 1997). The 3 Ps (process, positions, and paths) are a source of competitive advantage for a company in a changing environment. The dynamic capabilities approach specifically emphasizes internal organizational processes and reconfiguring internal and external resources and competencies, which can enhance a company's potential to achieve a competitive advantage.

Recently, another new model, known as "orientation–capability–performance," was proposed in an RBV empirical study combining organizational concepts from Barney's work with the capability approach (Sinkovics and Roath 2004). This model posits that company-level orientation will influence the development of a company's capabilities, which in turn improves its competitive advantage. We seek to increase the knowledge in this stream of research by proposing that customer orientation is a company-level orientation that influences two types of dynamic capabilities from the operations management literature: external supply chain integration and process management. These, in turn, lead to a positional advantage based on product innovation and product quality. We also propose that a product-based positional advantage can expedite financial performance. Building on this theoretical model, we hereafter argue and develop more detailed and testable hypotheses, as represented in Figure 19.1.

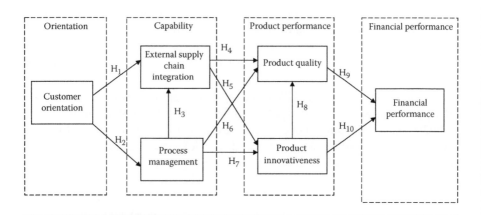

Figure 19.1 Hypothesized model.

19.2.2 Customer Orientation and Capabilities

Customer orientation is a company-level orientation that is based on developing a sufficient understanding of targeted customers in order to be able to consistently create superior value for them (Narver and Slater 1990). Customer orientation is defined as a set of beliefs that puts customers' interests first, while not excluding those of other stakeholders such as owners, managers, and employees, in order to develop a long-term profitable enterprise. Gatignon and Xuereb (1997) argued that a customer-oriented company has the ability and the will to identify, analyze, understand, and answer customer needs. Customer orientation helps a company understand the market's technical issues and provides an evaluation of possible segments, the importance of the market, and its growth rate. We follow the definition of Sitkin et al. (1994) that customer orientation is a company-level orientation that focuses on satisfying or exceeding customers' requirements. Customer orientation means that a company is able to create value for its customers because it understands their value equation (Reed et al. 1996). Customer orientation drives a company to assess customer expectations, manage customer relationships, and commit to customers, leading it to achieve better organizational performance (Dean and Bowen 1994). In empirical studies, customer orientation was found to positively influence profitability (Narver and Slater 1990), business performance, and innovativeness in technical and administrative areas.

According to the orientation–capability–performance logic of RBV, company-level orientation leads to the development of specific capabilities that develop over time, as a company deals with its problems from the perspective of its company-level orientation. We propose that customer orientation is associated with the development of external supply chain integration capability, driving a company to externally integrate with its customers and suppliers (Braunscheidel and Suresh 2009). External supply chain integration is the capability of a company to design products and improve processes through involvement with its supply chain partners. Many customer-oriented companies recognize the strategic role that suppliers can play, seeking to develop a high degree of integration with key suppliers, in order to better serve their customers. Customer orientation motivates a company to share information with its supply chain partners, including suppliers, customers, and working partners, so as to ensure their responsiveness. Customer-oriented companies involve their supply chain partners in product design and process improvement in order to ensure that products and processes are free of defects (Das 2001; Monczka and Trent 1993). Thus, we hypothesize a positive relationship between customer orientation and supply chain integration:

H_1: Customer orientation is positively related to external supply chain integration.

A second capability that we propose as associated with customer orientation is process management. Process management is the capability of a company to control and improve its processes, either incrementally or radically, in order to better serve its customers. It includes both product quality and product innovation. The relationship between customer orientation and process management is emphasized by the Malcolm Baldrige Quality Management framework (Flynn and Saladin 2001). Customer orientation drives a company to control and improve its internal processes so as to ensure that cost, quality, delivery and flexibility performance can be achieved and improved (Flynn et al. 1995; Wilson and Collier 2000). Customer orientation has a positive influence on organizational innovativeness, including technical and administrative areas, which will, in turn, improve process innovation and improvement. Thus, we hypothesize a positive influence of customer orientation on process management:

H_2: Customer orientation is positively related to process management.

Process management is an internally focused capability, focusing on process control and process innovation, while external supply chain integration is an externally focused capability, focusing primarily on relationships with customers and suppliers. Just as internal integration has been described as an antecedent to external integration (Braunscheidel and Suresh 2009), we propose that process management, as a kind of internal capability, is an antecedent to external supply chain integration. As a dynamic capability, process management influences resource allocation and development of other capabilities within and outside a company, such as external supply chain integration. Thus, we hypothesize a positive influence of process management on external supply chain integration.

H_3: Process management is positively related to external supply chain integration.

19.2.3 Supply Chain Integration and Product Performance

As capabilities, external supply chain integration and process management are related to competitive advantage. We examine competitive advantage in terms of product performance (product quality and product innovation) and financial performance. In the following sections, we develop hypotheses based on each of these.

Customers and suppliers, as important supply chain partners, play an increasingly important role in new product development, enhancing product quality and innovativeness. Customers can make different contributions to quality, including serving as a resource, worker (or coproducer), buyer, and beneficiary (or user), and product (Lengnick-Hall 1996). In empirical research, statistically significant relationships between customer integration and product quality have been documented (Koufteros et al. 2005). Customer integration was positively related to operational performance; however, they did not specially measure product quality.

The benefit of supplier involvement lies in ensuring that suppliers will be able to supply the components specified in a product's design and to make appropriate investments, in order to minimize the possibility of design errors. Other benefits of supplier involvement include helping to better coordinate communication and information exchange, improving relationships with the supply base, adding information and expertise regarding new ideas and technology, and reducing the internal complexity of projects (Ragatz et al. 2002). Building good relationships with customers and suppliers has been emphasized through many quality initiatives, including total quality management (TQM) and International Organization for Standardization (ISO) 9000. The findings of Frohlich and Westbrook (2001) demonstrate that integrating both suppliers and customers is positively associated with performance, including conformance quality and on-time delivery. Droge et al. (2004) indicate that external integration, including supplier development, supplier partnerships, and closer customer relationships, was related to product development time, product cycle time, and responsiveness. Thus, we hypothesize a positive relationship between external supply chain integration and product quality:

H_4: External supply chain integration is positively related to product quality.

External supply chain integration is related to product innovation through the role of customers as an information resource and co-developer (Fang 2008), providing a broad range of market information to generate ideas and opinions about product concepts, which is related to innovativeness. The broad knowledge that is acquired from customers gives a company greater flexibility and adaptability in responding to environmental changes (Fang 2008) and allowing it to draw upon the voice of the customer to enhance its product features and improve the innovativeness of its products. Thus, customer integration is positively associated with product innovation performance (Koufteros et al. 2005).

Similarly, supplier integration is associated with product innovativeness. Suppliers can be involved in product design, product testing, and product commercialization. Handfield et al. (1999) found that early and extensive involvement of suppliers greatly improved the success of new product development projects. The greater the supplier involvement in the radical innovation process, the more innovative a new product will be. Thus, we hypothesize a positive influence of supply chain integration on product innovativeness.

H_5: Supply chain integration is positively related to product innovativeness.

19.2.4 Process Management and Product Performance

Similarly, we propose that process management is related to both product quality and innovativeness. Process management improves quality performance through reducing process variance (Flynn et al. 1995), designing quality into a product during development, and building it in during production (Handfield et al. 1999). Process management helps to reduce the amount of scrap and rework (Ahire and Dreyfus 2000), which, in turn, improves product quality. Process management has been emphasized as a core quality management practice (Flynn et al. 1995), proposed to influence business results directly, according to the Baldrige framework (Flynn and Saladin 2001). Ahire and Dreyfus (2000) found that it was positively related to both external and internal quality. Anderson et al. (1995) found that process management had an indirect influence on customer satisfaction through continuous improvement and employee fulfillment. In Kaynak's (2003) research, process management was directly related to quality. In his meta-analysis of the relationship between TQM and performance, Nair (2006) showed that the relationship between process management and product quality was significant and was the strongest among the relationships between process management and aggregate performance, financial performance, operational performance, customer service, and product quality. Thus, we hypothesize a positive relationship between process management and product quality:

H_6: Process management is positively related to product quality.

As a company implements process management practices, it becomes increasingly skilled at producing outputs that leverage its existing knowledge about inputs, technologies, manufacturing techniques, and distribution channels (Benner and Tushman 2003). Thus, process management cultivates improved innovation performance (Prajogo and Sohal 2003), as its changes induce process improvement and innovation. Prajogo and Sohal (2003) found that TQM, which includes a process management component, was positively related to both product and process innovation. They concluded that quality management (a key element of process management) is a prerequisite for innovation management and that TQM is necessary for innovation. On the basis of the above arguments, we hypothesize a positive influence of process management on product innovation.

H_7: Process management is positively related to product innovation.

19.2.5 Product Performance and Financial Performance

Finally, we posit that both product quality and product innovativeness are associated with financial performance. Product innovation is hypothesized to have both a direct effect on financial performance and an indirect effect, through product quality. We begin with the indirect effect of product innovation through product quality, which occurs because of the way quality issues are discovered and addressed during a product development process (Koufteros et al. 2002). Product innovation is a means of accommodating the changing needs of existing and potential customers, which improves perceived product quality and customer satisfaction. Empirical studies have supported the argument that product innovation is positively related to product quality. It was found that product innovation was related to quality, with effects that were quite robust and invariant across environments with different levels of uncertainty and equivocality. Koufteros et al. (2007) reported that product innovativeness influenced external quality for both large and small companies. Prajogo and Sohal (2003) found that process innovation, product quality, and product innovation were highly correlated with each other. On the basis of the above arguments, we hypothesize a positive influence of product innovation on product quality:

H_8: Product innovation is positively related to product quality.

Kaynak (2003) described how quality performance improves financial and market performance, as a company acquires a strong reputation from delivering high-quality products, reducing waste and rework, and improving efficiency and productivity. This results in more customers with greater loyalty, which enhances a company's competitive position. Many other studies have supported the positive influence of quality performance on financial performance, including Koufteros et al. (2003), who found that quality positively influences profitability, and Curkovic et al. (2000), who found that all eight dimensions of quality performance were highly correlated with various types of financial performance. Thus, we hypothesize a positive influence of product quality on financial performance:

H_9: Product quality is positively related to financial performance.

The development of innovative products creates opportunities for differentiation and competitive advantage and hence positively impacts financial performance (Kleinschmidt and Cooper 1991). Product innovation allows a company to offer new features or products that are first in the market and thus command a premium price, which influences profitability (Koufteros et al. 2002). It was shown that product innovation was positively associated with market share, and it was found that product novelty was positively related to new product performance. Koufteros et al. (2002, 2005) found that product innovation can impact profitability through premium pricing. Thus, we hypothesize a positive relationship between product innovation and product quality:

H_{10}: Product innovation is positively related to financial performance.

19.3 Research Methodology

19.3.1 Sampling and Data Collection

With the assistance of the China Quality Management Association, we conducted a nationwide survey across 14 provinces in China. A stratified sampling approach was employed to draw samples based on industry (manufacturing vs. service), sales revenue (five levels), and ownership (state-owned, collective, privately owned, joint venture, shared, and foreign investment). We administered the questionnaire to one key informant from each of 5000 sampled companies. The unit of analysis is the company level. Of the 2675 usable questionnaires, we identified 560 brand manufacturers that had a top or middle manager as the key informant to use as our sample for this study. The demographics of the respondents are shown in Tables 19.1 and 19.2. Following Harman's single-factor approach (Sanchez and Brock 1996), we found that the single-factor model had inferior fit (χ^2 = 6138.677, df = 350, $\chi^2/$ df = 17.539, RMSEA = 0.172 [0.168, 0.176], GFI = 0.416, CFI = 0.526, TLI = 0.488), thus substantiating that the impact of common method variance was not a threat to our study.

19.3.2 Survey Instrument

In this study, the customer orientation and process management constructs are based on the framework provided by the Malcolm Baldrige National Quality Award (e.g., Flynn and Saladin 2001; Wilson and Collier 2000). We used four items to measure customer orientation and seven for process management. We developed new items for external supply chain integration based on previous research discussing customer and supplier involvement in new product development (Stump and Heide 1996) and our understanding from our field observations and interviews. We asked about the informants' extent of agreement with statements about their company's information and data sharing with its supply chain partners, involvement of its suppliers in quality improvement activities, acquisition and application of knowledge from its supply chain partners and internal employees, and involving suppliers in its projects early in the development process.

To measure product innovativeness, we searched previous research (Brockman and Morgan 2003; Gatignon and Xuereb 1997; Koufteros et al. 2007) to identify valid measures for related constructs. Product innovativeness was measured by asking informants about their agreement with four aspects: the sophistication of the technology adopted in their products, the extent to which their products are perceived as revolutionary, the extent to which their products are new to the market, and the innovativeness of a product designed by their company. We measured product quality using four items that asked informants about the extent to which quality is continuously improved, the existing quality level, the amount of unique features, and the level of technological superiority of their products. Building on

Table 19.1 Profile of Responding Companies (*n* = 560)

Industry	%	Industry	%
Chemical products	9.8	Medical	0.5
Food	8.8	Plastics and rubber	2.0
Pharmaceuticals	2.7	Wood	0.9
Construction	4.6	Automobiles	4.3
Metal	4.8	Transportation	0.7
Electronics	3.8	Consumables	4.6
Garments	2.1	Mining	0.2
Textiles	4.8	Jewelry	0.4
Electricity	4.3	Water	0.2
Equipment	22.3	Printing	0.7
IT	1.1	Miscellaneous	15.3
Agriculture	1.1		

Sales	%
<RMB5 million	28.8
RMB5 million–RMB10 million	12.4
RMB10 million–RMB50 million	20.8
RMB50 million–RMB100 million	10.0
>RMB100 million	28.0

Size	%
<100	17.9
100–1000	59.1
1000–5000	18.7
5000–9500	2.3
>9500	2.0

(*continued*)

Table 19.1 Profile of Responding Companies (*n* = 560) (Continued)

Ownership	%
State owned	20.4
Collective	5.4
Privately owned	54.1
Foreign investment	5.7
Joint venture	9.8
Shared	0.9
Others	3.7

Table 19.2 Characteristics of Informants (*n* = 560)

Position	%	Years in Current Position	%
Top management	25.9	<5 years	30.5
Middle management	74.1	5–10 years	27.0
		10–20 years	26.1
		>20 years	16.4

the work of Narasimhan and Kim (2002) and Vickery et al. (2003), financial performance was measured by asking informants to evaluate their company's growth in sales, return on investment (ROI), growth in ROI, ROS, and growth in ROS, relative to its industry.

After generating the initial questionnaire items, we translated the questionnaire from English to Chinese and then backward translated to it English. Wordings were refined as needed. We then invited three quality experts and one marketing expert in China to assess the content validity of the items. We further pilot tested the questionnaire with managers from 30 companies. Based on the results, some minor changes in wording were made.

19.3.3 Measurement Analysis

The 560 respondents were randomly split into two subsamples: a calibration sample and a validation sample. We randomly drew 150 cases to be used as the calibration sample for scale construction and purification, which included tests for unidimensionality and reliability using exploratory factor analysis (EFA) (Hair et al. 1998). The remaining 410 cases were then examined for validation purposes using

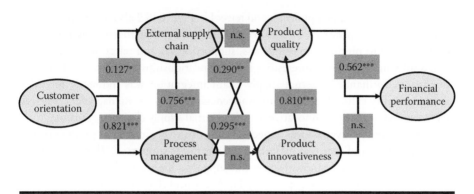

Figure 19.2 Research results. *** denotes that the path coefficient is significant at *p* < 0.001 respectively. n.s. denotes that the path coefficient is not significant at *p* < 0.05. Model fitness: χ^2 = 1047.28; df = 340; χ^2/df = 3.080; RMSEA = 0.061 [0.057, 0.065]; GFI = 0.874; CFI = 0.942; TLI = 0.936.

confirmatory factor analysis (CFA). Technical details of the measurement analysis are contained in Appendix 19.2.

19.3.4 Analysis

Structural equation modeling was used to test the hypotheses. The results of the structural model are shown in Figure 19.2. The overall goodness of fit was good (e.g., χ^2 = 1047.28, df = 340, χ^2/df = 3.080, RMSEA = 0.061 [0.057, 0.065], GFI = 0.874, CFI = 0.942, TLI = 0.936).

19.4 Results

There were significant direct relationships between customer orientation and process management and external supply chain integration, supporting H_1 and H_2. Companies with a higher level of customer orientation had higher levels of process management capability and external supply chain integration capability. Thus, our results are consistent with the literature that describes capabilities as developing from company-level orientation. Specifically, our results indicate that customer orientation was more strongly related to process management (an internal capability) than to external supply chain integration (an external capability). Hypothesis H_3 stated that process management would be positively related to supply chain integration, and the results support this hypothesis, lending support to the notion that external capabilities build on internal capabilities.

Figure 19.2 shows that external supply chain integration was positively related to product innovativeness. However, it was not significantly related to product quality; thus, the results support H_5 and reject H_4. Figure 19.2 also reveals that process management was positively related to product quality but that it was not significantly related to product innovativeness, supporting H_6 and rejecting H_7. However, our results indicate some interesting indirect relationships between capability and product performance. External supply chain integration was indirectly related to product quality through product innovativeness, and process management was indirectly related to product innovativeness via external supply chain integration.

Product innovativeness was expected to be positively related to product quality (H_8), and we found that this hypothesis was strongly supported. This means that a higher level of product innovativeness can support a higher level of product quality, rather than constraining it, supporting H_8. We found that that product quality was positively related to financial performance, supporting H_9. The effect of product innovativeness, however, on financial performance was not significant, rejecting H_{10}. However, product innovativeness was indirectly related to financial performance through product quality. Thus, when an innovative product conforms to customers' needs and specifications, the company will achieve financial gains. On the other hand, an innovative product that does not satisfy customers' needs or does not conform to quality requirements can cost a company a substantial amount of money, which is reflected in diminished financial performance.

19.5 Discussion

19.5.1 Theoretical Implications

We found that customer orientation provides the strategic direction for the development of internal and external dynamic capabilities in process management and supply chain integration. Customer orientation not only sets the stage for internal process management capability, congruent with the TQM literature (Flynn and Saladin 2001), but also enhances the degree of involvement with customers and suppliers. Companies that reported a high degree of customer orientation, such as systematically listening to and understanding the preferences of different groups of customers and designing the characteristics of their products based on the voice of the customers, had better process control, adjusting or improving the process based on quality information and customer feedback, acquiring more information and knowledge from external partners, and integrating with customers and suppliers on product design. Thus, customer orientation can induce a company to develop its internal process management capabilities and external supply chain integration capabilities. Customer orientation had a strong indirect relationship with external supply chain integration through process management (Table 19.3).

Contrary to expectations, external supply chain integration was not directly related to product quality. This is consistent with previous research results that found that supplier product integration and supplier process integration were not associated with product quality (Koufteros et al. 2005). The influence mechanisms

Table 19.3 Analysis of Direct, Indirect, and Total Effects (*n* = 560)

Factor	Effect	Process Management	External SCI	Product Innovativeness	Product Quality	Financial Performance
Customer orientation	Direct	.821	.127			
	Indirect		.621	.340	.434	.234
	Total	.821	.748	.340	.434	.234
Process management	Direct		.756	.150	.295	
	Indirect			.219	.214	.276
	Total		.756	.369	.509	.276
External SCI	Direct			.290	−.112	
	Indirect				.235	.061
	Total			.290	.123	.061
Product innovativeness	Direct				.810	−.028
	Indirect					.455
	Total				.810	.427
Product quality	Direct					.562
	Indirect					
	Total					.562

from supply chain integration to quality should be explored in future research. To make the external quality enabler effective, a company may need to implement some internal changes and align its external environment and internal capability to improve product quality. Our findings indicate that external supply chain integration is strongly related to product innovativeness, which is consistent with the results of Song and Di Benedetto (2008). Supplier chain partner involvement, through information sharing, involvement in quality improvement activities and product design, and external knowledge management with partners, is related to improved product innovativeness. One of the interesting findings of this study is that supply chain integration was not directly related to product quality. However, it was indirectly related to product quality through its influence on innovativeness.

Process management appears to be critical for product quality, which is consistent with the results of Kaynak (2003) and Nair (2006). Process management, which includes a variety of process controls and process improvement practices, helps to enhance product reliability, product durability, design quality, and perceived quality. As Benner and Tushman (2002) argued, process management focuses on variance reduction and efficiency, which is related to dynamic capabilities that decrease radical innovation and promote incremental innovation. Our findings complement their argument that process management was positively, but insignificantly, related to product innovativeness. Our findings build upon the findings of Prajogo and Sohal (2003) by showing that process management, as a key component of TQM, is indirectly related to product innovativeness through supply chain integration. A high level of process management can facilitate the acquisition of external knowledge and information, which are important in product design and enhancement. This finding fills the gap concerning the influence mechanism between process management and product innovativeness. Future research should continue to explore how process management influences other types of product innovativeness and examine the theoretical boundary conditions.

Concerning the relationship between product performance and financial performance, we found that product innovativeness was not directly related to financial performance, while product quality was. Our study enhances the findings of Koufteros et al. (2005) by operationalizing financial performance as a more comprehensive measure of business performance than profitability. One interesting finding is that product innovativeness was not directly related to financial performance. Nevertheless, it was indirectly related through product quality, which was directly related to financial performance. The relationship between product innovativeness and financial performance differentiates our study from previous research that argues for a direct relationship between them. We argued that product quality is positively related to financial performance, which was supported by our research context. Compared with product innovativeness, product quality was more strongly related to financial performance. Product quality creates more purchasing opportunities and higher levels of product margins than product innovativeness does. New features and innovative products that are not accepted by customers and require greater expenditures for promotion may decrease financial performance. However, highly innovative products of high quality can also lead to improved financial performance. Future research should examine the influence of different stages of product innovativeness on financial performance and explore the complementary effect of product innovativeness and product quality on financial performance from a dynamic perspective.

19.5.2 Managerial Implications

This study has several important implications for managers. First, managers nurturing customer orientation in their organizational culture or pursuing customer satisfaction as a strategic goal should strive to simultaneously develop internal process management capability and external supply chain integration capability. Thus, customer orientation will drive a company to develop its process management capability and then build its external supply chain integration capability via internal process management. Internal capabilities can enhance external capabilities, which provides another path to realize strategic and product performance objectives.

Second, in order to advance product innovativeness to achieve a competitive advantage, our results provide managers with several alternatives. On one hand, managers can nurture customer orientation, including carefully categorizing feedback from customer and market groups to accurately define and understand customers' needs, listening to and understanding the preferences of different groups of customers, designing the characteristics of products and services based on the voice of the customers, and taking the initiative to build partnerships with customers, in order to enhance external supplier chain partner involvement. On the other hand, managers can select the path from customer orientation to process management to external supply chain integration to product innovativeness. In order to promote product innovativeness, managers following this path should not only understand customer demands and listen to the voice of the customer but also simultaneously develop internal and external capabilities, reflecting the basic alignment between strategic direction and operational capabilities. However, a point that should be noted is that process management does not influence product innovativeness directly. When process management helps a company to share information with external suppliers and customers, better acquisition of knowledge from the outside applies it to internal product design and development, in order to improve product innovativeness. Process management should not only focus on internal efficiency and improvement but also be considered broadly as a means for synchronizing information, sharing knowledge, and elevating the involvement of external supply chain partners.

Third, managers should recognize that improving product quality can be achieved directly via process management, but not by external supply chain integration. To understand the influence of external supply chain integration on product quality, product innovativeness should be considered. Only when involving external supply chain partners to help design new features into products and adopt more advanced technology in product design will external supply chain integration lead to improved product quality. Otherwise, external supply chain integration can bring some disadvantages for a company, for example, increasing organizational complexity and becoming myopic. To make a final product with higher quality, a company should focus on process management to reduce process variance and then enable external supply chain integration to enhance product innovativeness.

Finally, managers should recognize that not all competitive advantages will promote financial performance. Product quality significantly boosts financial performance directly, which is different from the role that product innovativeness plays. A key point to note is that when adding new features and releasing new products, companies must cater to customers' needs and improve product quality, which in turn greatly influences financial performance. Otherwise, product innovativeness can have a negative impact on financial performance. Thus, the relationship between product quality and product innovativeness is not a tradeoff but is complementary.

19.6 Conclusions

This study extends the existing research on company-based orientation and capabilities in several important ways. First, we independently consider customer orientation, separating it from the broader construct of marketing orientation, as the antecedent to several capabilities. This provides us with an opportunity to make a comparison between marketing orientation and customer orientation, helping to address the debate about the relationship between company-level orientation and capabilities in the strategic management literature. We argue that customer orientation acts as the driving factor for other internal and external capabilities, which differentiates our research from the previous TQM research. Second, this study describes organizational capabilities from both the internal and external perspective, including both process management (an internal capability) and external supply chain integration. Our findings indicate that customer orientation influences internal and external capabilities differently, which fills the research gap concerning the influence mechanisms of customer orientation on competitive advantage. Third, our findings extend the previous literature by indicating that different organizational capabilities influence different types of product performance. Internal process management capability directly influences process quality, but not product innovativeness; however, external supply chain integration directly impacts product innovativeness, but not product quality. Finally, we link the two product performance dimensions with overall financial performance.

While our research makes a significant contribution to the TQM and orientation–capability–performance RBV literature and provides important managerial implications, there are some limitations and opportunities for future research. First, this research uses a cross-sectional research design, which can constrain causal inferences. Customer orientation, like other components of organizational culture, develops gradually. Similarly, internal process management capability and external supply chain integration capability develop gradually. Therefore, it will be fruitful for future researchers to explore the evolution of relationships between them using a longitudinal research design. Second, we collected data from manufacturing companies; therefore, future work should study the same issues in service operations. We conjecture that the paths in this model may be different for high-contact services because of the heavy involvement of customers in the service process* and the use of different quality criteria (Parasuraman et al. 1985). Third, we include only customer orientation as the antecedent of organizational capabilities. Future research should compare different company-level orientations, for example, technology orientation, market orientation, competitive orientation, and learning orientation.

---

* Service organizations can be further classified into mass services, service factories, professional services, and service shops. These types of services are different in their degree of customization and the degree of labor.

The importance of customer orientation has been emphasized across areas of research, including strategic management, marketing, and operation management. This study empirically addresses how customer orientation influences organizational capabilities, and then product and financial performance. To this end, we also provide some research avenues for future studies.

Appendix 19.1 Measurement Analysis (*n* = 150)

		Factor Loading	α
Customer Orientation Eigenvalue = 3.04, % of variance = 76.05%			
C3.1	Firm carefully categorizes customer and market groups so as to accurately define and understand customers' needs.	0.90	
C3.2	Firm systematically listens and understands the preference of different groups of customers and markets.	0.91	.89
C3.3	Firm designs the characteristics of products and services based on customers' voice.	0.85	
C3.7	Firm takes initiative to build partnership with customers.	0.83	
Supply Chain Integration Eigenvalue = 2.71, % of variance = 67.81%			
C4.7	Firm shares its data and information with suppliers, partners, and customers.	0.86	
C4.8	Firm actively requests suppliers to be involved in the quality improvement activities.	0.88	.84
C4.9	Firm acquires and applies knowledge from employees, customers, suppliers, and partners.	0.84	
C6.11	Suppliers are involved early in company's project in product/service design project.	0.85	

		Factor Loading	α
Process Management Eigenvalue = 4.22, % of variance = 60.28%			
C6.1	Key production/service processes have clear and measurable performance indicators.	0.83	
C6.2	Firm uses information collected from customers, suppliers, and partners in design processes.	0.78	.89
C6.3	Firm standardizes and documents production and service processes.	0.74	
C6.6	Firm uses statistical methods to control the variation of production and service processes.	0.80	
C6.8	Firm encourages front-line employees to be involved in process improvement activities.	0.74	
C6.14	Firm uses IT to radically improve production/service processes.	0.71	.89
C6.17	Firm systematically collects and analyzes quality information to adjust production/service processes.	0.83	
Product Quality Eigenvalue = 2.76, % of variance = 69.07%			
C7.6	Company's product quality is improving.	0.66	
C7.29	Products/services designed by company have better quality than the same types of products in the market.	0.89	
C7.30	Products/services designed by company have more unique features than the same types of products in the market.	0.90	.85
C7.34	Products/services designed by company have better technical performance than the same types of products in the market.	0.85	

	Factor Loading	α
Product Innovativeness		
Eigenvalue = 3.09, % of variance = 77.32%		
C7.25 Products/services designed by our company adopt more advanced technology.	0.87	
C7.26 Products/services designed by our company often cause revolutions in the market.	0.90	.90
C7.27 Products/services designed by our company are totally new to market.	0.88	
C7.28 Products/services designed by our company is very innovative.	0.87	
Financial Performance		
Eigenvalue = 4.19, % of variance = 83.86%		
C7.10 Growth of sales	0.88	
C7.12 Return on investment (ROI)	0.91	
C7.13 Growth of ROI	0.93	.95
C7.14 Return on sales (ROS)	0.93	
C7.15 Growth of ROS	0.93	

Appendix 19.2 Technical Details of the Measurement Analysis

In order to assess the unidimensionality and reliability of the measurement items, they were subjected to EFA on a subscale-by-subscale basis. Items for which the largest factor loading was greater than or equal to 0.45 (based on the sample size of 150) (Hair et al. 1998) and for which the cross-loading difference* is greater than or equal to 0.10 were retained (Nunnally 1978). The percentage of variance of the measurement items extracted by the construct should be greater than 50% or its eigenvalue larger than 1.0 (Hair et al. 1998), if the construct is unidimensional. The EFA results for the individual constructs are shown in Appendix 19.1, indicating that each construct had an Eigenvalue greater than 1.0 and variance extracted

---

* Note that cross-loading difference is the difference between the largest and the second-largest factor loading.

greater than 50%. The items that comprise each factor all had loadings greater than 0.45. The percentage of variance explained by each of the three process management dimensions was all greater than 50%.

The threshold for Cronbach's α (Nunnally 1978) was set at .70, in order to assess the adequacy of subscale reliability. As shown in Appendix 19.1, the results reveal that all constructs met this criterion.

CFA was used to assess convergent validity. Running CFA on the validation sample ($n = 410$) showed acceptable fit ($\chi^2 = 856$, df = 335, $\chi^2/df = 2.554$, RMSEA = 0.062 [0.057, 0.067], GFI = 0.865, CFI = 0.943, TLI = 0.936), therefore indicating convergent validity (O'Leary and Vokurka 1998). Convergent validity is further supported by the finding that the average factor loading of each construct was greater than 0.56 and by the statistical significance of each factor loading. Therefore, the scales exhibit acceptable convergent validity.

We followed the procedure of Anderson and Gerbing (1988) for assessing discriminant validity by first setting the correlation between any two constructs to 1.0 and then performing a χ^2 difference test between the constrained and unconstrained models. A positive and significant χ^2 value indicates that the constrained model has significantly poorer fit than the unconstrained model does, thereby providing evidence for the distinctiveness of the two constructs. This was repeated for all the possible pairs of constructs. Table 19.A2.1 shows that all χ^2 differences between the constrained and unconstrained models were significant at $p < .001$. Therefore, discriminant validity is confirmed.

Table 19.A2.1 Discriminant Validity (χ^2 Difference)

	Customer Focus	External Supply Chain Integration	Process Management	Product Innovativeness	Product Quality
External supply chain integration	227				
Process management	233	116			
Product innovativeness	876	648	774		
Product quality	494	410	418	72	
Financial performance	1270	770	1509	753	443

Note: All χ^2 differences are significant at $p < .001$ with $\Delta df = 1$.

References

Ahire, S.L. and Dreyfus, P. 2000. The impact of design management and process management on quality: An empirical investigation. *J. Ops. Mgmt.* 18(5): 549–575.

Anderson, J.C. and Gerbing, D.W. 1988. Structural equation modeling in practice: A review and recommended two-step approach. *Psych. Bull.* 103(3): 411–423.

Anderson, J.C., Rungtusanatham, M., Schroeder, R.G. and Devaraj, S. 1995. A path analytic model off a theory of quality management underlying the Deming management method: Preliminary empirical findings. *Dec. Sci.* 26(5): 637–658.

Barney, J.B. 1991. Film resources and sustained competitive advantage. *Journal of Management* 17(1): 99–120.

Benner, M.J. and Tushman, M.L. 2002. Process management and technological innovation: A longitudinal study of the photography and paint industries. *Admin. Sci. Qly.* 47(4): 676–706.

Benner, M.J. and Tushman, M.L. 2003. Exploration, exploitation, and process management: A productivity dilemma revisited. *Acad. Mgmt. Rev.* 28(2): 238–256.

Braunscheidel, M.J. and Suresh, N.C. 2009. The organizational antecedents of a firm's supply chain agility for risk mitigation. *J. Ops. Mgt.* 27(2): 119–140.

Brockman, B.K. and Morgan, R.M. 2003. The role of existing knowledge in new product innovativeness and performance. *Dec. Sci.* 34(2): 385–419.

Christensen, C.M. and Bower, J.L. 1996. Customer power, strategic investment and the failure of leading firms. *Strat. Mgt. J.* 17(3): 197–218.

Curkovic, S., Melnyk, S., Calantone, R. and Handfield, R. 2000. Validating the Malcolm Baldrige National Quality Award framework through structural equation modeling. *Int. J. Prod. Res.* 38(4): 765–791.

Das, D.K. 2001. Corporate governance and restructuring: A post-crisis Asian perspective. *Asia-Pacific J. Econ. and Bus.* 5(1): 21–25.

Dean Jr., J.W. and Bowen, D.E. 1994. Management theory and total quality improving research and practice through theory development. *Acad. Mgmt. Rev.* 19(3): 392–418.

Droge, C., Jayaram, J. and Vickery, S.K. 2004. The effects of internal versus external integration practices on time-based performance and overall company performance. *J. Ops. Mgmt.* 22(6): 557–573.

Eisenhardt, K.M. and Martin, J.A. 2000. Dynamic capabilities: What are they? *Strat. Mgmt. J.* 21(10/11): 1105–1121.

Fang, E. 2008. Customer participation and the trade-off between new product innovativeness and speed to market. *J. Mktg.* 72(4): 90–104.

Flynn, B.B. and Saladin, B. 2001. Further evidence on the validity of the theoretical models underlying the Baldrige criteria. *J. Ops. Mgmt.* 19: 617–652.

Flynn, B.B., Schroeder, R.G. and Sakakibara, S. 1995. The impact of quality management practices on performance and competitive advantage. *Dec. Sci.* 26(5): 659–691.

Frohlich, M.T. and Westbrook, R. 2001. Arcs of integration: An international study of supply chain strategies. *J. Ops. Mgmt.* 19(2): 185–200.

Gatignon, H. and Xuereb, J.M. 1997. Strategic orientation of the firm new product performance. *J. Mktg. Res.* 34(1): 77–90.

Hair, J.R., Anderson, R.E., Tatham, R.L. and Black, W.C. 1998. *Multivariate Data Analysis.* New York: Prentice-Hall.

Handfield, R.B., Ragatz, G.L., Peterson, K.L. and Monczka, R.M. 1999. Involving suppliers in new product development. *California Mgt. Rev.* 42(1): 5–82.

Helfat, C.E. and Peteraf, M.D. 2003. The dynamic resource-based view. *Strat. Mgt. J.* 24(10): 997–1010.

Henderson, R. and Cockburn, I. 1994. Measuring competence? Exploring firm effects in pharmaceutical research. *Strat. Mgt. J.* 15: 63–84.

Im, S. and Workman, J.P. 2004. Market orientation, creativity and new product performance in high technology firms. *J. Mktg.* 68(2): 114–132.

Kaynak, H. 2003. The relationship between total quality management practices and their effects on company performance. *J. Ops. Mgmt.* 21(4): 405–435.

Kleinschmidt, E.J. and Cooper, R.G. 1991. The impact of product innovations on performance. *J. Prod. Innov. Mgt.* 8(4): 240–251.

Kogut, B. and Zander, U. 1992. Knowledge of a company, combinative capabilities, and the replication of technology. *Company Sci.* 3(3): 383–397.

Koufteros, X.A., Cheng, T.C.E. and Lai, K.H. 2007. "Black-box" and "gray-box" supplier integration in product development: Antecedents, consequences and the moderating role of company size. *J. Ops. Mgmt.* 25(4): 847–870.

Koufteros, X.A., Vonderembse, M.A. and Doll, W.J. 2002. Integrated product development practices and competitive capabilities: The effects of uncertainty, equivocality, and platform strategy. *J. Ops. Mgmt.* 20(4): 331–355.

Koufteros, X.A., Vonderembse, M.A. and Jayaram, J. 2005. Internal and external for product development: The contingency effects of uncertainty, equivocality, and platform strategy. *Dec. Sci.* 36(1): 97–133.

Lengnick-Hall, C.A. 1996. Customer contribution to quality: A different view of the customer-oriented firm. *Acad. Mgmt. Rev.* 21(3): 791–824.

Monczka, R.M. and Trent, R.J. 1993. Supply base strategies to maximize supplier performance. *Int. J. Phys. Dist. Log. Mgt.* 23(4): 42–61.

Nair, A. 2006. Meta-analysis of the relationship between quality management practices and company performance—Implications for quality management theory development. *J. Ops. Mgmt.* 24(6): 948–975.

Narasimhan, R. and Kim, S.W. 2002. Effect of supply chain integration on the relationship between diversification and performance: Evidence from Japanese and Korean firms. *J. Ops. Mgt.* 20(3): 303–323.

Narver, J.C. and Slater, S.F. 1990. The effect of a market orientation on business profitability. *J. Mktg.* 54(4): 20–35.

Newbert, S.L. 2007. Empirical research on the resource-based view of a firm—An assessment and suggestions for future research. *Strat. Mgmt. J.* 28(2): 121–146.

Nunnally, J.C. 1978. *Psychometric Theory*. Englewood Cliffs, NJ: McGraw-Hill.

O'Leary-Kelly, S.W. and Vokurka, R.J. 1998. The empirical assessment of construct validity. *J. Ops. Mgmt.* 16(4): 387–405.

Parasuraman, A., Zeithaml, V.A. and Berry, L.J. 1985. A conceptual model of service quality an its implications for future research. *J. Mktg.* 49(4): 41–60.

Peteraf, M.A. 1993. The cornerstones of competitive advantage: A resource-based view. *Strat. Mgt. J.* 14(3): 179–191.

Prajogo, D.I. and Sohal, A.S. 2003. The relationship between TQM practices, quality performance, and innovation performance: An empirical examination. *Int. J. Qual. Rel. Mgmt.* 20(8): 901–918.

Ragatz, G.L., Handfield, R.B. and Peterson, K.L. 2002. Benefits associated with supplier integration into new product development under conditions of technological uncertainty. *J. Bus. Res.* 55(5): 389–400.

Reed, R., Lemak, D. and Montgomery, J. 1996. Beyond process: TQM content and company performance. *Acad. Mgmt. Rev.* 21(1): 173–202.

Sanchez, J.I. and Brock, P. 1996. Outcomes of perceived discrimination among his panic employees: Is diversity management a luxury or a necessity? *Acad. Mgmt. J.* 39(3): 704–719.

Sinkovics, R.R. and Roath, A.S. 2004. Strategic orientation, capabilities, and performance in manufacturer–3PL relationships. *J. Bus. Log.* 25(2): 43–64.

Sitkin, S.B., Sutcliffe, K.M. and Schroeder, R.G. 1994. Distinguishing control from learning in total quality management: A contingency perspective. *Acad. Mgmt. Rev.* 19(3): 537–564.

Song, M. and Di Benedetto, C.A. 2008. Suppliers' involvement and success of radical new product development in new ventures. *J. Ops. Mgmt.* 26(1): 1–22.

Stump, R.L. and Heide, J.B. 1996. Controlling supplier opportunism in industrial relationships. *J. Mktg. Res.* 33(4): 431–441.

Teece, D.J. 2007. Explicating dynamic capabilities: The nature and micro-foundations of (sustainable) enterprise performance. *Strat. Mgmt. J.* 28(13): 1319–1350.

Teece, D.J., Pisano, G. and Shuen, A. 1997. Dynamic capabilities and strategic management. *Strat. Mgmt. J.* 18(7): 509–533.

Teese, D.J. 1997. Explicating dynamic capabilities: The nature and microfoundations of (sustainable) enterprise performance. *Strat. Mgt. J.* 28(13): 1319–1350.

Vickery, S.K., Jayaram, J., Droge, C. and Calantone, R. 2003. The effects of an integrative supply chain strategy on customer service and firm performance: An analysis of direct vs. indirect relationships. *J. Ops. Mgt.* 21(5): 523–539.

Voss, G.B. and Voss, Z.G. 2000. Strategic orientation and company performance in an artistic environment. *J. Mktg.* 64(1): 67–83.

Wade, M. and Hulland, J. 2004. The resource-based view and information systems research: Review, extension, and suggestions for future research. *MIS Qly.* 28(1): 107–142.

Wang, C.L. and Ahmed, P.K. 2007. Dynamic capabilities: A review and research agenda. *Int. J. Mgt. Rev.* 9(1): 31–51.

Wernerfelt, B. 1984. On the role of RBV in marketing. *Acad. Mktg. Sci.* 42(1): 22–23.

Wilson, D.D. and Collier, D.A. 2000. An empirical investigation of the Malcolm Baldridge National Quality Award causal model. *Dec. Sci.* 31(6): 361–390.

Winter, S.G. 2003. Understanding dynamic capabilities. *Strat. Mgmt. J.* 24(10): 991–995.

Zott, C. 2003. Dynamic capabilities and the emergence of intra-industry differential company performance: Insights from a simulation study. *Strat. Mgmt. J.* 24(2): 97–125.

Chapter 20

Effect of Supply Chain Quality Management on Performance

Haiju Hu and Barbara B. Flynn

Contents

20.1 Introduction: Supply Chain Quality Management

Although traditional quality management (QM) requires the involvement of customers and suppliers, its primary emphasis is on the people and departments within a company (Vanichchinchai and Igel 2009). However, QM issues transcend the boundaries of a single company, and a quality problem can be caused by any link in a company's supply chain. For example, in Chapter 5, we described the catastrophic consequences of upstream supply chain quality problems for Chinese dairy companies. Thus, it is important for QM to focus on the interactions between all members of a supply chain.

Supply chain QM (SCQM) extends the traditional company-centric, product-based QM mindset to an interorganizational supply chain focus involving customers, suppliers, and others (Flynn and Flynn 2005; Foster and Ogden 2008; Kannan and Tan 2005; Lin et al. 2005; Robinson and Malhotra 2005; Saraph et al. 1989; Sila et al. 2006). This perspective is important in developing an understanding of how to best deliver value to customers in a globally dispersed supply chain (Robinson and Malhotra 2005). In previous research, QM and supply chain management have been treated as distinct and independent because of their differing foci; while QM focuses on quality improvement, supply chain management emphasizes primarily cost reduction (Vanichchinchai and Igel 2009) through synchronizing the decisions and activities of all members of a supply chain (Li 2007). Despite their differences, however, QM and supply chain management share many similarities (Vanichchinchai and Igel 2009), including their ultimate goal of customer satisfaction and the need for integration among internal functions and between internal functions and external constituents.

The prior conceptual work on SCQM has sought to develop a concise definition and propose various frameworks. Robinson and Malhotra (2005) defined SCQM as "the formal coordination and integration of business processes, involving all member organizations in the supply channel, to measure, analyze and continually improve products, services, and processes, in order to create value and achieve satisfaction of intermediate and final customers in the marketplace." Foster (2008) defined SCQM as "a systems-based approach to performance improvement that leverages opportunities created by upstream and downstream linkages with suppliers and customers."

Previous research (Kannan and Tan 2005; Lin et al. 2005; Lo and Yeung 2006; Sroufe and Curkovic 2008; Theodorakioglou et al. 2006; Vanichchinchai and Igel 2009; Yeung 2008) suggests that the conjoint implementation of QM and supply chain management will yield superior financial and business performance. For example, Romano and Vinelli (2001) found that a coordinated supply chain was better able to meet customers' quality expectations in the textile industry. Due to the inconsistency of the operationalizations of SCQM in the prior literature, however, the empirical results of the prior research is not comparable and can provide only limited implications for practice.

As we described in Chapter 8, SCQM is a holistic management system to improve quality, which includes supply chain leadership for quality, strategic supply chain design for quality, upstream quality management, downstream quality management, internal quality integration, and product recall systems. Because SCQM is holistic, it will not function effectively if any of the six components is missing. SCQM has a broader scope than traditional QM does. It emphasizes supply chain leadership for quality and strategic supply chain design for quality, which explicitly focus on supply chain interactions and are not considered in traditional QM. Although traditional QM has described the importance of involving suppliers, its prescriptions have been limited mainly to product design. However, learning from suppliers can take place in many other ways, such as through training and providing advanced knowledge. Similarly, the downstream element of SCQM moves beyond simply establishing a committed, long-term relationship with customers. The selection of customers has strategic implications for supply chain quality; a customer that lacks appropriate storage and handling capabilities can be the cause of consumer dissatisfaction with the quality of the company's products.

This chapter operationalizes SCQM's key constructs and investigates their effectiveness. It focuses on the perspective of a company with upstream suppliers and downstream customers, in order to develop a better understanding of SCQM.

20.2 Research Hypotheses

In this section, the hypothesized relationship among the six SCQM components and their relationship with quality performance are described. Each of the components is the basis for multiple hypotheses, which are described by the conceptual model in Figure 20.1.

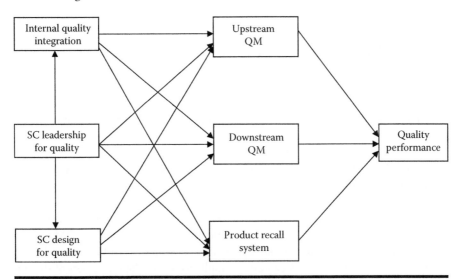

Figure 20.1   Conceptual model. SC = supply chain.

20.2.1 Supply Chain Leadership for Quality

Supply chain leadership for quality is the ability of a company to influence supply chain members in order to increase their compliance with and commitment to the leader's vision for the entire supply chain (Sinha and Kohnke 2009). The existence of a supply chain leader is important to the success of a supply chain since the supply chain leader is the driving force behind supply chain decisions (Sinha and Kohnke 2009). For example, in China, the influential leader in many supply chains is a foreign member or customer; for example, Guangzhou is home to a large Honda production facility, and many toy suppliers there produce toys for brand owners like Mattel or international retailers like Wal-Mart. The supply chain leader may be a manufacturer or brand owner, such as Motorola, a customer such as Wal-Mart, or even the supplier of a rare and critical component. What distinguishes the supply chain leader from other members of a supply chain is its ability to influence supply chain members' activities and their commitment to a particular supply chain vision. A company becomes the supply chain leader based on the resources or power that it possesses (Richey et al. 2004).

Supply chain leadership for quality refers to the importance that the supply chain leader attaches to quality. In the context of a single company, leadership is an important driver of company success; effective leadership should increase the effectiveness of other QM dimensions, resulting in improved company performance (Kuei et al. 2001). Extending this thinking to a supply chain context, supply chain leadership for quality lays the foundation for the quality orientation and commitment of the entire supply chain; thus, we begin with a comprehensive set of hypotheses related to supply chain leadership for quality as the driver of many other activities related to supply chain quality.

According to the resource dependence theory, a company adapts its structures, production strategy, external organizational links, and many other aspects of its organizational strategy based on the pressures of its dependence on external resources (Pfeffer and Salancik 1978). Because the supply chain leader controls the resources that supply chain members want, it can influence members' behavior and decisions about SCQM. Thus, if the supply chain leader promotes values related to quality, other members will readily incorporate these in their supply chain design decisions.

H_{1a}: Supply chain leadership for quality is positively related to strategic supply chain design for quality.

QM describes how activities to improve quality within a company cannot be accomplished by a single department or function in isolation. Rather, QM requires collaboration. This thinking about QM within a company can be extended to the supply chain context. SCQM can be accomplished only when members of the supply chain work together, beginning with each supply chain member implementing

QM in an integrated fashion across its own company. Thus, stronger supply chain leadership for quality will be associated with internal quality integration.

H_{1b}: Supply chain leadership for quality is positively related to internal quality integration.

The quality of purchased parts is a determinant of product quality. Effective supplier selection is important to ensuring supply quality (Lo and Yeung 2006), ruling out unqualified suppliers and ensuring their resource commitment (Choi and Hartley 1996). Supply chain leadership for quality drives supply chain members to select their suppliers based on quality criteria.

H_{1c1}: Supply chain leadership for quality is positively related to supplier selection.

The evaluation of existing suppliers is critical in ensuring supply quality (Araz and Ozkarahan 2007). Regular and effective supplier evaluation can motivate a supplier's quality improvement, as well as provide information that is important in future supplier selection decisions. Supply chain leadership for quality sets the stage for effective supplier evaluation.

H_{1c2}: Supply chain leadership for quality is positively related to supplier evaluation.

Supplier development is instrumental in improving product quality (Araz and Ozkarahan 2007; Lo et al. 2007) because it builds mutual trust and enhances communication and commitment between a company and its suppliers (Lo et al. 2007). When the supply chain leader emphasizes quality, supply chain members will focus on supplier development in order to contribute to achieving supply chain goals.

H_{1c3}: Supply chain leadership for quality is positively related to supplier development.

As a company develops a stronger relationship with its suppliers, it engages in valuable learning from them, improving its ability to design and produce better quality products. Supply chain leadership for quality lays the foundation for a company to learn from its suppliers about QM and to work with its suppliers to improve its products.

H_{1c4}: Supply chain leadership for quality is positively related to learning from suppliers.

A company's customers and their customers play an important role in a supply chain in terms of ensuring the quality of products before these reach the final consumers. Careful customer selection practices can help a company find customers with appropriate storage and handling capabilities, in order to keep products safe and free from defects. This is especially important for products that are sensitive to storage conditions, such as cold chain products. Customer selection is also important in developing opportunities for learning. Although the traditional thinking about customers has been that all customers are equally desirable, effective supply chain leadership for quality develops an understanding of the differential role of various customers in product quality.

H_{1d1}: Supply chain leadership for quality is positively related to customer selection.

An effective supply chain leader will stress the importance of working with customers to ensure that they have similar quality priorities and a thorough understanding of how to handle, store, and display its products.

H_{1d2}: Supply chain leadership for quality is positively related to customer development.

Customers can help a company to improve its quality by providing knowledge or information about the market and customers. As the final link in a supply chain, retailers are an important source of intelligence about consumer needs, buying behavior, and consumption practices. Downstream links can provide valuable insights about customers and their customers. An effective supply chain leader will stress the importance to a company of learning from its customers.

H_{1d3}: Supply chain leadership for quality is positively related to learning from customers.

In a complex supply chain, it can be challenging to keep track of the actual suppliers of every component, particularly if suppliers outsource their production. Yet, this is critical in quickly addressing quality problems that originate with purchased materials and components. Thus, tracking and tracing systems are important in reducing quality risk (Tse and Tan 2011) because they allow the source of defects to be quickly discovered and can help to prevent similar problems from recurring. Effective supply chain leadership for quality encourages systematic record keeping at all levels of a supply chain.

H_{1e1}: Supply chain leadership for quality is positively related to tracking and traceability.

Strong supply chain leadership for quality emphasizes the importance of top management making quality a priority. It is critical to the supply chain leader that supply chain members are able to effectively handle any quality problems. Consequently, the supply chain leader will work with the top management of the companies in its supply chain to ensure their commitment to quality.

H_{1e2}: Supply chain leadership for quality is positively related to top management commitment to quality.

Effective supply chain leadership for quality motivates supply chain members to follow high ethical standards. This will cause them to be more proactive in recalling a defective product, in order to protect the health and safety of their consumers. Without strong supply chain leadership for quality, a company may be more likely to focus on its own financial interests and not issue a recall unless it is mandated. For example, Chapter 13 showed that proactive recalls are much more common in China's automobile industry, which is characterized by strong supply chain leadership by foreign customers such as Honda and Ford.

H_{1e3}: Supply chain leadership for quality is positively related to product recall proactiveness.

The quality orientation of the supply chain leader is also instrumental in a company's philosophy about consumer compensation in the event of a product recall. If company feels a greater responsibility for product quality, it will be more willing to provide meaningful compensation to affected customers.

H_{1e4}: Supply chain leadership for quality is positively related to recall compensation.

20.2.2 Strategic Supply Chain Design for Quality

Supply chain design is "the process of planning a supply chain in order to guarantee smooth and efficient supply chain planning and execution, as to meet the targets set by supply chain management in terms of cost, time, quality, and service" (Freiwald 2005). There are three key supply chain design tasks: specifying the basic structure of the production and logistics network, defining the processes along the supply chain, and configuring the relationships among supply chain members (Fine 2000; Freiwald 2005).

However, supply chain design based on quality considerations differs in its goals from conventional supply chain design, which aims to minimize cost by allocating capacity among facilities (Chopra and Meindl 2007) and to maximize profit by balancing service level and costs, including transportation, inventory, and ordering cost. Because supply chains are driven primarily by economic factors, quality issues may be overlooked. However, researchers have recently advocated that product quality, safety, and risk issues be incorporated into supply chain design (Speier et al. 2011). In designing a supply chain, the most important decision is how it will be structured; that is, a company must decide who its supply chain members will be. Therefore, supply chain design for quality focuses on quality considerations as a company selects its customers and suppliers.

H_{2a1}: Strategic supply chain design for quality is positively related to supplier selection.

H_{2b1}: Strategic supply chain design for quality is positively related to customer selection.

Supplier evaluation is an important input in supplier selection. Strategic supply chain design for quality will be associated with better evaluation of suppliers' quality performance.

H_{2a2}: Strategic supply chain design for quality is positively related to supplier evaluation.

An effective supply chain design, based on quality considerations, will be structured to encourage communication and interaction among supply chain members, in order to facilitate the development of customers and suppliers.

H_{2a3}: Strategic supply chain design for quality is positively related to supplier development.

H_{2b2}: Strategic supply chain design for quality is positively related to customer development.

Learning from suppliers and customers requires frequent interaction and communications between a company and its supply chain members. Strategic supply chain design for quality can facilitate the exchange of knowledge and ideas about product design and other quality issues. Therefore, we propose the following:

H_{2a4}: Strategic supply chain design for quality is positively related to learning from suppliers.

H_{2b3}: Strategic supply chain design for quality is positively related to learning from customers.

One of the most important supply chain design decisions is the number of supply chain tiers, which is directly related to the ability to track products and easily trace them to their source. When supply chain design is based on quality considerations, minimizing the number of tiers is important.

H_{2c1}: Strategic supply chain design for quality is positively related to tracking and traceability.

When quality considerations are foremost in supply chain design, quality will also be at the forefront of the minds of the top managers of the constituent companies.

H_{2c2}: Strategic supply chain design for quality is positively related to top management commitment to quality.

When a supply chain is strategically designed based on quality considerations, quality is a priority among the companies that comprise it. In addition, supply chain design can facilitate communication among supply chain members about a quality problem or defect, which can help hasten the supply chain's response.

H_{2c3}: Strategic supply chain design for quality is positively related to recall proactiveness.

20.2.3 Internal Quality Integration

Internal quality integration refers to a company's efforts to facilitate quality improvement by integrating its own departments and internal processes. According to the resource-based view of the company, resources (physical capital, human capital, and organizational capital) have the potential to achieve a sustainable competitive advantage when they are valuable, rare, inimitable, and nonsubstitutable (Barney 1991). However, this potential will not be fully realized unless the company is well organized to facilitate exploitation of the resources' potential (Barney and Clark 2007). By integrating its internal processes, a company's capabilities will be enhanced, helping it to build up its supply chain network through selection and evaluation of its members.

H_{3a1}: Internal quality integration will be positively related to supplier selection.

H_{3a2}: Internal quality integration will be positively related to supplier evaluation.

H_{3b1}: Internal quality integration will be positively related to customer selection.

An internally integrated company is better able to facilitate development of its customers and suppliers. The quality capabilities that are related to integration provide resources, such as knowledge, that can be used in developing supply chain members that focus on quality.

H_{3a3}: Internal quality integration will be positively related to supplier development.

H_{3b2}: Internal quality integration will be positively related to customer development.

Distinct organizational mechanisms can influence a company's level of absorptive capacity (Cohen and Levinthal 1990). Therefore, higher levels of internal quality integration are associated with a higher level of learning from supply chain members.

H_{3a4}: Internal quality integration will be positively related to learning from suppliers.

H_{3b3}: Internal quality integration will be positively related to learning from customers.

Internal quality integration can make information flow more smoothly and increase the transparency of a company's internal processes, which improves supply chain tracking and traceability.

H_{3c1}: Internal quality integration will be positively related to tracking and traceability.

A company that is internally integrated with a focus on quality is characterized by an overarching commitment to quality at all levels, including top management.

H_{3c2}: Internal quality integration will be positively related to top management commitment to quality.

When a company is well integrated internally, its functions will be better able to work together to make timely recall decisions. Therefore, we propose the following:

H_{3c3}: Internal quality integration will be positively related to recall proactiveness.

When determining the amount of compensation for customers who purchased a recalled product, a company can better assess the potential loss from multiple perspectives if its internal departments are well integrated. Thus, the extent of internal integration is related to recall compensation.

H_{3c4}: Internal quality integration will be positively related to recall compensation.

20.2.4 Product Recall Systems

As a follow-up reaction to the discovery of a product defect, a product recall serves as a recovery measure and feedback mechanism that provides a base for future improvements. There are several key tasks associated with a product recall: identifying the source of the defect, managing the recall process, and reducing its negative effect. Tracking and tracing systems should be established throughout a supply chain (Kumar and Schmitz 2011; Roth et al. 2008), in order to facilitate quickly locating the source of any quality problems. Tracking and tracing systems minimize the number of potential sources of defects through backward tracing or minimize the number of potentially affected products through forward tracing (Zhang et al. 2011). Thus, tracking and tracing systems have both proactive and reactive value.

With an effective tracking and tracing system, each supply chain member's responsibility is clear. Therefore, if a defect is detected, the source of the quality problem can be quickly identified. In turn, this can reduce the time to issue a recall announcement.

H_{4a}: Tracking and traceability will be positively related to recall proactiveness.

When the source of a quality problem can be traced to a specific supplier, a company may ask the supplier to share the cost of remedying the problem or pay a penalty. Because the company's cost is reduced, it may be more willing to provide higher compensation to affected customers.

H_{4b}: Tracking and traceability will be positively related to recall compensation.

Top management is a company's driving source of improvement. When top management is committed to quality, a company is more likely to make proactive recall decisions, when necessary, in order to protect its consumers.

H_{4c}: Top management commitment to quality will be positively related to recall proactiveness.

Moreover, when its top management is committed to quality, a company is more likely to provide affected customers with meaningful compensation in the event of a recall.

H_{4d}: Top management commitment to quality will be positively related to recall compensation.

20.2.5 Upstream QM

A company's output is only as good as its input. Therefore, upstream QM is important in ensuring product quality. Tan et al. (1998) found that supplier evaluation and supply base management were related to better performance, while Shin et al. (2000) found that long-term supplier–buyer relationships, supplier-involved product development, quality focus in supplier selection, and reduced supplier base significantly improved quality performance. Lo et al. (2007) found that supplier integration, supplier selection, and supplier development were positively related to supply quality performance. We describe upstream QM systems as composed of supplier selection, supplier evaluation, supplier development, and learning from suppliers. According to the social capital theory, companies are embedded in social networks (Coleman 1988; Lin 2002; Tsai and Ghoshal 1998), for example, a buyer–supplier relationship. A company can capture social capital (Lin 1999) from its supply chains, as members' social ties provide it with access to knowledge, resources, markets, and technologies (Inkpen and Tsang 2005), which, in turn, creates the opportunity to generate competitive advantage.

Supplier selection serves as a gatekeeper by ensuring that suppliers meet specified quality criteria and commit an appropriate amount of resources (Choi and Hartley 1996). The social capital that a company gains from its ties with its suppliers will be increased, which will improve product quality.

H_{5a}: Supplier selection is positively related to quality performance.

With regular evaluation of its suppliers' quality performance, a company can get more information about them, which provides clues for adjustment or future supplier selection. Suppliers that are evaluated based on quality criteria will be better motivated to improve their processes. With a better supply network, a company gains social capital, improving its quality performance.

H_{5b}: Supplier evaluation is positively related to quality performance.

Supplier development is an important upstream QM practice. Supplier development refers to a company's efforts to improve its suppliers' capabilities, for the long-term mutual benefit of both parties (Hahn et al. 1990). Supplier development requires a long-term effort that indicates the company's commitment to maintaining the relationship with a supplier, increasing trust and mutual commitment. The company gains social capital from this relationship, which will help to generate a competitive advantage.

H_{5c}: Supplier development is positively related to quality performance.

Suppliers provide a company with information, ideas about product design, and advanced knowledge, which can reduce the possibility of design errors and supply uncertainty and increase product conformity and innovativeness. Li et al. (2011) found that such learning was positively related to quality performance.

H_{5d}: Learning from suppliers is positively related to quality performance.

20.2.6 Downstream QM

Downstream QM plays an important role in ensuring supply chain quality. Customer involvement is an important component of traditional QM (Flynn et al. 1994), which advocates that a company should listen to the voice of its customers and build customer relationships. Similar to what we have observed with upstream QM, the ultimate goal of involving customers is to learn from them; therefore, we include learning from customers as a component of SCQM. Learning from customers includes not only involving customers in product design and product development but also obtaining guidance in the production process and information from customers about quality and customer needs. Customer development is a company's efforts to improve its customers' capabilities for the long-term mutual benefit of both parties. This is manifested as providing customers with suggestions about how to improve, providing information about product and quality issues, or educating customers about how to store products.

The downstream supply chain is an important source of social capital. Similar to supplier selection, customer selection also can serve as a gatekeeper by its requirement that customers satisfy certain criteria. By building up a relationship with qualified customers, a company's social network is improved. Qualified customers provide it with good storage facilities, ensuring that inappropriate storage and handling will not occur. Therefore, customer selection is a way to safeguard and improve quality until a product reaches consumers.

H_{6a}: Customer selection is positively related to quality performance.

Customer development requires a long-term effort to the sustainable improvement of customers, which will improve the relationship between a company and its customers, increasing their trust and mutual commitment.

H_{6b}: Customer development is positively related to quality performance.

By using information learned from its customers, a company can generate new ideas and opinions about product concepts, innovativeness, and improvement (Amabile 1983).

H_{6c}: Learning from customers is positively related to quality performance.

20.2.7 Recall System and Quality Performance

Organizational learning is an importance source of competitive advantage, and product recalls can be an important source of learning. Previous studies have argued that supply chain visibility can help reduce supply chain quality risk (Tse and Tan 2011) and that traceability is useful for ensuring product quality and safety (Marucheck et al. 2011) because it helps to identify the source of a quality problem and provides a company and its supply chain members opportunities to learn how to improve. Therefore, we propose the following hypothesis:

H_{7a}: Tracking and traceability are positively related to quality performance.

A proactive recall indicates a company's willingness to learn, which, in turn, increases quality performance. Haunschild and Rhee (2004) found that a proactive recall resulted in more learning than a mandatory recall did, with learning measured as the reduction in subsequent involuntary recalls.

H_{7b}: Recall proactiveness is positively related to quality performance.

Recall compensation is an important method of communicating with the public. It can be proactively offered or reluctantly provided, based on the mandate of an enforcement agency. However, the amount of compensation is normally decided based on projecting the losses by the affected parties or based on negotiations. Therefore, it does not contribute to the learning process. We propose the following:

H_{7c}: Recall compensation is not related to quality performance.

Top management commitment to quality indicates the importance that a company attaches to quality issues. During a product recall, top management commitment can promote immediate adjustment both within a company and throughout its supply chain Moreover, it motivates employees to learn from the recall experience, in order to avoid the recurrence of quality problems in the future.

H_{7d}: Top management commitment to quality is positively related to quality performance.

20.3 Research Methodology

20.3.1 Questionnaire Development

Measurement items were identified in the literature, corresponding to the constructs in the SCQM model. They were adapted, as necessary, to make them relevant to the supply chain context. In addition, on the basis of our observations during interviews and case studies, we developed some new items to enrich the constructs. For the constructs where there were no existing measurement scales, we developed new measurement items based on our understanding of the relevant literature and our observations.

The questionnaire was first developed in English and then independently translated into Chinese by two Chinese-native PhD students in operations management. After translation, the students discussed items where their translation was not consistent or used different wordings. The Chinese version was then translated back to English by an operations management professor and used to check against the original English version for any discrepancies.

To ensure the validity of the questionnaire, extensive pilot testing was conducted. First, we administered the questionnaire during a plant visit, asking managers to complete it and note any issues or difficulties in responding to it. Second, we invited managers from eight companies that were participating in a QM conference to respond to the questionnaire. Third, we hosted a half-day seminar on SCQM for managers, inviting them to respond to the questionnaire. We obtained a total of 30 completed questionnaires during pilot testing. On the basis of the feedback and preliminary results, we further refined the questionnaire.

20.3.2 Sampling and Data Collection

The unit of analysis is a manufacturing plant that has suppliers and customers. It may or may not be the supply chain leader. Four industries (toys, food, automobiles, and pharmaceuticals) were targeted because they have attracted a lot of global attention because of their quality problems and product recalls. To ensure the representativeness of the sample, we used the manufacturing company list of the China Statistical Bureau. We strategically selected the Yangtze River Delta, Pearl River Delta, and Bohai Coastal Rim areas because they represent different stages of economic development. We contacted each company by phone to invite it to participate. We asked some questions before the invitation was made, in order to ensure that the company and informant were consistent with our targets. We administered each questionnaire face to face, collecting 400 usable surveys. The detailed sample distribution is listed in Tables 20.1 and 20.2. Overall, we obtained a response rate of 24.6%. Table 20.3 presents the demographics of the participating companies. All informants had been in their position for at least 2 years, ensuring their familiarity with the company (Table 20.4). On average, about 40 minutes were spent to finish the questionnaire; thus, they were not completed in rush.

Table 20.1 Respondents by Region

	Pearl River Delta	Yangtze River Delta	Bohai Coastal Rim	Total
Automobiles	30	35	35	100
Food	31	35	34	100
Toys	55	33	12	100
Pharmaceutical	22	35	43	100

Table 20.2 Response Rates by Industry

	Automobiles	Toys	Food	Pharmaceuticals	Total
Returned questionnaires	100	100	100	100	400
Declined to participate	523	491	420	189	1623
Response rate	16.1%	16.9%	19.2%	34.6%	24.6%

Table 20.3 Profile of Participating Companies

	Automobiles	Food	Pharmaceuticals	Toys	Total
Legal Status					
State owned	5	5	13	0	23
Collective	2	2	2	0	6
Private owned	27	40	51	42	160
Joint venture	17	19	14	10	60
Foreign	49	31	12	47	139
Other	0	3	8	1	12
Number of Employees					
<50	6	3	2	1	12
50–99	16	26	12	9	63
100–199	31	16	35	18	100
200–499	31	36	30	33	130
500–999	12	10	12	20	54
1000–4999	4	9	9	17	39
>5000	0	0	0	2	2
Total Sales (RMB)					
5–<10 million	12	13	5	16	46
10–<20 million	8	11	14	16	49
20–<50 million	22	22	16	20	80
50–<100 million	15	21	22	22	80
≥100 million	43	33	43	26	145

Table 20.4 Profile of Respondents

	Minimum	Maximum	Mean	SD
Time to finish the questionnaire (minutes)	25.00	70.00	39.29	7.51
Years in position	2	30	7.48	4.26

20.4 Analysis

20.4.1 Measurement Quality

Before testing the hypotheses, the reliability and validity of the measurement scales were assessed, following the steps described in Appendix 20.1.

20.4.2 Hypotheses Testing

To test the hypotheses, structural equation models were conducted using AMOS. All 400 cases were used as the input for this model. However, due to sample size limitations and the complexity of the conceptual model, we could not test all hypotheses simultaneously. Thus, we run three submodels, corresponding to the models used for the confirmatory factory analysis (CFA).

20.5 Results

The results of the hypothesis testing are shown in Figures 20.2 through 20.4 and are summarized in Table 20.5. The results for the first model (Figure 20.2) showed acceptable goodness-of-fit (χ^2 = 2078.45, df = 971, CFI = 0.905, GFI = 0.901, RSMEA = 0.054). All of the hypotheses were supported, except for the hypothesized relationship between supply chain leadership for quality and supplier development (H_{1c3}) and the relationship between supply chain leadership for quality and

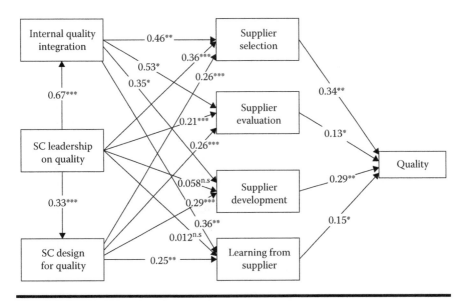

Figure 20.2   Results for Model 1. SC = supply chain.

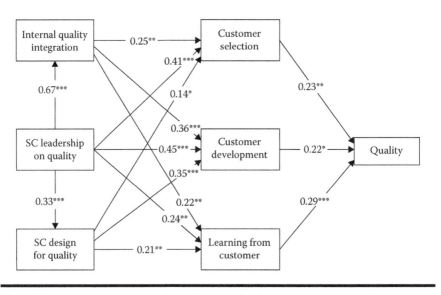

Figure 20.3   Results for Model 2. SC = supply chain.

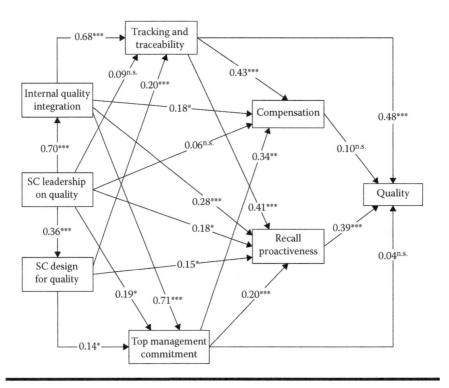

Figure 20.4   Results for Model 3. SC = supply chain.

Table 20.5 Summary of Hypothesis Testing Results

Hypothesis	Results
Leadership for Quality	
H_{1a}: SC leadership for quality→SC design for quality	Supported
H_{1b}: SC leadership for quality→internal quality integration	Supported
H_{1c1}: SC leadership for quality→supplier selection	Supported
H_{1c2}: SC leadership for quality→supplier evaluation	Supported
H_{1c3}: SC leadership for quality→supplier development	Not supported
H_{1c4}: SC leadership for quality→learning from suppliers	Not supported
H_{1d1}: SC leadership for quality→customer selection	Supported
H_{1d2}: SC leadership for quality→customer development	Supported
H_{1d3}: SC leadership for quality→learning from customers	Supported
H_{1e1}: SC leadership for quality→tracking and traceability	Not supported
Hypothesis	*Results*
Leadership for Quality	
H_{1e2}: SC leadership for quality→top management commitment to quality	Supported
H_{1e3}: SC leadership for quality→recall proactiveness	Supported
H_{1e4}: SC leadership for quality→recall compensation	Not supported
Strategic SC Design for Quality	
H_{2a1}: SC design for quality→supplier selection	Supported
H_{2a2}: SC design for quality→supplier evaluation	Supported
H_{2a3}: SC design for quality→supplier development	Supported
H_{2a4}: SC design for quality→learning from suppliers	Supported
H_{2b1}: SC design for quality→customer selection	Supported
H_{2b2}: SC design for quality→customer development	Supported
H_{2b3}: SC design for quality→learning from customers	Supported

(continued)

Table 20.5   Summary of Hypothesis Testing Results (Continued)

Hypothesis	Results
H_{2c1}: SC design for quality→tracking and traceability	Supported
H_{2c2}: SC design for quality→top management commitment to quality	Supported
H_{2c3}: SC design for quality→recall proactiveness	Supported
Internal Quality Integration	
H_{3a1}: Internal quality integration→supplier selection	Supported
H_{3a2}: Internal quality integration→supplier evaluation	Supported
H_{3a3}: Internal quality integration→supplier development	Supported
H_{3a4}: Internal quality integration→learning from suppliers	Supported
H_{3b1}: Internal quality integration→customer selection	Supported
H_{3b2}: Internal quality integration→customer development	Supported
H_{3b3}: Internal quality integration→learning from customers	Supported
H_{3c1}: Internal quality integration→tracking and traceability	Supported
Hypothesis	*Results*
Internal Quality Integration	
H_{3c2}: Internal quality integration→top management commitment to quality	Supported
H_{3c3}: Internal quality integration→recall proactiveness	Supported
H_{3c4}: Internal quality integration→recall compensation	Supported
Recall System Components	
H_{4a}: Tracking and traceability→recall proactiveness	Supported
H_{4b}: Tracking and traceability→recall compensation	Supported
H_{4c}: Top management commitment to quality→recall proactiveness	Supported
H_{4d}: Top management commitment to quality→recall compensation	Supported

(continued)

Table 20.5   Summary of Hypothesis Testing Results (Continued)

Upstream SCQM and Quality Performance	
H_{5a}: Supplier selection→quality performance	Supported
H_{5b}: Supplier evaluation→quality performance	Supported
H_{5c}: Supplier development→quality performance	Supported
H_{5d}: Learning from supplier→quality performance	Supported
Downstream SCQM and Quality Performance	
H_{6a}: Customer selection→quality performance	Supported
H_{6b}: Customer development→quality performance	Supported
H_{6c}: Learning from customers→quality performance	Supported
Recall Systems and Quality Performance	
H_{7a}: Tracking and traceability→quality performance	Supported
H_{7b}: Top management commitment to quality→quality performance	Not supported
H_{7c}: Recall proactiveness→quality performance	Supported
H_{7d}: Recall compensation→quality performance	Supported

Note: SC, supply chain.

learning from suppliers (H_{1c4}). The model fit indices for the second structural model (Figure 20.3) indicated acceptance of the model (χ^2 = 1071.59, df = 763, CFI = 0.929, GFI = 0.909, RSMEA = 0.056). All path coefficients were positive and significant, which meant the hypotheses related to downstream QM system were all supported. The third structural equation model's (Figure 20.4) fit indices indicated that it was also acceptable (χ^2 = 1403.42, df = 757, CFI = 0.925, GFI = 0.913, RSMEA = 0.046), supporting all hypotheses except those describing the relationship between supply chain leadership for quality and tracking and traceability (H_{1e1}) and recall compensation (H_{1e3}), recall compensation and quality performance (H_{7d}), and top management commitment to quality and quality performance (H_{7b}).

20.6 Conclusions and Discussion

In this chapter, we operationalized and tested the validity and effectiveness of the SCQM model. Survey data were collected from Chinese companies in the automobile, toy, food, and pharmaceuticals industries to test the hypotheses. Supply chain leadership for quality was found to be a driving factor for the success of SCQM since the supply chain leader is able to influence members' decisions about SCQM, including decisions related to strategic supply chain design for quality, internal quality integration, supplier selection, supplier evaluation, customer selection, customer development, learning from customers, recall proactiveness, and top management commitment to quality.

Supply chain leadership for quality did not directly influence supplier development, learning from suppliers, or tracking and traceability. However, it did have an indirect effect on all three constructs. This means that supply chain leadership for quality works through internal quality integration and supply chain design in its influence on supplier development, learning from suppliers, and tracking and traceability. In addition, supply chain leadership for quality was not directly related to recall compensation. However, it was indirectly related through top management commitment to quality.

Strategic supply chain design based on quality considerations helps to form a supply chain network that facilitates upstream and downstream quality and product recalls. Internal quality integration provides a structure for a company's internal quality capabilities and presents a uniform interface with customers and suppliers. Tracking and traceability were positively related to quality performance. An effective tracking and tracing system provides opportunities for organizational learning, which can help improve quality and prevent quality problems in the future. Moreover, recall proactiveness was associated with quality performance because of its impact on learning. As expected, recall compensation was not related to quality performance. Top management commitment to quality was not directly related to quality performance; however, it was indirectly related through recall proactiveness.

Overall, the data analysis results supported most of our hypotheses. We can conclude that there are significant causal relationships among SCQM components. In addition, SCQM can significantly improve quality, which indicates that SCQM is important to a company in managing its supply chain quality.

This study has important implications for practitioners. Supply chain leadership for quality drives SCQM, which, in turn, is related to improved quality performance. Therefore, a company should strive to be involved with supply chains where there is strong supply chain leadership for quality. Managers should take quality issues into account when designing a supply chain, rather than focusing on cost reduction only. To improve quality and competitive advantage, a company should restructure its internal processes, based on the understanding that quality is not solely an internal management issue but extends to the entire supply chain. By effectively managing its upstream and downstream members, it will be able to achieve better performance.

Product recalls are often regarded as a necessary evil for dealing with a product defect emergency. However, based on this research, an effective product recall system can also help a company to improve its quality performance, through its learning effects. Therefore, a company should be proactive in setting up a product recall system, paying particular heed to the tracking and traceability of its products in the field. This will help it to not only manage recalls effectively but also improve its own performance through learning.

Appendix 20.1 Technical Details of Measurement Analysis

Step 1: Subscale correlations were assessed. Items that were negatively or weakly correlated with other items in the same construct were removed (DeVellis 2003; Netemeyer et al. 2003; Robinson et al. 1991).

Step 2: Exploratory factory analysis (EFA) was conducted using 150 randomly selected cases as the calibration sample.

Step 3: The subscale EFA was conducted. Items were retained when the largest factor loadings were greater than .45 (for sample size of 150) (Hair et al. 1998) and the cross-loading difference was greater than or equal to .10 (Nunally and Bernstein 1978).

Step 4: Cronbach's α and item-to-total correlations were used to assess reliability. An item was deleted if its item-to-total correlation was less than .30 or if its inclusion did not improve α (Netemeyer et al. 2003), with .60 as the cutoff (Flynn et al. 1994). Steps 2–4 were performed iteratively to ensure unidimensionality and reliability. The results are shown in Table 20.A1.1.

Table 20.A1.1   EFA Results

Construct	Items	Factor Loadings	% of Variance	Eigenvalue	Cronbach's α
SC leadership for quality	LLQ1	.619	52.300	4.710	.882
	LLQ2	.763			
	LLQ3	.743			
	LLQ4	.653			
	LLQ5	.739			
	LLQ6	.741			
	LLQ7	.712			
	LLQ8	.814			
	LLQ9	.707			

(continued)

Table 20.A1.1   EFA Results (Continued)

Construct	Items	Factor Loadings	% of Variance	Eigenvalue	Cronbach's α
SC design for quality	QDQ1	.651	52.380	3.140	.816
	QDQ2	.732			
	QDQ3	.759			
	QDQ4	.768			
	QDQ5	.700			
	QDQ6	.725			
Internal quality integration	IQI1	.650	50.87	3.56	.836
	IQI2	.758			
	IQI3	.624			
	IQI4	.756			
	IQI5	.714			
	IQI6	.763			
	IQI7	.714			
Tracking and traceability	STT1	.793	54.11	2.71	.783
	STT2	.788			
	STT3	.711			
Tracking and traceability	STT4	.741			
	STT5	.633			
Top management commitment	STP1	.764	64.39	1.93	.72
	STP2	.826			
	STP3	.771			
Recall proactiveness	SPR1	.564	55.65	2.23	.73
	SPR2	.806			
	SPR3	.832			
	SPR4	.752			

(continued)

Table 20.A1.1   EFA Results (Continued)

Construct	Items	Factor Loadings	% of Variance	Eigenvalue	Cronbach's α
Recall compensation	SCM1	.848	66.25	1.99	.732
	SCM2	.847			
	SCM3	.743			
Supplier selection	USL1	.734	47.16	1.88	.623
	USL2	.642			
	USL3	.636			
	USL4	.729			
Learning from suppliers	ULR1	.774	49.87	3.49	.829
	ULR2	.612			
	ULR3	.684			
	ULR4	.740			
	ULR5	.718			
	ULR6	.707			
	ULR7	.697			
Supplier evaluation	UEV1	.673	50.6	2.02	.683
	UEV2	.701			
Supplier evaluation	UEV3	.705			
	UEV4	.764			
Supplier development	UDV1	.772	50.06	2.00	.732
	UDV2	.801			
	UDV3	.641			
	UDV4	.596			
Customer selection	DSL1	.833	59.18	1.78	.732
	DSL2	.816			
	DSL3	.643			

(continued)

Table 20.A1.1   EFA Results (Continued)

Construct	Items	Factor Loadings	% of Variance	Eigenvalue	Cronbach's α
Learning from customers	DLR1	.720	50.21	3.51	.83
	DLR2	.770			
	DLR3	.757			
	DLR4	.668			
	DLR5	.706			
	DLR6	.589			
	DLR7	.734			
Customer development	DDV1	.774	49.97	2.00	.65
	DDV2	.684			
	DDV3	.816			
	DDV4	.516			
Quality performance	PPQ1	.854	70.72	3.54	.896
	PPQ2	.857			
	PPQ3	.814			
	PPQ4	.835			
	PPQ5	.843			

Step 5: CFA was run using the validation sample ($n = 250$) to assess convergent validity and discriminant validity. A construct with indicator loadings greater than 0.5, a significant t value ($t > 2.0$), or both was considered to have convergent validity (Chau 1997).

Step 6: Discriminant validity was assessed by comparing the χ^2 statistics for the unconstrained and constrained models. In the unconstrained model, the correlations among constructs were freely estimated, while in the constrained model, we fixed the correlation between each pair of constructs to be 1, while freely estimating the other correlations. This process was followed for each possible pair of constructs. A significant χ^2 change indicates discriminant validity between a pair of constructs (Chau 1997).

Because the validation sample size was only 250 and the number of constructs was large, it was not possible to estimate all of the parameters in a single CFA model. Therefore, we tested three submodels, rather than a large model that contained all the constructs. The first CFA model contained the constructs related to upstream

SCQM. It had an acceptable level of fit (χ^2 = 1806.3, df = 961, RMSEA = 0.047, CFI = 0.908, GFI = 0.899), and all factor loadings were significant. Therefore, the convergent validity of these constructs was confirmed. Table 20.A1.2 indicates that all χ^2 changes were significant, which means that the discriminant validity among these constructs was acceptable. In the second CFA model, we tested the downstream QM system constructs, finding an acceptable level of fit (χ^2 = 1749.00, df = 758, RMSEA = 0.054, CFI = 0.925, GFI = 0.922) and significant factor loadings, confirming convergent validity. The discriminant validity of these constructs was confirmed by the significant χ^2 changes (Table 20.A1.3). The third CFA model

Table 20.A1.2 Discriminant Validity for Model 1

	1	2	3	4	5	6	7
1. SC leadership for quality							
2. SC design for quality	186.1						
3. Internal quality integration	239.3	251.4					
4. Supplier selection	183.8	167.5	248.9				
5. Supplier evaluation	173.4	154.5	223.2	126			
6. Supplier development	121.4	85.1	167.5	99.3	57.6		
7. Learning from suppliers	117.9	84.2	153.7	88.9	78.2	20.7	
8. Quality performance	219.8	187.2	273.6	219.1	195.4	99.4	123.7

Note: SC, supply chain.

Table 20.A1.3 Discriminant Validity for Model 2

	1	2	3	4	5	6
1. SC leadership for quality						
2. SC design for quality	189.2					
3. Internal quality integration	237.9	253.9				
4. Customer selection	140.8	136.5	202.8			
5. Customer development	117.8	93.1	172.4	59.0		
6. Learning from customers	121.5	104.8	177.7	62.9	21.9	
7. Quality performance	217.3	190.0	274.4	149.4	140.8	124.3

Note: SC, supply chain.

Table 20.A1.4 Discriminant Validity for Model 3

	1	2	3	4	5	6	7
1. SC leadership for quality							
2. SC design for quality	133.8						
3. Internal quality integration	195.4	213.9					
4. Tracking and traceability	112.3	111.9	171.3				
5. Top management commitment	163.2	178.1	245.5	113.5			
6. Recall compensation	106	94.3	172.7	57.2	117.9		
7. Recall proactiveness	102.3	110	173.5	47.9	81.4	61	
8. Quality performance	183.4	161	269.6	157.6	248.3	146.6	170.5

Note: SC, supply chain.

contained the product recall system constructs. It had an acceptable level of fit (χ^2 = 1252.3, df = 750, RMSEA = 0.041, CFI = 0.924, GFI = 0.906), and all factor loadings were significant. Therefore, the convergent validity of the product recall system measures was confirmed. Table 20.A1.4 shows that the χ^2 changes were significant, therefore, discriminant validity was acceptable.

References

Amabile, T. M. (1983). *The Social Psychology of Creativity*. New York: Springer-Verlag.
Araz, C. and I. Ozkarahan (2007). "Supplier evaluation and management system for strategic sourcing based on a new multicriteria sorting procedure." *International Journal of Production Economics* 106(2): 585–606.
Barney, J. (1991). "Firm resources and sustained competitive advantage." *Journal of Management* 17(1): 99–120.
Barney, J. B. and D. N. Clark (2007). *Resource-Based Theory: Creating and Sustaining Competitive Advantage*. Oxford: Oxford University Press.
Chau, P. Y. K. (1997). "Reexamining a model for evaluating information center success using a structural equation modeling approach." *Decision Sciences* 28(2): 309–334.
Choi, T. Y. and J. L. Hartley (1996). "An exploration of supplier selection practices across the supply chain." *Journal of Operations Management* 14(4): 333–343.
Chopra, S. and P. Meindl (2007). *Supply Chain Management. Strategy, Planning and Operation.* (3rd ed). NJ: Prentice-Hall Inc., 265–275.

Cohen, W. M. and D. A. Levinthal (1990). "Absorptive capacity: A new perspective on learning and innovation." *Administrative Science Quarterly* 35(1): 128–152.

Coleman, J. S. (1988). "Social capital in the creation of human capital." *American Journal of Sociology* 94: 95–120.

DeVellis, R. (2003). *Scale Development: Theory and Applications.* Thousand Oaks, CA: Sage Publications.

Fine, C. H. (2000). "Clockspeed—Based strategies for supply chain design." *Production and Operations Management* 9: 213–221.

Flynn, B. B. and E. J. Flynn (2005). "Synergies between supply chain management and quality management: Emerging implications." *International Journal of Production Research* 43: 3421–3436.

Flynn, B. B., R. G. Schroeder and S. Sakakibara (1994). "A framework for quality management research and an associated measurement instrument." *Journal of Operations Management* 11(4): 339–366.

Foster, S. (2008). "Towards an understanding of supply chain quality management." *Journal of Operations Management* 26: 461–467.

Foster, S. and J. Ogden (2008). "On differences in how operations and supply chain managers approach quality management." *International Journal of Production Research* 46: 6945–6961.

Freiwald, S. (2005). *Supply Chain Design.* New York: Peter Lang.

Hahn, C. K., C. A. Watts and K. Y. Kim (1990). "The supplier development program: A conceptual model." *Journal of Purchasing and Materials Management* 26(2): 2–7.

Hair, J., W. Black, B. Babin, R. Anderson and R. Tatham (1998). *Multivariate Data Analysis.* Upper Saddle River, NJ: Prentice Hall.

Haunschild, P. R. and M. Rhee (2004). "The role of volition in organizational learning: The case of automotive product recalls." *Management Science* 50(11): 1545–1560.

Inkpen, A. C. and E. W. K. Tsang (2005). "Social capital, networks, and knowledge transfer." *Academy of Management Review* 30(1): 146–165.

Kannan, V. R. and K. C. Tan (2005). "Just in time, total quality management, and supply chain management: Understanding their linkages and impact on business performance." *Omega* 33: 153–162.

Kuei, C. H., C. N. Madu and C. Lin (2001). "The relationship between supply chain quality management practices and organizational performance." *International Journal of Quality and Reliability Management* 18(8): 864–872.

Kumar, S. and S. Schmitz (2011). "Managing recalls in a consumer product supply chain—Root cause analysis and measures to mitigate risks." *International Journal of Production Research* 49: 235–253.

Li, L. (2007). *Supply Chain Management: Concepts, Techniques and Practices.* New York: World Scientific.

Li, Y., L. W. Wang and Y. Liu (2011). "Organisational learning, product quality and performance: The moderating effect of social ties in Chinese cross-border outsourcing." *International Journal of Production Research* 49(1): 159–182.

Lin, C., W. Chow, C. Madu, C. Kuei and P. Pei Yu (2005). "A structural equation model of supply chain quality management and organizational performance." *International Journal of Production Economics* 96(3): 355–365.

Lin, N. (1999). "Building a network theory of social capital." *Connections* 22(1): 28–51.

Lin, N. (2002). *Social Capital: A Theory of Social Structure and Action.* Cambridge: Cambridge University Press.

Lo, V. H. Y. and A. C. L. Yeung (2006). "Managing quality effectively in supply chain: A preliminary study." *Supply Chain Management: An International Journal* 11(3): 208–215.

Lo, V. H. Y., A. H. W. Yeung and A. C. L. Yeung (2007). "How supply quality management improves an organization's quality performance: A study of Chinese manufacturing firms." *International Journal of Production Research* 45(10): 2219–2243.

Marucheck, A., N. Greis, C. Mena and L. Cai (2011). "Product safety and security in the global supply chain: Issues, challenges and research opportunities." *Journal of Operations Management* 29(7–8): 707–720.

Netemeyer, R., W. Bearden and S. Sharma (2003). *Scaling Procedures: Issues and Applications.* Thousand Oaks, CA: Sage Publications.

Nunally, J. and I. Bernstein (1978). *Psychometric Theory.* New York: McGraw-Hill.

Pfeffer, J. and G. Salancik (1978). *The External Control of Organizations: A Resource Dependence Perspective.* New York: Harper and Row.

Richey, R. G., P. J. Daugherty, S. E. Genchev and C. W. Autry (2004). "Reverse logistics: The impact of timing and resources." *Journal of Business Logistics* 25: 229–250.

Robinson, C. J. and M. K. Malhotra (2005). "Defining the concept of supply chain quality management and its relevance to academic and industrial practice." *International Journal of Production Economics* 96: 315–337.

Robinson, J., P. Shaver and L. Wrightsman (1991). "Criteria for scale selection and evaluation." *Measures of Personality and Social Psychological Attitudes* 1: 1–24.

Romano, P. and A. Vinelli (2001). "Quality management in a supply chain perspective: Strategic and operative choices in a textile-apparel network." *International Journal of Operations and Production Management* 21: 446–460.

Roth, A. V., A. A. Tsay, M. E. Pullman and J. V. Gray (2008). "Unraveling the food supply chain: Strategic insights from China and the 2007 recalls." *Journal of Supply Chain Management* 44: 22–39.

Saraph, J. V., P. G. Benson and R. G. Schroeder (1989). "An instrument for measuring the critical factors of quality management." *Decision Sciences* 20: 810–829.

Shin, H., D. A. Collier and D. D. Wilson (2000). "Supply management orientation and supplier/buyer performance." *Journal of Operations Management* 18: 317–333.

Sila, I., M. Ebrahimpour and C. Birkholz (2006). "Quality in supply chains: An empirical analysis." *Supply Chain Management* 11: 491–502.

Sinha, K. K. and E. J. Kohnke (2009). "Health care supply chain design: Toward linking the development and delivery of care globally*." *Decision Sciences* 40: 197–212.

Speier, C., J. M. Whipple, D. J. Closs and M. D. Voss (2011). "Global supply chain design considerations: Mitigating product safety and security risks." *Journal of Operations Management* 29(7–8): 721–736.

Sroufe, R. and S. Curkovic (2008). "An examination of ISO 9000: 2000 and supply chain quality assurance." *Journal of Operations Management* 26: 503–520.

Tan, K. C., R. B. Handfield and D. R. Krause (1998). "Enhancing the firm's performance through quality and supply base management: An empirical study." *International Journal of Production Research* 36: 2813–2837.

Theodorakioglou, Y., K. Gotzamani and G. Tsiolvas (2006). Supplier management and its relationship to buyers' quality management. *Supply Chain Management: An International Journal* 11: 148–159.

Tsai, W. and S. Ghoshal (1998). "Social capital and value creation: The role of intrafirm networks." *Academy of Management Journal* 41(4): 464–476.

Tse, Y. K. and K. H. Tan (2011). "Managing product quality risk in a multi-tier global supply chain." *International Journal of Production Research* 49(1): 139–158.

Vanichchinchai, A. and B. Igel (2009). "Total quality management and supply chain management: Similarities and differences." *The TQM Journal* 21: 249–260.

Yeung, A. C. L. (2008). "Strategic supply management, quality initiatives, and organizational performance." *Journal of Operations Management* 26: 490–502.

Zhang, L., S. Wang, F. C. Li, H. Wang, L. Wang and W. A. Tan (2011). "A few measures for ensuring supply chain quality." *International Journal of Production Research* 49: 87–97.

Chapter 21

Concluding Thoughts

Barbara B. Flynn and Xiande Zhao

Contents

21.1 Introduction

In this book, we have examined research on product safety and product recalls from a variety of perspectives and in a variety of contexts. This is a fruitful area for research for several reasons. First, it is important. Product safety issues affect everyone, so these are both an important managerial problem and an important consumer problem. Second, it is all-encompassing. Product safety issues, and the recalls that result, are related not only to manufacturing in China. Product recalls occur all over the world and affect manufacturers, as well as distributors and retailers. Third, there is still much to learn in this area of research. Although we have presented a wide variety of research, we have only scratched the surface. There are many interesting and important research questions related to product safety and product recalls that remain to be investigated.

We began with a set of cases that illustrated the dark side of product safety. Through the discussion of classic cases like the burning Ford Pintos in the 1970s and more current cases, such as Mattel and the Chinese melamine-tainted milk, we described various sources of product safety issues. Although there is a tendency to blame manufacturers (particularly Chinese manufacturers) for quality defects and safety issues, in reality, many safety issues are the result of poor product design. We also discussed the supply chain as a source of product safety issues.

Drawing upon these "dark side" cases, we developed a framework for research in this important area, in Chapter 8. The cases and examples provided in this book illustrate the importance of each of the key dimensions described in this framework. Dongfeng-Peugeot-Citroen-Automobile Co., Ltd. (Chapter 9) provides a detailed examination of internal quality integration, while examples of effective customer quality integration are provided by an examination of retailers in Chapter 15, the consumer experiments in Chapters 16 and 17, and the discussion of Bright Dairy's cold chain management in Chapter 11. Models for effective supplier quality integration are provided in Chapters 11 (Bright Dairy) and 12 (CHIC). These cases are especially interesting because they deal with agricultural products and poorly educated farmers, two areas where quality is notoriously difficult to control. Changan Ford Mazda Automobile Com., Ltd. (Chapter 10) provides a detailed model of proactive planning for quality, particularly for the necessity of a product recall.

We introduce the concept of supply chain leadership in our model, where the supply chain leader can be located anywhere but exerts power over the entire supply chain. Bright, CHIC, and Mattel are all leaders of their respective supply chains, making tough demands on their supply chain members, both upstream and downstream, in order to ensure quality in the products that they deliver. Finally, Bright and CHIC provide particularly effective examples of information systems for supply chain quality management through their use of remote technologies to record detailed information from the farmers who are their suppliers.

21.2 Research Questions

Research in product safety and product recalls is inherently interesting because it draws upon important practical issues while driving rigorous, theoretically based research. The research reported in this book addresses some important research questions, while posing many more as opportunities for future research. Part of what makes this research interesting is that it builds upon a multidisciplinary foundation. Product recalls have significant financial implications, as the event studies described in Chapters 13–15 illustrate. Developing a more completed understanding of the financial implications of a product recall may help drive companies to invest more in prevention efforts. Product recalls also have significant consumer implications, as described by the experiments in Chapters 16 and 17. Consumers form their perceptions about products from what they experience with them, as well as what they hear about these products. Their perceptions drive their future purchasing behavior, so it is important to have a thorough understanding of what is important to consumers who are involved in a product recall, both what they like (e.g., a proactive approach or an appropriate level of compensation) and what they do not like (e.g., what they hear about illnesses and injuries that result from a product safety hazard). Combined, the finance-based and marketing-based research on product recalls provides an interesting set of research from both the perspective of investors and the perspective of customers, who have very different concerns, both of which are important to companies. The survey research illustrated in Chapters 18–20 shows important antecedents, consequents, and relationships between variables related to product safety and product recalls.

Future research questions should certainly draw upon this multidisciplinary research foundation. There are many important unresolved research questions within each of the disciplines. Perhaps the most significant research, however, will seek to merge them into a common perspective, rather than treating research in each of the disciplines separately.

The research questions that drive this book are inherently international because of our primary focus on product recalls in China and the United States. There are many reasons why we would expect the situation to be different in these two countries, including their recent economic history, government, institutions, and national cultures. There are numerous opportunities for future research that extends the research in this book to other regions of the world that have their own unique economic history, government, institutions, and national culture.

21.3 Theoretical Foundations for Research on Product Recalls

A strong theoretical foundation is critical for any high-quality research, forming a lens through which researchers can make sense of events and generate coherent explanations for their findings. Research with a practical bent is sometimes criticized for being atheoretical. The research in this book, however, draws upon a strong foundation of theory. In addition to making sense of recent product recall events, this theoretical foundation will lead to future research questions related to product safety and product recalls.

The theoretical foundations for this book include the institutional theory, which deals with pressures that companies face when adopting new practices, including practices related to quality and product safety. These can include both pressures from the government and other agencies and competitive pressures from customers. Signaling theory illustrates the importance of the message that a company sends to investors and consumers when it announces a product recall; both the words that it uses and its recall strategy (proactive vs. passive, compensation, etc.) send messages about the safety of the recalled product, which investors and consumers may interpret differently. Attribution theory provides a related perspective of a product recall, where customers have a tendency to make attributions about a company based on what they observe in its product recall strategy and actions. Prospect theory describes how potential losses loom larger than potential gains in the minds of consumers, who may be considering the effect of a product recall.

Agency theory is important when studying the distinction between customers and consumers. For example, when parents (customers) purchase a toy, they are acting as agents for their child (consumer), who is the principal; in this case, the principal and the agent may have very different perspectives on product safety. The notion of information asymmetry is important in understanding the perspective of a company vs. the perspective of a consumer. Consumers have less information about product safety issues than the company does, so they may try to fill in the gaps through attribution. This imbalance of information is also important from a legal perspective, providing a rationale for the need for consumer protection legislation.

There were many other theoretical perspectives used in the research described in this book, in addition to the sampling provided above. Thus, even though product safety and product recalls are very practical and important problems, there is a wealth of theoretical foundations available for framing research in this area. Drawing upon these and other theoretical perspectives will improve the quality of future research.

21.4 Methodological Approaches

The research in this book used a wide variety of methodological approaches. We began with in-depth research case studies, developed based on publicly available information from the media and other sources, site visits, and interviews with managers. They illustrate the serious consequences of a product recall, as well as lead to the development of a framework for research on product safety and recalls. The research cases also provide exemplars of companies that did an exceptional job of developing systems for addressing the causes of product recalls through making investments in prevention.

The research reported in Section IV draws upon the highly technical methods used by finance and economics researchers to study the stock market impact of a product recall announcement. By examining the cumulative returns before and after a product recall announcement, we showed that a product recall announcement is associated with a significant negative cumulative abnormal return. This was true across industries and countries. Thus, a product recall announcement is perceived negatively by investors.

In Section V, we used controlled experiments to examine consumers' perceptions of a product recall announcement. Through scenario experiments, consumers were asked to report their perceptions of actions taken by a hypothetical company and interpreted through the theoretical perspective of organizational legitimacy and the risk-as-feelings hypothesis. Critical factors were manipulated in the various scenarios, in order to observe the reactions of the consumers.

In Section VI, empirical surveys of organizations were used to gather data on a wide variety of factors related to product safety, product quality, supply chain integration, and product recalls. The researchers then statistically examined the relationship between the factors in order to learn more about the important drivers of supply chain quality management.

While each of these methods undoubtedly has its weaknesses, looking at product safety and recall issues from multiple perspectives allows us to capitalize on the strengths of each of the approaches. We can synthesize the findings from the various methodological approaches to highlight key overall findings.

21.5 Key Findings

There are many key findings from the research that was presented in this book. While some of it confirms what might have been expected, some presents new constructs and ideas that have not been previously considered.

Perhaps one of the most important themes from this book is that there are several sources of product defects and the safety issues that can result. In particular, we focused on product quality problems whose origin was in the supply chain, focusing on upstream quality integration, downstream quality integration, and internal quality integration.

Several new constructs related to supply chain quality management were introduced. The concept of re-outsourcing is particularly important. When a company like Mattel outsources some of its production, it may have no idea that its supplier may re-outsource production to a different supplier, which may also re-outsource it. Although Mattel started out with the best of intentions and provided more than adequate documentation, standards, and training to its supplier, the benefits of the documentation, standards, and training are often lost as re-outsourcing occurs. This can have devastating consequences for both consumers and for Mattel, whose brand equity can be destroyed.

A related construct is supply chain transparency. When a supply chain is not transparent, re-outsourcing may take place unknown to the brand owner. Similarly, from the consumers' perspective, when a supply chain is transparent, they know where the products that they purchased were produced and by whom.

Supply chain traceability is also critical to supply chain quality management. While this is related to transparency, it can also be related to the practices used by supply chain members. The classic example is the mixing of raw milk from different suppliers at a milk collection station, which completely destroys supply chain traceability. On the other hand, traceability was created by Bright's use of separate sealed jars for the milk from each cow at each dairy farm; although this represents a significant investment in equipment and time, it plays an important role in ensuring that a crisis like the melamine crisis will never occur again.

Research on supply chain management tends to focus on the relationship between a supplier and a manufacturer, or perhaps in a supplier–manufacturer–customer triad. While such research is tightly controlled and allows developing an understanding of the impact of various factors, it ignores the complexity of actual supply chains. This is particularly important in the context of product safety, where a safety issue in any link of a supply chain can have devastating consequences for both consumers and the brand owner. Our case research looks at supply chains from a broader, more realistic perspective, taking a dive into more remote links, including supplier's suppliers and re-outsourcing. On the customer side, supply chain management research tends to focus on the adjacent downstream link in the supply chain. We highlight the importance of more distant downstream links, including retailers and customers.

Another interesting set of findings deals with the impact of consumer protection legislation, the judicial system, and social media. In the United States, there is a long history of consumer protection, which is strongly upheld by the judicial system. China has had surprisingly good consumer protection legislation in place in the last several decades; however, there are not sufficient mechanisms in place for enforcing it. In its place, consumers have taken to using social media to fill the need to be informed and express themselves about products that they use.

Several of the chapters point out the need for harmonization of international quality standards. This is particularly important when there is international outsourcing. Suppliers, some of which are not particularly well educated about quality issues, are faced with a confusing variety of standards for acceptable levels of toxins in the different countries whose manufacturers they supply. Development of worldwide standards for things like the acceptable lead content in paint would help significantly with the quality of supply chain members and enforcement issues.

CHIC illustrates the strong, but benevolent, supply chain leader. Like a good parent, it cares about the welfare of its suppliers and provides many initiatives to help them to produce acceptable levels of quality in the fruit that they grow. However, it is correspondingly strict, not accepting any fruit that does not meet its standards and immediately terminating any supplier that does not follow its procedures. It does not hesitate to closely monitor the actions of its suppliers in order to ensure that they comply. In this way, it creates a traceable and transparent supply chain. CHIC realizes that it has substantial power in its supply chains, but it uses it in a constructive way, to help both its suppliers and itself to produce high-quality, safe fruit products. This role of a supply chain leader and the ways in which the supply chain leader exercises its power are potent topics for future research.

There are many other interesting and important findings in the research presented in this book. It lays the theoretical, methodological, and practical foundations for a wide range of future research on the broad topic of supply chain quality management and for more specific research questions that fall under its umbrella.

Index

Page numbers followed by f and t indicate figures and tables, respectively.

For Product Safety Concerns and Information please contact our EU representative GPSR@taylorandfrancis.com Taylor & Francis Verlag GmbH, Kaufingerstraße 24, 80331 München, Germany

T - #0004 - 230425 - C0 - 234/156/23 [25] - CB - 9781439815540 - Gloss Lamination